THE PROBLEM OF TRIESTE AND THE ITALO-YUGOSLAV BORDER

SUNY series in National Identities
Thomas M. Wilson, editor

THE PROBLEM OF TRIESTE AND THE ITALO-YUGOSLAV BORDER

Difference, Identity, and Sovereignty in Twentieth-Century Europe

Glenda Sluga

State University of New York Press

Published by
State University of New York Press, Albany

Printed in the United States of America

For information, address State University of New York Press,
90 State Street, Suite 700, Albany, NY, 12207

Production by Kelli Williams
Marketing by Michael Campochiaro

Library of Congress Cataloging-in-Publication Data

Sluga, Glenda, 1962-
    The problem of Trieste and the Italo-Yugoslav border : difference, identity,
    and sovereignty in twentieth-century Europe / Glenda Sluga.
        p.   cm. — (SUNY series in national identities)
    Includes bibliographical references and index.
    ISBN 0-7914-4823-1 (alk. paper) — ISBN 0-7914-4824-X (pbk. : alk. paper)
      1. Trieste (Italy)—History—20th centure.   2. Ethnicity—Italy—Trieste—
    History—20th century.   3. Italy—Boundaries—Slovenia.   4. Slovenia—
    Boundaries—Italy.   5. World War, 1914-1918—Territorial questions—
    Italy.   6. World War, 1939-1945—Territorial questions—Italy.   I. Title.
    II. Series.

DG975.T825 S58 2001
945'.39309—dc21   00-057355

10 9 8 7 6 5 4 3 2 1

Contents

List of Illustrations   vii

Acknowledgments   ix

Abbreviations   xiii

Introduction   1

Chapter 1. Difference, Identity, and Sovereignty, before 1920   11

Chapter 2. Liberalism, Fascism, and Italian National Identity,
            1918–1943   39

Chapter 3. Anti-Fascism and Antinationalism, 1943–1945   63

Chapter 4. Identity and Revolution, May–June 1945   83

Chapter 5. Gender, Ethnicity, and the Iron Curtain, 1945–1948   111

Chapter 6. "FreeTerritory," Nationalism, and the Cold War,
            1948–1954   133

Chapter 7. History and Sovereignty, after 1954   157

Notes   179

Bibliography   233

Index   249

Illustrations

FIGURES

4.1. Armor of The New Zealand Division Enters Trieste,
      2/5/45 (Imperial War Museum)   84

4.2. Partisans, Male and Female, Trieste, 2/5/45 (Mario Maganj)   87

4.3. Partisans, Male and Female, in Piazza Unità, Trieste,
      2/5/45 (Mario Maganj)   88

4.5. A Partisan from Marshal Tito's Forces, 2/5/45 (Imperial
      War Museum)   105

4.6. New Zealand Infantry and Tito's Partisans, 2/5/45
      (Imperial War Museum)   106

4.7. Transport Passes Through a Crowd of Cheering Italians,
      2/5/45 (Imperial War Museum)   107

5.1. Women's Demonstration, 23/6/46 (Mario Maganj)   128

5.2. Union Gathering, 23/6/46 (Mario Maganj)   129

6.1. Allegory of the Division of Territory, 6/10/46
      (Mario Maganj)   134

6.3. *Castel Felice*, 26/2/55 (Mario Maganj)   154

MAPS

Map 1.1.   Adriatic Littoral under the Habsburg Empire   12

Map 2.1.   Interwar Borders and Border Preferences   40

Map 2.2.   Italo-Yugoslav Border, 1924   46

Map 4.4.   The Morgan Line, 1945   100

Map 6.2.   The Free Territory of Trieste   142

Acknowledgments

I n the process of researching and writing this book I have relied on
many different people in many different places. Essential was the financial assistance offered by the Association of Commonwealth
Universities, the Australian Research Council, and the University of
Sydney. Giampaolo Valdevit, Raoul Pupo, Galliano Fogar, Sergio Zucco,
and Anna Maria Vinci at the "Institute for the History of the Liberation
Movement" in Trieste, oriented for me the historiography and archives
of that city. Aleks Kalc, Milan Pahor, and Dragica at the Historical
Department of the Slovene National Library in Trieste offered me alternative perspectives and alternative sources, including the indispensable
photographs of Mario Maganj. In Trieste I also drew on the advice of
Professor Jože Pirjevec of the University of Trieste, and was helped by
the personnel at the Biblioteca Civica Hortis; while Mira, Neva, Nadia,
Emma, Anna, Ljubo, and Licia Chersovani generously passed on their
memories of World War II. In Ljubljana, the helpful staff at the Institute
for Ethnic Questions made undusted files easily accessible, and
Professor Dušan Nečak of the University of Ljubljana shared his research. Metka Gombač and Aleš Gabric from the Slovene National
Archive reinforced my critical interest in the early history of Tito's
Yugoslavia, and Boris Gombač, Marina Grižnic, and Cathie Carmichael
introduced me to Ljubljana's intellectual life. The librarians at the Rome
Parliamentary library and archive provided essential bibliographical
assistance. In the United States, I benefited from the impressive facilities

of the Maryland-based National Archives. In London, the staff at the Public Record Office, the Imperial War Museum and Chatham House were consistently generous with their services. Sir Robert Andrews in London and John Rosselli in Brighton helpfully remembered their time in Allied intelligence; in New Zealand, Ambassador Hawk Mills discreetly shared his knowledge of the American State Department. For taking time to read or discuss my work as it progressed, and for their personal support I should like to thank: the postgraduate seminar group at the University of London's Institute for Historical Research, colleagues at the Sir Robert Menzies Centre for Australian Studies, Ruth Ben-Ghiat, Richard Bosworth, Barbara Caine, Michael Cathcart, Kate Darian-Smith, Patrizia Dogliani, Stephen Fender, David Forgacs, Stephen Garton, Moira Gatens, David Goodman, Kevin Murray, Ros Pesman, and Shane White. Special thanks are due to to Rod Kedward. Finally, the story I tell here has benefited enormously from the detailed critical advice of Alexander Zahar, now of the International Criminal Tribunal for Rwanda, who over the years read through every reincarnation of the text that has now become this book. I thank him for his unconditional support.

     Some of the chapters in this book have appeared in different forms elsewhere. Parts of chapter 2 were published as "Fascism, Anti-fascism, and *italianità:* Contesting Memories and Identities," in R. Bosworth and P. Dogliani (eds.), *Italian Fascism* (St Martin's Press and Macmillan, 1999) and as "Italian National Identity and Fascism: Aliens, Allogenes and Assimilation on Italy's North-Eastern Border," in G. Bedani and B. Haddock (eds.), *The Politics of Italian Identity* (University of Wales Press, 2000); chapter 3 (and parts of chapter 7) emerged from "Inventing Trieste: History, Anti-History, and Nation," *The European Legacy: towards New Paradigms,* 1 (1996): 25–30 (MIT Press); parts of chapter 4 exist in an earlier version as "No Man's Land: the Gendered Boundaries of Postwar Trieste," *Gender and History* 6 (1994): 184–201 (Blackwells). Portions of chapters 4, 5, and 6 were taken from "Trieste: Ethnicity and the Cold War," *Journal of Contemporary History* 29 (1994): 285–303 (Sage Publications); "Identity and Revolution: The History of the Forty days of May 1945," *Annales* 8 (1996); and "Inventing Ethnic Spaces: 'Free Territory', Sovereignty and the 1947 Peace Treaty," *Acta Histraie* iv (1998). Chapter 7 includes reworked sections of the article "The Risiera di San Sabba: Fascism, Anti-Fascism, and Italian Nationalism," *Journal of Modern Italian Studies* 3 (1996): 401–412 (Taylor & Francis). I would like to thank Mario Maganj and the Imperial War Museum for permission to reproduce photographs from their collections, and Erica Seccombe for her map designs.

My father died before I had a chance to show him any of this work. This book took me away from him for the final three years of his life, but it also brought us together. One of the last times I spent with him was in Trieste and its hinterland. It was there that he showed me that, whatever my argument, the politics and history of Trieste could never be as simple as taking sides.

Abbreviations

AFHQ	Allied Forces Headquarters—Mediterranean
AFZ	Anti-Fašistične Ženske/Anti-Fascist Women
AIS	Allied Information Service
AMG	Allied Military Government
AS	Slovene National Archives
BUSZ	British and United States Zone
CEAIS	Comitato Esecutivo Antifascista Italo-Sloveno/Antifascist Italo-Slovene Executive Committee
CLN	Comitato di Liberazione Nazionale/National Liberation Committee
CLNAI	Comitato di Liberazione Nazionale Alta Italia/National Liberation Committee for Upper Italy
CLT	Consiglio di liberazione di Trieste/Trieste Liberation Council (see also MOS)
DC	Democrazia Cristiana/Christian Democrats
EAM	Greek Liberation Front
FO	British Foreign Office

FTT	Free Territory of Trieste
G-2	United States Army General Staff, Division 2, Intelligence
G-5	United States Army General Staff, Division 5, Military Government & Civil Affairs
GSI	General Staff Intelligence
INV	Inštitut za Narodnosta Vprašanja/Institute for National Questions
ISMLVG	Istituto regionale per la storia del movimento di liber-azione nel Friuli Venezia-Giulia/Regional Institute for the History of The Liberation Movement in Friuli Venezia Giulia
MOS	Mestni Osvobodilni Svet/Trieste Liberation Council (also CLT)
NA	United States National Archives
NZEF	New Zealand Expeditionary Force
OF	Osvobodilna Fronta/Liberation Front
OZNA	Odsek za zaščitu naroda (Yugoslav Secret Police)
PCI	Partito Comunista Italiano/Italian Communist Party
PCRG	Partito Comunista della Regione Giulia/Giulian Region Communist Party
PCTLT	Partito Comunista del Territorio Libero di Trieste/Free Territory of Trieste Communist Party
PNOO	Pokrajinski Narodni Odsvobodilni Odbor/Regional Committee for National Liberation
PolAd	Political Adviser
PRO	Public Record Office
PWB	Psychological Warfare Branch
SACMED	Supreme Allied Commander, Mediterranean Theatre of Operations
SCAO	Senior Civil Affairs Officer
s.d.	senza data/no date

SecState	U.S. Secretary of State
sitrep	situation report
SNL	Slovenska Narodna in Študijška Knjižnica/Slovene National and Research Library (Trieste)
SOS	Seje Osvobodilni Svet/Liberation Council Meetings
SPFZZ	Slovenske Proti-Fašistične Ženske Zveze/Union of Slovene Anti-Fascist Women
SU	Sindacati Unici (General Union)
TLT	Territorio Libero di Trieste/Free Territory of Trieste
UAIS	Unione Antifascista Italo-Slava/Italo-Slav Antifascist Union
WO	War Office

Introduction

Trieste, a port town on the northeastern Adriatic, has often been accorded a historical significance on the changing map of twentieth-century Europe greater than its modest prospect might propose. Over the course of the twentieth century, each of the various governments that has administered Trieste has been eager to make it a symbol of its political aims and leave its cultural marks—Habsburg Austria (until 1918), the liberal and then Fascist Italian kingdom (1918–1943), Nazi Germany (1943–1945), pro-Yugoslav communists (May–June 1945), a British-American Military Government (1945–1954), and Republican Italy (1954–). At the end of both the First and Second World Wars, Trieste was also the subject of internationally mediated territorial disputes between Italy and Yugoslavia.[1] In 1919, it was implicated in the "Adriatic Question," a quarrel over sovereignty regarded as the test case for the idea that national borders should follow the territorial contours of racially—or ethnically—differentiated national groups. In 1945, Trieste became a site of contest between the Western allies and Tito's new Yugoslavia, the southern point of an "iron curtain" that had come to separate the communist East from the democratic West. At the end of the twentieth century, some scholars still find Trieste's role as a symbolic axis of Europe's cultural and ideological divisions helpful for delimiting chimerical borders. In academic and populist histories, Trieste is proffered as the point at which European nationalisms have bifurcated: west of Trieste nationalism was benign, but east of Trieste "it was likely to be horrible."[2]

1

Historians have commonly attributed Trieste's turbulent political past to the problem of nationalism. They have presented nationalism as a consequence of the cultural heterogeneity of the region and, ultimately, of the intrinsic differences between (Western European) Italians and (Eastern European or Balkan) Slavs. I argue that the twentieth-century history of Trieste as a "problem" is directly related to the increased political legitimacy accorded to national forms of identification that relied on the *representation* of cultural (ethnic) or "racial" differences, and to the convergent idea that a state's sovereignty is properly grounded in the homogeneity of its culturally or racially named people. Behind each political transformation of Trieste's identity and the imperatives for an Italo-Yugoslav border, lie the complex connections between representations of difference and conceptions of normative national sovereignty. This book traces the changing historical contours of those connections this century.

A HISTORICAL OVERVIEW

From the Enlightenment until the late twentieth century, intellectuals, travellers, commentators of all kinds who have looked at Trieste from the West, have characterized it as part of an Adriatic boundary region that, for changing reasons, divides Europe's Eastern and Western halves. In these accounts, the boundary region extends indefinitely along the Adriatic's luminous eastern shore from the robust Julian Alps to the indolent southern limit of the Adriatic, looking westward to the Italian peninsula, and eastward to the Danubian hinterland. By the late nineteenth century, Europe's Eastern and Western halves were also increasingly visualized as spaces filled with discrete cultural nations and racial groups. The Adriatic boundary region and Trieste were commonly portrayed as the confluence of three European races, German (or Teuton), Italian (or Latin), and Slovene (or "Slav"), each of which had related characteristics. Germans and Italians were regarded as cultural equals: bourgeois, modern, nationally evolved, and essentially Western. Slavs were backward peasants, lacking national consciousness, and Eastern. These prescribed differences sustained complementary conceptions of the evolutionary progress of states into nations, the national designation of territory, and national sovereignty as the political expression of a homologous national identity. Although Trieste was geopolitically part of the multinational Habsburg empire, classifications of the national diversity of Trieste's population gave rise to competing claims to sovereignty by Italian, Slovene, and German nationalists, both from within and outside the region. The most fervent in their attentions were Italian "irredentists" from across the Habsburg border in the Kingdom of Italy, who claimed that Trieste was a natural and unredeemed part of the Italian national corpus. Importantly, at the same time, Trieste's "boundary" status made it the subject of debates about the nature of cultural difference, and the relevance of those differences for determining sovereignty. Trieste was also represented as a zone where a border seemed impractical if not impossible.[3] It inspired models of sovereignty that could accommodate and represent multiple forms of individual or subjective identification, and the cultural diversity of groups who shared a particular territory. Modernists and socialists from the region argued that Trieste's boundary status was not so much exceptional as exemplary of the questions of political and cultural representation faced by an increasingly heterogeneous Europe.

The First World War, the demise of the Habsburg empire in 1918, and the creation of Yugoslavia as a nation-state partly out of Austria-Hungary's southeast European remnants, transformed Trieste and the Adriatic region into an international problem of a new kind. During the postwar peace process, international mediators used Trieste as barter to help resolve the dispute between Italy and Yugoslavia over territory in the Adriatic region, and as an affirmation of the efficiency of a new "principle of nationality" that equated (ethno-national) identity and territorial sovereignty. After Trieste had been awarded to Italy by the international community, Italian Fascist authorities exploited the principle of nationality in order to justify their often violent repression of political and cultural differences within Italian borders, and to initiate Italy's imperial mission in the Balkan East. The shortcomings of the principle of nationality were once again made evident at the end of the Second World War. The reprise of competing claims to Trieste by pro-Italian and pro-Yugoslav parties inspired challenges to the prevailing political emphasis on ethno-national differences, and renewed enthusiasm for alternative conceptions of sovereignty. For a very brief period the pro-Yugoslav Communist administration in control of Trieste attempted to assert a form of sovereignty based on "Italo-Slovene brotherhood." By contrast, the pressures of the Cold War encouraged the British-American Allied Military Government that succeeded the Communists to place their emphasis on the consolidation of a border between East and West, and the clearer delineation of class, gender, and even "racial" differences in order to separate Italians from Slavs. With Trieste's return to Italy in 1954, a spate of Italian and English-language histories celebrated the "successful negotiations" that had finally resolved the problem of Trieste.

At the turn of the twenty-first century, Trieste lies on the western side of a border between Italy and the new nation-state of Slovenia. While the location of that border has remained stable for half a century, the question of sovereignty in the boundary region has reemerged, particularly in Italy. During the wars that led to the breakup of Yugoslavia, Italian nationalists confidently renewed their interest in the coastline extending beyond Trieste and lost to Italy in 1954. Their challenge to the territorial status quo drew its authority from representations of this terrain as naturally Italian, and of the historical enmity between Italians and Slavs. At least some of the responsibility for that situation lies with historians, whose narratives of the past have authorized the view that the problem of Trieste was a consequence of its diversity, and of the natural differences and antagonisms between (Western) Italians and (Balkan) Slavs. As I show, the twentieth-century history of attempts made at international, national, and local levels to establish an ethnically defined national border in the Adriatic boundary region, also includes the history of the ambiguity of differences that the border was meant to separate, and the alternative conceptions of sovereignty that the experience of identity in the Adriatic boundary region invited.

DIFFERENCE, IDENTITY, AND SOVEREIGNTY

In the last decades of the twentieth century, Benedict Anderson's landmark work *Imagined Communities* and the emphasis placed by historians such as Eric Hobsbawm on the "invented" character of nations, helped consolidate a constructivist vocabulary for historical analyses of nations and the formation of national identities.[4] Their work renewed historical reflection on how national identities are made (often by elites) in specific social and political circumstances, and repudiated the persistent popular and academic view that nations are an excrescence of liberal and democratic progress.[5] Abetted by poststructuralist theories, and in particular the work of Edward Said on "Orientalism," historians shifted their attention to the discursive representations of difference that underwrite the "invented" and "imagined" constitution of nations and national identities.[6] Peter Sahlins, a historian of boundaries, has argued that "[n]ational identity is a socially constructed and continuous process of defining 'friend' and enemy."[7] This theoretical approach has helped historians to historicize the broad cultural oppositions *within* Europe, as well as the specific national differences nestled in those oppositions. Thus, Larry Wolff has shown that the idea of "Eastern Europe" was invented as a particular kind of space—essentially backward and barbaric—by "Western" intellectuals during the eighteenth and nineteenth centuries.[8] Wolff convincingly argues that the discursive invention of Eastern Europe was a process "whereby Western Europe also identified itself and affirmed its own precedence."[9] In another example, Maria Todorova has surveyed the literary construction of the Orientalist subcategory "the Balkans" by Western intellectuals at the turn of the twentieth century.[10] These studies reveal what Wolff refers to as the "perceived pattern of similarities and differences" that garnered widespread political and cultural authority in Western Europe since the Enlightenment.[11] They also provide insights into the influence of these broader differentiations on subjective identification. Todorova shows, for example, that although the Balkans is a place whose characteristics have been, in the main, discursively "imagined" by "Western European" intellectuals seeking self-definition, the "outside perception of the Balkans has been internalised in the region itself."[12]

Trieste's conventional delineation as part of a boundary region—an area of transition often marked by ambiguity—offers a promising vantage point for the study of both the oppositional discourses that shape national identities, and the fragile points of attachment and separation of "perceived patterns of similarities and differences." In the sense that national identities are constructed out of differences and in spite of ambiguities, boundary regions can typify what David Campbell refers to as "the attitudes and expectations at the basis of representations of core national identities."[13] Trieste's twentieth-century political history provides us with profiles of a range of core national identities—Habsburg, Italian, German, Yugoslav, Slovene, British, and American—and of the divergent ideological contexts (liberal, fascist, and communist) in which those identities have been shaped. It reveals the way in which each of these identities signifies broader cultural and political clusters: Italian as an identity that exists within and beyond, before and after the existence of the Italian nation-state; Slav as indicative of Yugoslav and Slovene national identities, and as representative of a shared Eastern European culture. It also provides a useful perspective on how and why specific representations of difference have held sway over others. What is most striking about the changing ideological and national contours of Trieste's political history, is the persistence and influence of specific perceptions of difference and of cultural and political oppositions. For most of the twentieth century, ways of knowing Trieste and its population, and the ways in which that population could know itself, have been couched in narratives that unwaveringly reiterate the antithetical differences between an East/Balkan Europe and the West, and constitute the East as the West's lesser "other." One aim of this book is to detail the historical meaning and value accrued by these narratives of difference over the century. A second related aim is to examine their changing political significance at specific historical moments by tracing their connections to prevalent conceptualizations of sovereignty.[14]

For most of this century in Europe, sovereignty has been defined implicitly as the authority of a political entity within a given territory that depends on the cultural (ethnic) or racial identification of the population within that territory. Sovereignty has involved what Richard Kearney describes as a "double crisis of representation," "[f]irst, the crisis of representative democracy . . . and, second, the correlative crisis of imaginative representation."[15] The authority of the political entity, and the extent to which citizens have access to representative democracy, have depended on the ways in which the identity of the community or territory is imaginatively represented. If the community or territory is imaginatively represented as mixed (as was predominantly the case with Trieste and the boundary region before the First World War), and the political entity seeks its authority according to simple ethnic or racial criteria, then either the criteria for the entity's sovereignty have to change, the community has to be differently imagined, or practices of assimilation and "cleansing" have to be introduced. Trieste's history as both Italian and as an international problem has coincided with the international legitimation of the ethno-nation as the appropriate basis of sovereignty, which has in turn corresponded to the imaginative representation of ethnically heterogeneous communities as a problem. It is no coincidence that the European use of the term Balkan (as resonant of antagonistic and fragmenting differences) expanded at the same time that Western liberals accepted (ethno-) nationality as the principle for the democratic reordering of state sovereignty in Central and Eastern Europe.

Historians and their historical narratives have had an important influence on imaginative representations of places and people, and the reproduction of an ethno-national understanding of sovereignty. There is a close relationship between the ways in which groups (whether named Italian or Slav, male or female, peasant or bourgeois) are imaginatively represented in academic and popular histories, and the power or authority they are able to exercise in order to claim their share in popular sovereignty.[16] J. G. A. Pocock argues that historical narratives (versions of the past which include representations of identities in the past) are potent attributes of sovereignty, since they are used to identify and determine the (national) limits or borders of a political entity's affairs.[17] Because categories of national identity, and descriptions of national differences, provide accepted commonsense ways of identifying the agents and characters of historical narratives, the influence of historians on the validation of ethno-national sovereignty has operated even when there has been no vested interest in building up a national identity. Historians have been implicated in the struggle for sovereignty simply through the manner in which they have imaginatively represented identities in their histories.[18] In writing this history, it was difficult not to give its protagonists national identities, but I use national categories to reflect their historical and political use—not to naturalize them—and without assuming that they directly correlate to subjective forms of identification in the region. I have paid attention throughout to the elision of ethno-national identity into political identity (for example, the assimilation of Slavs and communism, Italians and fascism). I have also used "pro-Italian" and "pro-Yugoslav" to distinguish between groups who had a specific political agenda and whose proclaimed cultural identity could be either Slovene or Italian, or neither, at different moments during this period. My intention is to record the history of difference, identity and sovereignty as a history of ambiguities, to incorporate voices that do not fit into the neat categorisations of ethnic, political, and gender identities assumed in arguments for ethno-national sovereignty.[19] I show how imaginative representations of differences, and specifically national identities, have influenced political choices and strategies at local, international, and national levels, how they speak to and mask the difficulty of acknowledging non-ethno-national forms of democratic representation within, and as constitutive of, communities.

Each chapter in this book focuses on the historically specific political contexts in which representations of difference in the Trieste region, and the narratives of identity and sovereignty in which they have been couched, emerged, persisted, and were challenged, their implications for perceiving Trieste as a problem and for local forms of national identification. Chapter 1 examines the intellectual and political debates regarding sovereignty inspired by Trieste's cultural "hybridity" in the final decades of the Habsburg empire. I then look at how, during the war and the peace process that followed, Trieste was transformed into an unproblematically "Italian" space and made politically a part of Italy. Chapter 2 surveys changing representations of Slavs in the context of Italian nationalist discourse between 1918 and 1943. In both the liberal period of Italian national government in Trieste from 1918 to 1922, and then during the Fascist *ventennio*, liberal-democratic, socialist, and Fascist intellectuals articulated the superiority and coherence of Italian national identity, and the legitimacy of Italian sovereignty in the boundary region, by emphasizing the assimilatory capacity of *italianità* and

the cultural inferiority and "alien-ness" of Slavs. In chapter 3, I consider
how the collapse of the Fascist state in 1943, and the opposing political
ideologies and forms of national identification of the two rival resistance groups in the region from 1943 until 1945, when Trieste was under
Nazi occupation, shaped the re-creation of Trieste as an international
problem. I analyze how local forms of national identification and preferred forms of sovereignty—preferences for the Italo-Slovene model
promoted by the Communist pro-Yugoslav Liberation Front, on the one
hand, and for Italian sovereignty supported by local Italian anti-Fascist
intellectual figures, on the other—were shaped in the matrix of predominant representations of Italian and Slav, Western and Eastern differences. Chapter 4 highlights the period of six weeks in May and June
1945 when Trieste was governed by Communist partisans who planned
to incorporate the region into a Yugoslav class-based federation of nations and whose ideals of "Italo-Slovene" (antinationalist) fraternity
challenged existing ethnic, class, and gender hierarchies. I reassess historical accounts of this period by looking at how narratives of difference
influenced and were influenced by anticommunist evaluations of the
ideal of "fraternity" and multicultural sovereignty. Chapters 5 and 6
look at the attitudes of the British-American Allied Military Government, which succeeded the Communists, toward non-national
forms of collective and individual identification and alternative models
of sovereignty. I focus in particular on the political impact of the Allied
Military Government's characterizations of the region's legitimate citizens as masculine, bourgeois, and Italian, and of a natural antipathy between Italians and Slavs.[20] In the final chapter, I examine the influence
of representations of Italian and Slav differences, and assumptions
about the importance of those differences for establishing sovereignty,
on memories and histories of the problem of Trieste and the Italo-
Yugoslav border since World War II. I also assess the ways in which the
much-maligned work of one Triestine historian, Fabio Cusin, invites us
to rethink the writing of identity into history. I argue that counternarratives of identity and history can provide a critical framework for historicizing representations of difference and related conceptions of
sovereignty, for understanding the continuing border tensions in the
Trieste region, and for analyzing the dissolution of the late-twentieth-
century Yugoslav federation. For a book that applauds pluralism, discussion of the Greek, Jewish, and Serbian Orthodox minorities in Trieste
is pointedly lacking. Neither have I included any analysis of the boundary region areas subject to Yugoslav rule after May 1945. But this history
is written in response to a historical canon that, in the case of Trieste,
has uncritically affirmed the early-twentieth-century principle of na-

tionality, reproduced complacent distinctions between good (Western) and bad (Eastern) nationalisms and even older stereotypes of the differences between Italians and Slavs, Western and Eastern (or Balkan) Europeans. My purpose is to unsettle the historical validity of these oppositions and value judgments as they were constructed from the West, to diversify the ways in which histories of difference, identity, and sovereignty might be rewritten, and Trieste's future as well as its past might be imagined.

1

Difference, Identity, and Sovereignty, before 1920

. . . the region abounds in streams which disappear underground and whose course and re-emergence is not yet known with certainty.

—René Albrecht-Carré, "The North-eastern Frontier of Italy"

The town of Trieste (or *Triest*, or *Trst* as it is also known by speakers of German and Slavic languages respectively) looks out to sea from the eastern shores of the Adriatic; west lies Venice, south Dubrovnik, and behind sits the limestone hinterland of the *Karst* (German)/*Carso* (Italian)/ or *Kras* (Slovene and Croatian), a main point of access to the expanses of Central Europe's Danubian plan. From the late eighteenth century until the end of the First World War, the Habsburg rulers of Trieste took advantage of the town's geographic position, developing its trading potential as a free port. A network of sea, road, and (by the early twentieth century) rail lines linked Trieste to Habsburg, Italian, and Ottoman cities alike. Trieste became the Habsburg empire's main seaport, and the most important town in the Habsburg-administered Adriatic Littoral, or *Küstenland*. The Littoral administrative area stretched from the provinces of Gorizia and Gradisca in the north, through Trieste (the name of the province as well as the town), to Istria in the south. By the middle of the nineteenth century Trieste had achieved a relatively prominent place on the map of a modernizing Europe. Rapid commercial expansion and urbanization brought with it

1.1. Adriatic Littoral under the Habsburg Empire

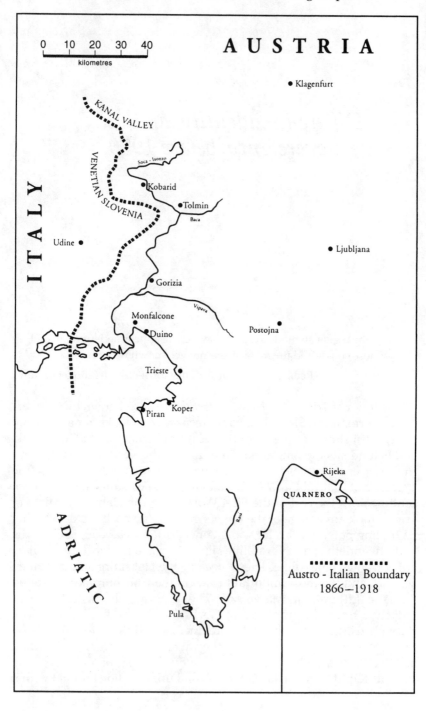

the diversification of Trieste's population and lent a heightened significance to its composite religious and cultural lifestyles. Trieste's free
port status attracted the politically and culturally displaced who supplemented the town's existing Catholic edifices with their Orthodox
and Evangelical churches, a synagogue, and a masonic hall. Censi conducted by the Habsburg administration keen to document this expanding population provided evidence of an attendant multilingual
competency in a range of languages and dialects, including Italian,
Ladin, Friulian, Slovene, Croatian, Serbian, German, Romanian, and
Greek.[1] At the same time, some members of the largest of these linguistic groups developed their own distinctive forms of geographical
orientation. Italian nationalists referred to the Habsburg Littoral as the
natural extension of the Italian-speaking Venetian region and named
it Venezia Giulia, in honor of an imperial Roman past. This imaginary
Venezia Giulia usually encompassed parts of the Austrian province of
Carniola and stopped just south of the port town of Fiume at the
Quarnero gulf, nominated by Dante in the thirteenth century as the
eastern limit of Italy. Alternatively, Slovene nationalists called the
Littoral *Julijska Krajina* (or the Julian March), in which they included
the Slovene-speaking areas that had been incorporated within Italian
borders in 1866, when the newly unified Italian state annexed the
neighboring Venetian and Friulian regions.

For a historian, the difficulty of introducing the population of
Trieste and the Adriatic boundary region surrounding the Italo-
Yugoslav border is the difficulty of knowing which perspective to
choose. Twentieth-century historians have tended to portray life in
pre–First World War Trieste and the Littoral as evidence of a "nationalities' struggle," which, they conclude, inevitably led to the disintegra-
tion of the Habsburg empire and creation of successor nation-states.[2]
Their histories of the Adriatic boundary region are informed by late
nineteenth-century representations of the differences between Western
and Eastern (or Balkan) Europe, and between Italians and Slavs (and
sometimes Germans). By the late nineteenth century, the numerous re-
searchers drawn to Trieste by its status as a commercial and cultural
hub imposed their "scientific" classifications of these differences without consideration of the complexity of subjective forms of local identification. Their observations do not so much provide a reflection of
Trieste as it was, as evidence of turn of the century ways of seeing.
They are exemplary of how the naming of places and describing the
nationality of people within a given territory had become instruments
for claiming authority over and possession of territory on behalf of homologous nations. In particular, their representations of the national

makeup of Trieste's population contributed to the conception of a nationalities' struggle in the Habsburg empire, and to a concomitant view of Trieste's diversity as a political problem.³ In turn of the century Trieste itself, increasingly confident local nationalists reinforced the idea that sovereignty in the region should be the prerogative of a single ethno-national group. This attitude conflicted, however, with the views of other local intellectuals, particularly socialists, who focused on the hybrid or ambiguous nature of identities in the region, and who thus questioned the premise that a democratic form of sovereignty entailed matching the territorial borders of states to the spatial limits of discrete ethno-national identities. The first part of this chapter traces the history of these two ascendant ways of representing national identities and difference in the Adriatic boundary region, and the divergent conceptions of sovereignty that they encouraged. In the second half, I examine how, in the course of the First World War, the view of diversity as a problem, and the idea that territorial sovereignty should be located in ethnically homogenous terrain, came to dominate the ways in which Trieste and the Littoral were represented in international contexts. This historical focus tells us little about how Triestines may have identified themselves in their everyday lives, but it does reveal that before the First World War the struggle in Trieste was between representations of difference and conceptions of sovereignty, as much as between nationalities. Only at the end of the First World War did the equation between (ethno-national) identity and (territorial) sovereignty provide an internationally legitimate formula for deciding and, most often, legitimating national borders. By then too, representations of national difference had become a powerful currency in the realm of international relations and in liberal discourses of democracy, with significant consequences for how people living in the region could identify themselves.

THE NATIONALITIES' STRUGGLE

Since the late eighteenth century Trieste has been situated on a heavily transected map of competing narratives of Europe as well as of nations. In 1774 the Abbé Alberto Fortis, a member of an international scientific expedition that had set off from Venice to explore the Adriatic's eastern coastline, portrayed the Littoral in his popular *Travels to Dalmatia* as the southernmost tip of an East/West division, separating *l'Europa colta*—the "polite parts of Europe" on its western side—from the "less polite" and "barbarous" east.⁴ In Fortis's narrative the eastern shores of the Adriatic were populated by so-called Morlacchi, who although "white as the Italians" shared the uncivilized characteristics of Eastern Europeans occupying an area stretching from the Adriatic to the Arctic.[5] As Trieste's population expanded and diversified in the nineteenth century, interest in the Morlacchi of the region declined. English travellers recorded the amalgam of "nations" that thronged the streets of Trieste, "Italians, Germans, English and Americans, with Greeks and Turks in their national dress."[6] By the mid-nineteenth century research into the region by outsiders focused more explicitly on the distinct class and cultural qualities of two groups: Italians and Slavs. Trieste was described as the urban creation of an Italian bourgeoisie. Local peasants were likened to a Yorkshire rural underclass and referred to as Slavs, a "middle race between the phlegmatic German and ardent Italian" who populated the marketplaces but were not Triestine.[7] Cathie Carmichael has argued that in these nineteenth-century accounts of the region, foreign merchants and "the wealthier of the country people" were seen as part of "an Italian milieu," but Slavs were doomed "'beyond the gate' to the ranks of . . . *strati subalterni.*"[8]

The identification of Slavs as peasants and outsiders, and Italians as middle-class and metropolitan, reflects the ways in which changing representations of Trieste drew on a shared, if mutable, European vocabulary of overlapping national and class differences. According to Larry Wolff, in the course of the nineteenth century, the category Slav increasingly served as the negative reflection of German as well as Italian nations, and of the bourgeois cultural and political characteristics of Western Europe as a whole. In the late eighteenth century, Johannes Herder had described Slavs as an "oppressed docile farming people," but only a few decades later, Francis Gibbon depicted them as racially inferior to Germans, savage, and lacking political organization.[9] By the 1820s "the equation of Eastern Europe and the Slavs was already axiomatic." This equivalence amplified antithetical representations of Slavs, on the one hand, and the individual nations deemed part of "Western" Europe, on the other, and the idea that Slavs posed a threat to (Western) Europe's natural political destiny.[10] In 1871 Ernest Renan (a philosopher famous for his antideterminist view of national identity), stated that the Slav "like the dragon of the Apocalypse . . . will one day drag behind him the herds of Central Asia. . . . Imagine what a weight will bear upon the balance of the world on the day when . . . all the Slavic populations of the Ottoman empire, group around the great Muscovite conglomeration."[11] When, in the 1890s, European geographers began classifying inhabitants of the "Balkans" (denoting the lands to the southeast of Fortis's dividing line) as Slavs, the new location was associated with a condition of political anarchy contrary to the order of Northern and Western Europe.[12]

Over the course of the nineteenth century, shifting geographical designations of Trieste and the Adriatic Littoral, and descriptions of their populations, reflected a perceived pattern of similarities and differences, and the changing political relevance of these differences. The classifications of cultural difference in Trieste and the Littoral crafted by late-nineteenth-century professional anthropologists and ethnographers are evidence of the influence of these patterned perceptions. Social scientists rendered the Austrian Littoral a crossroads of three major European nations/races—Teuton (or German), Latin (or Italian), and Slav—and portrayed these nations as locked in a contest for political as well as cultural predominance (varyingly referred to as a national, racial, or ethnographic struggle). Their assessments of the relative success of each of these nations/races in that contest accorded with influential evolutionary theories and presumptions about the inherent capacities of different nations and races for assuming political authority. The view of the Adriatic Littoral as a site of national contest also coincided with a growing interest among Italian intellectuals and politicians in the redemption of the so-called Italian *terra irredenta* (unredeemed land) of Trieste and "Trentino" or southern Tyrol to the north of Italy's existing border, which was also under Habsburg government.[13] In the Kingdom of Italy, anthropologists not only looked to the diversity of languages and peoples in the Adriatic Littoral as a site for testing out their taxonomic skills, they assumed that their classifications of the differences between the populations of that territory were meaningful for determining its political and cultural future. In 1885 Professor Giovanni Marinelli, a member of the Venetian Institute of Sciences and Letters, claimed that the Adriatic Littoral was populated by Italians, Germans, and Slavs engaged in two different "ethnographic struggles." In the struggle between Germans and Italians the artificial presence of German culture in the region meant that the Italians would prevail; in the struggle between Slavs and Italians, Italians would easily subsume the inferior culture of the Slavs.[14] Some anthropologists adopted a more benign image of the Italian role in this Darwinian struggle by modifying their representation of Slovenes, the largest Slavic-speaking group in the region. A study of Slovenes conducted in the 1890s by Italian anthropologist Francesco Musoni concluded that because Slovenes were on the whole a "simple, good, honest people with a meek spirit: not yet wild, nor ferocious, in their political passions" (a Herderian version of the Slav type) there was no competition between Slovenes and Italians;

instead, the cultural inferiority of Slovenes made them passively sub-missive to Italian influence.[15]

Anthropologists with no vested interest in the Littoral's Italian fate were more equivocal in their observations of difference and its political significance. In 1898 the French anthropologist Bertrand Auerbach published an extensive study of the races and nationalities of Austria-Hungary in which he argued that although language sta-tistics showed that in the province of Trieste Italians dominated "with-out contest" and that the Slovenes were peasants who lived in the mountain regions, if those statistics were used to prove the natural-ness of Italian sovereignty over the region, the value of that evidence was "more documentary than moral."[16] To support his argument he claimed that Austrian ethnographers had been able to show that "everyday language did not match the mother language, and race did not match nationality"; instead, the local processes of "hybridity" had "provoked the anxiety of philologists."[17] Conventional racial and na-tional typologies, Auerbach concluded, were at the least imprecise, and unhelpful for understanding the complexity of identity in the re-gion or for verifying the political claims of nationalist groups. The dif-ferent languages and dialects of the Littoral and Trieste, their mixed and hybrid forms, threw into stark relief the difficulties of distin-guishing absolute national differences, of matching national and racial typologies with the people they saw and the languages to which they listened, of settling on one version of a language as definitive of the national identity of a population, and of deciding which nationality was sovereign in that territory. Even Marinelli confessed that in dis-tinguishing between Slav, Italian, and German *stirpe* (a term that could connote a community of either cultural or racial descent) he was un-certain whether he should refer to the differences between bodies, skulls, skin color, or language. After settling on language, he worried about its efficiency for distinguishing singular national identities. Even in the case of an established nation-state such as Italy, if written language was the basis of deciding a *stirpe* then there was only one *stirpe* in Italy; but if it was the spoken language, then Italy itself con-tained many *stirpe*.[18] While Marinelli's concerns about classifying na-tional differences did not sway him from his belief in the Italianness of the Littoral, Auerbach believed that ethnographic evidence of the processes of hybridity, and of the presence of Slav, Friulian, German, Romanian, and Serbo-Croat speakers, meant that the region could only be described as a "great highway of traffic, . . . a theatre of fusions and mixtures," and that, as a result, its destiny lay with a multina-tional state such as the Habsburg empire.[19]

In the decades before World War I, images of the region as the site of a national struggle between culturally unequal Italians and Slavs (less frequently Germans) competed with representations of the Littoral as home to hybrid identities.[20] The political and social structure of late-nineteenth-century Austria-Hungary gave credence to both of the political conclusions that were generally drawn from these competing representations: that the empire's authority was under threat from a nationalities' struggle, and that the empire was fostering a progressive multinational form of sovereignty. The 1867 Austro-Hungarian constitution had awarded all nationalities and local languages equal rights, and, in the ensuing decades, the Habsburg empire established a political system that in principle recognized and reproduced diversity. The Austro-Hungarian state also placed increasing emphasis on classifying and distinguishing those differences through language censi and bureaucratic regulations, requiring individuals to identify themselves with one group rather than another.[21] Gerard Stourzh argues that in the final decades of the empire's existence "[t]he question of Austrian citizens *belonging* to a certain nationality, and the problem of finding out, when in doubt, to which nationality a person belonged" loomed large.[22] In some cases the Austrian legal experts resorted to (often unsatisfactory) cross-examinations and questionnaires in order to objectively determine the nationality of an individual.[23] The obsession with ethnic attribution assisted the transformation of individual imperial subjects into members of distinct national groups. Historians have suggested that there was an informal consensus about the relative historical and cultural worth of each of these national groups, and the respective power of the individuals named as their members. C. A. Macartney states that according to this consensus, "[c]ulturally, the Germans, Poles, and Italians stood far ahead of all the others," and that "[e]conomically, the Germans, Jews, and Italians were much stronger than the Slavs."[24] Robert Kann argues that, after Germans, Italians were treated most favorably in terms of language rights in school, court, diet, and administration.[25] With the introduction of universal male franchise in the Habsburg empire in 1907 "the Italians became the most privileged of all national groups from the angle of 'franchise arithmetic.'"[26] According to Robin Oakey, most favored status was as much a result of the cultural standing of different groups, what he terms the "power of stereotypes," as political opportunism. The weak political status of Slavs corresponded to depictions in travelogues and academic works of the "South Slav lands" as backwaters and Slavs as a group "unfit for modern life" who should be treated with firmness and benevolence by superior cultures.[27]

At the same time as Habsburg institutions and practices reified national identities and differences and fortified nationalist organizations within the empire, they created the conditions for national coexistence.[28] This latter political option was given a firm theoretical basis in the Austro-Marxist conception of nonterritorial nationalism, and non-nationalist sovereignty. Austro-Marxists envisioned the reorganization of the Habsburg empire into national-cultural units without territorial representation, and the restructuring of the state into a federation of territorial and national-cultural layers of political representation. It could be argued that their ideas were an amalgam of accepted national stereotypes, of the "scientific" and class-based perspectives of Marxist thought, and, to a lesser extent, of the modernist questioning of sexual, psychological, and social identities that flourished among the Viennese intelligentsia.[29]

Despite the ideological antipathy of socialists to nationalism, and the common depiction by Marxists of the bourgeois nature of national struggles, late-nineteenth-century Austrian socialists incorporated the question of national political rights into their class-driven programs. In 1899 the Austrian Social Democratic Party promoted as part of its political platform the principle of national federalism "on the basis of territorial autonomy."[30] Influential socialist intellectuals aspired to a radical means of reconciling the empire's cultural diversity with its ideological renovation. They proposed a socialist federal state that would discard the idea that national groups could only be politically represented by exercising sovereignty over nationally homogenous territory. Two socialists in particular, Karl Renner and Otto Bauer, were responsible for propagating an Austro-Marxist view of the relationship between national identity and territorial sovereignty. In the 1880s and 1890s Renner argued that the Habsburg empire had to be organized according to two principles, "a double network . . . an economic and an ethnic one."[31] The state's population would be identified twice "once nationally and once according to administrative requirements *(staatlich)*. In either case the territorial units will be different." Bauer supported and elaborated this program in his 1907 publication *Die Nationalitätenfrage und die Sozialdemokratie* (The Nationality Question and Social Democracy). His aim was "to strive to find the forms in which the nationalities can live together in the given frame of the state."[32] He argued both that individual national identities were usually the product of mixed or hybrid racial cultural influences, and that collective national differences could be empirically distinguished. For Bauer, a nation was an entity determined by will and destiny rather than by biology, but historically and culturally distinct national groups had to have collective political representation in a state aspiring to democracy.[33] The programs put forward by Bauer and Renner recognized the demands being made within the empire by particular national organizations for national representation, but rejected the idea that popular sovereignty for each of these national groups or peoples meant their political representation as national groups in nationally homogenous territory.[34] C. A. Macartney has explained that on Bauer and Renner's view, "[a]ll members of each nationality, whatever their residence, were to form a single public body or association, endowed with legal personality and competent to deal with all its national ('national-cultural') affairs."[35] The innovative aspect of their programs was the stipulation that nationality need not be politically represented on a territorially contiguous basis, and, further, that an overarching state's authority need not rest on a cultural or ethno-national definition of territorial sovereignty.

Renner and Bauer's ideas exerted substantial influence among socialists throughout the Habsburg empire. Macartney has commented on how writers (not all of them socialists) regarded the Austro-Marxist view that nationalist demands for popular sovereignty could be satisfied without sanctioning culturally based territorial sovereignty as a model for all Europe.[36] Similar approaches to the themes of difference and sovereignty emerged among Triestine writers in this period. According to an Italian literary critic, Triestine writers were "mixed in language, culture and often blood . . . usually intent on self-discovery, self-definition."[37] The pseudonym taken by Trieste's most famous writer, Italo Svevo, bore witness to a simultaneous self-consciousness of hybridity and national singularity: Svevo the literary persona was in everyday life the bank clerk Ettore Schmitz who transformed his Jewish-German sounding name to evoke an Italian-German identity as Italo Svevo (meaning Svevian or Swabian).[38] When Svevo explored the psychology of the self in his pre–First World War novels he made few references to national or cultural identification. By contrast, a younger generation of local writers, like the well-known Scipio Slataper, self-consciously represented Trieste as a cultural crossroads and their selves as culturally polygenous. In the opening lines of Slataper's fictionalized (Italian-language) autobiography, *Il Mio Carso* (1912), the narrator/protagonist avoids describing himself as either Italian, Slav, or German by invoking a voice fractured through the languages of the Carso—a territory that extends east and south into the Danubian lands beyond the port of Trieste—and identifies himself with an uncertain territorial genealogy: "I would like to say, I was born in the Carso . . . I would like to say, I was born in Croatia . . . I would like to say, I was born in the Moravian plain."[39] *Il Mio Carso* traces a personal voyage from this hinterland of multiple identities to the city of Trieste, where the narrator discovers a singular Italian national patriotism which he then rejects because, as he explains, even Trieste is a place where "everything . . . is double or triple."[40]

In the prewar essays *Scritti Politici*, Slataper presumed that questions regarding identity and sovereignty raised in the Triestine setting were relevant to Europe as a whole, and that their solution in Trieste would provide the basis "for a better Europe."[41] Together with the Stuparich brothers, Carlo and Gianni, Slataper planned the publication of a new journal called *Europa* to profile what he regarded as Europe's major cultural traditions: Northern, Western, and Central European, and Slav.[42] His political ideas relied on a less experimental narration of identity than his fiction, but they were still keenly attuned to the theme of multiple identities in Trieste and the Littoral. Slataper described Triestine identity as a combination of the three major racial and cultural groups recognized in the region by contemporary anthropologists: Italians, Germans, and Slavs. Trieste was Italian ("in a different way than other Italian cities are"), and Trieste's *italianità* (although a composite of *three* races) had a "double soul." Trieste's double soul was its German commercial identity and its Italian cultural identity; its third Slavic identity was culturally undeveloped and spiritually insignificant. Ideally, Slataper argued, Trieste's function as part of an Austria "of the people," and of a multicultural Europe, was to propagate *three* cultures—Italian, German, and Slav. "[T]he future of Europe," he proposed, was "not tied to one culture, but in the broadening and valuing of all three cultures that are present in Trieste."[43] For Slataper, ensuring peace in Austria and Europe entailed raising Slavic culture to an equal footing with Italian and German culture.

This literary and political trend in Triestine intellectual thought was taken farthest in the work of Angelo Vivante. Vivante's long essay on Italian irredentism, *Irredentismo Adriatico*, an Austro-Marxist political treatise published in the same year as *Il Mio Carso*, was more radical in its effort to combine a critique of national identification with political analysis. In *Irredentismo Adriatico* Vivante historicized the development of Italian nationalist aspirations in the Adriatic region, criticized the supposition that Italian irredentism was a natural and spontaneous symptom of the individual aspirations of Italians for national liberation, and argued that Italian irredentists had an impractical and unrealistic view of Trieste's future within an Italian state. *Irredentismo Adriatico* can be read as an attempt by Vivante to align the unstable contours of national identification with a class model of political organization and representation.

Like Slataper in his fiction, Vivante experimented in his political analysis with the narration of his own identity. In the preface to *Irredentismo Adriatico*, Vivante referred to himself in the third person, as if subjecting himself to a form of psychoanalysis. The "psychic structure of the person writing," he explained, accounts for his (Vivante's) lack of national identification. That person, Vivante argued, "has made a rigorous examination of his conscience, and feels in this regard perfectly tranquil."[44] Vivante presented his own lack of Italian national identification as exemplary of the ways in which Italian nationalism was a consequence of ideology, rather than a reflection of a particular physiognomy or an intrinsic national psychology. As further evidence he pointed to the changing descriptions of the Adriatic region and of Slavs in the region after Italian unification. It was only after unification, according to Vivante, that the Italian nationalist Pacifico Valussi used a description of Slavs as a rural plebeian people—dispersed and divided, unable to evolve into a nation and easily assimilable by Italian culture— to justify Italy's absorption of Trieste and the Adriatic region as Italian *terra irredenta*.[45] Before then Valussi had presented Slavs, like Italians, as an indigenous *stirpe* in a "neutral zone." Vivante claimed that too many people had allowed themselves to believe that *italianità* and *slavismo* in the Julian region were well-defined and rigidly antithetical terms: Italians as "clear-cut and definitive national individuals, even as if they were all direct descendants of Rome and of Venice," and Slavs as "the strangers, the new-comer conquerors, disciplined by the Austrian government and by foreign agitators to fight against the only indigenous group in the [Venezia] Giulia."[46] At the same time, Vivante preferred to describe Trieste and the Adriatic region as the "intersection of two nations," Italian and Slav.

Representations of Trieste and the Littoral as a boundary region populated by two, and only sometimes three, distinctive peoples (referred to as both nations and races) persisted in the work of these political radicals. Despite their interest in the ambiguity and multiplicity of identities,[47] and the existence of Jewish, Greek, and other cultural or religious organizations, languages, or dialects in Trieste, Vivante and Slataper resorted to representing Trieste as the crossroads or intersection of Italians, Slavs, and Germans. Slataper and Vivante's experimentation did not ensure an open-minded acceptance of all cultural differences, or the consideration of other forms of inequality (of all the distinctive groups that could be separated out in Trieste, Slataper most intentionally ignored Jews). At a time when feminist organizations were demanding political and legal rights for women, Slataper and Vivante (like other socialists writing on nationalism) made no acknowledgment in their work of gender disparity.[48] Instead, Vivante in particular was most concerned with the disparities between the political and economic situation of collectively identified Italians and Slavs, a concern that, according to Slataper in his obituary for Vivante, was considered radical. Although Slataper did not always agree with Vivante he maintained that Vivante, like the Viennese Austro-Marxists Bauer and Renner, "had tried to provide an absolutely new national solution to the mixed aggregate of peoples which is today Austria-Hungary, and which tomorrow will perhaps be new states surging from the monarchy, autonomous, but nevertheless impure as nations."[49]

Both the view that the Habsburg empire was engulfed by the struggle between its constituent nationalities, and that the future of the Habsburg empire rested in its reinvention as a federation of mixed nationalities, resonated in Triestine political life. The premise of national struggle was propagated by local nationalist organizations and political parties. Italian nationalism in Trieste was the provenance of an intellectual milieu linked to organizations based in Rome, such as the Dante Alighieri society and the Italian Nationalist Association.[50] The Trieste municipal council was dominated by the Italian Liberal National Party which consistently used its authority to prohibit the presence of Slovene-speakers and their schools and organizations in the city center. Their strategies reinforced the identification of urban Trieste with *italianità* and the hinterland with Slovenes and the foreign status of so-called Slavs. By the 1890s, Slovene-speaking clergy and Slovene nationalists in Trieste had attempted to improve their cultural status by establishing organizations such as the Cyril and Methodius Society, and Slovene language education programs, Slovene-language newspapers, and Slovene agricultural cooperatives. But because of the municipal authorities' objections, these organizations were mainly located on the city's periphery.[51] Marginalized by their local political representatives, obstinate Slovene-speakers and Slovene organizations looked to Vienna for political protection.[52]

Before the First World War in Trieste and the Littoral, the paradigm of racial and cultural struggle was also rivalled by support for the Habsburg empire's transformation into a "socialist" federation that could meet the demands of nationalist groups for political representation without fragmenting the state into territorially defined national units.[53] Richard Bosworth has claimed that there was more support in Trieste for political, social, and economic change as part of the Habsburg empire than for Trieste's unification with Italy.[54] Although there were reports of nationalist tensions spilling over into the streets of Trieste, this tension was often the result of ideological antagonism between socialists (who had achieved political prominence in the empire and who gave less political weight to their national identities) and the commercial middle class.[55] The views of nationalists and socialists were separated not only by their respective opinions of the existing economic hierarchy, but the political meaning each attributed to Trieste's diversity. Some Slovene nationalists regarded Austrian socialism as a means of achieving Slovene national liberation, and of realizing international, or multinational coexistence.[56] Aping the themes of Austro-Marxism, local Slovene socialists stated that nations were the "sum of single speakers of a given mother language which they, of their own will, recognised as their nationality," rather than "a sum of single inhabitants in a given territory."[57] Austrian socialism seems to have been as popular among self-identified Italians. At the 1907 elections, the first to allow universal male suffrage in the empire, socialists from the Italian branch of the Austrian Socialist Democratic Party in Trieste, led by Valentino Pittoni, won an absolute majority in the area from Triestine supporters who anticipated the empire's transformation into a federation of (nonterritorial) nations.[58] That success, however, was ultimately only a short-lived moment in a much longer history of ideological contest in the region.

For many contemporaries, the struggle between conceptions of identity and sovereignty was thought of in terms of the conflict between nationalists and socialists. During a conference of Italian nationalists in Florence in 1910, Scipio Sighele (an irredentist whose personal ties were closest to the Trentino *terra irredenta* on Italy's northern border) advised his audience that in the unredeemed territories still ruled by Austria, socialism was now more popular than nationalism. Nationalists such as Sighele regarded socialism as the negation of nationalism; in the context of Italian irredentism, they perceived socialism as the tool of a Habsburg and Slavic threat to Italian national aspirations. Although Sighele exaggerated the extent to which socialists rejected nationalism (as we have seen there were aspects of the nationalist view that most socialists accepted, including the naturalness and significance of national allegiance, and the salience of national-cultural identities), his warning echoed and reinforced fears articulated by Italian nationalist groups and in their presses, of the overlapping threat posed to Trieste by socialism and Slavs.[59] For Sighele, the delineation of national differences, and the borders between them, was critical to the legitimation of national sovereignty, which was in turn the natural result of the evolutionary struggle between races. Boundary regions such as the Littoral constituted a "neutral zone of territory" between "two races" and "two *civiltà*," where "bit by bit the strongest of these races linguistically absorbs the other."[60] Socialism, he argued, "neither recognised the diversity of languages nor natural frontiers,"[61] and was "the flag of a vast ideal that knows no division of nations or of races, and thus does not want to fight for one race or for one nation against another."[62] By contrast, on the view of nationalists, the political notion that nations had natural territorial borders (or frontiers) provided an important conceptual basis for cultural national identification. According to Barbara Spackman, in this same period F. T. Marinetti, the Italian Futurist-*cum*-Fascist, identified the threat of socialism as its elimination of "the boundaries between individuals, between classes, but most importantly between nations."[63]

Long before Italian irredentism existed, the territory projecting north from the Adriatic's axis and along its eastern shores had been imagined as a boundary region. Throughout the nineteenth century, Enlightenment representations of East and West, Italians and Slavs, the scientific concern for distinguishing and classifying cultural and biological differences, shaped perceptions of identities in this region. Until World War I, the political significance of difference was the subject of intense intellectual discussion. Italian nationalists such as Sighele bemoaned the Italian population's lack of the kind of geographical, historical, and political knowledge that might encourage their identification as Italian, and their commitment to the Italian *terra irredenta*. Sighele's proposed remedy was to encourage a new generation of irredentists who would devote themselves temporarily to the pen rather than the sword, that is, to the dissemination of nationally appropriate historical and geographical knowledge about the *terra irredenta*'s Italian destiny, and the awakening of Italian national consciousness. Their evocations of a historically and geographically ascendant Italian culture would lay the foundations, Sighele predicted, for the time when, as in the days of the mid-nineteenth-century Italian Risorgimento, a war would allow the Italian *terra irredenta* to be claimed by military means.[64]

THE ADRIATIC QUESTION, 1914–1920

The outbreak of war in 1914, between the Entente and the Central Powers, shifted the balance of rival conceptions of identity and sovereignty in Europe. It raised expectations amongst the enemies of the Habsburg empire regarding Austria-Hungary's demise, and placed the fate of Trieste and the Littoral more firmly in an international arena. In that arena, Trieste was rarely referred to as a place where national diversity demanded the reconceptualization of forms of political representation and sovereignty. Prevalent descriptions of the Adriatic as the meeting point of East and West, and of Italians and Slavs (Germans were no longer mentioned), implied a predisposition to political and territorial division. The common shorthand for this equation between identity and sovereignty was the principle of nationality, and in Trieste that principle buttressed the political premises of the prewar nationalists.

Only five years after Sighele had conceded the lack of support for Italian irredentism, the Italian press, politicians, and intellectuals of varying ideological persuasions began to popularize the idea that Italy was a territorially incomplete nation. Patriots rankled by Italy's lack of international status promoted the expansion of Italy's northeastern frontier as the proving ground for the nation as a major power.[65] For Italian irredentists in Trieste, the war provided Italy with the opportunity to conquer the *terra irredenta* and "to make itself great."[66] Consequently, when, in 1915, Britain offered Italy the *terra irredenta* as an inducement to enter the war on the side of the Entente, the Italian government happily accepted. In an earlier (failed) attempt by the Italian Foreign Minister, Sidney Sonnino, to negotiate with the Habsburg government Italy's neutrality or intervention on the side of the Central Powers, the price of Italy's involvement was only the transformation of Trieste and Istria into an autonomous state.[67] The "Secret Treaty of London" agreed to with Britain, promised the Italian government much more than it had demanded from the Austrians or had been dreamed of by irredentists before the war: Trentino, Trieste, Gorizia and Gradisca, Istria (excluding the port town of Fiume), islands off the coast of Istria, eastern Adriatic coastal territory extending to Dalmatia (including the Dalmatian islands), the Dodecanese in the Mediterranean, and African colonies.[68] Once Italy joined in the war, the pledged territory of the Adriatic Littoral became a key Italian military objective. In the years of fighting between Italian and Austro-Hungarian soldiers (which included Slovene and other "Slav" units) that followed, shocking numbers of casualties and the deaths of hundreds of thousands of soldiers provided a convincing backdrop to the potent prewar narratives of cultural struggle. Scipio Slataper, killed in the war fighting for an Italian Trieste, was transformed into a national martyr by Italian nationalists who disowned the writer's prewar dreams of an "Austria of the people."[69] Vivante's suicide (committed in unexplained circumstances a few months before Slataper's death) was offered as evidence of the pathology of the individual who could not identify with a national group.[70] Prewar narratives of the cultural struggle between Italians and Slavs now took on a fresh poignancy and validity. Studies

of Austria and the *terra irredenta* published by a "new generation" irredentist, Virginio Gayda, found new audiences. Gayda's views, like his
future philo-Fascism, exuded political extremism. But his books
reached a broad Italian public, and were published in English for international consumption. In these studies, Gayda described Trieste as the
"moral centre" of the "racial struggle" between Italians, Germans, and
Slavs, and claimed that its "history, its position, its large population,
and its general importance," its "proud Italian past" went "back to
Roman times, when it formed, with all Istria, a single province together
with Venetia."[71] In Gayda's view, Italians were indigenes or *autochthoni*
(a term which suggested that they had literally sprung from the terrain),[72] and Slavs were *invasori*, or "imports."[73] Gayda argued that
Austrians were pursuing "slavification" by encouraging Slav immigration into what was predetermined Italian terrain. Previous immigration
strains, "[c]olonies of Greeks, Armenians, Frenchmen . . . and later
Germans and Slavs," had all been successfully assimilated so that they
were "absolutely indistinguishable from the Italians," but in the
decades before the First World War the new wave of Slav migration
constituted "a veritable organized invasion, silently carried out, as an
artificial phenomenon, planned in cold blood."[74] He claimed that the
Austrian authorities had encouraged Slovene peasants into Italian
towns, and granted them positions in the bureaucracy and law courts,
but, because of the assimilatory capacity of Italian culture, the ongoing
influx of Slav migrants into the region did not affect its fundamental
italianità. Italian cities not only attracted Slavs, Gayda argued, they absorbed them. Gayda built on conventional representations of the differences between Italian (or Latin) types and Slavs, on their relative status
as insiders and outsiders, and added the specific "evidence" of assimilation within Italy and in Trieste. The history of Slavs in the Natisone
valley, annexed by Italy in 1866, "proved," he stated, that "[i]nstinc-
tively, Slovenes feel themselves attracted towards the Italian hearths of
the highest culture. . . . When the Slovene comes into contact with
Italians, even outside the city's walls, he spontaneously learns the
Italian language."[75] Bilingualism in Trieste was a Slavic trait, and symptomatic of the undeveloped character of Slovene culture; Slovene was
only a dialect not a language, and Slovenes had no spontaneous nationalist ambitions. Gayda maintained that because of the cultural inferiority and passivity of Slavs, once they were removed from the ambit of
Austria's insidious influence, they could become the "faithful spontaneous collaborators of Italians."[76]

　　More moderate Italian intellectuals such as Gaetano Salvemini
employed similar representations of difference to give force to their

"minimalist" arguments for Italian claims to the northeastern *terra irre-denta*. Salvemini was an independent socialist democrat and proponent of nineteenth-century Mazzinian ideas of "brotherhood" between nations. A resident of Florence, Salvemini was a hero of the Triestine avant-garde, and an admired acquaintance of influential British and American liberal-democrats. He was widely regarded within Italy and in Europe as an advocate of a "reasonable" nationalism, and irredentists such as Gayda, who renamed him "Slav-emini," considered him a national traitor. Yet Salvemini too enjoined the international community to *"delenda Austria"* (delete Austria)[77]—a prospect that immediately raised the question of the political future of the Adriatic region—and to acknowledge the *italianità* of the *terra irredenta*.

Salvemini's views on the "Adriatic Question" were first published in 1916 in *Questione dell'Adriatico*. Salvemini and his co-author Carlo Maranelli built their argument for the Adriatic's Italian destiny on representations of Trieste as part of a boundary region. They described the Littoral as a place of ill-defined nationalities and "ethnic zones": In Venezia Giulia, "the two nationalities mixed with each other almost everywhere"; Gorizia exemplified "the political indivisibility of the two ethnic zones"; Western Istria was a place where Italians and Slavs "found themselves so mixed up that it was not possible to create any territorial division between them"; in the "ethnically mixed" eastern Adriatic "neither of the two cohabitant nations could advance claims for an exclusive national right."[78] The statistics of Austrian censi showed, Salvemini added, that the provinces of Trieste, Gorizia, and western Istria were almost equally comprised of Italians and Slavs. The hybridity and ambiguity of ethnic identity in the "mixed" regions along the eastern shores of the Adriatic did not prevent Salvemini from proposing the inevitability of Italian sovereignty.[79] This proposal was based not on the predominance of a population that could be named Italian, nor on any evidence of the possibility of a border that might separate Italians from Slavs. Rather, Salvemini argued that the Italian character of the urban centers, the cultural superiority of Italian identity, and a culturally and historically defined "Italian experience" made the Italians of Venezia Giulia "the most cultivated and most refined social element" in "mixed areas," and gave Italy the right to rule over Slavs.[80] He dismissed the only other possibility that he considered, a Slav Trieste, as unimaginable and unreasonable because it would arouse hatred and rebelliousness among the Italians of the region, and suggested that the unequal cultural status of Italians and Slavs would make Italian sovereignty in the region acceptable to its Slav population. Despite Salvemini's censure of what he termed Italian nationalist "slavofobia" and his depiction of Italian claims to Dalmatia as "dal-matomania," the arguments he used to support Italian claims to Venezia Giulia and Istria illustrate the extent to which representations of the moral, historical, and cultural precedence of Italian identity, and of cultural antipathy between Italians and Slavs, could overwhelm contrary evidence of the nature of identity, and underwrite what were regarded as reasonable renditions of how to resolve the problem of sovereignty in a mixed boundary region.[81]

Even the dissemination of publications by Italian intellectuals such as Salvemini and Gayda may not have effectively contributed to the shift in the international balance of perspectives on Trieste and the Adriatic region's political destiny were it not for the growing currency of the principle of nationality among the influential intellectual elites of the Entente. By 1915, British and American liberals and radicals were generally propounding the view that the democratic reorganization of states and state borders in the postwar would rely on the application of the principle of nationality. According to this principle, the political borders of nation-states ideally corresponded with the ethnic borders of homogenous national identities. Despite the evidence from regions such as the Adriatic Littoral that nationalities in a given territory were never simply homogenous, and that individual identities were never solely or even saliently national, on both sides of the Atlantic liberals of all kinds presented the principle of nationality as the legitimate basis for reordering sovereignty in Central and Eastern Europe.

Among the most influential proponents of the principle of nationality and its application in regard to the Adriatic Question was Robert Seton-Watson, editor of the wartime fortnightly review *The New Europe*, founder of the University of London's School of Slavonic and East European Studies, and an important advisor at the British Foreign Office and its wartime Propaganda Department.[82] *The New Europe* published articles by leading European intellectuals (including Salvemini) and was widely read by the statesmen and "experts" who would play important roles in the postwar peace process. Reflecting in 1919 on the evolution of his own views on national identity, Seton-Watson explained that before the war he had believed in the democratic potential of a federal Habsburg empire. However, the war had made him realize that "it lay in the general interest—indeed, in the very logic of things" that the Habsburg and the Ottoman empires make way for a new European (and world) order determined "upon a mainly racial basis," that is, according to the principle of nationality.[83] For Seton-Watson, the source of the ills of the nineteenth and early twentieth century was the European map drawn in 1814 at the Congress of Vienna, which had cut across the natural borders of national difference. As a result there were four main "national questions" in Europe that needed resolution: "The Southern Slav or Adriatic, the Roumanian, the Bohemian and the Polish." In each of these cases, the principle of nationality would involve the establishment of more natural "racial" borders. Those borders would be discerned from maps and censi, from geography, history, and politics, and their rectification would ensure future peace. His own undisguised priorities were to assist the "liberation" of the Slav nations in Eastern Europe from Habsburg rule, and to create a South Slav state (also referred to as Yugoslavia). These objectives, he believed, required him to counter the prevailing image of the Slav as "uncivilised and barbarous."[84]

Although arguments for carving out a South Slav state from Habsburg terrain were made by Serb, Slovene, and Croatian supporters, its most influential proponents were British intellectuals such as Seton-Watson. As with arguments for Italian sovereignty, public discussions of South Slav sovereignty in the Adriatic region involved some demonstration of the salience of Italian and Slav differences and the appropriateness of a border separating them. Seton-Watson, for example, argued that "The True Lines of an Adriatic Settlement" were to be traced in census statistics that established the sum of quantifiable Italian and Slav national identities.[85] Despite the controversy surrounding the composition of Austrian language censi and their political manipulation,[86] Seton-Watson (like Salvemini) explained that the "national" composition of territory in the Adriatic region could be gleaned from the 1910 census: the city of Trieste was 62 percent Italian and 25 to 30 percent Slovene; "the suburbs" were "purely Slovene territory."[87] In Istria the "races" were "more mixed," but it was still possible to identify two zones, "the Western predominantly Italian (129,903 Italians, as against 58,373 Croats and Slovenes) and the Eastern, which is almost exclusively Slav (135,290 Croats and Slovenes as against 6,686 Italians)."[88] These statistics allowed Seton-Watson to spatially segregate discrete nationalities, and to imagine the possibility of a political border between Italians and Slavs.

Seton-Watson's determination to locate a border between Italy and a new South Slav state that would lend credibility to the principle of nationality, did not completely bury consternations that in the Adriatic boundary region there was no contiguous territorial basis for establishing a "scientific" or natural ethno-national border. Seton-Watson accepted that the "essence of the problem" was "to leave as few minorities as possible on the wrong side of the final line and to strike an average between ethnography and geography."[89] Other polemicists for the creation of a South Slav state tried to use the proposition of indivisibility to advantage. Bogumil Vosnjak argued that because "a distinction between the races there was impossible," and because Trieste was both Italian and "Yugoslav," an "Illyrian" Littoral (including Trieste, Gorizia, and Istria) should be created as an appendage of a South Slav state.[90] For Seton-Watson, however, like Salvemini, the region's indivisibility was not a basis for denying sovereignty to Italy. Rather, Seton-Watson proposed that the Adriatic region was "a centre of Italian culture and sentiment," and should be assigned to Italy "on moral and spiritual grounds." Despite their ideological differences, Seton-Watson and Salvemini presumed that by describing the bourgeois urban core of the Adriatic region's cities as culturally Italian, and by representing the Slav population as the inhabitants of suburbs and the outlying hinterland, they could prove that the political destiny of the region as a whole lay inside the Italian state. Seton-Watson's one concession was the creation in an Italian Trieste of a "free port" which, as in the Habsburg era, would allow the town to fulfill its multinational economic function as the main commercial outlet, transport and trade lifeline for the "Danubian lands," including the new South Slav state.[91]

Ultimately, the course of the war, and not the arguments of these men, decided the context in which the Adriatic Question was resolved. In November 1918, a year after the Italian forces had suffered devastating defeat and casualties at the hands of the Austro-Hungarian army in the battle of Caporetto, and had failed in their military attempts to "reclaim" Trieste, the Italian government gained the permission of the Supreme Allied War Council to occupy territory included in the 1915 Secret Treaty of London agreement.[92] With the Austrian army in disarray, Italian troops moved farther inland toward Ljubljana, beyond the traditional *terra irredenta*. This action galvanized the pro-Yugoslav factions from the region into immediately reconciling their political differences, agreeing on the creation of the Kingdom of Serbs, Croatians, and Slovenes (officially entitled Yugoslavia in 1927), and formalizing their own claims to the mixed territory of the boundary region now under Italian occupation.[93] Once the Entente had defeated Austria-Hungary and Germany, the Italo-Yugoslav border was completely transformed from the stuff of nationalist and intellectual speculation into a practical concern of international diplomacy. Importantly, the representations of difference that had characterized Western wartime speculation about the Adriatic Question shaped the debate's new diplomatic form. Those representations also decided Trieste's status in that debate as uncontroversially Italian.

At the postwar peace conference that commenced in Paris in January 1919 under the supervision of the political leaders of the United States, Britain, France, and Italy, the Adriatic Question was regarded as the test case for the official promulgation of the principle of nationality's democratic and pacific credentials.[94] Harold Nicolson, the British diplomat and junior delegate to the conference—a member of the committee assigned to determine the border between Italy and Yugoslavia—believed that if the principle of nationality could not be applied in the Adriatic, it would not stand up anywhere.[95] He also believed that if it was successfully applied, the principle of nationality would abolish the undemocratic diplomacy that had characterized the old world, and, in particular, the Secret Treaty of London, and would establish the limits of Italian and Yugoslav sovereignty in the Adriatic region on a democratic basis.

Despite Nicolson's faith in the democratic promise of the principle of nationality, the official Yugoslav and Italian memoranda of territorial claims presented to the peace conference reflected the potency and authority of now conventional representations of differences between Italians and Slavs, rather than any realistic discussion of democratic representation. An early draft of the Italian memorandum (written in French) demanded all the territory promised in the Secret Treaty of London, as well as the town Fiume (which the Treaty had not promised), and stated that Italian claims in the Adriatic were based on "communal traditions, indissoluble interests, the will and the conscience to safeguard *la Patrie*"; Italians were indigenous in the territory, Slavs were migrants.[96] To the "instinctive" Italianness of the Littoral was added Italy's need to have territory that would allow it to defend the West from *"barbares"* to the East.[97] The memorandum explained that previous annexations by Italy of territory that included *"allogenes"* (literally, of another kind)—French, Slovenes, and Germans—were proof that the introduction into Italy of new Slav minorities would not pose a problem. Indeed, the draft continued, only the assimilation of Slavs in an Italian state could guarantee the containment of the "menacing pressure" of Slavs and potential future Slav irredentism. Later drafts and the final *Italian Memorandum of Claims* made in February 1919 added that although the incorporation of Trieste, Istria, and Dalmatia meant "the inclusion in Italian territory of a certain number of people of foreign tongue and descent," those foreigners were only in the territory because of Austrian policies for the "infiltration and importation of foreign races within boundaries assigned by nature."[98] This memorandum also supported the national necessity for "geographical separation, natural defence, historic tradition and natural redemption," and described (in the liberal language of Ernest Renan) the impetus of an Italian national will:

> At every step from the sea to the mountains . . . the spirit and habits of which are predominantly Italian, even in those parts where infiltration has in the course of centuries interwoven new elements in their ethnical composition . . . the daily life of the people, which is truly, as Renan puts it, "a daily renewed plebiscite" testify to the spontaneity and harmonious participation of Julia Venetia in the secular movement of ideals and heroic action for the liberation and unification of Italy.[99]

For its part, the Yugoslav delegation demanded the coastal territory from Monfalcone (a shipyard town a few kilometers northwest of Trieste) south to Dalmatia and including Trieste—an area that they argued was "inhabited by Yugoslavs in a compact and continuous mass."[100] The Yugoslav memorandum recognized the power of standard representations of Italian and Slav differences in the region, and attempted to subvert them. It described Slovenes "as a highly cultured people" who "possessed a deep-rooted consciousness of their national unity with the other Yugo-Slav peoples." Accepting the conventional depiction of towns as Italian, it argued that since the "Slav element" was the majority everywhere except in those towns, the political fate of the territory had to be decided by that majority. It also stated that rather than favoring Slavs, Austrian policy had been antidemocratic and had privileged Italians.

British and American experts at the peace talks wasted no time debating Trieste's Italian identity, and with little discussion assigned it to Italy. They focused their energies instead on the competing Italian and Yugoslav claims to Fiume, a town that traditionally had not been a concern of Italian irredentists.[101] The intransigence of the Italian and Yugoslav authorities on the question of Fiume led President Wilson himself to suggest a compromise solution in April 1919. The "Wilson line," as it became known, almost paralleled the border proposed by the Secret Treaty of London, granting Trieste, Gorizia, and Istria to Italy. Fiume, however, was earmarked to become the "Free State of Rijeka"— Rijeka being the Slavic name for Fiume.[102] In September, with still no agreement on Fiume, the poet-statesman Gabriele D'Annunzio and a supporting cast of war veterans took it upon themselves to claim the town on behalf of Italy by force. Consequently, the Italian and Yugoslav delegations were pressured to negotiate a treaty between themselves. In November 1920 a domestically weak Yugoslav government signed the Treaty of Rapallo which established the Italo-Yugoslav border even farther east than the Secret Treaty of London line, but promised Sušak (regarded as a suburb of Fiume) and all of Dalmatia to Yugoslavia. Italy obtained Trieste and the Istrian peninsula, the islands of Cres, Lošinj, Palagruža, and Lastovo. Fiume became one of only two places on the European continent where the principle of nationality was explicitly abandoned because it was seen to conflict with the economic and social function of the disputed territory (the other was the port town of Danzig claimed by both Poland and Germany). In these examples the abandonment of the principle of nationality was inspired by more idealistic and realistic considerations than its pretended application in other cases. Yet, the "Free State of Rijeka" never saw the light of day. The Rapallo Treaty's rejection of Italian claims to Fiume and Dalmatia provoked outcries of a "mutilated victory" among some Italian nationalists and aroused support for the burgeoning Fascist movement. By 1922 when Fascists assumed power in Italy, there was even less opportunity to implement the Free State. In 1924 Fiume was legally incorporated into the Italian state by agreement between Italy and Yugoslavia. Bogdan Novak has argued that "[t]he Rijeka events in 1919 were an object lesson for Trieste. . . . A de facto occupation is better security than awaiting settlement at a peace conference."[103]

Historians of the postwar peace such as Rene Albrecht-Carré, Kenneth Calder, and Ivo Lederer have shown that the resolution of the Adriatic Question at the peace conference was decided by strategy and diplomacy rather than the application of the principle of nationality—which was ultimately impossible to apply. Albrecht-Carré states that at a time when Italy was being criticized for attempting to benefit from the old-style diplomacy involved in its secret agreement with England, the success of Italian claims to Trieste, Venezia Giulia, and Istria must be credited to Italy's leading statesmen.[104] Calder refers to the role of Seton-Watson in the promotion of both the Italian and Yugoslav causes, and the moral and political attack on the Habsburg empire.[105] He highlights the importance of the British government's support for the creation of a Yugoslav nation, but adds, "[w]henever there was a conflict of interests between the Italians and the Yugoslavs, the government supported the Italians."[106] Dockrill and Goold too have argued that in 1918 Britain and France were still committed to the provisions of the Treaty of London in Italy's favor, and that the United States alone refused to recognize this vestige of old diplomacy.[107] Alan Sharp describes the American president as an "instinctive friend of Slavs," but records that in January 1919 Wilson told Prime Minister Orlando that "the Trentino and Trieste had, as far as he was concerned, already been ceded to Italy."[108] By focusing on the weakness and division among the Yugoslav delegation, Lederer has emphasized the important role of the diplomats in deciding the Italo-Yugoslav border.[109]

In the context of the *Realpolitik* character of these diplomatic entanglements, it would be difficult to argue that the stock representations of Italian and Slav differences put forward by intellectuals and politicians to support either Italian or Yugoslav sovereignty in Trieste and the Adriatic boundary region determined the political fate of the territory. Certainly Italy's successful claim to the Alto Adige, the region north of Trentino predominantly represented as German-speaking, suggests the influence of strategic and diplomatic considerations rather than representations of national difference. However, the general respect that had accumulated internationally for the principle of nationality had given increased political legitimacy to representations of Italian and Slav differences.[110] During the period in which the fate of Trieste and the Littoral was being decided by peace experts and diplomats, the conception of the region as "a theatre of fusions and mixtures" was still germane to the problem of national sovereignty, but what had shifted was the credence given by European intellectuals, diplomats, and politicians to the criteria of historicity, cultural maturity, and national self-consciousness as justifications for claims to sovereignty. Both the Italian and Yugoslav delegations, and their various supporters, reduced the problem of separating out an Italo-Yugoslav border to the possibility of distinguishing between the relative value of different national (or racial) cultures in respect to these criteria. In 1918 Seton-Watson passed on to peace conference experts deliberating the Italo-Yugoslav border (in particular Nicolson who valued his opinion) his general concerns about "the utter impossibility of finding a line which shall satisfy both races and which shall leave no minorities on either side."[111] In place of the ideal of national self-determination, which he himself had touted, he suggested a historical border, "Italy's frontier in Roman times," which usefully corresponded with "the line of partition between Latin and Slav."[112] While reflecting on the peace process, Salvemini noted that faced with the indefinite nature of nationality in the Littoral even geographers were substituting the idea of a line marking a physical border with a boundary zone that could express a transitional space on either side of the border.[113] Salvemini's resolution was to insist that although national borders could be created "out of the conscience and will of men," in the case of the disputed territory between Italy and Yugoslavia the national border should be decided by an acknowledgment of Italian cultural and political precedence over Slavs. In December 1918, the Italian geographer and Republican Arcangelo Ghisleri imagined himself as Woodrow Wilson at the Paris peace conference: "in front of a large colored ethnographic map of the countries of Europe, which yesterday comprised the Austro-Hungarian empire" facing the problem of "how to mark out the lines in this mosaic of borders without giving rise to a chorus of Babel-like voices."[114] Ghisleri (like Salvemini and Seton-Watson) described nations as ideally the products of collective will and conscience rather than race, but in the *terra irredenta* of the boundary region *italianità* was the product of "the twice millenarian ethnic continuity" which predetermined the objectives of that will.[115] Mixed ethnic zones, he argued, were the artificial result of immigration. "Introduced" cultures (whether the French on Italy's northwestern border in the Val d'Aosta, or the Germans on Italy's "natural" northern border in Alto Adige) were "guests in someone else's house"; the indigenous culture had sovereign rights in that house.[116] All minorities were "guests" in Italian territory, but the Slovenes of Natisone and the Carso, and the Croats of Eastern Istria were not the cultural equals of the French or German groups within (preordained) Italian borders. Ghisleri argued that the Balkan nations (including the new Kingdom of Serbs, Croats, and Slovenes) lacked a heightened and developed sense of national conscience and a national mission. Balkan Slavs had arrived in a territory where an indigenous Italian population allowed them to participate in Italian *civiltà*, the civilization of "the indestructible Latin soul of our border territories."[117] The democratic-minded Ercole Bassi, a regular contributor to the Milan-based journal *La Vita Internazionale* (a journal labelled antipatriotic by orthodox irredentists such as Gayda and Sighele),[118] also took the view that "[i]t should never be allowed that even the simplest Italian centres that boast a much superior *civiltà* would have to be subjected to Slovenes or Croats who with their primitive mentality would continue to carry out the work of oppression of the Austrian imperial past."[119] In the same issue of *La Vita Internazionale*, Libero Tancredi argued that any failure to acknowledge the different evolution of culture and national consciousness of Italians and Slavs would inevitably offend the conscience of an Italian.[120] The Trieste-born Italian geographer Carlo Errera stated that although Slovenes were *invasori* in the naturally Italian territory of Venezia Giulia (the Italian nationalist name for the Littoral), they had been there long enough to forgo the status of a foreign people; he then stated that Italians in the region were linked by the superiority of the Italian language, expressive of a civilization and culture that had no equal in the Venezia Giulia region.[121] Errera explained that Slovenes and Croats had only new and superficial sentiments of solidarity that could not be the basis of national claims in the region.[122]

Conflicting accounts of the propriety of an ethno-national border and of the impossibility of drawing such borders, of the struggles between nations, and of national hybridization, gave international authorities a role in deciding and validating the location of an Italo-Yugoslav border. Their interventions were at least influenced by an accepted vocabulary of Eastern and Western differences, and a hierarchy of nations that may have placed Italians before Slavs, but rendered Italians the inferiors of Englishmen and Americans.[123] The relative status of national representatives at the peace conference merely reinforced accepted representations of the cultural and political characteristics and corresponding moral authority of the different nations as viewed not merely from the West, but from Britain and America. Historians have described the Italian Prime Minister Orlando as an outsider in the Big Four because of his lack of English, and his "Italianness."[124] Dockrill and Goold argue that the British regarded Italians as "objectionable" and "mischief-makers."[125] If Sonnino was respected by the English it was only, British and American delegates argued, because his "Scottish" ancestry made him more respectable.[126] Nicolson wryly observed in his diary *Peacemaking* that during the peace conference "liberated Slavs" were "the lost sheep over whom there was much rejoicing."[127] But Slavs were a group more conventionally perceived by British diplomats as having a doubtful capacity for self-government and as a threat to Western political values.[128] As Nicolson indicated in his own pessimistic reflections on the democratic future of the Adriatic region, Slavs traversed the territory from newly Bolshevik Russia to the Adriatic:

> I also have an uneasy feeling that it would be a mistake to give the Slavs too firm a footing on the Adriatic. What should we do with a Slav block from Vladivostock to Fiume, from Danzig to Samarcand? *Les Scythes ont conquis le monde*. This probably will be one of the great problems of my middle age. What will the new Russia care for the League of Nations?[129]

Seton-Watson may have been a successful proponent of the principle of nationality, and even of the creation of Yugoslavia, but it seems that he was less successful in modifying negative views of Slavs, to which, after all, he had contributed in his discussions of the Adriatic Question. In the aftermath of the Bolshevik revolution, and in the uncertain political and social climate of the postwar, the socialist threat to democracy, and the "pan-Slav spectre," became an interrelated feature of Western representations of Slavs.[130]

The post–First World War peace conference and the disputation that surrounded it not only put the final nail in the coffin of the

Austro-Hungarian empire, it muted discussion of alternative conceptualizations of identity and sovereignty. Before the war, Vivante had
maintained that Italian nationalism tended "at least in its phraseol-
ogy" to find refuge in a utopian line dividing the indigenous Roman-
Italian from the Slav in the Littoral region.[131] The more Italian
government demands for new territory had augmented, the more liberal opposition to the Habsburg empire as a remnant of a feudal age
intensified throughout Europe, the more that the principle of nationality was privileged as the basis for legitimating sovereignty, and the
more the relationship between identity and sovereignty in Trieste was
concentrated in representations of the differences between Italians
and Slavs, their indigenous and migrant status, and their relative cultural worth, the less utopian and more realistic the dividing line
between Italians and Slavs became. In Trieste, essentialized characterizations of Slavs corroborated and authorized the salience of Italian
national identity and of Western Europe. Before the war Trieste had
been the subject of some controversy and interest because it was seen
as a microcosm of the ways in which cultural diversity could be politically managed in Europe as a whole. But by 1918 the problematic relationship between identity and sovereignty was now depicted as
characteristic of territory along the eastern Adriatic coast south from
Trieste as far as Dalmatia and including Fiume/Rijeka, but not Trieste
itself. In 1920, the Austrian socialist Valentino Pittoni thought the possibility of an ethno-national Italo-Yugoslav border so unrealistic in a
boundary region that he continued to insist that Trieste be made a
state in the newly-truncated Austria.[132] Ironically, by then his preference was politically and culturally almost inconceivable in an international arena dominated by those other multinational states Britain and
the United States. After the war, the Adriatic region could still be con-
templated as a crossroads of East and West, of Slav, German, and
Italian, but images of Trieste nestled in a "theatre of fusions and mixtures," or of its German, Jewish, Orthodox, Evangelical, Greek, and
Serb influences, and the prewar discussions of the political modalities
that might best represent class as well as cultural diversity, or even hybrid identities, were of little political consequence internationally. In
the chapters that follow I examine the impact of this discursive shift
on local as well as national knowledges about Trieste and the boundary region, and on the region's political destiny for the remainder of
the twentieth century.

2

Liberalism, Fascism, and Italian National Identity, 1918–1943

According to the principle of nationality established at the peace conference of 1919, the Italo-Yugoslav border should have separated Italian and Slav populations. Instead, national "minorities" became a new feature of the political and cultural landscape on either side of the Italo-Yugoslav border.[1] The existence of minorities on the now-Italian side of the Adriatic boundary region brought to the fore Italian nationalists' anxieties about the homogeneity of the Italian nation. The area inside the Italian border remained a space of possible threat and potential expansion, national definition and national ambiguity.[2] During the war Gaetano Salvemini and Carlo Maranelli warned that the incorporation into Italy of what they estimated to be "half a million Slavs" would pose a problem for the Italian government, and the loss of Dalmatia to Yugoslavia (or, as it was still known, the Kingdom of Serbs, Croats, and Slovenes) would require the Italian state's vigilance on behalf of the Italians there.[3] After 1918, liberal and then Fascist Italian governments employed various strategies to "manage" minorities in the territory, which had been incorporated into Italy and renamed Venezia Giulia. The political ideals of Italian liberalism and fascism were ideologically distinct, but the liberal and Fascist Italian political authorities both represented minorities as a problem in nationally defined terrain. They both endowed the Slav-named minority with the status of an alien, anonymous, antagonistic, yet ultimately assimilable Other.[4] In the interwar period,

2.1. Interwar Borders and Border Preferences

and during World War II, these representations of minorities had crucial implications for the modalities of Italian national identity, and the everyday lives of individuals singled out in the new Italian provinces as foreign.

"FOREIGNERS" IN LIBERAL ITALY, 1918–1922

From November 1918 until the signing of the Treaty of Rapallo exactly two years later—a period during which Italian military forces occupied the territory promised by the 1915 Secret Treaty of London—and then until 1922 when the Fascist Party assumed power nationally, political authority in Venezia Giulia was exercised by appointed individuals who headed "quasi-autonomous regimes."[5] For the first eight months of Italian rule, an Italian military governor, General Carlo Petiti Di Roreto,[6] was given responsibility for the region. From August 1919, "Civil Commissioner-Generals" were appointed by the national government in Rome and granted extensive powers over each of the three new provinces that constituted Venezia Giulia: Trieste, Gorizia, and Istria.[7] The civil commissioner-general appointed to the province of Trieste by the Italian prime minister Francesco Nitti was Antonio Mosconi.[8] Before 1922, these provincial authorities had the same autonomy as previous governors in the Habsburg political system; the only Italian innovation was the expansion of that autonomy in order to assist the political and economic integration of the new provinces into the Italian state.

In Trieste, national integration was not as simple as the wartime representations of its indefatigable *italianità* had implied. At the most visible political level, the end of Habsburg rule aroused tensions among socialists divided by their nationalist, antinationalist, and class objectives. A minority of socialists led by Edmondo Puecher banded with the reformist wing of the Italian Socialist Party and supported an Italian future for Trieste as part of the Italian Kingdom. In 1918, the majority of socialists in Trieste supported their old leader Valentino Pittoni and his vision of a Republic of Venezia Giulia protected by the League of Nations.[9] A year later with Italian rule established in the territory de facto, many of these socialists turned to another faction led by Ivan Regent and Giuseppe Tuntar. This faction supported the creation of an Italo-Slav Soviet Republic in Venezia Giulia.[10] Postwar socialist conceptions of an antinationalist class struggle echoed earlier Habsburg ideals. But as with Regent's claim that Slav national rights could only be achieved by an Italian and Slav proleteriat-led fraternal revolution, they also evoked the contemporary example of the Bolshevik revolution in Russia.[11]

The ambitions of left-wing political groups in the newly Italian Trieste were exemplary of the variety of political responses to the peace process and Italian state's reinvention of Slavs as an alien minority. The Treaty of Rapallo had made the Yugoslav government responsible for Italian minority rights in the Dalmatian territory it was awarded, but had applied no such condition to the role of the Italian state in Venezia Giulia. In some instances, however, before and after Trieste was officially incorporated into Italy, Italian politicians took it upon themselves to informally address and confirm the linguistic rights of the new minorities.[12] In 1919 Prime Minister Nitti instructed the civilian provincial governors "to pursue a policy of freedom, justice and warm sympathy for the people of another race." Nitti argued, "[t]hey must have the feeling that Italy does not desire the denationalisation of the Slavs. Italy is a democratic country."[13] Dennison Rusinow, a historian of Italy's new provinces in the interwar, has shown that regardless of Nitti's instructions, from 1918 to 1922 the treatment of those individuals named as Slavs in each of the provinces of Venezia Giulia was inconsistent, their fate dependent on the discretion of provincial authorities and the "continued trends established during the period of military government."[14] Istria harbored the most regressive practices: "[A]ttacks on Croat institutions and individual Croats were legion and often conducted with the open co-operation of the authorities." In the province of Gorizia north of Trieste, Slovene organizations were left relatively unscathed. In Trieste, Rusinow explains, the treatment of Slavs was not as bad as in Istria, nor as good as in Gorizia. In all these cases, the representation of Slovenes as different rendered their status as citizens vulnerable. Antonio Mosconi, the Trieste civil commissioner-general referred to the new minorities as "aliens" who had to be treated "with equity and justice," but who were also expected to show "their loyalty and absolute respect for the State and for our national consciousness."[15] Mosconi generally described minorities within Italy as *allogeni*. He assumed that the national and cultural identities of these *allogeni* had been fostered by Austria as a weapon against the quantitative supremacy of Italians in the boundary region, and that they could be subdued by the pacifying and assimilating powers of an ancient and superior Italian *civiltà*.[16] The generic category *allogene* referred to minorities within Italy, while the relatively specific term *Slav* was used to emphasize the foreignness of socialist organizations. Although historians such as Elio Apih have argued that socialist organizations had no substantial power in Trieste, Mosconi looked on the local worker organizations and socialist parties as a threat to the vulnerable authority of the Italian state. For the duration of his tenure, from 1919 to 1922, Mosconi led an assault on socialists in Trieste by reinforcing Italian nationalist representations of a combined working-class and Slav cultural menace.[17] Mosconi's identification of working-class discontent and agitation as anti-Italian and pro-Slav fuelled the rhetoric of cultural struggle between Italians and Slavs in the boundary region. This rhetoric also intensified as a result of the demands by substantial pockets of socialists for either the greater autonomy of the new provinces or for their complete independence, and Gabriele D'Annunzio's proto-fascist military occupation of Fiume in September 1919.

As we saw in the first chapter, the synonymity of socialism and Slavs was a feature of prewar Italian irredentist discourse. Mosconi's speeches and actions lent a new national authority and local respectability to representations of Slavs as a restless, dangerous "mass" eager to "invade" Trieste.[18] His evocations of Slavs as aliens or foreigners in Italian terrain also translated into specific anti-Slav policies. Mosconi reneged on promises made by the Nitti government, and prohibited the use of the Slovene language in government institutions and the law courts. More significantly, Mosconi's policies and speeches encouraged and offered ideological protection to burgeoning extremist groups whose main targets were Slavs. In July 1920 Mosconi and the Giolitti-led liberal government that had replaced Nitti's voiced their disapproval of the torching by Fascists of the "Hotel Balkan" (the Trieste headquarters of Slovene cultural organizations also known as the *Narodni Dom*, or National Home).[19] By this time, Mosconi had already lent explicit support to Fascist attacks on working-class and Slovene organizations. These attacks ranged from physical harassment to grenade and bomb offensives.[20] Two months after the burning of the Hotel Balkan, Mosconi turned to the local Fascist Action Squads led by Francesco Giunta for help in disabling a general mass strike. After the Treaty of Rapallo legitimated Italy's claims to Trieste and Venezia Giulia in November 1920, Mosconi orchestrated attacks by Fascist squads against socialists and Slavs, and discouraged arrests of the Fascists responsible.[21] During the general election of 1921 Italian liberals in Trieste made the decision to form a "national bloc" with Fascists against the combined forces of the radicalized Slovene, Croatian, and Italian socialists who had reinvented themselves as members of the Italian Communist Party. The strategy of forming a "national bloc" with Fascists against Socialists and Communists was also adopted at the national level by Giolitti's liberal government,[22] further redefining ideological antagonisms as national antipathies. In Venezia Giulia the election resulted in the return of two (out of three) Fascist candidates and the one liberal candidate in that coalition, and a Communist who later transformed himself into a Fascist. Some historians have attributed the Fascist Party's success to the support of the Triestine bourgeois and commercial classes who sought a remedy to the diminishment of Trieste's shipping role and the contraction of markets that had resulted from Trieste's incorporation into the Italian national economy. The Fascist invocation of Italy's imperial destiny east of its new border promised these commercially oriented groups new trading opportunities. The Fascist victory can also be accounted for by its members' use of aggression, and the unintentional role of the provincial authorities in the validation of Fascist policies and practices.[23]

Whereas before the war the idea that Slavs in Trieste were foreigners was propagated mainly by irredentists, after the war that idea was publicly disseminated by state authorities who thereby defined the acceptable class and political interests of those individuals who wished to be recognized as legitimate Italians. The Triestine bourgeois and commercial classes, and the "newly arrived" pro-Italian intelligentsia that had replaced such intellectual icons of the prewar period as Slataper and Vivante, embraced the idea that Slavs were *invasori,* and that Bolshevism, like socialism, was fundamentally Slavic.[24] Representations of Slavs as "foreign" provided the justification for the redefinition of the Slav-speaking minority as allogene, and relegated Slavic culture to the margins of a Bolshevik and Balkan East.[25] By extension, not only were Italians indigenous, but working-class dissent and socialist agitation was un-Italian.

In the immediate postwar period, the national significance in Italy of a Slav-Bolshevik threat was directly related to anxieties about Italy's diminished national identity, as the "least of the great powers," and recitations of Italy's fate at the peace conference (the "loss" of Dalmatia) as a mutilated victory. The named minorities inside Italy's northern and northeastern borders acted as reminders of the political and cultural diversity of the Italian Kingdom, and of the territory that had been claimed as essentially Italian. Their existence provoked intellectual discussions outside the new provinces about the vitality and reality of Italian national identity.[26] A series of articles on "Foreign Languages and Foreigners in Italy" published in 1922 in the Milan-based reformist review *La Vita Internazionale,* illustrates the place of minorities in conceptions of Italian national identity among the most ostensibly antinationalist of Italian intellectuals. *La Vita Internazionale* was a weekly that published articles by Mazzinians, socialists, democrats, and feminists concerned with social justice. The author of the series on "Foreign languages and Foreigners in Italy," Antonio Marcello Annoni, speculated on what the results of a national census undertaken in the new Italy might reveal about the assimilation of the "foreigners" who had long resided in the old Italy: speakers of French, Slovene, Serbian, Albanian, Greek, Catalan, German-Bavarian, and the German-Vallese dialect. Annoni was optimistic about the capacity of these old "allofone [of another voice] populations in Italy" to live in harmony. He attributed this capacity to their small numbers, their dispersal and Italy's "great assimilatory *civiltà*."[27] Annoni argued that the proof that superior civilizations could absorb inferior ones was provided by the ancient Romans, and Italy's Roman inheritance deemed it an equally powerful assimilator. He assumed that Greeks, with their similarly ancient culture and inherent good business sense, and impressively masculine Albanians accustomed themselves almost naturally to the cultural freedoms of Italian society, while Slavs were easily governable because of the inferiority of their *civiltà*. Despite his general confidence in Italian national identity, Annoni was concerned that after 1920 the conditions under which *allofoni* had previously been assimilated had altered: the addition of new provinces had increased the number of Slav-speakers in Italy tenfold to three hundred thousand Slovenes, and nearly two hundred thousand Serbs.[28] Italy's acquisition of Alto Adige had increased the number of German speakers from fewer than ten thousand to three hundred thousand. Annoni feared that unlike the existing *allofoni*, the new foreigners (particularly the Germans he regarded as the cultural equals of Italians) might remain close to their co-nationals across their respective borders. The one exception was "the new Slav brothers" whose inferior *civiltà* rendered them especially assimilable. Annoni argued that incidents of "resistance" to assimilation among the Slovene cultural circles of Trieste would be quickly overcome, just as over the course of more than half a century the Slovenes of the Natisone in the Friuli region adjacent to Venezia Giulia had given up their language for Italian, and become invisible. "[T]he few *allofoni*," Annoni concluded optimistically, "are easily italianised."[29]

In the period after the Italian government took control of the new provinces, and before the establishment of a national Fascist government, liberals and socialists writing in *La Vita Internazionale* portrayed Italy as a place where there was no minority problem because minorities were left free to use their languages. At the same time, they argued minorities chose to forego that freedom because of their preference for Italian culture, and because of the intrinsic superiority of Italian civilization. Ercole Bassi, a regular contributor to *La Vita Internazionale*, stressed that in Italy allogene minorities were not a problem because

2.2. Italo-Yugoslav Border, 1924

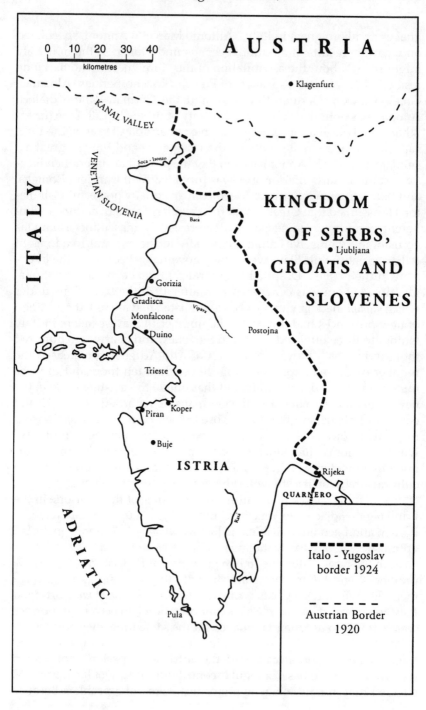

0 10 20 30 40
kilometres

AUSTRIA

● Klagenfurt

KANAL VALLEY

VENETIAN SLOVENIA

Soča - Isonzo

ITALY

Baca

KINGDOM

OF SERBS,

● Ljubljana

CROATS AND

SLOVENES

● Gorizia

Gradisca

Vipava

Monfalcone

● Duino

Postojna ●

Trieste ●

Piran ● Koper

● Buje

ISTRIA

Rijeka

QUARNERO

ADRIATIC

Raša

Pula ●

▬ ▬ ▬ ▬ ▬ ▬
Italo - Yugoslav
border 1924

– – – – –
Austrian Border
1920

Italy's "millennium of *civiltà*" had always demonstrated the maximum respect for small groups of *allogeni*.[30] That same *civiltà* ensured that there was no Zionist problem in Italy, just as there was no antisemitism or racial hatred.[31] Both Bassi and Annoni argued that one had only to compare Italy with the "Balkans inferno," where the lack of a dominant nation with the capacity to assimilate minor cultures had led to an endemic minority problem. Their arguments confirmed that the ideal nation was culturally homogenous by virtue of its ability to absorb and assimilate other cultures, and that the Balkans was the antithesis of this ideal.

Denison Rusinow has argued that in Venezia Giulia fascism was "centralizing, oppressive, and dedicated to the forcible Italianization of the minorities . . . many months before the Fascist regime had destroyed parliament and imposed authoritarianism on Italy."[32] It can also be argued that before the Fascist Party assumed national power, supporters of the liberal and democratic ideals of Italian society characterized minorities as a problem because of their foreignness, and posited Italianization through the assimilatory power of Italian *civiltà* as the solution to the problem of their difference. These views were in full accordance with representations of Italians and Slavs and the principle of nationality sanctioned internationally during the Paris peace process and, as we will see, from 1922 until 1943 they provided a foundation for Fascist strategies for rendering invisible political as well as cultural minorities.

THE FASCIST ITALIAN NATION, 1922–1938

In 1922, the Fascist government began the legislative integration of Venezia Giulia into Italy and, more erratically, into a Fascist vision of Italian national life. Prefects were appointed in the new provinces to directly implement Fascist legislation emanating from Rome. In 1923, toponomy laws reinvented the identities of these provinces, from their "street names and monuments to contemporary persons."[33] The process of renaming was a common feature of nation building in Italy and elsewhere in Europe in the late nineteenth and early twentieth centuries. In this case, the erasure of public traces of an alternative history was compounded by laws against the public expression of alternative linguistic identities. By 1924, throughout Italy, all "foreign-language" newspapers were required to publish Italian translations, and schools were prohibited from teaching in "foreign languages." The regions inside the north and northeastern borders were depicted as places where a natural Italian identity had been artificially muted, and where *italianità* had to be consolidated against the presence of minorities. In the first years of Fascism the full brunt of these laws was most ardently directed against the German-speaking population of Alto Adige—possibly because of the Germans' status as the cultural equals of Italians—but their force was soon extended to Venezia Giulia.[34] In 1925, when Mussolini announced his intention to "fascistize the nation"—to assimilate Italian and Fascist identity—he stated in a "Letter of the President of the Council of Ministers" that "the problem of the new provinces was to be resolved in terms of an Italian duty to content herself with having on her very borders subjects who should be obedient, but remain outside the nation."[35] Between 1924 and 1927 in the northeastern provinces the meaning of the phrase *outside the nation* was translated into policies that transformed five hundred Slovene and Croatian primary schools into Italian-language schools, deported one thousand "Slavic" teachers (personified as "the resistance of a foreign race") to other parts of Italy, and closed around five hundred Slav societies and a slightly smaller number of libraries.[36] In addition, by 1926 Slav surnames had to be changed into what were described as more "aesthetically pleasing" Italian versions.[37] All evidence of non-Italian names, even on old gravestones, was to be erased.

From 1926 the assimilation of Slovenes and other minorities into Fascist Italian life was more aggressively enforced by provincial and national governments. Carabinieri and other groups were directed to search houses for evidence of foreign-language literature. Alien cultural and athletic organizations were purged of their non-Italian content. The Italian Ministry for the Interior liquidated Slovene economic associations, including a thriving network of agricultural cooperatives and banks. Land and property were confiscated from Slovene peasant-farmers. Slovene residents were deported or relocated, and new Italian settlements were introduced.[38] By the late 1920s these policies supplemented the introduction of other nation-building ideals, particularly the supervision of demography through the control of reproduction, and the integration of the public and private identities of Italian subjects.[39] In the wake of Mussolini's 1927 Ascension Day strategies for the "defense of the race,"[40] Trieste hosted a meeting of the "Fascist Federal Secretaries" from the six frontier provinces to coordinate an Italianization program. Trieste's representative was a young Fascist enthusiast named Bruno Coceancig.[41] The meeting produced a memorandum on "Fascism and the *allogeni*" which stated that *allogeni* did not inevitably pose a problem, but any resistance by *allogeni* to assimilation would be construed as an act of disloyalty against the regime. The connotations of assimilation in this case were both political and cultural.

The Fascist Federal Secretaries described Italy as a nation that by nature treated minorities benevolently and justly, as long as those minorities were loyal. That loyalty was to be openly shown to Fascist Italy. This emphasis on assimilation served the purpose of undermining any culturally focused political opposition. Considering the German and Slavic-sounding names of leading local Fascists such as Coceancig (who changed his own name to Coceani) and Fulvio Suvich, the possibility of cultural assimilation may have also served the political ambitions of newly minted Italian-types eager to shed any nominal trace of a culturally hybrid past.

The idea that Slavs were politically as well as culturally assimilable was implicit in attempts to transform local minorities into good Fascists as well as good Italians. In 1928 the *Corriere della Sera* emphasized that the Fascist Italian state required,

> not trembling obedience, but the true and conscious consent of one who understands that he must be disciplined before he can share in the formation of the new Italian spirit. . . . Those who were but groups of Slaves [Slavs] until today are summoned by Italy to be her citizens, with equal rights and equal duties with all the other inhabitants of the peninsula.[42]

In the new provinces these duties were to some extent traditional (until 1942 men who spoke Slovene and who had once borne Slovene names were conscripted into the military). They were also connected to specifically Fascist political objectives. Fascist youth groups included the *allogeni*. Special live-in schools were established for Slav boys in order to indoctrinate them in the ways of Fascism and to remove them from the influence of Slav language and culture.[43] As a corollary to demographic ideals, Slav women were targeted as important agents for the assimilation of children as Italians and Fascists.[44] Federico Pagnacco, the editor of the Triestine pro-Fascist magazine *Italia* and an advocate of veterans' causes, believed that because Slavs were honest peasants led astray by Austria they were also "worthy of becoming real Italian citizens, like other Italian rustics." He even recommended that state creches be established to facilitate the earliest introduction of the children of mixed families to Italian and remove them from the possible influence of surreptitious private expressions of Slav language and culture.[45]

Gaetano Salvemini's documentation of the Fascist treatment of minorities recorded that between February 1927 and July 1932 a special court for crimes against the state, the *Tribunale Speciale per la Difesa dello Stato* sentenced 106 Slavs to 1,124 years in prison.[46] Salvemini noted that in proportional terms, "Slav criminals" far outnumbered Italians in the

Special Tribunal's sentencing and executions. This situation suggests either more widespread resistance among Slovenes, or that Fascist authorities paid more attention to dissent they could identify as Slav. The historian Anna Maria Vinci claims that the effect of Fascist Italianization policies was to disperse the disaffected communities, particularly Slovenes, and to annihilate their memory and identity.[47] Yet Vinci's own evidence suggests that between 1921 and 1931 there was no decline in the number of individuals in Venezia Giulia who identified as Slovene, or were judged to be *alloglotte* (of another tongue). If anything their numbers had risen slightly. The more the Fascist government introduced repressive measures to eradicate traces of political and cultural difference, the more resistance intensified, and the more Slovene-speakers identified as non-Italian and anti-Fascist.[48] Not all resistance was politically motivated, or took the form of terrorism, but measures directed against Slavs and political dissent were effectively creating an "external" Slav threat.[49] In the late 1920s and 1930s (political and/or cultural) anti-Fascists established bases across the border in Yugoslavia (the most notable were two underground terrorist movements known as TIGR and ORJUNA).[50] By the 1930s exiled Triestine Communists were planning the creation of an independent Slovenian workers' and peasants' republic in the boundary region straddling Yugoslavia, Austria, and Italy. This republic was to attach itself to any of these states "in which a Communist regime might be victorious."[51] In 1931, a journalist from the *Corriere della Sera* told his readers that the Italian boundary region exuded the "atmosphere of war."[52]

The intensification of anti-Fascist resistance in Venezia Giulia coincided with renewed efforts by the Fascist government to incorporate the "problem" of minorities into a national Italian history of political and cultural assimilation and conquest.[53] At the 1932 Rome exhibition of the Fascist Revolution the Slav threat was given national recognition. Arms and ammunitions said to have been found amongst the ruins of the "Hotel Balkan" destroyed by Fascists in 1920, were displayed as evidence of Fascist vigilance against the Slav enemy.[54] The burning of the Hotel Balkan was transformed into a foundation event in historical narratives celebrating Fascism's fight against Slavs along Italy's border. Publications such as *Il Fascismo nella Venezia Giulia: Dalle origini alla marcia su Roma* claimed that the Hotel Balkan had been a "foreign fortress in the heart of Trieste," a front for pro-Austrian, and pro-Yugoslav activities, the center of Slav propaganda, and "a nest of spies and secret agents."[55] In 1934, *Trieste* featured the burning of the Hotel Balkan as one of a series of critical moments in the history of Italian nation building.[56]

Just as previous liberal authorities had portrayed socialist activities as un-Italian, Fascist authorities consistently characterized anti-Fascism, like the Slavs themselves, as an import, an "artificial resistance," "a Balkan manoeuvre," "a foreign activity," and an extension of the history of Habsburg conspiracies against Italy in the past.[57] Yugoslavia, like Austria before it, was depicted as a state that fostered this Slav/Balkan enemy. In defending the work of the *Tribunale Speciale* in Venezia Giulia and its targeting of Slavs, Mussolini argued that "the centres of criminal infection are created and nourished from the other side of the border."[58] Bruno Coceani described three young Slovene men executed by the *Tribunale* in 1930 as Slavs from "beyond the borders" who had attempted to incite the local population against Italy and to hinder the civilizing work of Italy and Fascism.[59]

Over the period that Fascist laws and policies of enforced assimilation were being implemented in the boundary region, Fascists elaborated theories of Italian national identity, of the diversity of peoples or races in the Italian state, and the unifying and homogenizing spirit of the Italian nation.[60] Historians such as David Horn and Victoria De Grazia have stressed that "Italy was a nation in which 'admixtures' were not feared but were instead imagined to invigorate the stock."[61] Acknowledgments of Italy's heterogeneity were a feature of the assimilationist views of Italian nationalists. Under Fascism, nationalist emphases on a spiritual and racial, vitalist and eugenic conception of the assimilatory capacity of *italianità*, had explicit political as well as cultural implications.[62]

In 1922, Enrico Corradini, the principal theorist of Fascist nationalism, argued that the Italian nation was a racial as well as historical entity. Like France it comprised a diverse number of regional races or *stirpi* and "minorities" united by their "*anima*." "It is a common soul," Corradini explained, "which lies behind so many beings living between the borders assigned in its name."[63] Luca Dei Sabelli, the author of *Nazione e minoranze etniche*, a 1929 study of minorities within Italian borders sponsored by the Legal and Historical section of the National Fascist Institute of Culture, situated Italy in the context of a Europe where races had become mixed, and where the mettle of a *stirpe* was proved by that *stirpe*'s ability to expand and assimilate other cultures. Dei Sabelli argued that Italy had no minority problem because such a problem existed only where assimilation was not effective.[64] Fascist intellectuals distinguished their spiritual version of race from biological racial theories, but that did not make their views of Italian nationalism any less effective for legitimating political and cultural uniformity, or repression. Horn offers as an example of the Fascist idea of race an interview conducted with Mussolini in 1932 in which the *Duce* "explicitly rejected the notion of a 'pure' race and observed that 'it is often precisely from happy mixtures that a nation derives strength and beauty.'"[65] The possible political and cultural connotations of this view of "happy mixtures" were underlined in Mussolini's document "Doctrine of Fascism" that same year. By evoking Italy's "single will" and "single conscience" (terminology fundamental to contemporary liberal conceptions of the nation throughout Europe), Mussolini blurred the borders between the respectability of the theme of *italianità*'s assimilatory capacity and the Fascist preference for political conformity.[66] By 1932, the national Fascist government's homogenizing vision of the nation as a state "unmarred by conflicts between capital and labour, centre and periphery," had merged with the repression by local and provincial Fascist authorities of different ways of being politically and culturally Italian.[67]

The coincidence of aggressive assimilation practices in the boundary region and the theoretical articulation of the eclectic spiritual bases of Italian national identity, also corresponded to both the unflagging representations of minorities within Italy as anonymous *allogeni*, and of Slavs as inhabitants of a territory *oltre il confine* (beyond the borders) stretching from Serbia in the south to Russia in the north. According to Arturo Cronia, "what little was written about the people of the border" during the interwar period "was for reasons of legitimating the border or . . . to complete the picture and general panorama of Yugoslavia."[68] Cronia argues that after the creation of Yugoslavia in 1918, a few intellectuals felt it "necessary to clarify the ideas" about Slavs, about the "ethnic and linguistic stock" of Slavs, their successive "morphological, historical and spiritual differentiation," and their contemporary aspirations.[69] Two of these intellectuals were Francesco Musoni, whose 1923 ethnographic study of Yugoslavia borrowed the term *Balkans* and the classification of Yugoslavia into three "racial" groups (the Dinaric, Central, and Pannonian) from the Croatian/Yugoslav anthropologist Jovan Cvijič; and Francesco Pullè who published a four-volume work, *L'Italia—genti e favelle* in 1927, in which he argued that all the national groups in the Adriatic (particularly Dalmatia) were biologically Italian.

Trieste, because of its Habsburg past, was regarded by some intellectuals as an important conduit for knowledge about the Slavs who existed beyond Italian borders, and for disseminating Italian civilization among them.[70] In 1929 the Fascist Triestine journal *Italia* advertised a book series on *Il Genio Slavo* that featured original works (in translation) from Russia, Poland, and Yugoslavia.[71] The rationale for the series was that Slavs had become part of "the Italian cultural patrimony" and had "entered into the sphere of an Italian aesthetic sensibility." Mussolini, the advertisement claimed, had brought about friendship between the Slav and Italian peoples. *Italia* invited Italians "to penetrate the soul, the life, the history, of the various Slav races [*stirpi*]." The break in the relationship between Italy and Yugoslavia, which occurred that same year (1929 marked the end of the Treaty of Friendship and Co-operation between Italy and Yugoslavia, and the signing of the Concordat between Italy and the Vatican), was reflected in the short life of this advertisement.[72]

The second issue of *Italia* for 1929 presented Yugoslavia as part of *La Balcania*, a place where East and West clashed, and where there was no stability of government or borders, a volcanic terrain where a subspecies of nationality was the product of indefinable, confused, and intersecting ethnic groups.[73] This view of the Slav/Balkans east of Italy corresponded to the view propounded by Dei Sabelli's study of minorities in Italy published the same year. Denying the existence of a minority problem within Italy, Dei Sabelli concluded that "it was impossible to conceive of any parity of rights" between Italians and Slavs, because "the barbarian" was the enemy of "the civilised world."[74] Coincident with intensifying anti-Fascist resistance on Italy's northeastern border and deteriorating relations between Italy and Yugoslavia, the Triestine press militantly represented Slavs as a biological threat to the Italian body politic. Mussolini's description of anti-Fascists as a "criminal infection" echoed the language of local exponents of *Fascismo Bonificatore* (literally, the Fascism that had reclaimed the land). Publications such as *Popolo di Trieste* and *Italia* enjoined the Italian government to "cut deep into this festering sore and without mercy remove this ulcer,"[75] to take steps to "purify" the region against "the Slav swamp," and to eliminate "the residue of Austrian hybridity."[76] The journalist Livio Ragusin-Righi urged eradication of "Austrian cancers" to protect Italy from "infection."[77] He argued that only Fascism had been able to conduct the necessary "surgical and hygienic operation" that fended off invasion of the national body.[78] Ragusin-Righi portrayed Fascism's specific contribution to the Italian nation as its ability to more effectively spread "the breath of a superior *civiltà* among less developed populations than the preceding weak-kneed liberal government."[79]

In this Fascist period, Slavs were both an external menace and an assimilable allogene inside Italian borders, just as they had been during Mosconi's government. In 1930, the local Triestine newspaper *Il Piccolo* described allogene as a denomination that distinguished between Italian citizens.[80] The Italian historians, political scientists, anthropologists, and

Fascist politicians who referred to minorities within Italy preferred to use these generic terms. In his critique of the Fascist treatment of minorities, Salvemini believed that this preference was meant to accentuate the differences between Italians who naturally belonged and the other (allo) "kind" (gene), "voice" (phone) or "tongue" (glotte) minorities.[81] In 1929 Ragusin-Righi implied that these terms were indicative of the insignificance of linguistic minorities in Italy, leaving him to ponder whether even "to believe or not to believe in the alloglotte population."[82] His own conviction was that "for Italy *un problema allogeno* does not exist in Venezia Giulia, just as it does not exist elsewhere."[83] The *allogeni* were "new Italian citizens who still need to be cultivated/cultured" and who "with time . . . could become truly Italian, even in sentiment."[84] Slavs specifically were "a minority which did not exist," the artificial product of Yugoslav nationalism and "Balkan megalomania."[85]

Fascist representations of the concomitant invisibility and superficiality of the *allogeni* were bolstered by the argument that Fascism would provide the conditions under which *allogeni* could recover an original Italian identity. For example, Fascist apologists argued that the Italianization of surnames would restore lost Italian selves.[86] Fascism would help "*allogeni* recover their real being, liberating them from the encrustation of others' ideas," from "every external influence" and "every residue of a false past."[87] A similar supposition was made in respect to the lost Italian identity of the territory. In 1925 Mussolini described the Fascist policy for managing "the problem of the new provinces" as the restoration of Italian territory whose identity had been destroyed under foreign governments to its "natural" Italian state.[88] This view validated Fascist planning policies in Venezia Giulia and Trieste, the historical showpiece of the new provinces. Fascist municipal and national administrators began planning the reinvention of Trieste's urban center as the modern incarnation of an ancient Roman settlement. The focus of excavations was the area containing Roman temple ruins, adjacent to the city's central church San Giusto and the *città vecchia*. While much of the old town was destroyed in order to uncover the ruins of a Roman amphitheatre, the progress of the amphitheatre's excavation was intensively promoted at national and international levels. The culmination of this promotional activity occurred when the *teatro Romano* was completed in time for the *Bimillenario Augusteo*, which lasted from September 1937 until September 1938 and featured Trieste and Venezia Giulia.[89]

The disinterment of the ancient Roman past conflated the ambitions of late-nineteenth-century and early-twentieth-century Italian nationalists and interwar Fascists. Italy's Roman ancestry had been an important aspect of nineteenth-century Mazzinian nationalism, which represented a unified Italy as the "Third Rome."[90] Excavations, like the toponomy laws enacted in 1920s and 1930s, were common to the late-nineteenth-century process of Italian unification and the creation of an Italian identity.[91] Gino Bandelli has shown that plans for digging up Trieste's Roman past had been elaborated in the late 1800s. Under Fascism, however, the recovery of material traces of Trieste's Roman past involved the symbolic removal of the layers of a "foreign" Habsburg history and the German and Slav features of the landscape as well as of its population.[92] The philo-Fascist Triestine historian Attilio Tamaro depicted each archaeological discovery as a "reply to the predatory aspirations of Slavs or a lesson to unconscious Austrian Italophobia."[93]

The archaeological revelation of the boundary region's Roman past was supplemented by the imposition of new layers of a material culture intended to highlight Trieste's simultaneously Fascist and Italian identity.[94] The city of Trieste was chosen as a national seat of the *Littoriali dell'Arte e della Cultura*. When Mussolini visited in September 1938, he viewed the *teatro Romano* and laid the foundations for the construction of the *Casa del Fascio* or Fascist Party Headquarters opposite the *teatro*, at the foot of the *zona capitolina*.[95] He also inaugurated the new university, which was to be built in the monolithic *stile littorio* on an elevated eastern site. The university's mission was to shine "the light of Italian culture and *civiltà*" "towards the villages of Trieste's hinterland and to the regions of the East."[96] In December 1938 Bruno Coceani declared before the Italian parliament that the university would function as "the spiritual defence of the border and of the cultural expansion of *nostra stirpe*."[97]

The phrase *nostra stirpe* could be understood as a reference to the spiritual dimensions of Italian national identity, but the prevailing premises of the relative value of different nations and cultures, and the assimilatory and civilizing role of *italianità*, rendered *stirpe* as potentially deterministic as biologically-based forms of racial identification. Two months before Mussolini's arrival in Trieste, a group of Italian scientists had published a manifesto attesting to the existence of biological races, and the Aryan origins of the Italian race.[98] By then, spiritual definitions of race and nation had provided adequate validations for the state-authorized repression of political and cultural differences.

RACE, NATION, AND WAR, 1938–1943

In the biological period of Italian racism inaugurated by the July Manifesto and by Mussolini's evocation of a nationwide "Jewish problem" on his visit to Trieste in September 1938, the national status of the boundary region was reaffirmed.[99] During this period, groups of young Fascists had organized attacks on Trieste's synagogue and provoked a climate of "racial" tension in the region. By November, a month after the signing of a military agreement between Italy and Germany (the Rome-Berlin Axis) the Fascist government had introduced laws aimed at resolving the "Jewish problem."[100] These laws prohibited all Jews, regardless of their political loyalty to Fascism, from participating in schools, commerce, professions, or politics. The application of these laws in Venezia Giulia transformed Trieste from the most prominent Italian center of Jewish culture into an epicenter of Fascist antisemitism.[101]

During the final five years of Fascist government (and for most of the Second World War), Jews throughout Italy were the focus of an official campaign to educate the Italian population in a biological understanding of Italian national identity that significantly mirrored the Nazi view of the world. Contributors to new Fascist journals such as *Razza e Civiltà* and *La Difesa della Razza* detailed the biological threat of Jews—and other "non-Europeans" such as Africans—to the purity of the Italian race.[102] Even though Nazi racial ideology provided a biological grounding for anti-Slavism, in the new Italian racial propaganda there was no biological explication of the racial alterity of Slavs. A 1940 issue of *La Difesa della Razza* featured the ethnographic work of a Slovene (educated in Germany), Božo Škerlj, whose views of race in the Adriatic region were displayed over four colorful pages. Škerlj argued that Europe had ten to twelve races that were subspecies of the white race. He used his method of racial classification to prove that Dalmatians were not Italian—an argument disputed by the editors of *La Difesa*, who were otherwise pleased to have a racial microstudy of the region. Škerlj emphasized that the border between Italy and Yugoslavia separated two racially distinct groups, Italians and Yugoslavs. The editors of *La Difesa* countered that the same Italian race occupied both banks of the Adriatic.[103]

There were other continuities between views of the significance of Slav difference during the periods of interwar assimilationism and wartime racism. Vinci argues that the intolerance cultivated in Trieste against a Slav enemy for nearly two decades had prepared the local population for the politically motivated antisemitic campaigns that took place during World War II.[104] Four years before the introduction of the racial laws, Salvemini had tried to alert the world to Fascism's treatment of minorities, including Slovenes, Serbs, Greeks, Albanians, Germans, and Masons, and had given special mention to evidence of Fascists singling out Jews as inherent enemies of the state.[105] In 1937,

Achille Starace, the national secretary of the Fascist party, proposed that one enemy of the Fascist revolution—the "red Slavs"—had been eliminated, but another, "masonic liberal Jews," remained.[106] Even after the introduction of the racial laws, some Fascists continued to describe the Italian "race" in spiritual terms as *una razza dell'anima e dello spirito* (a race of the soul and of the spirit). Giacomo Acerbo, a key figure in the Fascist Party and national government, wrote in 1940 that "the great people of Italy" were composed of "many *stirpi*." The nation was "an ethnic mixture," but the "ethnic complex of the Italian people" had survived generations, just as its "sentiment for a unified destiny" had not been exhausted.[107] That destiny was guided by the assimilatory spiritual forces of *italianità* and millennial, immortal Roman *civiltà*.[108] The bibliography of Acerbo's study *The Principles of the Fascist Doctrine of Race*, devoted to an impressive array of English-, French-, and Italian-language discursions on nations, integrated his interpretation of Italian national identity into a mainstream Western European intellectual tradition.

The introduction of the racial laws did not affect the engagement of municipal, provincial, and national Fascist authorities with a Slav-Bolshevik threat from *oltre il confine*. Rather, as anti-Fascist and Communist resistance grew more organized and efficient in the region, and as the Fascist government made plans for "imperial expansion" into territory across Italy's northeastern border, Slavs from beyond the borders were increasingly referred to as the beneficiaries of an Italian civilizing mission.[109] In fulfillment of a promise made to Fascist supporters almost two decades earlier, Trieste was to be transformed into the bulwark of a new Italian empire. Songs celebrated Trieste as "the bridgehead of Italy towards the East," the "centre of the spiritual radiation of *romanità* in the nearby lands beyond its borders."[110] *Geopolitica* (1939–1942), a review based at the Geography Institute of the University of Trieste and dedicated to expressing the "geographic doctrine of the Empire," described Trieste as the emblem of "national unity, and . . . of the new shores of expansion and conquest in the Balkan Orient."[111] Published under the auspices of Giuseppe Bottai, editor of *Critica Fascista* and a member of Mussolini's Grand Council, *Geopolitica* involved the participation of academics from the Milan Catholic University, the Political Science Faculty of the University of Pavia, and large numbers of Triestine intellectuals, including the geographer Carlo Schiffrer who, ironically, had cultivated a reputation for writing objective and even anti-Fascist history.[112] Vinci argues that the review was one more scientific instrument for promoting the respectability of Italy's national mandate of cultural and territorial expansionism in the

Balkans, and for creating an Italian *"spazio vitale"* in the Mediterranean and Balkans.[113]

Italian military forces were not sent across the Italo-Yugoslav border to establish Italy's imperial destiny in the Mediterranean and Balkans until 1941, after the Yugoslav state had collapsed under the force of a German offensive.[114] After 1941, these forces occupied parts of Yugoslavia, effectively dissolving the border's relevance. Italian military administrations were established in the Slovene capital, Ljubljana, and Dalmatia. Despite the urging of the Triestine Aldo Vidussoni (a secretary of the national Fascist Party) that all Slavs in the occupied territory be exterminated, Fascist authorities awarded their new subjects rights in principle that Slovenes and Croatians living within the interwar borders did not have. The Italian forces hoped that these rights would gain them popular support and prevent possible challenges to their administration from their German allies, who had imperial ambitions of their own in the region.[115] James Walston has argued that in practice Slavs in occupied Yugoslavia were treated with no more respect than inside Italy's legal borders, where civilian authorities incited pogroms against Jews and Slovenes, and destroyed any of their remaining businesses.[116]

After 1941 too, Communists from Venezia Giulia who had gone into exile returned to organize mass resistance. As Italian-, Slovene-, and Croatian-based Communist organizations established an anti-Fascist network inside the territory occupied by Italian forces and on both sides of the old Italo-Yugoslav border, the Italian Fascist government felt even more under siege from a Slav threat.[117] The anti-Fascist and Communist resistance was now labelled by authorities as Jewish as well as Slav and Bolshevik. Between 1941 and the spring of 1943, Fascist death squads operating in Venezia Giulia exacted summary justice against suspected subversives, regardless of whether they were identified as Jewish, Slovene, or Italian.[118] From 1942, a Special Italian Inspectorate of Public Security terrorized the city and its peripheries. It was headed by a former specialist in the Italian state's campaign against Sicilian *banditi*. The Italian military erected concentration camps *per scopi repressivi* (for the purposes of repression) in Venezia Giulia, in which they interned "able-bodied people from ethnic minorities" living inside and outside Italy's pre-1941 borders.[119] In early 1943 an Italian army order called for the internment of individuals from Venezia-Giulia identified as *allogeni* "between the ages of 42 and 55 and non-able-bodied people from 19 upwards and families of rebel supporters." The number of so-called allogene internees (including mothers and children) was nearly 70,000 out of a regional Slav population that Italian censi numbered at 360,000.[120] The most notorious of these camps was at Gonars near Trieste, and on the Adriatic island of Rab. The Rab camp held Slovene and Croatian civilians, many of them originally from Dalmatia.[121] According to Walston, the annual mortality rate was at least 18 percent, "[t]ens of thousands of internees died of disease and malnutrition."[122]

War had provoked all sides to participate in atrocities within and beyond the old Italo-Yugoslav border. Widespread views that Slavs were foreigners on Italian soil, and that assimilation was evidence of the superiority of Italian *civiltà*, had an important role in determining what was remembered about the responsibility of each of these sides for atrocities, and the meaning attributed to their actions. With the collapse of Mussolini's government in 1943 the history of the Italian military's civilian concentration camps, and the chauvinism that had led to their creation were soon forgotten. As Walston argues, the wartime events in the Balkans "have not become part of history or general knowledge in Italy."[123] The attribution of the 1938 Fascist racial laws to Nazi influence, has encouraged historical views of Italians as a characteristically *brava gente*, and racism as an anomalous chapter in Italian history.[124] Events in the boundary region during the interwar period have been described as peripheral to the mainstream of Italian politics and forms of national-ism. Wartime events have been historically interpreted as a struggle be-tween two antagonistic nations, rather than conflict between a state and its citizens.[125] Some historians who have focused on Fascist policy in the boundary regions before 1938 attribute policies in the provinces to the pressure exerted by extreme nationalists from these areas on an other-wise dispassionate national government. Rusinow argues that the ap-pointment of Fulvio Suvich (a Triestine) as Under-Secretary at the Italian Foreign Office in 1932 coincided with the intensification of offi-cial Slavophobia.[126] However, in the 1930s Salvemini had argued that Fascist assimilation policies directed against cultural minorities were an extension of the general Fascist repression of political opposition, with even more tragic consequences. The interwar history of Italy's north-eastern boundary region also suggests that the predominant represen-tation of minorities as cultural "others" was integral to the mainstream conceptualization of the homogenizing nature of a spiritual Italian identity, and a validation of the Italian nation itself. Fascists exploited rather than created representations of the place of minorities in the na-tion—of Italian and Slav, and then Jewish and Italian differences—in or-der to justify political uniformity within its borders, and to assert Fascist as well as Italian sovereignty in the boundary region.[127] Liberal and Fascist authorities alike had iterated the differences between an

Italian self and Slav other, and emphasized the assimilatory capacity of *italianità* in order to secure the borders between Italy and Yugoslavia, between Italy and the Balkans, and between their preferred social order and the various forms of political opposition that, they believed, jeopardized Italian national sovereignty.

In 1932 the Triestine writer and journalist Silvio Benco confidently declared that in Trieste, the "anxious preoccupation" with identity on Italy's northeastern border was over: "Trieste in the past has been a crucible of peoples; today it is a city which can refer to itself as having one nationality alone."[128] For Benco, homogeneity was one of the great achievements of a decade of Fascist government in Italy. Yet the problem of cultural difference in the new border provinces continued to preoccupy local, provincial, and national Italian governments throughout the 1930s. In the closing phases of the Second World War, the English geographer Arthur Moodie commented on the recent history of the Italo-Yugoslav border by recalling that when he visited Venezia Giulia in 1931 and 1937 he observed "the widespread occurrence of Fascist slogans, catch-phrases and inartistically-drawn emblems and posters, inscribed in enormous letters or painted in flamboyant colours on the walls of almost every building, in town and village alike."[129] He believed that this "window-dressing" had been effective in convincing visiting Italians of the region's Italianness:

> [L]arge numbers of Italians have been brought annually to Venezia Giulia by every kind of cheap excursion and from all parts of the Kingdom. When they have seen the decorated walls of the towns and villages, they return home convinced of the "Italianita" of the region and presumably have more faith in the administration of their Government.[130]

Moodie argued that these material markers of *italianità* could not be used "as objective evidence of the culture of the people" because they were staged. Although his skepticism about the performance of Italian national identity in the Venezia Giulia region was an expression of his ideological disaffection with Fascism, rather than doubt regarding Trieste's Italianness, it exposed the problem with the principle of nationality validated internationally during the 1919 peace process. This principle presupposed the political representation of an intrinsic and homogenous collective national identity. Yet, in practice, liberal and Fascist governments in the Trieste region based their authority on the symbolic and discursive representations of Italian national identity and of the differences between Italian and Slavs. When German forces occupied Venezia Giulia in late 1943, the boundary region was once again more explicitly vulnerable to identification as "a hybrid zone, fractured, without an identity."[131] Under these circumstances Italian intellectuals of almost all political persuasions turned their attention to the restoration of representations of the territory's *italianità* as the basis for redeeming the region's Italian sovereignty. As we will see in the following chapter, those members of the Triestine population who had found the political experience of Italian sovereignty unsatisfactory, were galvanized instead by the alternative conceptions of the relationship between Italians and Slavs, and between identity and sovereignty, on offer from the Yugoslav Communist resistance.

3

Anti-Fascism and Antinationalism, 1943–1945

I n 1941 the political leaders of Britain and the United States, Winston Churchill and Franklin Roosevelt, signed the Atlantic Charter which stated that the ethical basis for British and American cooperation in the war was the defense of national sovereignty and "self-government," the ability of "all nations" to dwell "in safety within their own boundaries."[1] The same year Italian and German military forces had negated the post–First World War Italo-Yugoslav border by invading and then occupying Yugoslavia. From October 1943, German military occupation also undermined Italian sovereignty within pre–1941 Italian borders, including Venezia Giulia. By then the progress of the war in Venezia Giulia was shaped by the question, which border was the expression of the "self-government" of which "nation" and in what territory. At various times after the collapse of Mussolini's national government, Republican Fascists, Italian nationalists, the Littoral National Guard, the Slovene Home Guard (Domobranci) , Croatian Ustaše and Serbian Četniks all collaborated with German forces in the boundary region in the hope of realising their respective nationalist territorial goals. Anti-Fascist forces in the region coalesced into two major resistance movements, each championing its own view of a future Italo-Yugoslav border, and the form of national sovereignty and self-government that would guarantee democracy in the postwar.

From 1941 an ever-growing number of people in Venezia Giulia joined the Slovene Liberation Front *(Osvobodilna Fronta)*. Their motivations varied. Some fought just to survive, some for the national liberation of Slovenes from Italian and German occupation, others for a new "antinationalist" order promised by the Communist ideal of "Italo-Slovene brotherhood" in a future federal Yugoslavia. The Liberation Front's popularity and the challenge posed to Italian sovereignty by the occupation of Venezia Giulia by the German military provoked pro-Italian anti-Fascists, many of them left-wing and Mazzinian intellectuals with established community standing, to form an alternative resistance organisation, the Venezia Giulia National Liberation Committee *(Comitato di liberazione nazionale* or CLN). The Venezia Giulia CLN was connected to the Milan-based Upper Italy National Liberation Committee *(Comitato di Liberazione Nazionale Alta Italia* or CLNAI), an umbrella organization that had emerged after September 1943 from a coalition of Italian liberal, socialist, nationalist, and communist parties.[2] Although the CLNAI cooperated with the Liberation Front, the explicit aim of the Venezia Giulia CLN was to offer an anti-Fascist and anticommunist alternative to the Liberation Front and to defend the 1920 Italo-Yugoslav border. The pro-Italian anti-Fascists of the Venezia Giulia CLN regarded the Liberation Front as an alien and anti-Italian Slav organization. They disputed the authenticity of any Italian support for Italo-Slovene brotherhood, arguing that Italian identity was the expression of a sophisticated bourgeois urban culture, and Slavs were a culturally inferior "racial" group extending from the Urals to the Balkans.

The competition between these anti-Fascist movements reinvented Trieste as a problem in terms similar to those established during the First World War. In this chapter I examine first the significance for some Triestines (Italian and Slovene) of the Liberation Front's political program of Italo-Slovene brotherhood and the idea of a federal communist Yugoslavia, and second, the forms of national identification that shaped the anti-Fascism of Venezia Giulia CLNists. This juxtaposition allows a closer focus on individual forms of national identification (Italian and Slovene or Yugoslav), the reproduction and negotiation of those identities in specific historical contexts and in relation to other forms of political, class, and gender identification. The struggle by anti-Fascists in the boundary region to authenticate and empower either communist or Italian identities, to establish the cultural and ethical foundations for their respective claims to territorial sovereignty in Trieste, was a struggle over the nature and significance of nationalism, and more specifically, narratives about the differences between Italians and Slavs.

COMMUNISM AND THE ITALO-SLOVENE

The Slovene Liberation Front was created in 1941, after Yugoslavia was occupied by the Italian and German armies. It operated in the territory of Slovenia (Yugoslavia) and Venezia Giulia (Italy), and acted as the resistance organization of the Slovene Communist Party. Initially it was organized on the model of the Popular Fronts of the interwar period in France and Spain and included noncommunist members. From 1943 it developed stronger ties with the Tito-led Yugoslav resistance movement based in Bosnia. Throughout its existence it officially proclaimed a commitment to both antinationalist support of the international interests of the working class, and national liberation as a response to the Fascist treatment of Slovenes. By 1943, Liberation Front intellectuals envisioned Slovene national self-determination within a new federal and Communist Yugoslavia. Rusinow describes the historical significance of the Liberation Front as twofold: firstly, it was "the first armed Resistance movement on the soil of either Italy or the German Reich (in Venezia Giulia and [Austrian] Carinthia)"; secondly, "in its ranks and its spirit the Slovene people, one of the most 'unhistoric' of Europe's nations, found themselves at last and laid the foundations of the Slovene national renaissance that has played a vital role in the post-1945 history of Yugoslavia."[3] Whether or not we can judge if the Slovene people "found themselves," the Liberation Front can be described as the vehicle for alternative, and not uncontradictory, conceptions of the relationship between identity and sovereignty. The Liberation Front's promise of a new postwar order that would transcend the national oppositions of the past and privilege class identities, was as influential in the political landscape of wartime Venezia Giulia as its military presence.

Historians who have attempted to analyze the contradictory nature of the national question in Yugoslavia have pointed to the Communist leadership's inconsistent evocation of national "rights" during the Second World War. In 1940, the leader of the Communist resistance in Yugoslavia, Josip Broz Tito, disowned the "bourgeois ideal of the Fatherland," but as Walker Connor argues, during the war Tito also spoke "as though his audience were composed of members of national groups motivated by ethnically inspired goals, rather than Marxist-Leninists inspired by proletarian nationalism."[4] These same inconsistencies are evident in the Liberation Front's wartime attempts to deal with the question of Slovene and Croatian national self-determination in nationally disputed territory. In 1941 the Slovene Liberation Front created a "Border Committee," its headquarters hidden away in

Ljubljana. The Border Committee's function was to advise on Slovene national self-determination in the regions bordering Austria and Italy. Like the Front itself, this committee comprised a range of Slovene political groups, Christian Socialist as well as Communist.[5] In 1943, Prežihov Voranc, a communist member of the committee, produced a popular underground pamphlet entitled "On Slovene Borders" and bearing the slogan "Proletarians of the World Unite." Voranc wrote that faced with popular criticisms of the Liberation Front's lack of interest in Slovene national borders, he was attempting to reinvent Slovene nationality out of the regional differences that interrupted the existence of an homogenous Slovene identity. Although Voranc described conventional historical, strategic, or economic justifications of borders as "imperialist," he added that a Slovene people had already begun to mark out borders that signalled their natural national, economic, and cultural inclinations.[6] He reminded his readers of the Allies' promise that in the postwar self-determination would be achieved even for the smallest of "peoples" (possibly a reference to the Atlantic Charter),[7] and stated that the borders of the new Slovenia, as part of Yugoslavia, would be determined by the right of the working people to determine themselves. Where Voranc was cryptic, the cover of his treatise was more explicit. It bore a map of Slovenia that showed Trieste, Gorizia (a part of Italy in the interwar), and Klagenfurt (a part of Austria) inside the Slovene border under the protection of a Yugoslav flag bearing a Communist star.

The Liberation Front had begun operating in the Adriatic boundary region, and specifically in Trieste, soon after setting up in Ljubljana in 1941.[8] Its strongest support came from the industrial surrounds and labyrinthine shipyards of Trieste and Monfalcone (a town just northwest of Trieste), and from Workers' Unity (*Unità Operaia/Delavska Enotnost*) a clandestine "mixed" Italian and Slovene makeshift union organized by Liberation Front operatives. Workers' Unity provided a successful base for disseminating the communist ideal of brotherhood, and for recruiting fighters for the Liberation Front units. Before 1943, the Liberation Front also gained some local momentum from cooperation between the Italian and Slovene Communist Parties. In 1942, an Italian Communist Party declaration recognized in principle the right of Slovene self-determination and the unification of Slovenian territory everywhere except Trieste, Monfalcone, and Istrian coastal towns, where the population were to determine for themselves which state they preferred. Some historians have commented that considering the Slovene Liberation Front's territorial aspirations in Venezia Giulia, cooperation between the Italian Communist Party and the Slovene

Communist organizations was naive on the part of the Italians.[9] Nevertheless, we know that by the end of 1942 the Italian and Slovene communists of Venezia Giulia had established at least thirty mixed Italian and Slovene committees as well as Workers' Unity.[10] In June 1943, while Trieste was still under Italian rule, the Slovene and Italian Communist Parties agreed to make Trieste the seat of the Littoral Committee of the Italian Communist Party and its cultural front, the *Comitato Fronte Nazionale d'Azione*. At this time too, members of the National Council (a Triestine middle-class and Slovene underground organization created two years earlier) joined the Liberation Front, despite their lack of communist sympathies.[11] After the German occupation of Venezia Giulia and Slovenia, there were even more examples of attempted cooperation between Italians and Slovenes, and communist and noncommunist anti-Fascists. In Trieste, the Liberation Front organized the Alliance of Slovene-Italian Anti-Fascist Women (*Antifašistične Slovenske Italianske Ženske Zveze* or ASIZZ), with separate Slovene and Italian committees: the Alliance of Anti-Fascist Women (*Antifašistične Ženske* or AFZ), and Italian Anti-Fascist Women (*Donne Anti-fasciste Italiane* or DAI). These groups were linked to sister AFZ organizations all over Yugoslavia, as well as to the Slovene Communist Party. The principal task of the leaders of provincial branches of Anti-Fascist Women was to establish smaller groups in every village in order to expand the network of communist influence, and develop the organization's grassroots base. Younger men and women joined local branches of either the Anti-Fascist Italian Youth or its Slovene equivalent. Recruits were promised that Yugoslavia would deliver justice for workers and women in a state united through the bonds of anti-Fascist class struggle rather than nationality.[12] The Liberation Front coordinated nationally distinct military units, including "Garibaldi Brigades," made up of Italian recruits under Slovene command, and including women. As the Liberation Front forces consolidated their military gains, locally organized cells instituted administrative governments or Liberation Councils. Branches of both the Italian and Slovene Communist Party secretly distributed pamphlets pronouncing their united anti-Fascist mission and Italo-Slovene brotherhood ideal. In 1944 the Liberation Front set up a number of clandestine Italo-Slovene Anti-Fascist Coordination Committees in mixed areas, and a special "joint civic committee" of Italian and Slovene Communist Parties in Trieste under the leadership of the Liberation Front's Rudi Uršič (a Triestine born at the end of the First World War who had become a communist by the 1930s, and was placed under Fascist arrest between 1938 and 1943). Although the term *Italo-Slovene* was specific to the Trieste region, it had a less successful equivalent in the

Istrian version of "Italo-Croat" fraternity.[13] In all its various organizational manifestations Italo-Slovene brotherhood presumed the possibility of cooperation between Italians and Slovenes on the basis that they were distinctive but equal identities. Rather than describe a form of hybridity, or a new identity, Italo-Slovene fraternity suggested a bridge between discrete cultural identities and implied their common future in a Communist Yugoslavia that was a federation of nations. Importantly, in Italian and Slovene versions of the new fraternity, the generic identity "Slav" was rarely used.

The Liberation Front's military and ideological success in Trieste and the boundary region was influenced by decisions taken internationally, in London and Belgrade, as well as Ljubljana. By the beginning of 1944, the regional status of the Liberation Front and its aims were enhanced by the British recognition of Tito's partisans (including the Liberation Front) as the legitimate resistance force in Yugoslavia.[14] Allied recognition was not accompanied by guarantees of Tito's or the Liberation Front's postwar aims. Tito was aware that British and American combined forces were planning to occupy Venezia Giulia after they had fought their way into northern Italy. Once the pro-Yugoslav partisans and British and American forces began cooperating against the German army in southeastern Europe, both groups agreed that the Allied Supreme Commander, Field-Marshal Alexander, would have authority in Trieste and Venezia Giulia, while Tito's forces would assume authority in the territory to the east, including Fiume.[15] Despite this agreement, in September 1944 Tito reminded his British and American allies of his territorial aspirations for the new Communist Yugoslavia. In a radio broadcast he demanded the Littoral, Austrian Styria, and Carinthia, adding, "We do not want what is not ours, but we shall not renounce that which is ours."[16] The Yugoslav Communist leadership also took up with the Italian Communist Party the question of postwar sovereignty in the boundary region. Edvard Kardelj (Tito's most important strategist and a Slovene) wrote to the new secretary of the Italian Communist Party, Palmiro Togliatti, explaining his plan to have the Slovene 9th Corps of the Liberation Front occupy the formerly Italian Venezia-Giulian provinces of Trieste, Gorizia, and Friuli before the Allies arrived. Togliatti agreed, in the expectation that the Liberation Front would be able to keep the same British and American military forces, which were disarming communist partisans in Italy, out of Venezia Giulia and Friuli, and secure the communist future of those regions.

The agreement between Togliatti and Kardelj did not ensure a settlement of the future Italo-Yugoslav border.[17] Togliatti's sympathetic view of the Liberation Front's role in Venezia Giulia was compromised by negotiations and altercations over which national communist party had precedence in what terrain—negotiations that rehearsed the dispute over national sovereignty. When Triestine leaders of the Italian Communist Party were arrested by the German military, Italian communists already suspicious of the territorial intentions of the pro-Yugoslav Liberation Front alleged that the Triestine leaders had been betrayed by their Slovene comrades.[18] Although unproven, these allegations have persuaded some historians of the Slovene nationalist and even irredentist character of the Liberation Front and its Italo-Slovene ideal. While historians agree that the Liberation Front's relative military strength in the boundary region before 1944 was a result of the small number of Italian communists involved in any resistance, and, consequently, of the "moral" precedence of the Liberation Front in the resistance struggle, they have also suggested that decisions about where the different Slovene and Italian brigades would fight, for example the creation of a Slovene 9th Corps City Command in Trieste, were influenced by the Front's Slav nationalist aspirations.[19] A letter sent by Kardelj to the Central Committee of the Slovene Communist Party, dated October 1, 1944, confirms that the Yugoslav communist leadership viewed the question of a border as a cultural as well as ideological issue. Kardelj's description in that letter of the broader significance of the boundary region and the Italo-Yugoslav border, suggests that the problem of territorial sovereignty was entangled in older representations of the boundary region's cultural significance. Kardelj argued that "Italian imperialists" portrayed this border (*meje*) as politically separating two peoples (*narodoma*) and as culturally dividing the "two worlds" of Eastern and Western Europe. "On this basis," Kardelj continued, "[they] are calculating on the support of the western world over the question of our borders." For Kardelj, "[t]he problem of these borders" had become "a general European political question," which had to be "resolved in such a manner that it will not be possible to have major discussions regarding this question."[20] His strategy was to have Fran Zwitter, the Director of the Liberation Front's "Scientific Institute" (*Znanstveni Inštitut*, a transmutation of the Border Committee), prepare a paper on the border that would convince international opinion of the legitimacy of Yugoslavia's territorial claims. In his instructions to Zwitter, Kardelj stressed that the paper should place less emphasis on strategic, economic, or commercial justifications of a border, and more on the principle of nationality.[21]

The German occupation of Ljubljana had forced Zwitter's Scientific Institute to conduct its research and propaganda tasks out of huts hidden in communist-liberated Slovene forests. One of the Scientific Institute's objectives was to collect and prepare scientific material that the Slovene Liberation Front could use in the postwar to establish its social, educational, and economic policies. It also provided discussion papers on the borders that a future Yugoslav and communist Slovenia would share with Italy.[22] Originally from northern Slovenia (Novo Mesto), Zwitter had studied geography and history in Ljubljana and in Vienna in the 1920s, and had been president of the Border Committee that published Voranc's work.[23] As the Director he made the north and northwest borders of Slovenia (bordering Austria and Italy respectively) a priority of the Institute's work, in the expectation that the ethno-national basis of these borders could be determined scientifically. Under his leadership too, the Institute aimed to validate the cultural and scientific credentials of the interrelated Slovene, Yugoslav, and communist claims to political sovereignty in Trieste by countering images of the cultural inadequacies of Slavs and communists. Zwitter complained that Italian bourgeois nationalists had always regarded Slovenes as less worthy. It was this view of Slovene culture, he argued, that also colored Italian nationalist perceptions of the prospect of a Slovene Trieste. He tried to validate the Italo-Slovene ideal by claiming that the Liberation Front enjoyed the cooperation of Triestine Italians in its preparations for transforming Trieste into the center of a new Mazzinian fraternity for "the mutual acquaintance of Italian and Yugoslav, and possibly all Slavic cultures."[24] In the paper that Zwitter prepared for Kardelj, *The Borders of Yugoslavia, The Borders of Slovene Territory* (published in English, Slovene, and Russian), he added a subverted historical imperative to this ethical argument for establishing communist Yugoslav sovereignty in the boundary region. Zwitter described many Triestine Italians as originally Slovene, and a pre–First World War trend in Trieste of expanding Slovene influence as evidence of the success of Slovene culture. He also turned the conventional geographical imagery of interwar Italian maps on its head: Italians were present in small bourgeois settlements outnumbered by the sea of Slovenes.[25]

Attempts by communist intellectuals in the Liberation Front to legitimate Yugoslav sovereignty in territory that had been granted to Italy by the Treaty of Rapallo required them to negotiate prevailing assumptions about East and West, Slav and Italian differences, their relative cultural worth, and the significance of identity for establishing territorial sovereignty. These discursive assumptions, and their polemical negotiation, tell us little directly about how the populations may have thought of themselves, or what national identification might have meant to them by the early 1940s. Histories of the Italian Communist Party intimate that the Liberation Front's objectives and the propaganda disseminated from Ljubljana and Belgrade regarding postwar territorial sovereignty in the boundary region, created an uneasiness between the Slovene/Yugoslav and Italian Communist parties, and their resistance forces.[26] The military precedence of the Slovene-led Liberation Front and their support for a Communist Yugoslavia (the borders of which might include formerly Italian territory) made communism "un'identità difficile" for Italian patriots.[27] In a discussion of the appeal of communism in Europe during the war, the historian Paolo Spriano (himself torn between the confession of patriotism and class ideology) maintained that "[t]he Communist felt a genuine love of country, which was linked to their love of the USSR—no other term is accurate—in a manner that none of them considered contradictory."[28]

The memoirs and memories of local communists often indicate that the question of ideological victory took precedence over the issue of national borders, and was perceived as an answer to the politics of chauvinism, which had predominated under Fascism. Licia Chersovani, for example, was a communist Italian who attempted to reconcile her national identity with her political convictions. In her early twenties, while studying physics at the University of Trieste, she became an important resistance figure in the youth wing of the Italian Communist Party. She has reflected on the motivations of many like herself to join a cause whose operations in the Trieste area were being guided by *slavi*, concluding that "there is no doubt that the fundamental motive was the aspiration to be part, once the war was over, of the communist world, or better still, to be one of its outposts." The war for her was not between nations but between ideologies.[29]

For some Liberation Front activists and fighters, or members of its adjunct organizations, the Yugoslav communist and antinationalist ideal was the only alternative to Italian Fascism and German Nazism. Ljubo (a bilingual former Liberation Front partisan I interviewed in 1989) recalled that in 1941 he had been sent to Germany to a labor camp. When he escaped he returned to Trieste but was told the Germans were looking for him. He joined the Liberation Front and fought to free Trieste not, he said in retrospect, for any communist ideal, but to liberate Trieste from the Germans and "the Fascist Italians."[30] The historian Alessandro Volk has drawn on a series of interviews with former Liberation Front activists from the Venezia Giulia region who identify as Slovenes, to show that in a significant number of cases the decision to join the Liberation Front may have initially been nationalist—in order to rebel against their lack of political and cultural rights in interwar

Italy—but that the resistance experience radically altered their motivations and self-identification. The Italo-Slovene ideal gave some partisans the courage to divulge Slovene identities. One of Volk's interviewees, Roberto, explained that of the young men he knew, "many were Italians, but they weren't Italians. They were Slovenes. But I only found out that some of them were Slovenes when I met them again in '43 or in '44 among the partisans, and they spoke Slovene. When we saw each other again I asked them: 'What, you speak Slovene? You are Slovene?' 'Yes' [they replied]."[31] When interviewed by Volk in 1996, Patrizia, who had joined the Liberation Front in the village of Banne, explained: "[I]t was said that we should never support nationalism, that we shouldn't support any nationalism. Slovene included. To be a nationalist was wrong, you had to be a proletariat, you had to be for everyone equally."[32] Sandro, a member of the Communist Party youth organization at the time, remembered that "[for those] who were more Communist, it did not suit them that . . . the partisans had a Slovene flag. They weren't pleased. They said: 'We are for the hammer and sickle,' they meant Bolshevism."[33] Another historian, Marta Verginella, has argued that interviews with former partisans conducted between 1950 and 1983 indicate that during the war some partisans exchanged their Slovene identity for a communist one, a few revealed their Slovene-ness, others for the first time heard and gained an appreciation for the word *brotherhood*, either in its Italian form as *fraternità* or Slovene as *bratstvo*.[34]

The heightened self-consciousness of Italian and Slovene/Slav identities, and the scarred relations between Italians and Slovenes that had resulted from the rhetoric and policies of the interwar Italian governments in Venezia Giulia, were obvious obstacles to non-nationalist or antinationalist resistance cooperation. In some cases, the Liberation Front experience brought Slovenes from more isolated parts of the hinterland into personal contact with "Italians," and encouraged them to revise their prejudices. For example, Slovenes learnt that Italians and fascism were not synonymous.[35] Volk's oral histories describe some of the processes by which the resistance movement affected relationships between Italians and Slovenes. Lino, a member of a Slovene partisan formation remembers entering a forest near Comeno while the war was still raging, and hearing a meeting take place in Italian:

> "What on earth is this?" [we said to ourselves]—at the time we were nationalists. It was *compianto* Franc Štoka, who was holding a political meeting with [Italian-speaking] workers from the Monfalcone shipyards, who had come along as volunteers. They were all in blue overalls, and I said to

myself, "What do you know?" And then I saw how it is, that it was about a struggle against fascism that did not recognize nationality.[36]

Volk concludes that particularly after the collapse of the Italian Fascist government in 1943, when Slovenes and Italians came into increased contact through the Liberation Front, in the majority of cases Slovene partisans began to discriminate more readily between Fascists and Italians.[37]

These examples suggest that cooperation between Slovene and Italian communists under Slovene and Yugoslav command was at least temporarily successful in propagating the expectations of Italo-Slovene brotherhood, and that brotherhood became the most distinctive feature of memories of the Liberation Front and its political meaningfulness. During the war Italo-Slovene brotherhood entailed, and allowed, redefinition of what it meant to be Slovene (i.e., being able or choosing to speak the Slovene language in public), and Italian (i.e., being able to identify as Italian and anti-Fascist). It also appealed to women, a constituency that the Fascist Party had addressed as mothers, but Italian liberals in the region had ignored in their preoccupation with Italian national sovereignty.

The involvement of women in European anti-Fascist resistance movements has been the historical subject of a number of national studies. Anna Teresa Iaccheo has argued that in Italy some women in the communist resistance bore arms as a means of "self-affirmation, the realisation of ideals and ideology, and the conquest of a utopian world of equals."[38] Italian historians explain that female involvement in the Italian anti-Fascist resistance was an exercise in Italian patriotism, a consequence of the pressure to prove that women deserved the right to don military uniforms and fight for the Italian nation.[39] Barbara Jančar-Webster, a historian of women in the Yugoslav communist resistance has described three reasons for their participation: to fight against the invader, to fight for national recognition of their respective Yugoslav nation (for example Slovenia or Croatia), or to fight for communism and in opposition to the Royalist Cetniks of Serbia.[40] Pro-communist anti-Fascist women's groups in the boundary region included Italians, but there is no evidence of attempts by their main organization, the AFZ, to contact the sister Union of Italian Women established in northern Italy under the auspices of the Italian Communist Party. The oral histories I have already mentioned indicate that the communist women who joined the ancillary organizations of the Liberation Front in the boundary region of Venezia Giulia (sometimes as civilians, sometimes as fighters), found it difficult to justify nationalist motivations.

In contrast to the Italian communist resistance, the Italian and Slovene women who assisted the resistance movement and donned uniforms and armory were important to Liberation Front iconography. They were used to symbolize the extent and depth of the revolutionary aims of communism and brotherhood in Yugoslavia. Volk has remarked on the frequent references to women in the recollections of former Liberation Front male and female partisans in Trieste.[41] However, feminism was a controversial aspect of female participation in Communist organizations. Slovene Communist Party female ideologues argued that the Yugoslav communist version of women's liberation was explicitly not "feminist"; that is, communist women were not interested in privileging women's emancipation over class emancipation.[42] The sex bias of this class priority was evident in the everyday lack of status of women involved with the pro-Yugoslav Liberation Front and Venezia Giulia Communist parties. Male Communist ideologues regarded women, like youth, as the most susceptible to fascism and thus most in need of political education.[43] Yet the extent of female participation raises the question of how anti-Fascist women themselves saw their role in the Liberation Front and its auxiliaries. Licia Chersovani and "Patrizia" were two of a substantial number of Triestine women from backgrounds regarded as lower-middle-class to working-class, from within the city and outside in its villages, who joined (unisex) Communist youth groups and supported the Liberation Front. Chersovani's educational and class background also made her the exception. Most of the women who joined the communist Liberation Front cause were channeled into specifically women's organizations. These women were generally seamstresses, clerks, or "workers" aspiring to be shopkeepers, shopgirls, or office workers. In the hinterland they were often farm women or hairdressers. Others had higher aspirations: to be musicians, administrators, or businesswomen.[44] Some were from peasant families and were drawn into the resistance as an extension of their family roles, or they were women from working-class families seeking economic and political independence through their involvement with the Liberation Front.[45] Some were born in Trieste, some identified as Italian, others as Slovene; most had Italian citizenship as a legacy of the interwar period. Many were bilingual in Italian and Slovene, and others had a knowledge of German. The ASIZZ, AFZ, and DAI combined general political participation with a concern for women's issues—which sometimes meant demanding equal pay and the provision of educational resources for women, or at other times social welfare and holiday camps for children. Regardless of the variation in specific causes, the executive of the Anti-Fascist Women's committees strove for women's right to be politically informed, politically active, and to raise the consciousness of the next generation of women. The Anti-Fascist Women appear to have shared the belief that they had earned their place as political citizens by being active in the anti-Fascist resistance, whether by bearing rifles, gathering intelligence, undertaking administrative tasks, or providing health care. Even when active in conventionally female roles (such as social welfare, education, and soup kitchens) they saw themselves as upholding the right of women to participate in a public arena dominated by men. Their activities show that they perceived women's issues as an integral, if not predominant, aspect of partisan politics.[46] They imagined that in the new society distinctions between men and women, Italians and Slovenes, would have less political relevance.

The liberation of the proletariat, national liberation, Italo-Slovene fraternity, and female emancipation were to divergent degrees all anticipated features of the Communist Yugoslav experiment in Trieste and the boundary region. As we have seen, their simultaneous promotion by the Liberation Front and its ancillary organizations was fraught with contradictions and inconsistencies. The concept of Italo-Slovene fraternity did not reflect the complex interrelation between subjective forms of national, class, and gender identification, and provided an uncertain indication of the future relation between national identity and political sovereignty in a communist Yugoslavia. But for certain sectors of the population Italo-Slovene fraternity was particularly meaningful in the context of the coincidence of Fascist representations of Italian and Slav differences, and the Fascist repression of Slovenes in the name of Italian nationalism. The Italo-Slovene was an identity that promised national liberation and, at the same time, transcended national identification; like Austro-Marxism, it implied both a new relationship between identity and sovereignty, and the reaffirmation of equal national-cultural rights. For patriotic Italians, it also confirmed the gender and class dimensions of the threat that a communist, Slav-coordinated victory against Nazism as well as Fascism, posed to their own ideals of *italianità* and *civiltà*.

ANTI-FASCIST ITALIAN NATIONALISM

According to the Italian historian Mario Isnenghi, after September 1943 patriotism overwhelmed the political meaning of the war throughout Italy: "Neither during the war of independence nor at the moment of intervention in 1915, nor in any other phase of its post-unification national life, had the word Italy ever mobilised so much civic passion and active participation."[47] Nazifascists, Communists, Liberals, Socialists, Catholics amongst others shared a patriotic vocabulary: "Each side killed or died for Patria, Italia, Nazione, Popolo, Risorgimento, Garibaldi and Mazzini." The language of Italian patriotism was deployed in defense of a panoply of incompatible political ideals. Although Isnenghi's description does not fit the locals on the Italian side of the Italo-French border who formed a CLN in order to secede the territory of Val d'Aosta to France, it describes well the Venezia Giulia CLN, a self-consciously Italian anti-Fascist resistance movement that opposed the Liberation Front. Formed in the absence of an Italian government in Venezia Giulia, its members felt responsible for upholding the continuity of the Italian state, and used their cultural authority as a form of scaffolding. The Venezia Giulia CLN included former First World War veterans, *legionari* who had accompanied D'Annunzio on his Fiuman campaign, members of the conservative Italian Liberal Party, the Italian Communist Party, the Italian Socialist Party, the Republican Party, and the centre-left party of intellectuals, the Action Party [*Partito d'Azione*]. On different occasions, the Venezia Giulia CLN fought not just against the Liberation Front, but for Trieste's regional autonomy, and the "old Italian frontier." In 1944, members of the Action Party, the most influential faction in the Venezia Giulia CLN, denounced the injustice and nationalist violence of the Fascist period, which they argued had placed Italy's eastern borders in peril. They also promoted the prospect of a regionally autonomous Trieste within an Italy that was part of a federal Europe.[48] One Action Party member, Emanuele Flora, went so far as to propose a plan for uprooting existing communities and linking them to each other by internationally supervised connecting roads. Italian and Slav enclaves could be created to force "an atmosphere of collaboration between Italy and Jugoslavia."[49] "[T]he internationalisation of streets under the aegis of the UN," Flora argued, "would have to prevent or at least reduce the friction." Even if it allowed ethno-national communities to coexist within the same state, the enclave plan reinforced the idea that Italians and Slavs could be and should be segregated.[50]

The CLN's sense of national purpose was first alerted by the policies of the German military forces that occupied Venezia Giulia in late 1943. The German administration restored the old Austrian *Küstenland* province, promoted nostalgia for the Habsburg past in radio programs with titles such as *"Trieste saluta Vienna,"* and fostered the Slovene language—a policy intended to win over Slovenes from their support of the Liberation Front.[51] In Gorizia, where the Slovene *Domobranci* collaborated with their Nazi governors, these policies were relatively effective in increasing the local profile of Slovene language and culture. But in Nazi-occupied Trieste, the strength of protestations by the collaborators Bruno Coceani and Cesare Pagnini (respectively the Nazi-installed prefect of the region and mayor of Trieste) against any concessions to Slovenes meant that the only manifestation of a Slovene "bias" was the Slovene-language radio program.[52]

Fears of Slavic nationalism among the Venezia Giulia CLN were only compounded by the policies of the Milan CLNAI. In early 1944, the left-wing-dominated executive of the CLNAI encouraged cooperation with the Slovene Liberation Front as a "communal struggle of the combatants of the two nationalities in mixed zones," which would create the conditions for "the total elimination of national intolerance, contributing to the friendly cohabitation of the two peoples." Even more worrying for the CLN was the CLNAI's evasion of questions regarding the future national border between Italy and Yugoslavia; to what extent and under whose sovereignty would those two peoples cohabit? Members of the Venezia Giulia CLN attempted to convince the CLNAI that because of an intrinsic antipathy between Italians and Slavs, cooperation with the Slav command of the Liberation Front was dangerous, naive, and unrealistic. As proof they pointed to an uprising that had taken place in Istria in October 1943 when, they claimed, local peasants threw still-living members of the Italian Fascist administration into limestone chasms (called *foibe*). The CLNists emphasised that not all the *foibe* victims were Fascists, and that the peasants had been incited to rebel by anti-Italian Croatian communists. Professor Gaetano Gaeta described the Istrian *foibe* killings as rehearsals by Slav communists of their preferred methods and objectives. He argued that events in Istria validated stereotypes of Slav ferocity, and of Slavs as a people who needed to be civilized and controlled.[53] After the war, Carlo Schiffrer, a socialist and perhaps the most respected intellectual figure in the Venezia Giulia CLN, wrote that, at the time, the Istrian *foibe* episode confirmed to the CLN their suspicions about the Slav hatred of Italians, and the fate of Trieste should Slavs take control:

> The possibility of an occupation of the city on the part of . . . a ferocious Balkan militia animated by sentiments of hatred against Italians was not to be taken lightly. Certainly looking back we could say that no such thing happened, but this does not make the CLN's preoccupations any less real.[54]

Schiffrer's own role in the Venezia Giulia CLN contributed to the realism of the CLN's perception of Slavs. His professional and personal opinions are evidence of the accruing political influence of representations of an intrinsic antipathy between Italians and Slavs, and their explicit contradiction of the Communist ideal of Italo-Slovene brotherhood.

Schiffrer was born in 1902 in Habsburg Trieste. His biographer has described his family as "petty-bourgeois German" in origin.[55] At the age of twenty Schiffrer began a historical thesis in Florence under Salvemini's supervision on the origins of Italian irredentism in Trieste.[56] *Le origini dell'irredentismo triestino* (published in 1937) was regarded by Italian reviewers as critical of the Fascist regime and of a polemical tradition in nationalist Triestine historiography.[57] Schiffrer's main concern was to provide a democratic historical validation for an Italian Trieste. He argued that the absence until the late nineteenth century of an Italian irredentist movement in Trieste did not signal the inadequacy of local Italian consciousness. Instead, Italian consciousness was inherent in the democratic tendencies of a local version of Italian *civiltà*. The thesis implied the historical existence of an authentically democratic Italian national culture distinct from the Italian nationalist irredentism that had fostered Fascism.[58] The distinction between a good, democratic, and bourgeois Italian national culture, and a bad, populist, and mass-based Italian nationalism informed Schiffrer's more general view of Italian history and politics. In 1925, Schiffrer wrote from Rome to his fiancée describing the crowds he witnessed in the ancient capital celebrating the Fascist-organized *festa del lavoro*. "Doesn't the nationalist intoxication we see around us irritate you?" he asked, "Misunderstood nationalism. Doesn't it seem to you a Balkan megalomania?"[59] Schiffrer's reference to the Balkan characteristics of bad nationalism supports Maria Todorova's general thesis about the negative image of the Balkans in the twentieth century.[60] For Schiffrer, the mass affects of Fascism and a Balkan culture alien to Italy posed identical threats to the tradition of rational, democratic Italian *civiltà*.

After September 1943, Schiffrer joined the local anti-Fascist *Giustizia e Libertà* group, and then became the Italian Socialist Party's representative in the Venezia Giulia CLN. In 1944 he formed the University Political Committee, a secret body housed in the University of Trieste, the "scientific" work of which mirrored the Liberation Front's Border Committee and Scientific Institute. Schiffrer's committee provided the Venezia Giulia and Friuli CLN organizations with statistical interpretations of the ethnic makeup of the boundary region to use in negotiations with the Milan CLNAI, and to insist on its Italian future.[61] Under Schiffrer's guidance, those interpretations postulated the superiority of Italian bourgeois and civic culture, which easily absorbed an inferior Slav non-culture. The work that Schiffrer undertook for the committee presented the boundary region as a "transition zone" where the natural domain of Italians was the town and the Slavs dwelt in the rural hinterland, which serviced civic centers.[62] In cases where Slavs from the countryside migrated to Italian cities, Schiffrer concluded that the masculinity and vitality of *italianità* both assimilated and expunged them.[63] As the city of Trieste expanded, Schiffrer explained, it "expelled the Slav population—a totally spontaneous phenomenon—further and further from the centre."[64] Although Schiffrer defined nationality as a spiritual complex of sentiment and will,[65] he implied that language, as the prime vehicle for the expression of sentiments, the most natural form of the identification of the self with nation, and the means by which the self was inducted into a national culture, was also a determinant of nationality.[66] On Schiffrer's linguistic map, bilingualism was a trait of less-developed national identities in the process of being assimilated.[67] Italians were, as a result, constituted as individuals who did not speak a second language. The offspring of mixed marriages (which, Schiffrer argued, tended to join Italian men with Slav migrant women who came to Trieste to seek employment as the housemaids of Italian women),[68] were spoken to in Italian, so that "even if these women cannot be considered Italian, the Slovene nation loses its fecundity."[69] Schiffrer's only fear was that the Italian language and culture that prevailed in urban areas of the transition zone could be statistically distorted by bilingual Slavs who either masked their knowledge of Italian for nationalist motives or passed themselves off as Italians. These theoretical accounts of Italian and Slav differences insinuated their way into Schiffrer's political activities.

In April 1945, on the eve of an expected Allied victory in northern Italy, local members of the Liberation Front approached the Venezia Giulia CLN with the intention of creating a mixed committee that would work to overthrow the Nazi forces in Trieste and establish a provisional government. The Liberation Front sought the CLN's cooperation in order to gain the respectability that the support of the Italian middle class and its intellectuals could offer their movement. The Venezia Giulia CLN chose Schiffrer to negotiate an agreement, but the negotiations failed.[70] When the Liberation Front proposed that two-thirds of the mixed CLN and Liberation Front committee be comprised of Italians and one-third Slovenes, Schiffrer demanded that seven of the members, including the chairman and vice-chairman, should be authentic Italians without party affiliations, the other five should be Italian members each representing a political party including the communists.[71] More importantly, Schiffrer's retrospective reports of his private meetings with local members of the Liberation Front indicate his concern about the number of persons identifying as Italians who belonged to the Liberation Front's "mixed" brigades of partisans under Slovene communist command, and who were ultimately loyal to Tito. He recounted that his role was to unmask bilingual Slovenes claiming to be Italians. Everyone knew, Schiffrer claimed, that the Italian who spoke Slovene was the exception. He was convinced that a bad accent or grammatical mistakes could reveal Slavic impostors. In one encounter with an Italian-speaking member of the Liberation Front called "Pino," Schiffrer recalled sensing that "even he has to be a Slovene who has passed himself off as an Italian for the occasion" and that "the Slavs were playing on ambiguities, it is easy for them to pass off as Italian one of their own faithful bilingual units."[72] He also maintained that the Front's claim to have the support of female Italians was unfounded since the Front's designated Italian women's groups had no members. The so-called "Italian" representatives among the women spoke amongst themselves in Slovene. In effect, Schiffrer argued that since no Italian would support what was obviously a Slav cause, those individuals who supported the cause and claimed to be Italian had to be Slavs. Moreover, as in his ethnographic work, he implied that Italians had only one essential identity, while Slovenes were capable of cultural transgression and transformation because they had no true selves.[73] Thus, what disturbed Schiffrer most in this anti-Fascist communist setting was that in the communist Liberation Front the lines between Slav and Italian had blurred. It was difficult to tell in this environment, he despaired, "who is Italian and who is a Slav?"[74]

Schiffrer's training as a geographer and historian only partly explains his preference for clearly defined ethnic, linguistic, and historical identities. His account of negotiations with the Liberation Front suggests that the ambiguity of national identities also threatened his personal identification as both Italian and anti-Fascist. According to Enzo Collotti, after 1943 Italian intellectuals generally believed they had been "defrauded of the destiny of conquest boasted by Mussolini" and that they were "bound to defend themselves from the dangerous Yugoslav partisan movement."[75] It could also be argued that from the perspective of pro-Italian anti-Fascists, the presence of men and women identifying as Italians in a movement supporting Yugoslavia potentially undermined the cultural validation of an emphatically *Italian* anti-Fascist resistance. The CLN focus on a Slav threat was related to a crisis of Italian national identity generated by the Fascist appropriation of Italian nationalism on the one hand, and by the example of Italians who had joined the Slovene Liberation Front on the other. The emphasis of intellectuals like Schiffrer on Italian and Slav differences challenged the authenticity of Italo-Slovene fraternity and moved the focus of resistance away from the difficult relationship between anti-Fascist and Fascist Italian nationalist objectives.

The defense of Venezia Giulia's and Trieste's *italianità* had brought the Venezia Giulia CLN and other sympathizers into an unofficial and uneasy alliance with Nazi collaborators such as Bruno Coceani and Cesare Pagnini who could mobilize their private police force and administrative and intellectual networks in support of a shared national cause. In 1944, for example, Pagnini exploited his position as mayor to reconvene meetings of the prestigious local historical organization Minerva. Against the backdrop of Allied bombings, and Nazi and Fascist exterminations of political and cultural opponents, writers such as Pier Antonio Quarantotti Gambini and Giani Stuparich joined Pagnini at these meetings in preparation for Trieste's postwar cultural and political renewal as a site of Italian culture. They studied what a historian of the Minerva society has described as "the documents of civic history in order to discover in them the traces of Trieste's inevitable destiny."[76] Similarly, when the Venezia Giulia CLN needed to conduct political meetings, it was often Pagnini or Coceani who provided the secure space, confident that they shared the same aspirations for the protection of Italian culture and Italian sovereignty in the region.[77] Coceani and Pagnini also exploited Schiffrer's version of the Italo-Yugoslav border to the same ends as the CLN—as they successfully argued in their postwar trials—to defend Trieste's *italianità* from its Slav enemy. While prefect of Nazi-occupied Trieste, Coceani wrote to Mussolini at Salò decrying the fact that under Nazi jurisdiction "the Slovene tongue and Slovene singing could be heard again in the streets and public places of Trieste."[78] But neither Pagnini nor Coceani protested against the operation of the notorious Risiera, a former rice-processing factory in the working-class Triestine suburb of San Sabba which the Nazis had converted into a concentration camp with purpose-built cremating ovens— the only camp of its kind in Italy. In the last two years of the war, the Risiera's victims included civilians (identified as Jews, Slovenes, and Italians) as well as members of the Liberation Front and CLN resistance.[79]

Mazzinian nationalists such as Schiffrer did not approve of collaboration with Nazism and saw themselves as spokespersons for a democratic and civilized Italian culture. They struggled to salvage an Italian *civiltà*, and their own Italian national identification, from the errors of the Fascist past. Yet their concentration on a Slav danger to the Italian state in the midst of the operation of the Risiera camp, and in the context of that Fascist past, only blurred the borders between Italian anti-Fascism and collaboration in the region. In a postwar report to the Italian Socialist Party, Schiffrer defended the Venezia Giulia CLN's preference in the final stages of the war for forming a national Italian front that embraced the Italian extreme right, rather than cooperating with the Slovene Liberation Front.[80] He referred to a Triestine tradition of Italian unity against foreign, non-Italian oppressors, and the cultural collaboration possible amongst the different pro-Italian political groups who intuitively feared political collaboration between Slavs and Italians. For Schiffrer, the Liberation Front's call for the union of Italian culture in Trieste with a "progressive" Yugoslavia was "a dreadful bastardisation."[81] Schiffrer insisted that the communist Liberation Front could not have been trusted to fulfil a commitment to keep the city from the hands of Balkan nationalists, a category, he argued, that included the communist Liberation Front, pro-monarchist Serb Četniks, and Slovene fascist Domobranci, even though during the war these groups fought against each other.[82]

In 1944, the Liberal historian Benedetto Croce made a well-publicized speech at the Roman Eliseo exalting the creation of a national front against Italy's national enemies: Germans and Slavs.[83] Croce identified the special role in this national front of "thinking people"; intellectuals were the progeny and progenitors of Italian nationality.[84] In Trieste, the themes of a German (Austrian) and Slav enemy, and the Italian intellectual's privileged national identity, acted as rationalizations for both the anti-Fascist Venezia Giulia CLN and Nazi collaborators. In Trieste too, these themes were explicitly under challenge from the ambiguities of national and ideological identification. The cultural indeterminateness of Italo-Slovene brotherhood, and the difficulty of distinguishing between Fascist and anti-Fascist narratives of Italy's intellectual heritage, intimidated democratically minded Venezia Giulian Italian patriots.[85] Faced with the problem of "securing an ordered self" and verifying an "ordered world,"[86] many of these democrats concentrated instead on the search for a scientifically and culturally unambiguous political border between Italy and Yugoslavia, and on their version of the importance of national identity for deciding sovereignty. Their determination to sustain the hierarchy of Italian and Slav differences, and the idea of Italian-Slav antipathy as the basis of their own national identification, only reinforced the local resonance of the Liberation Front's similarly utopian, but markedly more egalitarian, conception of Italo-Slovene fraternity.

4

Identity and Revolution, May–June 1945

B y early 1945, the Allied governments recognized that the demarcation of military authority in the Adriatic boundary region could determine the postwar resolution of the problem of the Italo-Yugoslav border. At the Yalta conference held by the Allies in February 1945 to plan the transition to peace, Anthony Eden, the British foreign secretary, proposed a border for dividing up military responsibility that placed Trieste and Gorizia, and the territory linking them to Austria, in British and American hands and, on the basis of the "ethnic principle," made Tito's forces responsible for the Adriatic boundary region east and south of that line.[1] After February, the New Zealand 2nd Division (which included the 28th Maori battalion) and the 43rd Indian Gurkha regiment of the British Eighth Army, which had been fighting their way up the Italian mainland from the Gotha line since 1944, headed for the Isonzo river (north of Trieste) under the command of the United States Main 13th Corps. They then turned south toward Trieste with the intention of liberating it from Nazi occupation and establishing an Allied Military Government. Unknown to the British soldiers, in March Tito ordered the Yugoslav 4th Army to advance north from Dalmatia and reach Trieste by 1 May. The 4th Army arrived on time and 2,500 pro-Yugoslav partisans rose against the German military and their collaborationist forces in Trieste.[2] By 2 May, the Trieste City Command of the Liberation Front, the Yugoslav 4th Army, and Slovene 9th Corps had together taken credit for the liberation of the city and

Figure 4.1. Armor of The New Zealand Division Enters Trieste,
2 May 1945

Courtesy of the Imperial War Museum.

assumed authority on behalf of the "Yugoslav Executive-Supreme Slovenian-Command City of Trieste-Command."[3] The Allies arrived in Trieste only to find that, contrary to earlier agreements, Tito's partisans had got there before them.

After the war, the debate over "who liberated Trieste?"[4]—whether or not Tito purposely stalled the New Zealand division so that his partisan forces could get to Trieste first, whether the Venezia Giulia CLN had liberated Trieste before the Liberation Front's arrival, and to what extent each of these groups had the support of the local population—featured in the competition between the British and American Allies, the Venezia Giulia CLN, and the Liberation Front to determine the political future of the boundary region. The question "who liberated Trieste?" usually invited consideration of the short period of pro-Yugoslav communist rule in Trieste that followed the liberation of 1 May 1945. In Italian historiography this period is commonly referred to with deliberate biblical resonance as "the forty days." At the end of the twentieth century, in the post–Cold War era, "the forty days" has even provided a convenient emblem for invalidating communist anti-Fascist resistance throughout Italy.[5] Although there has been no detailed historic study of the Liberation Front's views of nationalism, historians have tended to focus on the forty days as an indication of the irredentist and anti-Italian machinations of foreign Slav communists.[6] This interpretation has been complemented by the themes of political competition and cultural differences between the British-American and Liberation Front forces.

At stake in the narratives of the end of the war in Trieste and Venezia Giulia are assessments of the region's political destiny, and its political past. The point of this chapter is to revisit the history of the forty days by drawing on Liberation Front archives that historians have ignored. Over what was in fact forty-two days, from 1 May 1945 to 12 June 1945, the Liberation Front had a brief opportunity to put into practice their promises of class, national, and female emancipation, and Italo-Slovene brotherhood. My concern is not to rehabilitate the communist aims of the pro-Yugoslav partisans, but to situate the images of natural racial antagonisms reiterated in Allied sources and predominant in English and Italian-language accounts of the forty days in the context of local support for the Liberation Front's agenda of antinationalism and the incorporation of Trieste into a federal Yugoslavia. The juxtaposition of these views allows us to examine both the complex Cold War narratives of ideological competition and cultural and racial incompatibility that have textured histories and memories of this period, and the counternarratives of cultural equality and coexistence embedded in mid-twentieth-century communist revolutionary utopianism.

"THE FORTY DAYS"

By assuming military authority in Trieste on 1 May 1945, the Liberation Front endeavored to ensure international acceptance of the region's future as the seventh republic of the communist Yugoslav federation. In order to make their point, pro-Yugoslav partisans immediately advanced the town's public clocks one hour to match the time in Belgrade. Major General Dušan Kveder of the Yugoslav 4th Army assumed the powers of town commandant, with local partisans Major Giorgio Jaksetich as his deputy, and Franc Štoka as political commissar. The new Liberation Front government made the town hall its headquarters, ignoring the protestations of the Venezia Giulia CLN who had tried to house their own alternative administration there. All armed groups not affiliated with the Liberation Front or Yugoslav Army, including the recalcitrant members of the Venezia Giulia CLN, were ordered to give up their arms to the new authority.[7] The Trieste City Military Command was almost immediately transformed into a civilian Liberation Council responsible to the Regional National Liberation Committee (known by its Slovene acronym as PNOO), which governed the Trieste region. The Trieste region included the Karst (*Carso* or *Kras*), and the Littoral (*Litorale* or *Primorje*) from Monfalcone south to Rijeka/Fiume.[8] Although the Liberation Front partisans guaranteed the autonomy of Trieste, the Regional National Liberation Committee had close links with the new Slovene Communist government, and the Slovene government conferred with Belgrade.[9] The Yugoslav 4th Army, a military force taking its orders from the Belgrade-based Yugoslav central government, remained to patrol the town. The threat to their command of Trieste was made obvious by the equally obtrusive presence of the New Zealand soldiers in control of Trieste's foreshore, the troops of the British Eighth Army and the United States 2nd Corps who had arrived as reinforcements, the Allied officers ensconced at Miramare Castle on Trieste's outskirts, the half dozen small ships of the British Royal Navy moored at the port, and the lone Allied destroyer that skulked farther out in the harbor.

When the Liberation Front forces first assumed authority in Trieste, local support for its objectives was not lacking. It could be found among the Front's worker strongholds (such as the ship-building town of Monfalcone), "independentist" groups that preferred "brotherhood" to a nationalist solution to the problem of Trieste, and the peasants and small landholders who expected release from a feudal tenant system and their own land.[10] Reports from the Antifascist Women's branches written out in both Slovene and Italian suggest that their members responded enthusiastically to the liberation celebrations. Many women assertively abandoned their housework for a number of days in order to participate. Unfriendly sources reported that the city seemed to have been "invaded" by men, women and children coming "down from the hills." Costumed in their Sunday best, joined by workers' groups, peasants carried flags and banners proclaiming Tito, Churchill, and Stalin. This was a ritual meant to join the city center with its hinterland, and with its working-class suburbs. The accompanying Slovene cry, "*Trst je naš*" (Trieste is ours), became the symbolic claim of belonging for those groups long ostracized from Trieste's cultural and political identity by the prerogative of *italianità*.[11] Jože Pirjevec, a Triestine historian, has evoked the overlapping gender, class, and ethnic dimensions of the forms of liberation resonant in these reclamations of Trieste. As the Liberation Council established its authority in the city, a Slovene woman whose Italian artisan husband had for years forbade her to speak a single word of her language in his presence, took a white, red, and green flag and burned it in the kitchen stove.[12] The liberation, one observer commented, had "transformed a servant people into an heroic peo-

Figure 4.2. Partisans, Male and Female, Trieste, 2 May 1945

The day after Trieste's liberation, Communist Partisans (male and female) relax in the city centre

Courtesy of Mario Maganj, SNL Photographic Archive.

ple."[13] The Liberation Front partisan Ljubo remembers feeling that after years of hardship, sleeping in forests, illness, and doing without food, he felt that he had come home.[14] In the early days of May 1945, like everyone else, he took to the streets. He shared with other partisans, communist and noncommunist alike, a sense of personal suffering at the hands of "Italians." In his recollections, those Triestines who hid in their houses peeking through shutters waiting for the partisans to leave were "Fascist Italians."

As these accounts suggest, not all Triestines were invited to share in the liberation. The posters that the Liberation Front administration plastered on the walls and pillars of the newly liberated Trieste stressed

Figure 4.3. Partisans, Male and Female, in Piazza Unità, 2 May 1945

Courtesy of Mario Maganj, SNL Photographic Archive.

Italo-Slovene fraternity between the citizens of Trieste and the forces of Marshal Tito, but they also identified fascism and the pro-Italian CLN as the enemy.[15] On 5 May 1945, the same day that the Yugoslav military banned outward manifestations of nationalist sentiment, Triestine witnesses recorded that "Yugoslav soldiers" opened fire on demonstrators carrying Italian flags, killing three.[16] Even if such events were outside the control of the new government, the ambiguity that surrounded the Liberation Council's emphasis on fascist epuration reinforced the atmosphere of uncertainty. Early in its administration, the Liberation Council established a Propaganda Commission in Trieste to deal with "fascist indoctrination" (the lower case "f" intimated its more general application). These epuration processes were to target Slovene as well as Italian Fascists, or ex-Fascists.[17] Businesses and industries were to be purged at all levels of fascist workers and managers. Delegates were appointed to industries to report on suspected fascists and maintain vigilance against continuing fascist practices.[18] Suspects were to be dealt with by a people's court, the *Tribunale Popolare*. The Liberation Council also created The "People's Defense" (*Guardia del Popolo or Narodni Zaščiti*), a 2,500-strong civilian body of former partisan units, whose role was to restrain any looting and anarchy provoked by the food, fuel, and accommodation shortages that had resulted from wartime damage, and to incarcerate any individuals who had abused anti-Fascists and Slovenes in the name of Fascist Italy.

Although the arrest of Fascist police, security forces, and war criminals, and vigilance against so-called political crimes were outside the council's jurisdiction and were the domain of, respectively, the Yugoslav 4th Army and the Yugoslav secret police, OZNA,[19] the actions of these units, along with the enrollment of some ex-Fascists in the People's Defense (in order to increase the manpower available for these duties), did not help the Liberation Council's reputation and implicated it in the very recriminatory excesses that it was meant to "manage."[20] An inquiry conducted by the British and American forces in July 1945 alleged that in the first days of liberation there were mass killings of non-Fascists, as well as persons who had been employed in the Fascist security organizations—the *Questura, Pubblica Sicurezza, Guardia di Finanza, Carabinieri*, and *Guardia Civica*.[21] Most of the recriminatory killings and deportations in Trieste and Venezia Giulia seem to have taken place between 2 and 15 May, a period long enough to arouse suspicions about the pro-Yugoslav forces even amongst those individuals who were relatively protected from reprisals. Local eyewitnesses sympathetic to the communist anti-Fascist forces reported two main types of retaliation, similar to the recriminations the United

States 5th Army noticed in northern Italy in April 1945: Casual murders for personal revenge, and summary justice effected by partisans "at the direction of their leaders, possibly after some form of so-called trial, such as is alleged to have been given Mussolini and the others arrested with him."[22] In Trieste, there was a further Yugoslav dimension to recrimination. A Liberation Front partisan in Trieste, Roberto, recalls hearing at the time that OZNA and the People's Defense were hunting out fascists and taking them to Ljubljana.[23] Andrea, a member of a Communist youth organization who had been imprisoned in an Austrian *Strapflager* until the end of the war, remembered returning to Trieste and noticing the strange behavior of some partisan groups. He referred to their use of the slogan "*caccia ai fascisti*" (hunt for fascists) to describe the arrest and deportation of fascists, and thought the partisans involved in these "hunts" included former criminals.[24] In addition to the massive deportations—the officially organized aspect of the Yugoslav-coordinated *caccia ai fascisti*—Communist partisans were allegedly burying their opponents in mass graves in the *foibe* around Trieste, natural abysses in the fractured limestone of the Carso countryside.[25] On the basis of interviews British and American investigators were able to discover that in Basovizza, a village high above Trieste, executions had indeed taken place. Don Malalan (described problematically in the Allied reports detailing his evidence as a "fanatic pro-Slav" and "bitterly anti-Italian") was a priest from a locality neighboring Basovizza. Malalan happened to be in Basovizza on 2 May to officiate at a burial of partisans because the local priest was absent. While there, he noticed that in a nearby field there were about 150 civilians, "who," he claimed, "were recognisable by their faces as members of the QUESTURA," facing the wrath of a populace determined to have their revenge. Officers of the Yugoslav 4th Army questioned and tried the prisoners in the presence of locals. As soon as one of the alleged fascists was interrogated, four or five women would rush up and accuse them of having murdered or tortured one of their relatives, or of having burned down their houses. The accused were butted and struck by the soldiers and eventually always admitted the crimes ascribed to them. They were then all shot. On 3 May 1945 Malalan was again at Basovizza and witnessed 250 to 300 civilians and about forty German soldiers being executed in the same place. Don Sceck of Cognale (also described by the Allied Committee as a "rabid anti-Italian") had refused to administer sacraments to some of the prisoners on the grounds that it was not worthwhile. Malalan claimed that Sceck *had* administered last rights to one victim from Trieste's *Pubblica Sicurezza* but not without berating the prisoner at the same time: "You have erred until now, you have amused yourself by torturing the Slavs. . . . The punishment about to be given you has been full deserved." Malalan himself approved the killings on the grounds of their "legality," claiming that at the time there was a great deal of confusion, and many people were suspected of being traitors or spies for the Germans. All the prisoners, he added defensively, had been tried and were dead before being thrown into the Basovizza *foiba.*

In the months and years that followed the forty days, some sources claimed that the pro-Yugoslav forces had arrested in total six thousand persons in Trieste and neighboring Gorizia, of which 4,150 were later released; that 1,850 persons had been deported, and 1,150 had never returned.[26] By contrast, a British intelligence officer in Trieste, Geoffrey Cox, reflected that although the arrest of fascists in Trieste was widespread, these must have "followed no coherent plan" since "[a] good portion of Gestapo agents and Fascists of some seniority came unscathed through the Yugoslav clutches to fall into our hands later."[27] More recent historical studies have shown that names on the compiled lists of missing were often repeated, invented, or corresponded to names of individuals who had in fact returned, and it is estimated that deportations conducted by Yugoslav authorities in the Trieste region in May 1945 totalled a few hundred rather than thousands—many of the deportees eventually dying in appalling conditions in Yugoslav camps.[28] Later excavations of the most infamous of the *foibe* in Basovizza revealed only eight bodies and dismembered corpses, their nationality and cause of death indeterminable.[29]

What actually happened in the first weeks of May 1945 is difficult to document with any precision, primarily because controversy surrounding the extent of unjustified epuration, its perpetrators (whether they were local partisans or the representatives of the Yugoslav secret police), the numbers of the deportees and *foibe* victims, and their ethnic and political identities, was kept fuelled by rumor, and the strategic efforts of the CLN and the British-American forces to undermine the credibility of the Liberation Council.[30] The archives of the Venezia Giulia CLN reveal that its members regarded the anarchy of the postwar as an inevitable consequence of the Slavic nature of the Liberation Front administration, and that they did not require much evidence to believe rumors of indiscriminate killings. After their eviction from the town hall by the Liberation Front, the CLN had established their own headquarters in the city's library from where they began a cultural counter-campaign that relied upon depictions of the "Balkanness" of the partisans.[31] Its members wrote to the Allied military command in Trieste responding to the rhetorical question, "What do the *Triestini* want?"

with the demand that Trieste's Italian identity be defended.[32] Triestines, they argued, were part of a population that had given history Roman civilization, Western Christianity, and the Renaissance; thus, it was contrary to any principle of liberty to place Italians under the protection of a people who, however courageous or hardworking, were a long way from sharing any common traditions or any ethnic or cultural affinity.[33] CLN propaganda repeatedly invited the Italian citizens of Trieste to exercise their *alta civiltà*, to distance themselves from the barbarism of the Yugoslavs, and thus to remain *"padroni* of their own destiny." While Liberation Council rule had abandoned Trieste to a "Balkan people whose totalitarianism was the equivalent of fascism, and the death knell for this purely Italian city," the CLN wanted Trieste to develop as a politically and administratively autonomous Italian city, fulfilling its historical role as a center of world trade and as a bulwark of the West erected against the East.[34] They stressed the foreignness of the Yugoslav army and what they called the Yugoslav administration. They offered examples of ungrammatical and ill-written Italian documents issued by the ministries of the Liberation Council as proof that Liberation Front supporters were illiterate and unable to speak Italian.[35] The CLN portrayed the idealized Yugoslavia as a federation of three races who had fought each other brutally. By inserting Venezia Giulia into that system, they argued, it could be expected that in a short time the region would also lose its demographic distinctiveness, its *civiltà*, and become deformed, barbarian, and sequestered from the world.[36]

Similar representations of differences between Italians and Slavs framed the reports by British and American military personnel who had arrived in Trieste. On a visit to Trieste between 10 and 13 May, Major Floyd E. Weidman of the Air Corps, described an environment tense with national antagonisms.[37] Weidman distinguished between a local Italian population and the "Jugoslavs." He attested that during his stay he heard "no one say a good word for the Jugoslavs," had seen no Italian "communistic" demonstrations in Trieste, and that "[e]ven the Italian policeman who acted as the interpreter for the Jugoslav sentry at the entrance to the Jugoslav command Headquarters told me he hoped the Allies would come into the city very soon."[38] He was convinced that if a plebiscite were held at that time the "Jugoslavs" would lose because the "Jugoslavs" were not an urban people, they may have understood mountain fighting, but "when it comes to occupying a modern city they just don't know the score." "Their very appearance," he stated, "apparently is revolting to the Italian city-dweller who feels he is being humiliated by the present condition." Major Smith, political adviser to the U.S. Main 13 Corps, reported that the Trieste administration was an alien force in Italian eyes. As a result of what he called twenty-five years of "calculated ITALIAN policy in Venezia Giulia," "SLAVS" were "considerably below cultural and intellectual level of racial ITALIAN." Now the tables had turned and the Slavs had the superior forces that might allow them to "establish themselves as master race." Although Italian airs of superiority annoyed Slavs, Slavs had found it useful to "detail intelligent ITALIANS for election" in order to display the "joint purpose of the two races," and, Smith assumed, "probably reap advantage of superior ITALIAN education under SLAV supervision."[39]

Some Allied observers were prepared to praise the Liberation Council's immediate attempts to repair and restore the economic and social infrastructure. As the population of Trieste swelled from 250,000 to an estimated 400,000, the Liberation Council created a plethora of ministries and instigated requisitioning programs to manage fuel, food, and accommodation shortages.[40] Although a report on 13 May by an adjunct for Brigadier Eve (Trieste's "Allied Commandant") stated that the local population were for the most part lying low, and there was little enthusiasm or sense that the city had been liberated, Brigadier Eve himself thought "the Jugoslavs had done well in getting the city going."[41] There had been considerable requisitioning and looting, but little shooting. Even those "influential Italians" who had earlier been arrested by the pro-Yugoslav forces had mostly been released.[42] A British Psychological Warfare Branch Area Report for the first two weeks of May 1945 observed that the "behaviour and discipline of Jugoslav soldiers" was judged to have been consistently "good," with respect shown to Allied officers "in the majority of occasions."[43]

The inconsistency of Allied depictions of the new government reflect both the influence of perceptions of the Liberation Council as a Slav entity, and the contradictory features of the Liberation Front government itself. The archives of the Liberation Council reveal its members were intensely preoccupied with local complaints about disappearances, repression, and murder. The intention behind the institution of formal epuration processes had been to underscore the council's antifascist priorities, and to manage the outbreaks of violence and recrimination. Instead, their processes had compounded the atmosphere of fear. Some council members openly declared their dissatisfaction with the spirit of vengeance that had been allowed to overwhelm their plans for orderly epuration. Others were extremely sensitive to the ways in which persecution of fascists was being interpreted as racially motivated, and itself fascist.[44] They feared these criticisms were eroding their traditional support bases. A regional official reporting on the state of the pro-Yugoslav press in Trieste acknowledged that workers at a

Trieste factory showed little enthusiasm for celebrating Tito's birthday (7 May) "since it all reminds them of fascism."[45] The council members were also sensitive to the fact that a few supportive teachers and lawyers were beginning to criticize their lack of representation, and that representatives of the lower middle classes, especially bank and office workers, were almost completely absent from the council's ranks.[46]

Two weeks after assuming government, Ivan Regent, a member of the Liberation Council and one of the leaders of the Italo-Slovene Communist movement in Trieste in the interwar period, reminded his colleagues that, in order "to show our new work," more Italians had to be recruited into the council's administrative organs.[47] The Liberation Council's first opportunity for exhibiting that work and their inclusive government came a few days later on 17 May, during a carefully staged evening ceremony to elect a new Liberation Council and a *Consulta* or supervisory body. The nominees for election were to be selected and voted for by the representatives of various Triestine political and worker bodies connected to the Liberation Front. The election took place at the Politeama Rossetti Theatre, named for the Italian patriotic figure Domenico Rossetti. The Garibaldi Brigade, the Italian Communist partisan unit fighting under Liberation Front command, stood guard. The stage was deliberately decorated with Italian colors, the Trieste halberd, Yugoslav, and Allied flags.[48] As the orchestra struck up the Garibaldi hymn—a hymn traditionally celebrating Italian nationalism—it was enthusiastically applauded by the audience.[49] The Yugoslav national anthem followed.[50]

The election evening's program included equivocal speeches of support by members of the Allied Command who had been invited as witnesses. For those cynical about the proclamation of fraternal government, the most suggestive speech was made by Major Jaksetich, second in command in the former military administration. Jaksetich was a Triestine who knew no Slovene. He spoke only Italian and had studied at the University of Turin.[51] He had participated in the Spanish Civil War with Communist brigades, and, between 1927 until 1943, he was successively imprisoned, exiled, and interned for his anti-Fascist activities by the Fascist Italian government. During one of those periods of imprisonment Jaksetich met Antonio Gramsci. After 1943 he joined the Garibaldi Brigade operating in the Trieste hinterland, and acted as a liaison with the Liberation Front.[52] In 1944, Jaksetich had distanced himself from the Venezia Giulia CLN because he believed that it was fighting against Slav communists rather than German Nazis. On the evening of the May election, Jaksetich used this personal history to evoke the connections between international anti-fascism, Italianness, and support for the new Yugoslav order. Trieste was to be part of a Yugoslavia where a new identity would be forged for populations on both sides of the old nationalist frontiers, and particularly for those who been subjected to more than twenty years of fascism. The key to this new identity was the union between Slovenes and Italians who, he argued, had together fought in Spain, suffered exile and imprisonment.[53] Their task was to build a new Trieste and to "direct it towards progress."[54] According to Jaksetich, what distinguished the Liberation Front from the pro-Italian CLN (which he argued encouraged only hatred between Slovenes and Italians) was the theme of fraternity.

For those with no vested interest in the preexisting order, there was something exhilarating about the idea that history had been defeated, that the identity of the city and its inhabitants had been liberated from the cultural and political burdens of the past.[55] The Liberation Council's Rudi Ursič tried to develop this theme:

> The union between the Slovene and Italian peoples already realised at a political level had to pass the ordeal of fire. . . . It is absolutely necessary to clear the air, it is necessary to remove in a reasonable way the obstacles that consciously or unconsciously interfere between Italians and Slovenes, it is necessary to show to the world that the common struggle has really generated an indestructible fraternity between Italian and Slovene elements. . . . There is no future for the city if it does not occur in the context of the fusion of the will of the Italians and Slovenes of Trieste.

Ursič claimed that the war had forged links between Triestines and other Yugoslav national groups, including the Croats, Dalmatians, and Montenegrins of the Yugoslav 4th Army, who were likewise to be remade into Yugoslavs.[56] According to Fulvio Forti, the council's newly elected secretary, the idealistic Triestine would support the new civil authority because he or she valued the principle of fraternity that it represented.[57] They would recognize that hatred between peoples was "artificial and horrible," and that it could be understood as the product of historical-cultural forces, the laws of which were now to be rewritten.

The partisan government had planned that the result of the May 17 election would reflect the inclusive and fraternal basis of their authority. Unsurprisingly, the elected Liberation Council was reported to consist of eleven Italian and seven Slovene members, all born or resident in Trieste. The *Consulta* comprised eighty Italians, thirty-six Slovenes, and one Albanian. Amongst these were thirteen women. The new representatives were described as professors, doctors, writers, bookkeepers, engineers, workers, technicians, artisans, businessmen, students, the "unoccupied" (usually women), nurses, lawyers, butchers, a "phonographer," tram-conductresses, barbers, electricians, gas workers, innkeepers, and chemists.[58] The election of each of these individuals was validated by a carefully recounted history of anti-Fascist participation, in the Spanish Civil War or the Second World War, insurrectionary activity, and commitment to the "democratic cause."[59] Much as the recounting of individual nationality or "race" had proven claims to membership of the nation in the past, citizenship was now anchored in an antifascist identity.

Armed with its antinationalist and antifascist brief, the newly sanctioned Liberation Council also tried to reinvent Trieste as "a city of mixed inhabitants each with respected rights regardless of their nationality."[60] On the day of the election, Franc Štoka, the council's political commissar, met with the employees of Lloyd's shipping company, one of Trieste's largest and most important firms. Formerly a fisherman, Štoka had been a member of the Communist youth in the interwar period, and in 1933 the Italian Fascist government had intered him on the island of Ponzo. During the war he had been active in the Italian Communist Party in Monfalcone, fought with the 14th Garibaldi Brigade, and was a well-known figure in Workers' Unity. At the meeting with the Lloyd's workers, Štoka responded to cries of "*Viva Trieste Italiana*" with the rejoinder, "Yes, *viva Trieste Italiana*, even I say so, but in Trieste not only Italian will be spoken, but also Slovene and, with respect, Turkish."[61] As the workers around him reportedly struck up a chorus in Triestine dialect of an old Italian nationalist and anti-Austrian anthem—"[i]n the homeland of Rossetti only Italian is spoken"—Štoka warned that in the new Trieste this song would no longer be tolerated. On other occasions, Štoka and other members of the Liberation Council insisted that it would now be possible to hear the voices of all minorities, including those of Austrians and Turks.[62] (Spokespersons for the CLN retorted that even if Turks or Arabs sought exile in "our city," it did not give them the right to claim it as Turkish or Arabic.)[63] The Liberation Council promised full support to a local Austrian Committee of Liberation whose object was to unite and represent antifascist Austrophiles in Trieste and the coastal region.[64] Although sectors of the Jewish and Greek communities and local representatives of the Greek Liberation Front (EAM) supported the council and petitioned it for the return of assets confiscated by the Nazis, the council was mostly silent on the place of the Jewish and Greek populations in their new pluralist version of the city and region. At the same time that the Liberation

Council promised to do away with the cultural and economic bases of past injustices, it placed *renewed* emphasis on the significance of Italian and Slovene cultures and their separate needs. Rather than create bilingual (or even multilingual) schools, it separated Italian and Slovene-language education, and divided responsibility for the education ministry between an Italian and a Slovene.[65]

Both the aspirations and limitations of the new government's view of liberation were evident in the experience of the Anti-Fascist Women's organizations. The day after the 17 May election a member of the Trieste committee of the Anti-Fascist Women declared: "we haven't just battled against the occupiers, but we've created a revolution in our home, listen well, I said a revolution."[66] The focus for the Anti-Fascist Women's ideological preoccupations and "progressive" aims was the new Yugoslavia, and political liberation through antinationalism. Records of committee meetings held between 1945 and 1948 indicate that the most common theme of the Anti-Fascist Women's discussions was "the pacific co-existence of peoples of diverse nationalities on a democratic basis."[67] In 1945 an Allied press summary reported that the local Anti-Fascist Women were out to "destroy chauvinism."[68] But the Anti-Fascist Women's interest in political liberation, their conflation of class, gender, and national liberation, foundered on the barriers of class and religion, on preexisting ethnic and cultural prejudices, and on their own obsession with ethnic and class credentials. From the first weeks of the May government, Anti-Fascist Women members spent much of their time trying to involve as many women as possible from Italian-speaking and middle-class areas, and organizing conferences independent of the mainly male pro-Yugoslav communist organizations. Their views often combined the traditional with the "modern." Support for communist organizations and partisans was on one occasion shown by the sacrifice of gold rings—a ritual emulating the symbolic attachment of women to the patriarchal Fascist state and to the church. The new "Italo-Slovene" woman was to be politically aware, but she was also to combine being a good worker with being a good mother, raising her children in the consciousness of the revolution.[69]

The new government's acceptance of the idea that national identities were unambiguously discrete was complemented by its preference for the separation of sexually differentiated spheres of political activity. The Liberation Council's promise that all would "finally be arbiters of their own destinies," *padroni* in their own homes, had lacked specificity, and *padroni*, like *fraternità*, was not a word whose meaning implicitly extended to women.[70] Although the *Consulta* and other partisan institutions had some women members, the powerful council had none.

Often impoverished women activists found it difficult to gain economic support that matched the Communist Party's nurturing of its male representatives.[71] A historical overview of the partisan government of May 1945 compiled by male members of the partisan administration later that same year, blamed women for the Liberation Council's failure to provide a secret ballot in the 17 May election. The official history implied that the continued presence of fascists in Trieste meant that women might have been swayed to vote for representatives of the Right.[72] This could have been an argument the former council members decided upon retrospectively, hoping to exonerate themselves. But by deploying the threat of a potentially conservative female vote in a primarily Catholic region as an argument against more inclusive democratic proceedings, they inadvertently allied themselves with the gender conservatism of their pro-Italian CLN opponents and the Allied forces.

The issue that most explicitly distinguished the Liberation Front government's views from those of the British-American forces was the political and cultural status of the differences between Italians and Slavs/Slovenes. While the Liberation Front saw the boundary region as an integral space, the diversity of which allied it with the multicultural experiment of Communist Yugoslavia, the British and American military personnel tended to see it as a faultline. This latter view was based on no less ideological or contradictory presumptions about difference, identity, and sovereignty than the communists' cultural and political ideal of Italo-Slovene brotherhood. In the official history of the Allied administration in Italy, C. R. S. Harris argues that the Allies' rejection of the validity of the partisan governments in Venezia Giulia was legitimate "in view of the racial tension between Italians and Slovenes."[73] Yet it is this characterization of Trieste and the boundary region that the supporters of the Liberation Front were attempting to challenge, and for which, despite all its shortcomings, the Liberation Council stood.

After the May election, the Allied view of the Liberation Council retained its inconsistent cast. A British intelligence report of the election ceremony emphasized that "few Italians" were in attendance and that the "three quarters Slav" audience were "imported from the suburbs and the surrounding country." The intelligence officer also looked suspiciously on the absence of Yugoslav propaganda:

> The outstanding feature of the publicity campaign was the disappearance of Yugoslav flags and TITO's photographs from the streets. Yugoslav flags now fly only from buildings occupied by Yugoslav military and all slogans have been taken from trams and in a few cases replaced by small Italian communist flags pasted on the windows.[74]

Two days after the elections, Major Smith summarized the situation as "outwardly calm though requisitioning and arrests by Jugoslavs continues. BALKAN methods adopted distasteful to Allied soldiers who cannot intervene and sympathise with Italians."[75] Despite efforts to appear inclusive and legitimate in the eyes of local antagonists and Allies, the Liberation Front and its administrative ancillaries were still regarded as "Jugoslav," Balkan, and an alien occupying force. This perception of the Liberation Front was as much a symptom of the competing military aims of British–American forces in the region as a cause. By mid-May, Allied command was exploiting the idea of Italian and Slav antipathy, and the foreignness of Slavs, for its own purposes. In a directive issued on the same day as the election by Field Marshal Alexander, the Supreme Allied Commander, the Liberation Council was identified as part of an alien Yugoslav force: "feeling against Jugoslavs is more strong and is getting stronger daily. . . . It is now certain that any solutions by which we shared an area with Jugoslav troops or Partisans or permitted Jugoslav administration to function would not work."[76] Alexander depicted his decision to undermine the authority of the Liberation Councils operative throughout the boundary region as a necessary response to a groundswell of feeling amongst the local population and the British and American troops against the Yugoslavs. Allied command implied it was acting in defense of the moral intuitions of the local people and its own men.[77] Yet the British Eighth Army had received its instructions "to impose Allied Military Government using as a medium whatever administration is found irrespective of nationality" as early as 3 May 1945, before any evaluation of the Liberation Front's government was possible.[78] Regardless of the strategic reasons for Alexander's 17 May intervention, the argument he employed fortified a racially based view of the illegitimacy of the Liberation Front at the expense of the ideal of fraternity. As we will see, a critical re-reading of key Allied texts of May 1945 does not support this view of events or cross-cultural relationships in Trieste.

On 21 May, Tito, under pressure from Alexander and the governments of the Allied forces, accepted the border demarcating the limits of Yugoslav and Allied areas of military occupation as proposed by General William D. Morgan, chief of staff to Alexander. In exchange Tito demanded that some units of the Yugoslav army be allowed to remain in the Allied area and that the Allies accept the existing civilian authorities established by the Liberation Front forces. On 9 June 1945 Tito and the Allies reached a compromise (known as the Belgrade agreement) according to which Venezia Giulia would be separated into two zones on either side of the Morgan line until a new Italo-Yugoslav border was

4.4. The Morgan Line, 1945

AUSTRIA

• Klagenfurt

KANAL VALLEY

ITALY

VENETIAN SLOVENIA

Soča   Isonzo

• Kobarid

• Tolmin

Bača

YUGOSLAVIA

• Ljubljana

• Gorizia

Vipava

Monfalcone

• Duino

• Postojna

Trieste •

Koper

Piran

ISTRIA

• Rijeka

QUARNERO

Raša

ADRIATIC

Pula

0 10 20 30 40
kilometres

•••••••••••••
Morgan line

- - - - - - -
Austrian Border 1920

formally decided upon at peace talks. Zone A, which included the city of Trieste, would be administered by the Allies; Zone B, which included the Istrian coast (but not Pula) would be placed under a Yugoslav caretaker government. There would be no restrictions on movement between the two zones for the local populations. Further, it was agreed that the Yugoslav army would leave Trieste and Zone A, but that the Liberation Front administrations would be retained where they were functioning efficiently. Tito's negotiations for the future of Trieste and Venezia Giulia seem to have taken the Liberation Council by surprise.[79] They struggled to retain their authority in the face of the Belgrade agreement (despite the undertaking that efficiently functioning Liberation Council administrations would be retained) and damaging accusations that they were "murderers and hunters of Italians."[80] Their political and legal offices were inundated with protests, some originating from the Public Prosecutor's office and the Higher People's Court for the Slovene Littoral.[81] Petitioners queried the detention of persons for long periods without reason, or without trial. The public prosecutor for Trieste, Dr. Stanko Peterin sent a report to his counterpart for the Littoral outlining the number of people who had come to his office complaining that their friends or relatives had been arrested or gone missing.[82] He stated that the makeshift offices of the British and American command were also besieged daily with requests and denunciations.[83] When the local representatives of the Allied forces complained to the council that nationalist rather than anti-Fascist motivations were guiding epuration, that Slovenes were judging Italians rather than anti-Fascists judging Fascists, one council member's response was to object: "Many still do not understand the reason for all these arrests, we cannot forget that we were downtrodden for all those years."[84] At a Council meeting for 25 May, Comrade Ferlan was more critical, charging that the process of epuration had alienated Italian support. There were too many arbitrary arrests, and more caution was needed: "It is true," said Ferlan, "that we have also suffered a lot, but it would not be right if we now executed reprisals. I appeal to the Slovene comrades, that they mediate with the responsible authorities, and in that way facilitate the cooperation of Italian elements."[85]

By this time, however, "the cooperation of Italian elements" had been decidedly undermined by the Venezia Giulia CLN, who portrayed "cooperative" Italians as victims of Yugoslav communist propaganda, insisting that no Italian could comfortably regard as equal a people they had always presumed inferior.[86] With the help of the Allies, the CLN also took steps to deter what they deemed collaboration by intimidating Italians who tried to cooperate with the Liberation Councils.[87] For example, the Liberation Council President, Dr. Zoratti, was kidnapped by members of *"il nucleo d'azione patriottica"* (NAP) and taken into Italy with the assistance of a member of the Allied forces. On 3 June 1945, Rudi Uršič, the Liberation Council secretary, opened the meeting of the Council Executive by listing all those absent, many of them having resigned under pressure from the CLN.[88] The Liberation Council's command of the local situation had been critically diminished not only by its lack of control over Yugoslav and Slovene army units, its failure to limit the People's Guard's powers of detention, but by the increasing stigma suffered by Italians supporting the pro-Yugoslav government.[89] At the same time, for those Italians who resisted accusations of collaboration, the Italo-Slovene ideal continued to be the most significant feature of the anticipated revolution. Three days after the meeting of the Liberation Council executive, Comrades "Visintin" and "Pobega" appeared before the Regional National Liberation Committee in Trieste to declare their continuing support as Italians for Trieste's communist and Yugoslav future. Visintin stated that Italians like himself represented the weakest part of the Italo-Slovene antifascist union. Pobega invited Italians to stand beside fellow Slovenes in this difficult hour.[90] Their efforts had little effect, however, and within a week a British and American Allied Military Government had replaced the Regional National Liberation Committee and the Trieste Liberation Council.

The difficulty of evaluating the representativeness of Pobega's and Visintin's testimonies is akin to the difficulty of evaluating the forty days itself, of peeling back the narratives of difference that have shaped the historical significance of this period: Trieste's *italianità*, communism's Slavness, Slavic Balkanness, and Italian and Slav antipathy. By May 1945, the Liberation Front government had invested the legitimacy of their sovereignty in Trieste in the Italo-Slovene ideal; they had also compromised their ethical credibility by emphasizing an ethical border between fascism and antifascism which they were at liberty to interpret and enforce indiscriminately. By contrast, British and American soldiers and officers increasingly turned to assumptions about natural racial antipathies to validate their own role in the region. The influence of the view that Italians and Slavs shared no common ground and that their cultures were unequal is evident in the descriptions disseminated by Allied personnel and "Western" observations of communist Slavs, of the intrinsic Italianness (and bourgeois character) of the Triestini.

Sylvia Sprigge, a correspondent employed by the *Manchester Guardian* to report on the war in northern Italy, arrived in Trieste with the New Zealand 2nd Division in May 1945 and stayed on for nine days of what she called "the occupation."[91] Later that year, the in-house journal of the Royal Institute of International Affairs in London, *The World Today*, featured Sprigge's account of the Venezia Giulia question. Sprigge's article was based on a diary she had kept during her time in the newly liberated Trieste; in its published form it was divided into two sections, "From the West" and "From the East."[92] At the outset of this article Sprigge sympathized with the aspirations of the subaltern classes unleashed by the liberation:

> [T]he workers of Trieste and the peasants in the region for the first time in many years felt they were the most important people in the city, whose hopes and ideals would at last be realised and . . . in the movement and under Yugoslav occupation, fraternisation between Italians and Yugoslavs really existed.[93]

She also explained that her account would exclude details of the hardship under which much of the worker and peasant population in Trieste were living, and the constructive efforts made by the pro-Yugoslav partisan government to alleviate their conditions, with the rationing of housing, meat, and provision of soup kitchens.[94] The reason for that exclusion was her preference for a supposedly less naive, more realistic interpretation: The world was divided into two blocs, and Trieste was at the center of a revolutionary plot in the mould of October 1917, inspired by similar Bolshevik, Slav tendencies.[95] Sprigge reported that there was a considerable working-class population employed in the shipyards, who inhabited the same suburbs of Trieste as the Slovenes, who might have identified as Italians and *Triestini*, and who simultaneously supported the Yugoslav government as communists. The Slovenes who had been absorbed into the middle class and who were ready to support Italian claims in order to repel communism also regarded themselves as *Triestini*. Sprigge concluded that Slovenes were more commonly working-class, and espoused an Eastern, communist, totalitarian ideology. They were also the most likely imitators of the Bolshevik revolution, "ready to scrap everything, just as Soviet Russia nearly thirty years ago was prepared to do without a penal or civil code, a stock exchange, landlords, and factory owners and managers, in order to create a new order,"[96] and to "make a tabula rasa of our civilisation and start 'fresh', as though 'freshness' were a privilege belonging only to the dockyard workers, tramwaymen, and shipbuilding hands of Trieste and Monfalcone."[97] Within the extremes that the ethno-political identifications Italian and Slav represented, Sprigge regarded the Allied British and American forces, like herself, as rational, and "serene" in "the midst of so much passion."[98]

Sprigge's own views of the ideological and cultural difference of the supporters of the Liberation Front were repeated in Geoffrey Cox's postwar autobiographical account of the New Zealand 2nd Division's journey to Trieste, *The Road to Trieste* (1947).[99] Cox emphasized the racial dimensions of the ideological differences between the British and American troops, on the one hand, and the Yugoslav partisans, on the other:

> At the crossroads, on every bridge, the local partisans and the Tito troops stood in irritated silence alongside the British and American sentries. On the great cornice road which is cut into the rock above the sea between Monfalcone and Trieste, our supply trucks wound in and out of columns of marching Tito troops, some of them Mohammedans with faces as dark as Moors.[100]

In Cox's story there were few Triestine Slovenes, and mainly Yugoslavs who were in competition for the city with Italians. He described the "ordinary soldier in the British American and New Zealand forces" as antagonistic to the Yugoslavs because of the struggle between Yugoslavia and Italy for the possession of the city: "[the ordinary soldier] did not mind Frenchmen bumping off Frenchmen or Italians hanging other Italians. That was their own business, and was no doubt the way they preferred to settle their political disputes." In Trieste, as far as the troops could see, it was "a question of one nation running another, and this seemed in the face of it, wrong."[101] When he lectured the British soldiers on the "tangled racial background of the Balkans and on the way this border area had been constantly grabbed and torn from both sides," the troops instinctively retorted, "'Maybe these are only Eyeties [Italians]. . . . But that's no reason why the Jugoslavs should push them around. After all the city is more Eyetie than Jugoslav. No one can deny that'."[102]

For Cox and other observers of the struggle for power between communist and anticommunist forces, gender was an indefinite but crucial category for marking out territories of cultural and political opposition. Gender relations were inextricable from the ways in which class and ethnic conflict were understood and imagined. Cox compared the "barrier of reserve" shown by the local Slovenes and the Yugoslav Army toward the Allied soldiers[103] with the "Viennese"-like "natural friendliness" of the *Triestini* (presumed Italian).[104] Relations between the Allied soldiers and locals identified as Italians were, Cox asserted, much closer than with the Slovenes because the soldiers became acquainted with local Italian blondes in two-piece bathing suits:

As a result the ordinary soldier heard the Italian case from every angle, and heard very little of the Tito case. He had come, moreover, to regard the Italians as full allies, not, as did the Yugoslavs, as very recent enemies who had invaded their country only four years before. The New Zealander saw that there was an Italian majority in Trieste itself, and that there were Italians elsewhere throughout the area. And he argued that the Yugoslavs had, therefore, on the face of it, no final right to run the place.[105]

Similarly, Cox's account of the welcome that the British Army received as they approached Venezia Mestre, about two hundred kilometres

Figure 4.5. A Partisan from Marshal Tito's Forces

Here the flag borne aloft by both Allied and partisan soldiers is a Yugoslav flag with the red star. NA24804: 'A Partisan from Marshal Tito's Forces presents a flag to a New Zealand tankman,' taken by Sgt. Menzies, 2nd May 1945

Courtesy of W.O.Ass.No.645, Imperial War Museum, London.

Figure 4.6. New Zealand Infantry and Tito's Partisans

The photographer's aim here seems to have been to capture the image of Allied cooperation, of soldierly camaraderie between the New Zealand infantry and the Partisans. NA24806: 'New Zealand infantry and some of Tito's partisans get together over a cigarette,' taken by Sgt. Menzies, 2nd May 1945

Courtesy of W.O.Ass.No.645, Imperial War Museum, London.

west of Trieste, centered on the relationship between the troops and the Italian "girls" of the town: "lithe girls with shining hair and with greeting and invitation in their eyes; northern Italians with blue eyes and sweeping eyebrows and high cheekbones in round faces; girls in white cool frocks with flared skirts like Americans, smiling, waving, laughing." While the Italian men greeted the Allied soldiers with a warm reserve, the eyes of the women, Cox stated, gestured "something akin to ecstasy," with arms thrown wide "as if they would embrace us all."[106] There is an obvious contrast in Cox's narrative between the welcome the Allies received in places that Cox designated as Italian and thereby familiar, and his descriptions of the partisan women the British soldiers encountered as they moved east, where the pro-Yugoslav partisan forces had assumed control. By detailing the responses of women to the advancing New Zealand division, Cox located the British Army in politically and culturally alien territory "between Eastern and Western Europe." Once on the eastern side of the Isonzo River, on the approach road to Trieste, the women turned aside "instead of waving back," the men did not understand "our dog-Italian" and, according to Cox, the Allied troops found themselves in a "No Man's Land." "We felt," Cox

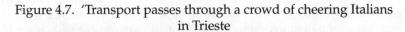

Figure 4.7. 'Transport passes through a crowd of cheering Italians in Trieste

The Imperial War Museum archive commentary identifies the crowd welcoming the Allied troops as Italian, but it would have been impossible to identify the political or national allegiances of the persons in the photograph. Rather, the photograph shows an individual stepping out of the crowd to offer his hand to a member of the arriving troops, perhaps a Maori, who extends his own hand in return. NA24809: 'Transport passes through a crowd of cheering Italians in Trieste,' taken by Sgt. Menzies, 2nd May 1945

Courtesy of W.O.Ass.No.645, Imperial War Museum, London.

wrote, "like strangers in a strange land, as if at the Isonzo we had passed some unmarked but distinct frontier. As indeed we had."[107]

For all their concentration on the racial, gender, and cultural differences that ostensibly marked the differences between the "Western" Allies (and Italians) and "Tito troops," both Cox and Sprigge give away alternative views of May 1945 in their own texts. Sprigge reports the local involvement and support for the pro-Yugoslav forces and the local significance of political and cultural change, even if only to dismiss it as irrelevant. Cox's narrative includes marginal references to the friendships established during May between the soldiers of the 28th Maori Battalion and those of the Liberation Front who used their common knowledge of Italian to dissipate the linguistic barriers between them.[108] Cox explained that the "Dalmatian blood" in Maori veins, "derived from settlers from the Dalmatian coast who had emigrated to New Zealand and inter-married," helped them overcome the language barrier with the speakers of Slavic languages.[109] Where language failed, their shared propensity to song, according to Cox, "rapidly provided one more common bond between these two strange groups."[110] The official New Zealand History of the 28th Maori Battalion contains descriptions of the Maori's ability to "communicate" and develop a rapport with the "sullen" Partisans. So successful were relations that, despite initial opposition from "higher spheres" to fraternization, "the battalion put in a dance every night of the week; civilians, Tito's men, and the troops were soon on the best of terms."[111] The author of the official history of the 43rd Indian Gurkha Brigade similarly stresses the Gurkhas' ability to find points of individual and human contact with Liberation Front partisans in the region during this period.[112] For the author, the Gurkhas' mediating role was also indicative of a new relationship in the postwar era between the British and Indians, as equals rather than master and subaltern.

Comprehension, hostility, and misconception between New Zealanders (some of them Maori) and the pro-Yugoslav partisans (not reducible to Slav) were as negotiable as the racial, class, and gender differences that Cox, like Sprigge and the Allied command, reiterated in order to shape narratives that brought together the interests of Italians and British-New Zealanders and set them against Yugoslavs. In May and June 1945, the antitheses of East and West, Balkan/Slav and Italian, oriented the view of Trieste "From the West" as if in anticipation of the later more intensified phase of the Cold War, when the problem of difference in the boundary region and its resolution became inextricable from the ideological reinvention of the political and cultural mission of the West. For the British and American Allies, and pro-Italian groups, representations of the Slavic identity of communism were an important means of undermining the Liberation Council's authority in Trieste, and naturalizing their own moral and political legitimacy as the representatives of Western democratic cultures, even at the cost of eliding the Fascist Italian past. Thus, in September 1945, the Allied Commission investigating the *foibe* confidently concluded that despite an absence of evidence, "without doubt" during the "Yugoslav occupation" "many thousands of persons were thrown down *foibe*."[113] The Allied Commission's tendentious conclusion is indicative of the extent to which readings of the events of May 1945 have been burdened by the political imperatives of the developing Cold War and by convenient representations of difference.

In mid-July 1945 a member of the AFZ wrote that it was with a heavy heart that she had watched the Yugoslav army leave Trieste, and all her hopes with them.[114] She believed that the Liberation Front had increased the autonomy of women as citizens of Trieste. Yet, for its part, the Liberation Council had hidden behind a simplistic division of the world into fascists and antifascists that allowed it to impose a political hegemony while it preached cultural pluralism. That there was no evidence to support the most damning Allied interpretations of the "Yugoslav occupation" does not mean that AFZ idealism did not coexist with cynical abuses of power by members of the Liberation Front movement, or that the Carso terrain might not one day reveal evidence of the extent of violence that ended the war. I have tried to extricate from the Liberation Council's failures, its inconsistencies and contradictions, the aspirations for alternative (more inclusive and representative) ways of imaginatively representing communities in Trieste which it encouraged and exploited. The history of the forty days of May 1945 is important not only because of the existence of these counternarratives, but because it reveals the ideological work that underlay constructions of "the problem of Trieste" as simply a problem of nationalism and natural antipathies. In the chapters that follow I explore in more detail the influence that British and American personnel and the local pro-Italian intellectual élite have had on interpretations of the history and politics of difference, identity, and sovereignty in Trieste. Even though the eyewitness accounts of individuals such as Sprigge and Cox inadvertently reveal inconsistencies in the attributed national differences and antipathies that framed "Western" interpretations and validation of events and actions, during the ensuing Cold War these narratives of difference became the most available and authoritative means of identifying the local population and of defining their political aspirations.

5

Gender, Ethnicity, and the Iron Curtain, 1945–1948

𝒯 he Cold War has evoked images of a conflict between two political conglomerations on either side of an impenetrable and manipulable "iron curtain" separating East from West Europe, and stretching from "Stettin on the Baltic Sea to Trieste on the Adriatic."[1] David Campbell has described this mapping of political oppositions around an ideological and cultural faultline as a "Cold War moral cartography."[2] If, as Roberto Rabel has argued, Trieste was "a microcosm of [an] unfolding Cold War,"[3] it was also a microcosm of the political and cultural antitheses that marked out that moral cartography. In 1944, Edvard Kardelj, the major spokesperson for the Yugoslav Communists, complained that the Italo-Yugoslav border was being portrayed by "Italians" as a border separating "two worlds," and that the British and American Allies were equating an Italian cause with the defense of Western culture.[4] As we saw in Geoffrey Cox's Cold War orientation of the road to Trieste, Western culture denoted presumed ethnic and gender identities, and relations between ethnic or racial groups, as well as between men and women. In this chapter I look at the gender and ethnic dimensions of a "Western" Cold War moral cartography that had its axis at Trieste, and the impact of that cartography on the different forms of political identification and agency available to male and female, Italian and Slovene, "peasant" and bourgeois Triestines. During the decade of Allied Military Government (AMG) in the Venezia Giulia region, from June 1945 until October 1954, British and American attempts to resolve the problem of Trieste and demarcate an Italo-Yugoslav border in the midst of the threat of renewed international conflict, involved the reproduction and transformation of "perceived patterns of similarities and differences" that had fashioned representations of Eastern and Western Europe since the Enlightenment, had resonated in the early twentieth century invention of Trieste as a problem and which, in the Cold War, gave the iron curtain its cultural and political texture.[5]

THE "BRITISH-AMERICAN WAY OF LIFE"

C. R. S. Harris claims that during World War II the United States and Britain conceived of their role in northern Italy to fight the war against Germany, and to establish, through the organization of military administration, "a more permanent 'objective'—the re-creation . . . of democratic institutions capable of surviving after the withdrawal of the occupying troops."[6] Supported by this democratic objective, and by the assurance of its "neutrality," on 12 June 1945, the British-American AMG assumed authority in the territory demarcated as Zone A of Venezia Giulia west of the Morgan line and including the towns of Trieste, Gorizia, Monfalcone, and Pula.[7] The AMG's governance of Zone A relied on characterizations of the intrinsically democratic national cultures of Britain and the United States. In the war correspondent Sylvia Sprigge's words, British and American nationals were "rational" and "serene" in "the midst of so much passion."[8]

On the first day of its tenure the AMG removed the flag of the city of Trieste from the town hall and replaced it with the national flags of the United States and Great Britain. At the same time it outlawed the raising of any other national flags from public buildings. The AMG occupied the former Liberation Council's headquarters, the town hall, and the "Casa del Popolo." In the place of the Liberation Council's laws and People's Court, it reinstated the legal system as it had existed in September 1943 and created new courts: General, Superior, and Summary Military Courts with jurisdiction over all persons except members of the Allied Forces and prisoners of war. These courts dealt with offences against AMG orders, laws of the territory, and the laws and usages of war. Offenses against AMG sovereignty included the incitement of "any inhabitants of the occupied territory to insurrection against military authority," or the organization of "any public demonstration or assembly for such purpose." In some cases these offenses were punishable by death.[9] There were other offenses that incurred fines or imprisonment, including breaking of curfews, publishing material "detrimental or disrespectful to the Allied Forces or any member thereof, to the Government of any of the United Nations or to the Allied Military Government," uttering any "hostile or disrespectful" speech or words.[10] All private means of communication, all photographic and related equipment had to be authorized. Meetings, assemblies, publications, newspapers, all needed written permission from the AMG, unless the activities were for religious purposes, or for the operation of courts of law, universities, schools, and educational establishments and ordinary functions of government. Any assembly could be dispersed by a Civil Affairs Officer if it threatened public order. The AMG military forces could arrest or hold suspects in detention, and could requisition property without warrants for the purposes of inquiry or investigation. Detention for reasons to do with hostility toward the Allied Forces or the AMG could be enforced for up to a period of three months before granting a trial. As with the government they had replaced, the AMG deemed it necessary to have a curfew, and to control travel out of the city center by issuing authorizations. All Liberation Front measures taken for requisitioning were cancelled. Allied Military "Lira Notes" became legal currency. All transactions, foreign trade and exchange, rationing, wage and price fixing were to be controlled by the AMG. For nearly a decade after the end of the Second World War, while the problem of a border separating Italy and Yugoslavia awaited formal resolution, the population of Zone A was subject to these conditions of British and American military rule with only minimal amendments to the extent of the AMG's sovereignty.

The ultimate authority in Zone A was the Supreme Allied Commander, Field Marshal Alexander. Beneath Alexander stood the Allied Commandant "in loco," General Harding, commander of the United States 13th Corps. In Trieste, Allied authority was represented by the Senior Civil Affairs Officer (SCAO). The first appointed SCAO was Colonel Nelson Montfort. Within a month he was replaced by Colonel Alfred Bowman, an American lawyer who had previously directed the AMG in the Pisa-Rimini combat zone. Bowman's term lasted until 1947, when British General Terence Airey took the helm.[11] The SCAO worked with three Area Commissioners, one each for Gorizia, Pola/Pula, and Trieste. In contrast to the AMGs in Northern Italy, the AMG in Zone A of Venezia Giulia operated autonomously. According to the promulgation of General Order 11, the AMG was "the only government in those parts of Venezia Giulia occupied by the Allied Forces and . . . the only authority empowered to issue orders and decrees and to make appointment to public or other offices."[12] SCAO Colonel Bowman would later confirm that consequently, for the first time in the

European experience of Allied Military Government, military rule existed de facto.[13] The AMG also had two separate political advisers who placed it in constant contact with the British Foreign Office and the American State Department.

The AMG's extensive practical and political authority was bolstered by the imposition of the Italian legal and administrative infrastructure that had existed in Trieste in 1943, before the Allied-Italian armistice. Some of that infrastructure was inherited from pre-Fascist Italy but tainted by the Fascist political experiment. Thus General Order 11 established the AMG's complete political and legal authority in Zone A by reimposing the prewar form of civil administration controlled by appointed Prefects (Podestà) responsible to the Italian state, but in this instance a Commanding Administrative Officer was responsible to the AMG.[14] If a local commune rejected the authority of the AMG, as occurred in a number of staunchly pro-communist villages, then a Commanding Administrative Officer merely assumed the powers that the Fascist state had bestowed on the Podestà or mayor.[15] Supporters and members of the former Liberation Council were invited to be involved in creating a Communal Council led by an appointed municipal president, but refused on the basis that the Belgrade agreement had stipulated retention of Liberation Councils; they instead demanded elections. Consequently, even though a few Slovene anticommunists played roles in the civil administration, the AMG bureaucracy was overrepresented by Italians from the former CLN and Italian nationalist groups.[16] Those groups who felt excluded by the AMG practices either because of their ideological preferences or their ethnicity thought that similar processes of political homogenization underway in Zone B under the Yugoslav Military Administration better represented their interests. In Zone B's three administrative areas, Croat Istria, the Slovenian Littoral, and the city of Rijeka, Liberation Councils were retained as the organs of the new military administration. These administrations recognized only the Venezia Giulia Socialist Party, the Independentist Front, and the Communist Party as legitimate political parties, but they awarded Slovenian, Croatian, and Italian equal status as official languages in "mixed territories." In Zone B all Italianized surnames were "restored" to their original form; in Zone A official permission had to be given to have one's name changed back from its enforced Italian version.[17] In Zone B, land was partitioned among the peasant farmers who owned it privately, although they lacked the resources and capital for individual farming. In Zone A, the AMG returned large tracts of land given to the peasants by the Liberation Council to the previous landowners (even though some of this land had been confiscated from "Slav" owners during the Fascist *ventennio*) and reimposed the preexisting sharecropping or *mezzadria* system.[18] The AMG categorized resistance by peasants to its reimposition of the *mezzadria* as "agrarian disorders." In one example of agrarian disorder, a young farmer explained that he was driven by the injustice of the *mezzadria* to kill a prosecutor defending the landlord's interests.[19] The historian Bogdan Novak has interpreted the significance of the respective socioeconomic changes in Zones A and B as highlighting the extent to which communist reform and "Slavic nationalism" were entangled, because most of the old landowners identified themselves as Italian and their peasants as Slovene.[20] Alternatively, these changes suggest that in the shaping of a new postwar order, the historical legacy of cultural and political identities (British, American, Italian, and Slav) and the class preferences that accompanied them, had to be negotiated, and that in 1945 AMG neutrality, like Yugoslav democracy, was a matter of perspective.

As with the Trieste Liberation Council, the AMG provided for the local epuration of Fascist organizations and employees, and for the local repeal of Fascist and specifically anti-Jewish laws.[21] But the AMG provisions did not apply to any anti-Slav laws, laws passed before the date of the Allied-Italian armistice, 8 September 1943, nor to any Fascist crimes committed before then.[22] Faced with pressure from pro-Communist and often pro-Yugoslav trade unions, disruptive strike activity, and outbreaks of violence in the shipyard areas, AMG used Fascist antistrike legislation to pursue and imprison labor activists linked to the Communist unions.[23] William Sullivan, the AMG's British political adviser, argued that, in an environment of labor disorder and unrest, the AMG's use of Fascist laws was necessary to defeat communism.[24] However, in reports to the British Foreign Office, Sullivan also mentioned that General Order 11 had "unconsciously adapted without too close scrutiny the Fascist model," and that it was difficult to justify the AMG's use of what he called "Draconian" antistrike laws since they were no longer being enforced even in Italy.[25] The political ambiguities that the conflation of Italian, Fascist, and AMG legislation produced were evident in the inaugural inspection of the AMG-instituted Venezia Giulia Police Force in October 1945. British bobbies had been imported to teach locals "impartial traditions" of civilian policing. The new locally recruited police, however, took up their placements wearing "black shirts reminiscent of Fascist militia and carrying automatic arms."[26] The controversial costumes worn by the new police force only highlighted the problem that a "fair proportion" of the 3,950 police gathered together were "ex-Fascists." The AMG investigations of the almost daily attacks on civilians by neo-Fascist gangs, shooting incidents, the wounding and killing of suspected communists and Slavs which occurred throughout late 1945 and 1946, placed some responsibility for the provocation of these events on members of the Venezia Giulia police force.[27] Sullivan explained that the greater part of the police force were "undoubtedly anti-Slav and anti-communist," but this was due to the refusal by "pro-Slav and communist" elements to collaborate with the AMG, hindering "the creation of a proper national equilibrium in the recruiting of personnel."[28] An earlier report made by Major Smith for the U.S. Main 13th Corps contended that "Yugoslav" and "Italian" representatives of the Trieste Liberation Council had "expressed [the] desire to cooperate and feared fascist disturbances." Smith concluded that not all "Slav" authorities wanted to subvert AMG and, more significantly, that opposition to AMG rule could not be reduced to local or even Slav communist influence.[29]

The AMG's prerogative of neutrality was invested in the concept of a "British-American way of life" representing fair play, equanimity, judiciousness, and a predisposition to democracy. The role of the Psychological Warfare Branch in Trieste, which controlled all official media outlets in the area, was to "project" Great Britain and the United States and this "way of life" to the wider population, to explain that although the AMG in Zone A was not itself completely democratic, it would help to bring about a democratic government.[30] At the same time, official instructions from the Psychological Warfare Branch advised the censoring of all press, radio, and official references "on the subject of elections in local government, particularly in England or the USA and elsewhere."[31] The AMG was to give prominence to "all official statements, and statements by prominent politicians in England and America" on the subject of "one form of totalitarianism following another" in Eastern Europe and on the subject of "elections in various Balkan countries not being run on truly democratic principles."[32] In the place of Balkan corruption, and of the Liberation Front's investment in Italo-Slovene fraternity, images of cooperation between Great Britain and the United States, "their aims, achievements and way of life," were to prevail. And in the face of the friction that permeated British and American foreign policies and the Allied military structure,[33] the Psychological Warfare Branch was to "picture these two nations in their peaceful pursuits and report their gradual process of turning swords into ploughshares, but avoid emphasising them as lands of plenty and luxury."[34]

The representations of a shared view of the British and American way of life that gave authority to the AMG, and to its image of neutrality, were the subject of some cynicism among Allied personnel. On his tour of the European Allied Military Governments in 1945 Edmund Wilson (the American Marxist and literary critic) observed that despite its American Senior Civil Affairs Officer and the presence of the United States Main 13th Corps, Trieste was regarded as a mostly British operation.[35] Benedict Alpers, an American officer who in July 1945 had taken up the position of "Director of Prisons for the Department of Public Safety of the Military Government for the Occupation of Trieste," thought of the British as ex-colonial administrators "who regarded everyone—often including their American allies—as colonials."[36] Some of the political differences among the Allies in the region emerged out of the war. Geoffrey Cox records in his memoirs that, during the war, officers within the British Eighth Army (including a Cambridge history scholar named Captain Rendall whose task was to liaise with Italian and Slovene-organized anti-Fascist partisan formations) were "struggling for full recognition and retention of the partisan forces as fighting units." Allied policy, though, was to detain these forces in concentration camps and replace their local civilian administrations with AMGs.[37] The Cold War exacerbated these internal political divisions. Dr. John Rosselli, the son of a leader of the Italian anti-Fascist left-wing *Giustizia e Libertà* group, who grew up in England, has recounted his time as a Field Security Officer in the Intelligence Corps in Trieste from July 1947 until February 1948—the height of Cold War tensions in the region—reflecting on the fractures amongst British and American personnel, and signalling that the Cold War perspectives of the AMG did not necessarily reflect the opinions of its itinerant personnel:

> [S]ince my father had been very strongly anti-Fascist . . . my sympathies were rather left-wing anyhow. I think looking back the other chaps in the unit, the section, we all tended, I think ('46, '47, '48, one was easily rather left-wing, if you were young and so on, you know the climate in Britain at that time) so I think we tended on the whole to sympathise with the Slovenes. And the Italian nationalists were so unpleasant, and these things like the *viale* boys [neo-fascist youth] beating people up and so on. The only thing is of course the Cold War was on, the British government and army were hostile to Yugoslavia. And I suppose, that we were supposed to do something about the OZNA, the Yugoslav secret service, if we had a chance . . . but, on the whole, I think the chaps I was with, and I, tended to sympathise more with the Yugoslavs, although that wasn't the official—with the Slovenes—that wasn't the official line.[38]

Not all AMG personnel saw the boundary region from the same perspective, but neither were they all in a position to publicly articulate or enforce their counter-views. Alpers railed at what he perceived to be the injustices perpetuated by the AMG, at times openly, but more usually quietly in letters to his wife and over a stiff scotch. Ultimately, conventionalized representations of difference provided officials with a refuge from the criticism directed at them, just as such representations had left the Liberation Front vulnerable to attack. The British and American political advisers responded to criticism by referring to the intrinsic judiciousness of British and American character. They justified the AMG's use of pre-armistice Fascist laws and structures by invoking the politically transcendent authority and status of the Italian nation.[39] From the outset of the AMG's rule, nationalist narratives and the representations of difference that sustained them—the salient characteristics of British, American, and Italian or Western societies and individuals—provided institutional, discursive, and ethical bases for legitimating the AMG's political authority, and its de facto sovereignty. The AMG's moral authority was anchored in the cultural projection of the democratic sovereignty of Britain and America at home, and a relationship between Britain and America that transcended any single national interest—a politically respectable Western version of transnational fraternity.

POPULAR SOVEREIGNTY

In September 1945, at a meeting with France Bevk, president of the usurped Regional National Liberation Committee (the PNOO), Colonel Robertson, the AMG Deputy Civil Affairs Officer, declared that the difference between them was they would never agree on a definition of "the people."[40] As far as Robertson was concerned, the Regional National Liberation Committee's claim that it continued to represent the views of the local population was not credible because it only had the support of Slovenes. For his part, Bevk rejected Robertson's portrayal of the Regional National Liberation Committee as Slovene and criticized Robertson's assumption that "the people" in Trieste were Italian and middle-class. Most galling for Bevk was Robertson's lack of interest in the principle of Italo-Slovene fraternity, the cultural cornerstone of the committee's regional authority. Bevk and Robertson could not agree on who "the people" were because they could not agree on the identity of the authentic Triestine citizen, or on the range of democratic rights that Triestine citizens could demand.

Almost from its inception, the AMG's preferred definition of "the people" was influenced by orders from British and United States authorities to discriminate between Italians and Slavs. It was explained that this discrimination would provide a means of evening up the inequalities of the political resources at the service of pro-Yugoslav and pro-Italian forces, and of ensuring a "pluralist" political presence.[41] The use of the term *fascist* to describe Italians was to be discouraged.[42] The "Italian" viewpoint was to be promoted by facilitating its propagation and publication, "without appearing in any way to support such Italian views."[43] AMG personnel also brought with them assumptions about the relative status of Italians and Slavs/Slovenes in the area. For example, the advice given to the Regional National Liberation Committee by Lieutenant Colonel Armstrong, the Trieste Area Commissioner, that it made sense that Slovenes should concede to Italian language and culture, just as the Scots and Irish spoke English, reflects a premise about the subaltern status of Slovenes in the region.[44] Although these directives and assumptions affected the political future of Trieste and Venezia Giulia, determining who "the people" were or what they wanted was not as simple as Armstrong or Robertson implied. AMG records suggest that while the AMG's official view of "the people" influenced their perceptions of the relative political credibility of the opinions voiced by the Triestine population, observations by Allied personnel of people and events in Trieste did not always comfortably corroborate AMG objectives.

In August 1945, an Allied intelligence officer reporting on a pro-Yugoslav celebration in Piazza Unità of the British Labour Party and Clement Attlee's victory at the British elections, described communist sympathizers as, in the main, "Italian-speaking":[45]

> It is true that there were several contingents of Slovenes with their flags and "icons" but the gathering consisted in striking majority of Italian-speaking workmen, lustily singing "Bandiera Rossa" and "Su fratelli su compagne." Moreover of the half-dozen speeches, only one was spoken in Slovene.[46]

Language was a problematic indicator of national identification because it could not prove (although it was often inferred) that Triestine Slovenes were not joining in the Italian-language songs. But the scene observed by the Allied intelligence officer challenged conventional views of the Slavness of Triestine communism, since the Italian language was being used to express communist allegiance. A few days after the Labour victory celebrations, an AMG observer attending the first congress of the UAIS (*Unione Antifascista Italo-Slava—Slovenska-italijanska antifašistična unija*), an umbrella group organized by the Regional National Liberation

Committee to link organizations that supported either Trieste's autonomy or its inclusion in Communist Yugoslavia, found himself confronted
by a similar confusion of identities and symbols.[47] The observer's secret
report described being "welcomed with great warmth" and cries of
"Viva Gli Alleati, Viva Attlee."[48] The hall had been decorated with Triestine flags, "with a large size Stars and Stripes and a Red Ensign on either
side of the hall." The key flags were arranged behind the platform: "a
large Italian tricolour flanked by a Jugoslav flag and a Russian flag with
a Fiume flag in the corner." Portraits of Truman, Attlee, and Stalin shared
space with smaller drawings of Tito and Garibaldi. The staging of this
event (like the celebration of the Labour Party's victory in England) il-
lustrated that supporters of the pro-Yugoslav option for Trieste were trying to situate themselves symbolically in a common international
domain of left-wing democratic ideals. But the careful distribution of national and political symbols merely served to arouse the observer's suspicions about the political sincerity of the audience. The large proportion
of women amongst the two thousand delegates suggested to him hyste-
ria and populism. The observer stated his impression that "it was impossible for anyone who knew Italy before the war not to hear echoes of
the familiar Du-ce, Du-ce, Du-ce, chant." According to this account there
was a genuine spontaneity to the event, but the mass audience and the
female component of this pro-Yugoslav and left-wing congress reminded the observer of a Fascist past.[49]

Within a few months of assuming government, the AMG adopted
a more methodical approach to the assessment of popular sentiment. In
September 1945 an Allied commission reported on its "scientific" survey
of the local population. Its aim was to clarify the nature of popular sentiment among "the people" inhabiting the territory within the borders of
Zone A of Venezia Giulia.[50] Like ethnographers, anthropologists, and geographers before them, the commissioners Colonel R. R. Cripps and
Major Temple grounded their study in statistics, in this case the 1921 Italian census, which they regarded as relatively uninfluenced by nationalist objectives. According to Cripps and Temple this census described a
region comprised of Italian cities and Slovene hinterlands, and a Trieste
that was "overwhelmingly Italian with the Slovenes living in the suburbs." In Trieste the ratio of Italians to Slovenes approached six to one, as
opposed to the three to one stated in the earlier 1910 Austrian census. To
this existing statistical map Cripps and Temple added their observations
of "popular sentiment." They identified "Italian opinion" as "still in the
process of changing and dependent on economic factors to a large extent
and on nationalistic factors to a smaller extent." Membership of the pro-
Italian national parties was "embryonic," and groups affiliated with the

Venezia Giulia CLN were weak. The "Italians," Cripps and Temple stated, were *Triestini* who for economic reasons supported an autonomous city with British and United States protection. Although Cripps and Temple paid scant attention to the variety of religious or ethnic communities in Trieste, they did note a 5,000-strong Greek population (a number they claimed had been diminished by Fascist policies) in their survey but argued that because these Greeks owned 25 percent of the city's wealth they could be described as Italian. By comparison three-quarters of the peasants were Slovene, and they covered 60 percent of Venezia Giulia. According to Cripps and Temple these Slovenes were mostly interested in preserving their own culture, but not necessarily in becoming part of Yugoslavia. While the small farmers were interested in communism because they believed that it might lead to a better existence on the land, a majority of the large agriculturalists favored an autonomous Slovene state under international protection. Those individuals who were members of the Communist Party had joined for social reasons rather than any identification with an exclusively Slavic or working-class cause.[51] Similarly, communist allegiance was directed toward a number of bodies; there was more support for the pro-communist trade union, *Sindacati Unici,* they argued, than for the pro-Yugoslav Regional Liberation Committee.[52] Cripps and Temple concluded that the population under AMG government generally supported either a pro-Yugoslav solution or an autonomous state—whether under Yugoslav, Italian, United Nations, or British-United States protection. Their report advised that feeling in Trieste varied, but dissatisfaction with the past and present was manifest in support for autonomous non-national sovereignty and for "independentist" parties.[53]

Although Cripps and Temple had begun their survey with assumptions about the significance of the Italian and Slav makeup of the territory, they concluded that the AMG was overemphasizing the importance of ethnic differences. Economic or political differences, and class perspectives, were just as, if not more, significant in shaping popular sentiment. Expressions of a political solution to the problem of the border were not consistent with the declared or decreed "nationality" of those individuals they had interviewed. Cripps and Temple also questioned the extent to which popular sentiment had been distorted by "high pressure" and "propaganda": "even the attitude of the populace might not reflect their true feelings," they warned, "[d]aily there has been a fluctuation of opinion, tempered by world as well as local events."[54]

Considering Cripps and Temple's emphasis on the relative irrelevance of ethnic differences, it was ironic that the impact of international and local events contributed to the ethnic polarization of the Zone A communities. An American military report submitted during the period of Cripps and Temple's survey sympathetically noted that country doctors, most often Italian speaking, who had worked "happily among the Slovene population" for ten to twenty years, were being rejected by patients who refused to speak Italian to them. As a consequence the doctors found themselves without employment and were concerned for their own safety.[55] Triestines who identified as Slovenes and felt inspired by communist political and social ideals regarded the cooperation of other Slovenes with the AMG as a betrayal of a common Slovene cause. Cases of kidnapping became so common that the AMG had to transport its Slovene "collaborators" to their places of work in the rural communes, and then guard them in their offices until the evening, when they were returned to the city.[56] The changing history of the local Communist Party is further evidence of "ethnic" pressures on ongoing attempts by the communist left to salvage and maintain the ideal of fraternity. During a local Italian Communist Party congress held in August 1945, pro-Yugoslav communists took the opportunity to create a Venezia Giulia Communist Party which was to give local communists an alternative non-national form of communist organization. By the end of September the national branch of the Italian Communist Party under Palmiro Togliatti's leadership retreated from its support for the incorporation of Trieste in Yugoslavia. Togliatti, the leader of the Italian Communist Party who, in 1944, had been prepared to surrender Trieste and Venezia Giulia to a revolutionary fate as part of Yugoslavia now insisted that "the Italian character [italianità] of Trieste must be defended."[57] According to AMG reports, the local branch of the Italian Communist Party was encouraging its members to remain involved in the Venezia Giulia Communist Party in order to "uphold the Italian standpoint in that otherwise Slavophile organisation."[58] The Venezia Giulia communists, for their part, accused the local Italian Communist Party of "being exploited by crypto-Fascists."[59]

To an important degree, the behavior of political parties was particularly affected by their recognition of the importance of impressing on AMG personnel, foreign journalists, and other outsiders in Trieste that they represented "the people." Galliano Fogar, active at the time in the Action Party and the CLN, has argued that "control of the piazza" was a main objective of the local groups struggling to have their claims to Trieste and their political ideals recognized by the AMG and by visiting international delegations:

[W]e had to show . . . that it was Italians who had conquered the piazza, that the mass of the population in the piazza was all made up of Italians with shared sentiments. On the other hand we also sought to contest any presence in the piazza of mass processions which would demonstrate the opposite.[60]

The struggle for control of the piazza polarized Italian and Slav political identities. It grew difficult for CLNists to control the types of demonstrations and the violence that occurred in the piazza on behalf of Italy. In effect, the piazza became the monopoly of the neo-Fascists who took it upon themselves to be the spokespersons of *italianità* and Italian patriotism. Spurred on by the AMG's failure to prevent Fascist and squadrist violence directed at their branches and institutions, Slovenes and communists retaliated with strikes. Giampaolo Valdevit has argued that the postwar atmosphere of strikes and class war provoked the British Foreign Office and American State Department's interpretation of the problem of Trieste as the problem of Italian and Slav antagonism.[61] Yet according to Fogar those strikes were a response to AMG policies, particularly the AMG's failure to curb neo-Fascist groups, as much as a strategy to undermine the AMG. The national polarization of the Triestine community was to a significant extent the consequence of AMG political strategies and "ways of seeing."

The trial of Giorgio Jaksetich at the beginning of August 1945 is illustrative of the complex ways in which AMG institutions and practices encouraged the conflation of political and national identities, and the delegitimation of a non-national view of "the people" and their sentiments. Jaksetich, a former Garibaldi partisan, had been a keynote speaker at the Liberation Council election in May 1945. As an Italian supporting the Yugoslav cause, he was the definitive communist anti-Fascist working-class hero, the individual whose political convictions overrode other forms of cultural or personal identity. After the Yugoslav Army's retreat in June 1945, Jaksetich had remained in Trieste. A month later he was arrested in his apartment by AMG police on the charge of possessing a firearm, an offense punishable by death according to AMG law.[62] When the police forced their way in, Jaksetich was in bed, *"in orgasmo,"* he explained. When asked if the pistol was his, he confusedly answered yes. Later, Jaksetich protested that the pistol belonged to a comrade (whose uniform, boots, and documents the police had found in Jaksetich's home) killed by the Germans. When Jaksetich's trial took place on 1 August 1945 in the *Corte d'Appello,* the highest court authority in the AMG administrative zone, it was witnessed by Sylvia Sprigge reporting for the *Manchester Guardian* and her husband Cecil who wrote for Reuters. To the surprise of the courtroom, the prosecution's recommendation that Jaksetich be released on probation was overruled by the president of the court who stated that the charge was grave enough to entail the death sentence and that "under a regime other than the American or the British the accused would run the risk of being shot."[63] Jaksetich was sentenced to eighteen months in prison.[64] In protest, the Regional National Liberation Committee immediately called a general strike for that afternoon.[65] Sections of the public came out to show their solidarity and to denounce the new legal authority.[66] Jaksetich's supporters quickly sent petitions to Prime Minister Attlee accusing the AMG of bias and staging.[67] Reporting to the British Foreign Office on the trial and the stir that it had caused, Sir Noel Charles (British Ambassador to Italy), defended Allied military justice as fair and equitable, if legally pedantic.[68] He clarified that Jaksetich had only been informed about the nature of the charge at 18:30 the day before the trial, and the arrest had been aggressively pursued. However, he felt that the judge was justified in that many Italians wished Jaksetich's sentence had been even more severe because they regarded him as the major obstacle to the Italian solution of Venezia Giulia. Charles also noted that these Italians, members of the Socialist and Action parties, claimed that Jaksetich was Yugoslav:

> [F]ew of these men have troubled to find out anything about Jaksetich. For the most part they believe, in all good faith, that he is Jugoslav. One member of the Party of Action was taken to task by other party members in the presence of an Allied Officer for saying that he had known Jaksetich in the "twenties when he was a schoolmaster in Trieste" and that he believed him to be an idealist and as far as he knew an honest anti-Fascist.

For Charles, Jaksetich was "a typical communist intellectual—as usual of non-proletarian origin—much more akin to the Italian communist . . . than to the cruder Balkan variety."[69] Jaksetich's travels had placed him in contact with communists and anti-Fascists from all over Europe, but he had never been to Russia, did not speak "Serbo-Croatian or Slovene, only German and French," and his "mother tongue" was "certainly Italian." Despite the British ambassador's description of Jaksetich as Italian, AMG personnel and Italian intellectuals in Trieste transformed Jaksetich into a Yugoslav/Slovene. Col. Hammond, an AMG legal adviser, described Jaksetich as "a Slovene who has been an outstanding Antifascist and leftist leader in Venezia Giulia."[70] Allied military intelligence reports interpreted references to "Italo-Slovene brotherhood" at the demonstrations demanding Jaksetich's liberation as another communist ploy.[71]

A month after Jaksetich's trial, Allied Information Services again reported that communists who spoke of Italo-Slovene fraternity were trying to "submerge" the national issue.[72] While AMG personnel officially attributed the policy of refusing local elections to the problem of

Italian and Slav antagonism, internal AMG reports detailed the strength of communist sentiment among Italians and the popular class nature of pro-Yugoslav support, as a prime motivation.[73] The AMG also effectively manipulated the symbols of national sovereignty and transnational cooperation. In 1945 the AMG only accepted the public display of internationally recognized national flags: an Italian flag with a red star in the middle (viz., the flag that represented Italian Communism and which had insistently appeared in liberation celebrations throughout Italy) was definitely not a national flag and could not be raised.[74] In 1947, however, the UAIS found cause to complain that their May Day plans had been sabotaged by the AMG's insistence that *only* the communist "red" flag could be used by the UAIS.[75] The AMG had changed its policy regarding flags for the occasion—a tactic that the UAIS believed was meant to undermine their credibility as a mainstream political organization. The banner of communism was to be seen to represent only Slavs.[76] Yet, for the UAIS, the May Day festival provided an occasion to make a political statement about autonomy for the region, the union of all "democratic" forces, of youth and women, and the creation of a single front that would have allowed them to be *i padroni a casa nostra*.[77] The parade was intended as a visual manifestation of their general representativeness:[78]

> the red flag symbol of workers, the Slovene and starred Italian flag, symbol of the struggle for liberation and symbol of unity, and the Yugoslav flag with the star, and the Italian without the star signifying that the population of Trieste desires friendship between Italy and Yugoslavia.[79]

The UAIS also complained that the AMG had refused them a permit to stage the celebrations in the Piazza Unità. Like the AMG and local Italian patriots, the UAIS recognised that the Piazza Unità, which fronts the Adriatic and looks out toward the Italian mainland with Trieste and its hinterland ranged about it, was the symbolic heart of the town. The AMG had decided to divide up the town for the 1947 May Day celebrations, allocating the Piazza Unità to pro-Italian groups. The UAIS was allocated what were defined as working-class, communist, and Slav spaces. The UAIS' response to the AMG's attempted ethno-national ghettoization of Trieste was to use any means possible to enter areas designated as nationally off-limits. Funeral processions which traversed the policed ethno-national spaces of the town were the most popular forms of transgression, and the most frustrating for the AMG.[80] But pro-Italian parties maneuvered the spatial strategies of the AMG more effectively by lobbying within the AMG civil administration to prevent Slovene being spoken in the Piazza Unità, and to block the development of what they defined as Slav businesses and residences in Italian areas.

The AMG's skepticism toward the idea of Italo-Slovene fraternity was in part itself a strategic response to accumulating examples in their own Situation Reports and special studies of communist affinities across ethnic borders, and of noncommunist interest in a non-Italian solution to the problem of Trieste.[81] The AMG also pursued its anticommunist campaign and contributed to the redefinition of local political aspirations by emphasizing the overlapping ideological, national (or ethnic), class, and gender characteristics of communists on the one hand, and legitimate political actors on the other. Communist demonstrations were discounted not only on the basis of their Slav identity, but on the assumption that support for communism itself did not and could not be the manifestation of an authentic popular sentiment. In post-mortems of the May Day celebration in 1947, the SCAO Colonel Bowman detailed to his AMG personnel the importance of distinguishing an authentically democratic demonstration from the overly disciplined, and therefore unspontaneous and manipulated, communist-type demonstration:

> Two of you have mentioned the discipline of the Communists' procession and demonstration, and I don't want these minutes to sound like a hymn of praise for Communist discipline. It is true that it makes it easier for the Police and we should be very grateful if everybody would demonstrate in the orderly way these people did on 1 May. At the same time, Democracy, Western style, is not characterised by excessive discipline but rather by a controlled degree of undiscipline, which is another name for freedom. I don't want constant reference to the discipline displayed in these demonstrations to give the impression that discipline is all we think about. We do admire the way these people march and the way they behave themselves in a group, even under greater provocation, but we must remember that the kind of discipline which results in this perfect order is, in its way, also a threat.[82]

In his autobiography Bowman recounted that the AMG found it difficult to believe in the spontaneity of the arrival in the town of hundreds and thousands of people, "poor, harried Slovene country people who had tramped all night in order to demonstrate all the following day," who were "from the hinterland, [and] who in the normal course of their lives had not been in the city half-a-dozen times."[83] He maintained that the events, demonstrations, marches in which they participated were obviously organized and staged. Despite Bowman's attitude of implied

sympathy toward peasants, he viewed their political involvement as il-
legitimate. They could not represent Triestine popular sentiment since
they lived beyond the city walls. It was not only the perceived orchestrated nature of communist demonstrations, but perceptions of the
peasant and female composition of the demonstrators, which undermined the political credibility of the pro-Yugoslav cause:

> There comes to mind the spectacle of several hundred middle-aged and
> elderly women, all in black from head to toe, as if in uniform, who would
> from time to time present themselves before the building that housed the
> seat of my government, at exactly four o'clock in the afternoon, to chant
> and cry about the starvation to which their families were being subjected.
> At some time from a half hour to an hour later, these ladies would at pre-
> cisely the same instant terminate their lamentations, pick up their baskets
> and shawls and be out of sight in an instant. It was time, I am sure, to start
> thinking about dinner.[84]

Bowman tried to dismiss the relevance of the political activity of these
women by describing their simple dress (as "uniforms") and their sup-
posed lack of spontaneity. But the fear of revolt by locals against food
shortages was a real concern for the AMG, and it was women who were
most vocal about their grievances on this issue and others. When AMG
sources reported that on 16 June 1945 women and children participated
in communist demonstrations, Bowman responded that they probably
demonstrated in return for extra food, as if their political allegiance was
insincere and had been bought.[85]

The photographs taken by a local Triestine, Mario Maganj, a UAIS
sympathizer, during the early days of AMG administration suggest that
locally organized women, whether wives of striking union members, or
members of the AFZ, DAI, or the new women's ancillary of the UAIS—
the UDAIS *(Unione delle Donne Antifasciste Italo-Slavo)*—were determined to play a disruptive role. In June 1946, Maganj, a UAIS
sympathiser, photographed groups of exasperated women (conscious
of the photographer) being watched and patrolled by military police.
They held signs in Italian stating that their children were hungry and
demanding a halt to AMG retrenchment policies. Documents from
Anti-Fascist Women organizations indicate that the women who took
part in these demonstrations were provoked by the AMG's dismantling
of most of the structures that the Liberation Front had set up to deal
with the problems of food and housing shortages, and unemployment.[86] Many of these same women activists barely maintained an
existence at poverty level, yet their faith in organized activity and

Figure 5.1. Women's Demonstration, 23 June 1946

Cummunist women participated in the struggle for control of "the pisazza."

Courtesy of Mario Maganj, SNL Photographic Archive.

demonstrations remained intact.[87] The Anti-Fascist Women's executive claimed that their role was to petition the AMG and to influence the discussions between Britain, America, and Russia on the problem of Trieste.[88] When some of the rank and file plotted to overturn fruit stalls in the San Giacomo market because of exorbitant black market prices, the executive of the Anti-Fascist Women was able to convince them that the more mature approach would be to protest in an organized fashion in front of the major food supply organization run by the AMG.[89]

Maganj may have exaggerated the poses of communist women demonstrators for his own political purposes, but a list of UDAIS public demonstrations from 1945 until 1947 supports the impression that the presence of impoverished-looking women in Trieste's piazzas bothered the AMG.[90] The AMG's tactics against the presence of particularly communist women in Trieste's piazzas was to first evict them from their various offices and block their funding.[91] The local branch of the Allied Information Service created a display for public consumption entitled "Types of Men and Women," as if communist women might be domes-

Figure 5.2. Union Gathering, 23 June 1946

Female protesters conscious of their political role and of the camera.
Courtesy of Mario Maganj, SNL Photographic Archive.

ticated by the promotion of a model of sexually appropriate political
and public behaviour for women.[92] Bowman also decided to give his
wife responsibility for "Women's Hour"—broadcast on AMG Italian-
and Slovene-language radio stations—in the hope "that the political
tone will be materially altered and that the listeners will receive trans-
missions suitable to the title of the programmes."[93] These strategies reflected the importance of gender norms in the AMG's view of social and
political order, and in their view of "the people." When the AMG con-
templated holding administrative elections (which eventually took
place in a limited form in 1949) there was no debate that women would
vote alongside men. But when the UDAIS followed the protocol of asking AMG permission to hold peace conferences and collective meetings
with invited foreign speakers, the AMG refused on the grounds that the
women were not to become involved in issues that the AMG dealt with
on their behalf.[94] When the AMG did act on unemployment issues their
strategy was to remove women from unemployment listings and institute a policy that favored male employment.[95] Women's participation in

public workplaces was only justified, as in the case of afforestation workers, if the pay was so low that no man would want to do the same work.[96] When the AMG itself employed women, it was to patrol known prostitution areas.[97]

The AMG's view of gender norms also implied overlapping national distinctions. Under AMG law the rape of British or American women could earn a local the death penalty, but Italian or Slovene women who "fraternized" in any way with British or American men were defined as immoral and criminal. The involvement of AMG staff and its military on intimate terms with the local population defined local women (whether as friends, protesters, or prostitutes) as potentially threatening social transgressors, and drew the "trustees" of the city into Trieste's everyday life on a level that compromised quite concretely their stance of "neutrality." Sexual disorder reflected poorly on social order; the AMG's American and British respectability, and authority, was bound up with the imposition of a code of gender normality. Policies to manage prostitution partly reaffirmed a familiar gender double standard, but its less controllable consequences—whether physical infection or the establishment of relationships across increasingly policed national, ethnic, class, and political boundaries—could also threaten the AMG's claims to be the representatives of an authoritative political and moral order.[98] Bowman acknowledged that some of the women targeted by his rehabilitation program as prostitutes were guilty of no more than having legitimate relationships with British or American men. He described a large number as "border-line women approaching the 'fiancée' status."[99] Bowman's observation, like the protests of Benedict Alpers, did nothing to halt the AMG's enthusiasm for imprisoning prostitutes, and exposing and condemning "fiancées."

In each of the competing social-imaginaries of democracy and popular sovereignty in Trieste conventional representations of women delimited in some way the possibilities for individual women to be constituted as responsible citizens. Women's activity was overtly scrutinized by all sides, and used as a means of negatively defining the accepted criteria for authentic political behavior. All sides in the contest for political representativeness and authority portrayed politically active women as a potential fifth column, as independent subverters of morality, or as mindless objects of manipulation. Women were less of "the people" than a symbol or metaphor for defining "the people" and political preferences. Pro-Italian groups and pro-Yugoslav sympathizers exploited gender prejudices as they struggled to challenge the sincerity and spontaneity of their opponents' political convictions. They both represented women as a vulnerable constituency—through their "fraternization" with the "other" side, as girlfriends, lovers, prostitutes, and spies. Despite their open promotion of women's organizations and their supporting activities, the Venezia Giulia Communist Party shared the same hostility to women acting "spontaneously" and beyond their control.[100] Local communist newspapers conjured up images of immoral women who betrayed the political ambitions of their class by "selling themselves" to Allied soldiers.[101] Italian nationalists charged the AMG command with taking Slav mistresses who swayed the Allies toward favoring Slavs.[102] They also focused on the underground activities of pro-Yugoslav women. The Venezia Giulia CLN reported cases of female Slav spies—women who had been "left in the city by the Slavs" in order to elicit information "by tricking the drunk soldiers," and "spreading subversive propaganda amongst the Indian soldiers."[103] It was alleged that these women were active in rapidly increasing numbers, and were trying to convince soldiers to abandon their arms if the Yugoslavs came into conflict with the Allies. In return Yugoslavia and Russia seduced the women with the promise of "true liberty" in Europe and independence in India as well as in Trieste. On 3 July 1945, the Trieste-based United States Main 13th Corps reported an accumulation of evidence suggesting that Yugoslavs had surreptitiously placed women agents in employment with the AMG before withdrawing from the city on 12 June.[104]

Between 1945 and 1947, as the ideological oppositions of the Cold War consolidated, the AMG's authority crumbled around it, and cracks began to appear in the facade of the British and American "way of life."[105] High-ranking AMG officers were found guilty of embezzlement and defrauding public funds; AMG forces used violence against local citizens, sometimes wounding and killing them; AMG prisons were full of detainees held without trial for up to fifteen months, and its courts were prone to iniquitous judgments against members of left-wing groups while AMG personnel and local neo-Fascists received relatively light sentencing.[106] The UDAIS openly blamed AMG policies—the freeze on wages and extensive retrenchments—for the economic difficulties of the general population and a flourishing black market. They argued that the predominance of a low standard of living encouraged the prostitution that serviced the soldiers and staff of the military government. A 1948 UDAIS report claimed that over the previous three years hundreds of women had been arrested by the AMG, one woman and a child had been killed, eight women made invalid by the Civil Police, hundreds of women harassed, beaten, intimidated, and retrenched because of their connections with the UDAIS, nine thousand prostitutes arrested. Trieste had the second highest infant morality figures in

Europe, there were no creches for women workers, who received 30 percent less pay than men, thirteen thousand women were unemployed, 80 percent of whom were the family breadwinner. The UDAIS also accused the AMG of intensifying police terror against "democratic organizations," and of favoring the work of those in the territory who fomented war by sowing discord and hate.[107] Whatever its propaganda purposes, this picture of the AMG contributed to the greater cynicism and resentment of large segments of the population not in the AMG's direct employ.

In the "microcosm of the unfolding Cold War" that was Trieste, the struggle between communism and anticommunism became profoundly inscribed in the conception of a cultural as well as political border, an "iron curtain" separating Communist Yugoslavia from an anticommunist West.[108] Individuals within the AMG structure might have sympathized with Yugoslavs, or felt superior to Italians, but when Intelligence Officers and government officials saw ambiguity or class conflict, they resolved their confusion by turning to familiar tropes of national character, of gender and class relations, and familiar principles of sovereignty, and made sense of them in the context of the ideological oppositions of the Cold War. Regardless of the origins or intensity of these tropes, their reassertion in AMG responses to local support for communism reinvented "the problem of Trieste" and of a border separating Italy from Yugoslavia, as the problem of the disorder of women, peasants, and Slavs. AMG propaganda against disorderly women bound together and discredited the relevance of women's issues, the views of Slavs, communists, peasants, and antinationalists. The AMG was not unique in its attitudes toward the democratic aspirations of these groups, and, ultimately, for the Allied representatives of the British and American governments in Trieste the task of fighting communism was more important than the problem of women, or ridding Trieste of a Slav presence (the concern of the local nationalist Italian intelligentsia). At the same time, the Cold War polarization of political alternatives reinforced the democratic credentials of nationalists and of their conception of ethno-national borders as the solution to the problem of Trieste. Faced with an influx of Zone B pro-Yugoslav residents into British-American Zone A on the occasion of the 1946 May Day celebrations, Lieutenant Colonel Smuts (the Trieste Area Commissioner) called for a "cordon sanitaire" to be erected around the urban perimeter.[109] By 1947, a time we conventionally associate with the beginning of the Cold War, one Foreign Office commentator defensively remarked, any attempt "to pull down the barrier between the two [British-American and Yugoslav] zones," had to be resisted.[110]

6

"Free Territory," Nationalism, and the Cold War, 1948–1954

In the spring of 1945, the Italo-Yugoslav border was only one of a number of pre–Second World War borders suddenly open to challenge as a result of the defeat of German and Fascist military forces in northern Italy. In April, regional CLN militia operating inside Italy's interwar northwestern border with France helped French troops occupy the Val d'Aosta, Briga, Trento, and Ventimiglia in the hope of ceding that territory to France.[1] On Italy's northern border with Austria, the German-speaking population complained about the Allies' imposition of an alleged Italianization policy, and demanded incorporation into Austria.[2] By 18 May the French occupation in Val d'Aosta had given way to a diplomatic agreement granting the region autonomy (including cultural autonomy) and privileging the French language in the region.[3] In the north, similar agreements with the German-speaking minority were mediated by the Allied forces as a temporary measure before internationally sanctioned peace talks decided the more permanent fate of the Alto Adige. The nationality question on Italy's Austrian border was regarded by one Allied officer as "the same problem as Venezia Giulia," but in the latter case it was "the outside influence," the Yugoslav presence, that made it more complicated.[4] The resolution of the Italo-Yugoslav border (not formally achieved until November 1954) was also more complicated because, as we have seen, representations of Slav and Italian, East and West differences were profoundly constitutive of the encounter between communism and anticommunism. The

133

Figure 6.1. Allegory of the Division of Territory

In October 1946, locals from Vojščica, a Venezia Giulia village, dressed up in military uniforms and symbolically acted out the absurdity of the division of a village on the border of Zone A and Italy, which the adoption of the "French" line would effect.

Courtesy of Mario Maganj, SNL Photographic Archive.

political and cultural oppositions of the Cold War in Trieste were in important ways at cross purposes with another postwar trend—intellectual skepticism toward nationalism and ethno-national borders. At the end of the Second World War, consideration of the special nature of identities in boundary regions became the focus of discussions about the principle upon which an uncontroversial political border separating Italy and Yugoslavia could be established. In this chapter I look at how during the Cold War, the Italo-Yugoslav border—like the iron curtain—was put into place in the context of the changing political significance of borders, and in defiance of evidence of the ambiguities, complexities, and inconsistencies of local political and national identities. Nationalism, I argue, was less a cause of Cold War border making in the Adriatic boundary region, than a repercussion.

"ONE SYMBOL OF THE WAY THINGS ARE GOING"

Toward the end of World War II, and immediately after, the involvement of Communist Yugoslavia in the disputation over Venezia Giulia was only one context in which Western intellectuals were discussing the problem of an Italo-Yugoslav border. Geographers, historians, and diplomats determined not to repeat the mistakes of the 1919 peace busily proposed a variety of ways to avoid future conflicts over territorial sovereignty.[5] In 1944, E. H. Carr argued that "[t]he tradition which makes the drawing of frontiers the primary and most spectacular part of peace-making has outlived its validity. . . . The urgent need now is to alter not the location but the meaning of frontiers."[6] Other British Foreign Office experts such as Arnold Toynbee (like Carr also a historian) saw merit in the creation of small city-states under international supervision, or a new federal conglomerate in the Balkans and Central Europe.[7] In an extensive study of the idea of national self-determination, Alfred Cobban, yet another historian, advised more conservatively that "[f]rontiers . . . can and should follow national lines where they can be determined";[8] where they could not, in "borderlands . . . with a special life of their own," the transfer of populations was preferable to "leaving bitterly hostile populations side by side in the same state."[9] As far as Cobban was concerned, only an international authority could be objective in determining where the border separating nationalities lay: "A settlement left to the local nationalities, whether it is disguised as self-determination or not, would be a bloody and probably an unstable one."[10] Early in 1945, the geographer Arthur Moodie drew on a different understanding of identity in order to underscore the problematic nature of national borders in his book-length study of the "Italo-Yugoslav boundary."[11] In Moodie's view, the prospects of an ethnic Italo-Yugoslav border were diminished because of the "zone of strain" that lay between the "watershed of the Julian Alps" and the Adriatic. This zone was exemplary of regions throughout Europe where linear borders were inappropriate because of the absence of "enclosed watertight [ethnic] compartments."[12] For the historian A. J. P. Taylor, the problem of Trieste and the Italo-Yugoslav border was a test case for the status of "frontiers" in general. In September 1945, Taylor aired his views on a BBC World Affairs radio program, presenting proposals for the transformation of Trieste into a free city as "one symbol of the way things are going":[13]

> If the scheme [for a free city] works it will make nonsense of all our present ideas of passport and customs. And if it works it won't stop at Trieste. . . . The frontier area between Italy and Jugoslavia has always been an area of conflict, and conflicting ways of life still meet there today. Latin and Slav, Eastern and Western. They conflict but they meet . . .[14]

Taylor resorted to generic modes of identifying Trieste as a confluence of West and East, of Latin and Slav, differences. But his speech captured the intellectual investment of European liberals, democrats, and Marxists in the problem of Trieste as one symbol of the problem of borders, and the place of cultural (or "ethnic") diversity in the composition of nation-states.

Gaetano Salvemini's renewed intervention in the Adriatic question in June 1945 offers further evidence of the extent to which intellectuals melded alternative conceptions of national borders with conventional representations of identities and differences. When Salvemini considered the problem of national borders in Europe, he thought that the Swiss model of federation should be applied to the whole continent. Like pre–First World War Triestine intellectuals, Salvemini now regarded Trieste as a model for solving the problem of national sovereignty in Europe as a whole.[15] He also argued that because of the difficulty of telling Slovenes from Italians, the region of Venezia Giulia should be granted autonomy. Contrary to his claims during the First World War, at the end of the Second World War Salvemini now described Trieste as well as Istria as territories in which "Italians and Slavs are indissolvably confused." In Trieste, Italians were not a socially or politically homogenous group, and socialist Italians promoted justice for Slav as well as Italian workers and were trying to create cordial relations between them. Yet, as if to contradict his own description, Salvemini also warned that "the history of all mixed territories in Europe except Switzerland is the history of hatred and brutality"; he argued that the 1919 Wilson line (which coincided "almost perfectly with that dividing the mixed Italo-Slav territory from Slav territory") should become the new Italo-Yugoslav border.[16] Salvemini's emphasis on territorially distinct ethnic groups represented by segregated political and social institutions recalls the proposal for enclaves put by the Action Party's Emanuele Flora in 1943. Salvemini suggested that in mixed territory the Wilson line could be applied so as to give maximum autonomy for Slavs in their rural communities and Italians in their municipalities; mixed municipalities would have separate schools and provincial councils moderated by a neutral International Court of Justice. The border between Italy and Yugoslavia would be administrative, not political or economic, and would allow free movement, "like moving between New Jersey and Connecticut and New York." Yet, on the premise of the endemic antipathy between nations, Salvemini absolutely opposed the idea of a "free city" because in Trieste "national rivalry divides the population," and "an external force has to intervene to maintain peace."[17]

In July 1945, as reports of the Allied excavations of alleged *foibe* sites in Venezia Giulia reached the world, the Allied "Big Four" met at Potsdam and assigned a Council of Foreign Ministers representing the Soviet Union, the United States, Britain, and France to draft a peace treaty with Italy, and to decide the fate of Trieste and the location of an Italo-Yugoslav border.[18] In contrast to the insignificance of Trieste in the peace talks at the end of World War I, Trieste was now critical to the Adriatic question, and the Italian sovereignty agreed to in the 1920 Treaty of Rapallo was vulnerable to challenge on moral and national (or ethnic) grounds. At the first meeting of the Council of Foreign Ministers in London in September, Edvard Kardelj (now vice-president of Yugoslavia) argued the case for reviving the pre–First World War Austro-Italian border as the new Italo-Yugoslav border, and for retaining Trieste in Yugoslavia as an autonomous region. The ethical basis of his case was Yugoslavia's wartime sacrifices for the Allied cause, but he also insisted on the existence of a salient ethnic line separating Italians from Slovenes which coincided with the old Austro-Italian border.[19] In the light of official Yugoslav support for an ethnic border, the complaint by Ivan Velebit, the Yugoslav Vice-Minister for Foreign Affairs, that at the peace talks the Italian delegation spurned his attempts to discuss the border as their ethnic compatriot, resonates with a sad irony. "I was to a certain extent a relative of the Italians," claimed Velebit, "I speak Italian, being a Triestino. My cousins are Italians, professors in Padua and in Venice."[20]

The Italian delegation led by the foreign minister Alcide De Gasperi (and including Schiffrer) also supported an ethnic border separating Italians from Slavs, but located along the 1919 Wilson line. Their justifications for that line renewed old cultural arguments: Trieste and Gorizia were Italian urban centers with Slav hinterlands, and the precedence of Italian urban culture meant the region as a whole was Italian. Their demands for a Free State of Fiume and an autonomous Zadar (both at the time under the caretaker jurisdiction of Yugoslav Zone B) were defended on the grounds that under Yugoslav rule thousands of Italians had been and continued to be subjected to "cruelty and methods which have even surpassed what the Germans themselves accomplished."[21] Any immediate agreement on a border among the council's British, American, French, and Russian foreign ministers was made difficult by Russia's inclination to protect Yugoslav interests, Italy's vulnerability to the popularity of left-wing and communist ideals, and the competing ethical status of Yugoslavia as a wartime ally and victim of Fascism, on the one hand, and Italy as a Western ally and victim of Yugoslavs, on the other. The only agreement they did reach was in regard to Italy's northern border. Despite the presence and protestations of a German-speaking majority in Alto-Adige, the disputed region on Italy's northern border was to remain Italian territory. By contrast, on Italy's northeastern border, the "ethnic principle" was to be applied to determine the national status of disputed territory. In this case, the ethnic principle was presented by the Council of Foreign Ministers as a "scientific" solution transcending conflicting political interests. The task of drawing a border that deviated as little as possible from the ethnic line between Italy and Yugoslavia was assigned to a special boundary commission, a representative cross-section of the conflicted ideological interests of the council itself.[22]

As Triestines awaited international deliberations and the arrival of the boundary commission, some took to the piazzas to support Italian or Yugoslav claims, others questioned the international process that would decide their fate as either Italian or Yugoslav. In September 1945 *The Times* published a letter by Dr. Pierpaolo Luzzatto-Fegiz, professor of Statistics at the University of Trieste, proposing that "scientific ingenuity" should be applied to reconceptualize international affairs: "One goal to be reached is the abandonment of the old idea of borders: a border should no longer be considered an impassable wall, fixed for all times to come."[23] Fegiz planned that in the interim before the creation of a federated Europe that would undermine the need for territorial borders, a neutral mixed area could be created with special governing committees. Even the most stalwart of pro-Italians situated their aspirations for reunification with the Italian state within a larger model of European federation. Edmund Puecher (the leader of the reformist faction of the Italian socialists in 1918, and the AMG-appointed president of the zone from 1945 until 1947) argued that any new solution to the problem of Trieste had to entrench Italy in Europe and the West. Puecher also stated that the denial of Trieste's inclusion within Italian borders would be tantamount to a betrayal of international justice.[24] Giovanni Paladin (of the Action Party and CLN) came up with a "Terza Forza" project, which secured the borders of Italian nationalism within an anticommunist, anti-Balkan federal Europe.[25] Carlo Schiffrer, who had taken part in the peace talks as an expert for the Italian delegation, published his studies of the national limits of Italy and Yugoslavia, which reiterated familiar propositions about Italian and Slav differences and the precedence of Italian culture. But he too advised that the region should become part of a federated Europe that would render the Italo-Yugoslav border practically irrelevant.[26] Allied reports on the growth of independentist parties, and general support for autonomy as a solution to the problem of Trieste suggest the extent to which ethno-national sovereignty was out of favor.[27] Allied observers noted that more than one thousand extremely poor anarchists led by Giordano Bruch, a clockmaker, were preparing for the revolution that would dispense with borders, political parties, and all other forms of organization.[28] More mainstream manifestations of interest in an alternative to ethno-national sovereignty included the emergence of political parties such as the Independence Front *(Il Fronte dell'Indipendenza)* created by former supporters of the Liberation Front, Teodoro Sporer and Mario Giampiccoli. It boasted the adherence of socialists, small shopkeepers, and skilled workers, and its own newspaper, *Il Corriere di Trieste.*[29] A second more right-wing independentist group, *Il Blocco Triestino* (the Triestine bloc), was led by Mario Stocca. It represented commercial, industry, and finance groups anxious to expand their markets. Stocca had also supported the Liberation Front during the war, and now favored a "free territory."

In October 1945 a Triestine delegation of CLNists—Edmond Puecher, Michele Miani (the AMG-appointed president of the commune or mayor), Ferdinando Gandusio (a Freemason and Liberal appointed president of the Zone Council by the AMG in 1946), and Bruno Forti (president of the Commune Council)—approached the Italian prime minister Ferrucio Parri about the possibility of initiating a direct treaty between Italy and Yugoslavia.[30] Parri, a member of the Action Party and former deputy commander of the combined Italian resistance forces, was amenable to the idea of direct local negotiations over the problem of Trieste. Gandusio immediately began communicating with the representatives of the Regional National Liberation Committee and Slovene communities. He was authorized to promise that in the new Italy the Slovenes of Venezia Giulia would have the right to speak their language at home and in public, and that an autonomous region would be created in Venezia Giulia that would act as a bridge or neutral zone for the Italian and Yugoslav national governments.[31] Gandusio's attempts to realize a more fraternal solution to the problem of a border, to lay "the foundation stones" for a bridge between the communities, presumed that bridge would be built on an agreement about the conditions under which Trieste and Venezia Giulia might be returned to Italy.[32] He focused his conciliatory efforts on a fellow ex-Dachau inmate, Giuseppe Mihelčič, who was, by this time, a spokesperson for the pro-Yugoslav UAIS. Gandusio wrote to Mihelčič stressing the urgency of a local solution to the problem of Trieste, before barriers to cultural understanding were irrevocably erected. Never again, Gandusio warned, would the moment to lay the foundations for more productive relations occur: "Woe betide us if a we build a wall on this eastern border. . . . We have to absolutely impede the construction of any wall."

By the time the boundary commission finally arrived in Venezia Giulia in March 1946 to locate an ethnic border, Parri had been replaced as Italian prime minister by the conservative Christian Democrat Alcide De Gasperi, and the Italian government's support for the CLN initiative had been withdrawn. The population of the disputed territories turned their attention to the British, United States, French, and Russian experts who had come to document local political preferences. While the boundary commission's guidelines privileged proof of *italianità* or of "Slavness" as a means of deciding the ethnic border, almost all political organizations campaigning for their preferred vision of Trieste's economic and political future tempered their ethno-national ideals. The intimidation of the local population by neo-Fascist *squadristi* and the local authorities during the commission's visit (there were at least two killings of suspected pro-Yugoslav sympathisers by the AMG locally recruited police force in this period) accentuated the urgency of a mediated solution to the problem of Trieste.[33] But the boundary commission returned to the peace talks in Paris in May 1946 no more able to reconcile the different viewpoints of its commissioners and proposing four different ethnic borders. According to Jean-Baptiste Duroselle, apart from a general acceptance of the idea that territorial sovereignty should be determined by ethnicity, there was very little agreement among the commission's experts on what even constituted the ethnic identities they were meant to be mapping.[34] The idea of an ethnic border masked the problem of determining not only who "the people" were, but how

Italians and Slavs could be objectively distinguished, and how population movement over time affected the stability and legitimacy of ethnic borders. The British experts concentrated on statistical information because they considered observation and interviews of little value to the determination of ethnic facts. The United States delegates found contact with the population more useful, but only in combination with analyses of demographic trends undertaken by the Italian state since the Austrian census of 1910. The historian Jean-Baptiste Duroselle has argued that the Russians considered an inhabitant of the region a Slav "if he was of Slav origin and spoke Italian."[35] Ultimately, the American and the British "experts" both opposed the Yugoslav annexation of Trieste, and the Russians supported it. The French seemed to have two objectives: to balance the number of minorities, and to trace a mid-path between the American and Russian lines.

The failure of the boundary commission to provide the peace talks with a scientific border, or strategy for the Venezia Giulia and Istria regions that might have distinguished an objective ethnic line or a predominant local preference, or transcended the political differences amongst its experts, led to more serious consideration of the idea of a "free territory." The free territory had in its favor support in Trieste for an alternative solution, and its recommendation by British intellectuals as "one symbol of the way things are going." The idea of a free territory was also retrospectively described by its American supporters as an extension of the transnational ideology of the developing United States Marshall Plan for a "unified Western European economy."[36] Ivan White, from the British Foreign Office, believed that the future of the free territory lay with the transcendence of economic and labor borders in the forging of a new Europe.[37] When the decision to create a free territory was taken in mid-1946, the British delegate at the peace talks justified it more pragmatically, as a necessary compromise in the face of "an impassable rock in Trieste."[38]

According to the Paris Peace Treaty of 10 February 1947, the Free Territory of Trieste would cover 738 square kilometres of land between the boundary commission's French line and the eastern shores of the Adriatic. The Free Territory would have no homogenous ethnic or political character, and it would recognize three official languages: Italian, Slovene, and Croatian.[39] The Free Territory government would comprise a governor appointed by the UN Security Council, an executive council, and a popular assembly. In order to establish the neutrality of the new government, the Free Territory was promised its own currency, official flag, and coat of arms: the Triestine "silver halberd on a blood-red background."[40] Special Free Territory stamps were to be printed, and produce from the region was to be marked

6.2. The Free Territory of Trieste

ITALY
Monfalcone

ZONE A/
B.U.S.-
ZONE

Trieste

ADRIATIC SEA

Punta Sottile
Debeli Rtič

Piran
Pirano

Izola
Isola

Koper
Capodistria

ZONE B/
YUGOSLAV
ZONE

YUGOSLAVIA

Border of the
Free Territory of Trieste

Border between
Zones A and B

Italo-Yugoslav border
since 1954

"Made in the Free Territory." In the words of Colonel Bowman, the SCAO, the Free Territory was to be "neither a State nor a Nation."[41] He advised his AMG personnel that appropriate adjectives to describe the Free Territory were "public," "general," or "territorial." Although the creation of a free territory included the restoration of those parts outside it to Italy and Yugoslavia on an "ethnic" basis, the potential innovation of the plan were its implications for ethnic identity within the Free Territory.

The Free Territory of Trieste was "free" only insofar as citizenship was not officially predicated on any intrinsic ethnic identity. Citizenship was not an open privilege. It depended, in the first instance, on historical precedent, on being an Italian citizen "domiciled on June 10 1940 in the area comprised within the boundaries of the Free Territory," or the child of those Italian citizens.[42] Once the Free Territory government had come into existence it was to reconsider the rules for the inclusion of new citizens. The provision that the United Nations Security Council would appoint the Free Territory's key officials (including the governor) and that none of them could be citizens of the territory so as to avoid possible national (and political) bias, suggests the limit of international faith in the concept of a Free Territory identity. Fears that the Free Territory could fall into communist hands and undermine British and American influence in the region influenced the Western powers' decision not to have local figures in positions of power, and not to provide the new state with a fully democratic apparatus.[43] While the Free Territory awaited the appointment of a governor by the UN Security Council, it was to remain divided into two zones and to continue to be supervised by Allied and Yugoslav military governments. Zones A and B were now renamed the British-United States Zone and the Yugoslav Zone. Those areas outside the borders of the Free Territory that had previously been part of Zone A and Zone B were incorporated into Italy and Yugoslavia respectively. On this basis Yugoslavia quietly gained Istria and Fiume, and Italy resumed its sovereignty over Gorizia and Monfalcone.[44]

When the Council of Foreign Ministers first announced their Free Territory compromise, reports from Trieste to the British War Office and Foreign Office intimated that there was a sense of finality about the prospect of a free territory among the local population.[45] Sullivan reported to the Foreign Office that the practicality of the Free Territory scheme was limited by the extent to which "national and ideological fanaticism" could be overcome and a "corporate consciousness" fostered, but he regarded the scheme as the only long-term plan likely to work, and described the average Triestine as reacting well to the Paris decisions.[46] Colonel Bowman announced his skepticism by arguing that "it would possibly take two generations for [Free Territory citizens] to become assimilated and for them to consider themselves as members of a sovereign state rather than either Slovene or Italian,"[47] but business groups in the Free Territory expressed their enthusiasm for the creation of a free port and potential improvement in trade. Gandusio, now president of the Zone Council, shared these economic expectations for the new territory, and believed that the Free Territory should cover a maximum area for political reasons.[48] There was some evidence that groups from the old Zones A and B left out of the Free Territory also desired to be included within its borders. The Allied Military Government recorded receiving fifty-eight petitions addressed to the Paris Conference demanding incorporation into the new Free Territory. These petitions bore 4,263 signatures from Gorizia and neighboring Slovene-speaking villages destined for inclusion in Italy. In the villages of Zone B adjacent to the Morgan Line and earmarked for incorporation into Yugoslavia locals expressed a first preference for inclusion in the Free Territory, and a second for union with Catholic Austria into a kind of "Switzerland of the Adriatic" embracing Austria, Friuli, and Slovenia in a democratic Christian federation.[49] The pro-Yugoslav movement fatalistically accepted the FTT as a lesser evil than co-option of Trieste into the Italian state, but demanded that the Free Territory include Monfalcone and exclude northwest Istria, which, like Gorizia, should be made part of Yugoslavia.[50]

The Paris Peace Treaty also inspired profound discontent. Italian political and intellectual figures such as Carlo Sforza and Benedetto Croce criticized it for depriving Italy of her "dignity and legitimate pride."[51] Italian patriots looked on the Free Territory as an eccentricity that denied Italy Trieste and the Istrian coastline. A military report for the end of September 1947 confirmed that the peace treaty had exasperated local extremists:

> Disorders broke out in Trieste on 15 September. They began by "right wing" Italian elements proclaiming a day of mourning for the crucifixion of Venezia Giulia. "Action squads" were in action in the city enforcing the closing of shops and attacking Communist and pro-Slav organizations. Hand grenades and sub-machine guns were used, and the total casualties were three dead, three seriously wounded, and twenty-two detained in hospital.[52]

In Pula, Maria Pasquinelli, described as a former Fascist, assassinated Brigadier General Robin de Winton, commander of the local British garrison.[53]

Equally tragic was the displacement that resulted from the drawing of borders. The Italian government advised Italians in Pula/Pola to leave the newly Yugoslav city; "anti-Tito Slavs" also left the port town on their own initiative. Along the northern reaches of the Isonzo/Soča

River similar decisions were being made by Italians and Slovenes anxious about their future in a communist Yugoslavia. According to the AMG, Slavs were fleeing "westwards to a country that will probably be a little less unsympathetic to them than that which they are fleeing."[54] The movement was not all in one direction. In April 1947, Sullivan reported that several hundred workers from the Monfalcone shipyards felt intimidated under the new Italian government and had left for Yugoslavia.[55] In other former zone areas handed over to Italy, locals who had worked with the AMG lost their jobs and the Italian government was threatening recriminations for their "disloyalty." Their options were to retreat to the new Free Territory zones or to migrate farther afield.

The dismal prospects of the 1947 Paris Peace Treaty were to a significant extent the consequence of the escalating Cold War, evident in the UN Security Council's failure to agree on a governor. Adding fuel to the Cold War fire, the pro-Yugoslav and independentist groups began to accuse the AMG of sabotaging the international state with the aim of creating "such a situation of disorder in Trieste that a permanent military occupation will be necessary."[56] The AMG authorities for their part officially rejected these accusations, and blamed a communist conspiracy to erode Allied influence in the region. Their strategy to defeat that conspiracy coincided with the anticommunist objectives of increasingly vigilant British and United States foreign policies. In October 1947, Colonel Robertson, the AMG deputy civil affairs officer, recommended the programming of "constant and effective anti-communistic propaganda by radio," and the discouragement of bilingualism "as this immediately brings in the national aspect."[57] Support for anticommunist organizations, or noncommmunist Slovene organizations, was to be consolidated, and communist organizations, including "Slav-communist" papers, gradually "liquidated." General Terence Airey, the new SCAO in the British-United States Zone, established a temporary military governorship with himself as executive to coordinate military and government policy and prevent a communist coup.[58]

Early in February 1948, Airey reported to the UN Security Council overseeing the creation of a Free Territory that Triestines had "disclosed no evidence of a real, disinterested and ready disposition to build up a local Triestine political consciousness distinct from, but not necessarily antagonistic to, Italian or Jugoslav national and racial ideology."[59] A month later, the Free Territory plan was officially abandoned.[60] On 20 March 1948, in an agreement known as the Tripartite Declaration, the leaders of the United States, Great Britain, and France agreed to a border that would grant to Italy both the British-United States and Yugoslav Zones, and render the Free Territory redundant. The parties to the Tripartite Declaration justified their unilateral decision as a necessary step in the face of antipathy between Italians and Slavs. They also referred to the existence of an ethnic line that two years earlier they had been unable to agree upon. They accused the Yugoslav government of having assimilated its zone "by procedures which do not respect the desire expressed by the Powers to give an independent and democratic statute to the Territory . . . Trieste which has an overwhelmingly Italian population must remain an Italian city."[61] Reports emanating from the Foreign Office prompted the belief that the Yugoslavs had "in the classic Slav manner" created an efficient and widespread network of agents trained to take over political control, and that it was only the presence of "Anglo-U.S. Military government and troops" that guaranteed the aversion of a civil war.[62]

Historians such as Giampaolo Valdevit have shown that the decision taken by British, American, and French governments to reject the counsel of the Russian government and to disband the Free Territory was an extension of the same anticommunist aims that earlier had motivated their support for the Free Territory's elitist political structure.[63] In the early period of AMG rule, strategies for containing communism were translated into policies for controlling nationalism. Increasingly however, the AMG explicitly referred to nationalism as an irrational force that pervaded the local (particularly Slav) population, and as a *raison d'être* for its own authority. In the immediate postwar the concept of ethno-national sovereignty was considered a problem. As the Cold War intensified, the erection of an ethnic border, the validation of national sovereignty in ethnically defined territory, was presented as the answer to the problem of nationalism.

RETURN

The obstacles to the peaceful enactment of the Tripartite Declaration, the return of both zones of the Free Territory to Italy while one of those zones was under a Yugoslav military administration, meant no immediate resolution to the problem of an Italo-Yugoslav border and, instead, led to an even longer period of AMG administration in the defunct Free Territory. British and American advice to AMG continued to enjoin the consolidation of an Italian anticommunist hegemony in the region. This strategy was moderated to some extent after the Cominform split between the Soviet Union and Yugoslavia in 1948. The redefinition of Yugoslavia as a potential Western ally coincided with a limited reevaluation of Slovene interests in Trieste. The AMG created an Office for Minority Affairs to deal with discrimination against Slovenes and finally overruled existing Fascist legislation that had outlawed Slovene in the Triestine surrounds and even on gravestones. Triestines could now choose to abandon the Italianized versions of the names they had assumed during the Fascist regime, if they could provide documents proving that the change had been forced. The reconstitution of Slavs as a "minority problem" had little impact on the representation of Trieste as incontrovertibly Italian. In deference to Italian nationalist demands, the AMG refused to allow what it deemed "Slav buildings" in the city center, and it reduced the number of Slovene schools. Italian refugees in the British-United States Zone were given residency and voting rights, but these same rights were refused to Slovenes born there.[64] The AMG also decreed Italian the only official language in its zone (its one concession was the use of Slovene in district municipal councils)—an explicit contravention of the 1947 peace treaty.[65] General Airey argued that by accepting "pro-Slovene" policies such as bilingualism the AMG would only encourage Slovene nationalism, and, in turn, Italian anger.[66] In June 1949 Airey told his political advisers that "the Slovene problem was, of course, the primary reason for our presence in Trieste." His policy, he added, had been and still was,

> directed towards complete equality for the Slovene population and to encourage the dangerous inflammation caused by the Slav-Communist influx of 1945 to heal up. . . . I am determined that nothing shall be done to retard the healing process or to open old wounds by reviving lost causes and stimulating excessive Slovene nationalism.[67]

The reinvention of the presence of Slovenes/Slavs as a minority problem raised for the British and American advisers an older dilemma of how to cater for minority rights in a territory identified with a single ethno-national group. When the AMG acquiesced to demands for local elections in 1949 (because the Cominform break had split communist support in the British-United States Zone to the benefit of anticommunist parties), the United States political adviser, Charles Baldwin, began reflecting on the place of minorities in the form of democracy being cultivated in Trieste by the Allies.[68] According to Baldwin, the "ways of the West" and the "benefits of capitalism with or without democracy" were being tested by the role of the United States and Britain in Trieste, and he worried that the AMG's failure to defend minority rights might work to the advantage of communists.[69] In a report to the secretary of state in Washington detailing strategies for the election and for fighting communism, Baldwin also assessed the "Slav minority problem."[70] He began by outlining his understanding of the problem's history:

> Among the many ills which beset the troubled area of which Trieste is the center, the problem of the Slav minority has long been a festering sore, inflamed by rampant nationalism and the accumulated resentments of centuries. This situation provides fertile ground for the seeds of Communism and is a challenge to the ingenuity and wisdom of the forces opposing Communism.

Baldwin partly blamed Fascist Italy for ignoring ethnic considerations. In expanding Italian territory Fascism had "rekindled the traditional Italo-Slav hostility." He also added that the "cruelty and terrorism" of the forty days of May 1945 had only strengthened "the Italian belief that all Slavs are essentially uncivilised," and accentuated "the emotional aspects of the racial problem":

> The problem is complicated, to an even greater extent than in many minority situations, by the bitter personal antipathy between the Italian and Slavic groups. Slavic descriptions of Italians are often punctuated with such adjectives as "cowardly," "corrupt," "weak-charactered" and "treacherous," while many Italians, particularly of the older generation, are inclined to regard the Slav as an almost sub-human individual.

Although Baldwin emphasized the role that chauvinist representations of Italian and Slav differences had to play in validating local nationalisms, he himself hardly deviated from these assumptions in his own assessment of the "caste distinction" between Italians and Slavs. He argued that the Italian government had been at fault in the past only insofar as "a more benevolent policy toward the Slovenes might have speeded their Italianisation and their adoption of the older and richer Italian culture." When Baldwin turned to the history of AMG policies in the region, he described early AMG policies as neutral in their intention "to hold a balance between the Italian and Slovene racial groups in the Zone." He argued that the shift in policy before the Tripartite Declaration was a necessary response to Italian claims that "AMG policy had the effect of encouraging Slovene penetration in the city." The earlier policy, Baldwin explained, had aroused resentment: "There were frequent physical clashes between Italians and Slovenes, a serious instance being the destruction by Italians of a Slovene book store in the heart of the city." Baldwin lay the blame for the AMG policy shift not with extremist and neo-Fascist groups, but with the "people of the Zone" who were "a highly volatile element which must be reckoned with both in day-to day administration and in planning future policies for the area."[71] These people were "moved emotionally by deeply-rooted racial antipathies and nationalistic sentiments, and influenced psychologically by the uncertainty of their status."

From the perspective of the AMG, nationalism was an irrational and pervasive force and Trieste was an uncontroversially Italian space with a troublesome nationalist Slovene minority. These images, however, were disrupted by historical and political inconsistencies. Baldwin advised that although antagonism between "the Slovene and Italian elements of the population" was "deeply rooted" in the "accumulated resentments of centuries," one way of reducing ill-feeling was to recognize Slovene minority rights in the courts and within the AMG infrastructure, thus combining "considerations of practical political importance with established American principles of justice and fair treatment."[72] The State Department replied to Baldwin by agreeing with the principles behind his recommendations but dismissing them as politically impractical because they would ultimately threaten the protection of freedom for Slovenes by arousing Italian hostility.[73] Margaret Carlyle, the author of a Foreign Office Research Department review of "Italy's treatment of her Yugoslav minority in the period between 1918 to 1949," suggested that minority rights in Trieste would have to be safeguarded before any handover to Italy could take place. Carlyle was made to revise her paper and omit her suggestion that Italian retaliatory measures against minorities would have to be actively prevented.[74]

For the most part, after the disbanding of the Free Territory plan, images of antipathy and hatred between Italians and Slavs dominated public discourses about the problem of Trieste. They influenced the political maneuvering and decision making of the British-American military government and helped rationalize those decisions. Yet from 1947 until 1954, the categories of friend and foe, like nationalist, social, and ideological aims, were as mutable and confused as they had been at the end of the war, to the extent that the friction, dislike, and distrust that predominated in Trieste could not merely be reduced to relations between Italians and Slavs. Some local communists formerly loyal to Yugoslavia were outraged by Tito's "nationalist deviation" from the internationalist Moscow-led brotherhood. Others just as fervently supported Yugoslav independence from Stalinist imperialism and hated so-called "Cominformists." Conflicting antinationalist pro-Cominform, and anti-Soviet pro-Yugoslav allegiances tore apart married couples, families, and friends. The women's organizations that had grown out of the Liberation Front movement were dispersing into national and ideological corners, reunifying around either Cominformist or Titoist groupings, both of which supported the resurrection of the Free Territory idea. Some communist women succumbed to a general disillusion with party politics and the lack of interest in "women's issues." They felt they were being ignored and exploited not only by their ideological opponents but by their male counterparts. They expressed deeply felt grievances about the reduction of politics to ethnic and Cold warfare, and its affect on their everyday lives. There was no less tension and fracturing among the anticommunists. Slovene liberals and Catholics were suspicious of each other despite their shared anticommunist convictions. Italian sympathizers were increasingly anxious about the favored status granted by the Western powers to post-Cominform anti-Russian Yugoslavia and its possible impact on Italian interests. Figures in the upper echelons of the AMG believed that the Italian government and certain Triestines were conspiring against their authority. Despite the AMG's support for politically conservative Italian parties at the elections, when the elected Christian Democrat Council took power in Trieste its economically irresponsible initiatives became the object of AMG criticism. Even Italian patriots in Trieste distrusted the imported Italian bureaucrats who were increasingly taking up positions in the AMG and civilian administration because they were suspicious that centralized administration from Rome would lead to Trieste's economic marginalization. The Americans distrusted the British, the British did not always understand the Americans, and General Airey felt his authority under threat from the American forces stationed in his zone.

From 1948, there was little confidence among the AMG, or the Italian government about the forms of democracy that an Italian solution to the problem of Trieste might ensure. As neo-Fascists cultivated an organized local presence, more moderate pro-Italy groups found it increasingly difficult to coalesce around a simply anticommunist conception of Italian sovereignty in Trieste. At the 1949 local administrative elections (which did not affect AMG control of important and influential areas of administration and policy making) an Italian bloc led by the Christian Democrats successfully orchestrated an anti-Slav campaign focused on the perils of the *foibe* and the antireligiosity of communists, and garnering the support of many women voting for the first time. The second British-United States Zone elections held in 1952, still only administrative and symbolic, were a year overdue because of the Italian government's fears that the Christian Democrat party would be defeated in Trieste. Even though the Christian Democrats were returned again, the pro-independentist parties gained over a third of the vote, doubling their representation since 1949. Ironically, as Trieste moved closer to becoming part of the Italian state, independentist movements were reported to be an increasingly popular local option, but not always for antinationalist reasons. An AMG report in June 1953 described support for a return to the Free Territory among Italian Socialists and Trieste's staunchly pro-Italian and pro-Christian Democrat bishop, who now proposed an expansion of the idea of the Free Territory as a means of removing Istria from Yugoslav influence.

In the final years of AMG rule, AMG functionaries reinforced the relative status of Italians and Slovenes as citizens in ethnically defined territory. They also affirmed the validity of the nationalist legislation introduced during the Fascist period. When in 1953 the mainly Slovene-speaking and pro-communist seaside commune of Duino, north of Trieste, was refused permission to erect bilingual road signs, J. A. Grant, from the British Foreign Office, justified the restriction: "The short answer, I presume, is that AMG are bound to administer the existing laws without regard to the character of the governments which originally passed them."[75] A debate ensued that underlined the contradiction between the AMG's refusal of the bilingual sign on the basis of an Italian Fascist law prohibiting bilingualism, and an AMG proclamation that made "illegal the Fascist party and its affiliated organisations."[76] Grant supported his initial argument by claiming that this clause could not be read as if "it automatically repeals any law which any Tom, Dick or Harry may choose to consider discriminatory: or that it justifies unauthorised action by local authorities."[77] AMG authorities displaced responsibility for local tensions onto the perceived natural state of Italian and Slav relations in the region. The assistant British political adviser wrote to Churchill stating that "Slovenes" were only about one-fifth of the population. "The fact," Laurence explained, "that the two ethnic groups are mutually suspicious and latently hostile has its causes in history and not in the present state of affairs."[78] In justifying the AMG's failure to take special measures to deal with claims of discrimination against Slovenes, the British political adviser, Phillip Broad, maintained that Fascism had subjected only Jews to "legalised spoliation." Thus, on this view, the AMG use of Fascist laws could not involve anti-Slav measures.[79]

By 1953, political disarray among the Right in Italy, and the prospect of improved relations between Yugoslavia and the United States, spurred the Italian Christian Democrat government to press for an immediate resolution of the fate of the still-disputed region. Negotiations continued for more than a year and were punctuated by military standoffs between Italy and Yugoslavia, and violent demonstrations in Trieste orchestrated by the Christian Democrat Mayor Gianni Bartoli.[80]

The signing of a "Memorandum of Understanding" between Italy and Yugoslavia on 5 October 1954 precipitated the handover of the caretaker zones to Italy and Yugoslavia, but only after another Boundary Commission had been deployed to resolve the ongoing disagreement over the ethnic assignation of territory bordering the British-United States and Yugoslav zones. The new border closely followed the border between the existing zones, and preserved a free port in Trieste. No principle of sovereignty was decided upon in the agreement, but among its special conditions were guarantees of the rights of minorities, and of "the ethnic character and the unhampered cultural development" of Yugoslav and Italian minorities on each side of the border.[81] Although the Italian parliament refused to ratify the agreement because it sacrificed Istria, south of Muggia (a small fishing village on the southern outskirts of Trieste), in 1954 the AMG oversaw the creation of a border between Italy and Yugoslavia that made the division of the two zones official.

By the time British and American government in Trieste began to be dismantled, the problem of Trieste and of the Italo-Yugoslav border had come full circle from the interwar period. As at the end of the First World War, the border was decided according to contingent political circumstances and the rules of *Realpolitik* rather than any principle of sovereignty. At the same time, negotiations relied upon conventionalised representations of Slav and Italian, East and West differences, and an implicit conception of ethno-national territorial sovereignty. In 1954, just prior to the AMG's departure, the administration decided that a new Slovene cultural center should replace the "Hotel Balkan," which had been burnt down by Italian extremists in 1920. The AMG had refused detailed demands by Slovene organizations for costly reparations to rectify interwar Fascist confiscation of the proceeds and assets of Slovene banks and cooperatives. The Slovene cultural center was to be offered as a form of compensation for Yugoslavia losing Trieste in 1954. This attempt to compensate the Slovene community for incorporation with Italy reaffirmed, however, the ordering of Triestine political space along ethnic lines. Allied government personnel had located a property in the suburb of Barcola, on the road leading west to Monfalcone. When this site was rejected as unsuitable, Colonel Broad explained that Trieste was composed of separate and distinct Italian and Slovene areas, and Italians would not tolerate a Slovene incursion. Thus, a Slovene building (presumably along with its inhabitants) could not be introduced into an Italian space:

> [The site] cannot now be accurately described as being in a predominantly Slovene area. This has in fact become largely an Italian residential

district. Furthermore the building is located on the main road from Italy into Trieste which would make it unsuitably conspicuous for use as a Slovene centre.[82]

The arguments that made an ethnic border meaningful were supported by representations of difference and conceptions of sovereignty, by a visualized logic of ethnic space and territory that the AMG themselves had fortified, and that made Italian-Slovene antagonism seem inevitable.

Conventional representations of Italian and Slav differences were a common means of political and cultural orientation before the phase of the Cold War initiated in 1947; from the inception of the AMG, these ways of knowing Trieste had constituted a convenient answer to the communist ideal of Italo-Slovene fraternity, and a means of disentangling the confusion of ideological and national ambitions that confronted the British and American personnel responsible for Trieste. The local community with which the AMG had most in common politically, the CLN, continued to promote this view of Trieste too by denouncing the "Yugoslav occupation," or "*sagra carnevalesca*," as another episode in the ongoing contest between Italians and Slavs.[83] These views of the problem of Trieste contributed to the idea that a "utopian" ethnic line existed and had to be fortified in order to separate naturally antipathetic Italians and Slovenes/Slavs/Yugoslavs. After 1947, British and American authorities had retreated to the view of national antipathy between Italians and Slavs as a validation for their own continuing presence in Trieste, and in order to more clearly distinguish Italian from Slav communist aims in terms that suited the Cold War polarization of East and West. Nationalism was repeatedly defined as a form of political and emotional excess characteristic of "the people" of Trieste, and more expressly of a Slav minority, despite contrary evidence provided by the Western Allies' own experiment with the idea of a free territory. Nationalism became a way of seeing or interpreting the problem of Trieste that belied the role that the Allies themselves had played in pitting ethno-national identity against communist internationalist class fraternity. British and American views of events on the ground as the problem of Slav nationalism were part of "a specific sort of *boundary-producing political performance*"[84] that reprised the narratives of difference and conception of sovereignty that had prevailed at the end of the First World War, and finally "returned" Trieste to Italy.

After the Italo-Yugoslav border was formally drawn in 1954, criticisms were voiced in some English-language literature of the "unnatural territorial division between Italy and Yugoslavia," and the absence of a "definitive solution."[85] These criticisms merely reminded readers

Figure 6.3. The Ship *Castelfelice* Leaving Trieste

The ship *Castel Felice* leaving Trieste loaded with emigrants heading for
Astralia, 26 February 1955
Courtesy of Mario Maganj, SNL Photograph Archive.

that although an ethnic solution to the problem of the border had not
been found, it should be.[86] There were other more dissatisfying aspects
to the history of "return." On 30 July 1954 the Italian parliament passed
a law that aimed to prohibit civil servants with Italian citizenship who
had "committed specific acts unequivocally directed towards prevent-
ing the return of the Free Territory to Italy" from being re-employed in
the Italian administration in Trieste.[87] An AMG report to the Foreign
Office remarked on the incumbent Italian government's exclusive application of citizenship rights and the denial of citizenship to individuals whose political preferences were antipathetic to the Christian
Democrat orientation of the Italian state. Broad wrote to the Foreign
Office that a "small number of persons" had had their Italian identity
cards taken from them by the elected Commune and had been told to
consider themselves Yugoslav citizens on the ground that their option
to retain Italian citizenship was being challenged by the Italian government.[88] After the Italian naval ships gracefully made their way into

Trieste's harbor, just as they had in 1918, other ships not belonging to the Italian fleet came to take the local population and the refugees temporarily settled in Trieste away. This exodus repeated other displacements that had become part of the history of the Italo-Yugoslav border.[89] Vittorio Vidali, the pro-Cominformist Trieste Communist Party leader has written of his return in 1954, "to the city without peace." He could not help but notice the amount of people leaving Trieste: "We sensed a catastrophe, and the Castelverde, so white, appeared like a sepulchre which entombed our people. . . . Trieste was going to Australia. Who could have imagined it!"[90]

7

History and Sovereignty, after 1954

$\mathfrak{H}$ istories of the problem of Trieste and the Italo-Yugoslav border provide telling examples of how imaginative representations of difference and identity read and written into the past have both empowered and disempowered individuals and communities, spoken to and delegitimated political choices and possibilities, and how they have helped determine the limits of sovereignty. The simple image of ships leaving Trieste after 1954 laden with Triestines in search of an economically and politically more secure world should have vitiated the political legitimacy that more celebrated images of Italian naval ships arriving in Trieste after its return to Italy that same year afforded to the ethno-national sovereignty of the Italian state. Although the transnational and migratory experiences of many Triestines have had little impact on the historical narratives of the problem of Trieste, they should remind us that the history of nations, like the history of identity, has no final point of arrival. In this chapter I look at how after Trieste's return to Italy the production and reproduction of national identities and nationalisms continued to involve a complex constant engagement between public and private spheres, between official and personal histories, effected across local, national, and international spaces, and in the writing of national and international histories. I examine how the ideological work of reinventing national identities, and the relationships between nationally defined groups, took place in the context of attempts by intellectuals and political activists to signpost the limitations of ethno-national sovereignty and to articulate alternative imaginative representations of identity and the significance of difference. In the early twentieth century, the Austro-Marxist Angelo Vivante historicized changing representations of Italian and Slav differences and by doing so questioned their primordial political status. In the middle of the century, Fabio Cusin, a Triestine historian, coined the term *anti-history* in order to critique what he regarded as the chauvinist practices of Italian historians. Despite his marginality, Cusin's work, like that of Vivante, reveals other paths to Trieste's past by underlining how the history of Trieste as a "problem," and reductive explanations of that problem as "nationalism," have been reinforced in historical narratives. This chapter looks first at Cusin's work, and then surveys how the nationalist historical narratives that he criticized have been cast in national and international histories of Trieste, and in Trieste's material landscape in the latter half of the twentieth century.

ANTI-HISTORIES AND NATIONAL HISTORIES

In the crucial years of Italian anti-Fascism in the Venezia Giulia region, and during Trieste's postwar decade of British and American military government, the Triestine historian Fabio Cusin publicly criticized the compulsion toward a nationalist reading of the past and the unreflective writing of national identities into history. Cusin was born in 1904 in Trieste, to a Jewish father, and Catholic mother.[1] In the latter half of the 1920s, he joined a group of radical young intellectuals led by the anti-Fascist (socialist) pediatrician Bruno Pincherle. During this time Cusin wrote a thesis arguing that the idea of an autonomous Trieste, independent of ties to an Italian motherland, had no historical basis.[2] Along with Carlo Schiffrer's contemporary work on irredentism, Cusin's thesis was deemed by some Triestine reviewers to augur a new tradition of non-polemical Triestine historiography that would salvage the integrity of Trieste's intrinsic *italianità* from the taint of Fascist Italian nationalism at the same time as it reinforced Trieste's Italian destiny. In the 1930s, it was Cusin's "Jewishness" rather than his anti-Fascist politics that was said to count against him in his search for academic employment. In 1940 Cusin missed out on a position in modern history on the University of Trieste law faculty because, as the federal secretary of the Trieste Fascist Party insisted, he was "racially mixed."[3]

Before the war Cusin had written nationalist histories of Italy's borders; by the early 1940s he began to develop a critical perspective of those national histories. From 1943 to 1946 Cusin published four books that radically diverged from his interwar research and methodology: *Introduzione allo studio della storia* (Introduction to the Study of History, written in 1943 and published in 1946); *Antistoria d'Italia: Una demistificazione della storia ufficiale* (Antihistory of Italy: A demystification of official history, written between 1943 and 1944, and published in 1945); *L'Italiano: Realtà e illusioni* (The Italian: Reality and Illusion, 1945); and *La liberazione di Trieste* (The Liberation of Trieste, written in 1945 and published in 1946).[4] At a time when Benedetto Croce was deploying history as a "rational positive discourse" that affirmed "the integrity of Italy, of Italians and the Italian tradition," and defining Fascism as "an invading foreign virus,"[5] Cusin argued that Fascism had created its own mythical national history in Italy and that scholars such as Croce had helped endorse the nationalist underpinnings of those historical myths, even as they distanced themselves from Fascism.[6] In *Antistoria*, Cusin described the ossification of history as a discipline and its subservience to a privileged elite.[7] In *L'Italiano* he expressed his concern that representations of the Italian ideal of "woman-mother" and family culture had been exploited by the Fascist regime in order to introduce Fascist conformism into everyday life.[8] At the end of the Second World War, the use of history by both pro-Yugoslav and pro-Italian sides to legitimate claims to national sovereignty in the region was attacked by Cusin as "racist historicism."[9] He saw no inconsistency between this criticism and his personal identification with *italianità*, his avowal of the *italianità* of Trieste, and his desire for a more democratic and egalitarian society along the lines being promoted by the left-wing Action Party. However, the Trieste branch of the Action Party saw things differently, and toward the end of 1945, one month after completing the manuscript of *La Liberazione*, they expelled Cusin and Bruno Pincherle, his old anti-Fascist ally, for favoring "a rapprochement with the Slavs."[10] Undeterred, six months later Cusin and Pincherle published a manifesto "appealing for a return to a peaceful life based on mutual respect" between the different political and cultural groups in Trieste.[11] In 1945, they teamed up to create a "Centre for Political Culture," and two years later began publication of a new journal *Ponterosso* (The Red Bridge) which brought together other like-minded Triestine intellectuals. An editorial for *Ponterosso* written in 1947 described "our Trieste" as "so strange and difficult," as a place where civilizations converged, and the cultural status of these was "never the privilege of one nation, or the predominance of one nation over another."[12] The journal also encouraged criticism of Italian post-Fascist historiography.

Cusin followed the shortlived *Ponterosso* with his most radical historical venture, an applied "anti-history" of national identity and national sovereignty in Trieste, *Venti secoli di bora sul Carso e sul Golfo* (Twenty Centuries of the Bora in the Carso and Gulf, written in 1949 and published in 1952). For Cusin, in postwar Trieste the historian's real task was demystification, critiquing and discarding the nationalist historical narratives of adventure-romance.[13] Cusin parodied the ahistorical national identities reproduced in conventional histories of Trieste by "our historians" who were "guided by a misunderstood nationalism which arbitrarily interprets or invents history" and claimed that "we no longer believe in this past."[14] His own ironic narrative of twenty centuries of Triestine history was accompanied by cartoon caricatures of past events. Together, the pictures and text undermined the historical continuity of national identities and states, and re-presented Trieste as "a city of the world."[15]

Cusin's premise in *Venti Secoli* was that "the complex, un-unified history of our city, subject across the centuries to many and diverse influences" could not "be reduced to a single source."[16] In the first chapter, entitled "One of Our Almost Fellow Citizens of Fifty Thousand Years Ago," Cusin ridiculed the idea of inherited national characteristics by depicting local inhabitants who consumed pieces of their dead compatriots in order to "acquire something of each other."[17] The title of the *Venti Secoli*'s fourth chapter, "How Rome Came to Stick Its Nose in Our Business," reconsidered the genealogy of a Roman Trieste and transformed Romans into an alien occupying force.[18] The final chapter lampooned a dispute over territorial sovereignty in the Adriatic sea— an issue that has since come to dominate relations between the nation-states along the eastern Adriatic coastline.

In 1950 Cusin was dismissed, "owing to his political views," from the University of Trieste where he had occupied a junior post teaching medieval history since 1945.[19] He was accused of being involved with the independentist newspaper *Il Corriere di Trieste*, regarded by patriotic Italian intellectuals as *filojugoslavo* (pro-Yugoslav).[20] Reviewers of Cusin's work depicted his iconoclasm as symptomatic of a disturbed psychological condition—a judgment that echoed criticisms of the work of Angelo Vivante.[21] Despite these attacks, in 1952 Cusin acquired local political prominence by being elected to the Trieste Council as the representative of a center-right Independentist Party, which supported the creation of a Free Territory of Trieste. Cusin used the Trieste Council forum to pursue his criticisms of the relationship between the academy and nationalist politics. His most specific charge was levelled against Carlo Schiffrer's statistics on "the distribution of Italians and Slavs" in Venezia Giulia.[22]

Cusin could not help but be aware, and perhaps even resentful, that as his own academic reputation had plummeted, Schiffrer's community standing as a dispassionate academic ready to fulfil his civic duties had grown.[23] Schiffrer was regarded by the AMG authorities as "a reputable and objective statistician and ethnologist," and "one of the few local politicians who has an enlightened attitude towards the Slovenes."[24] Even while Schiffrer was acting as secretary of the Italian Socialist Party in Venezia Giulia, the AMG had appointed him to a range of positions in the AMG bureaucracy (including vice-president of the British-American Zone [1948–1952] and head of the department of social welfare).[25] In the Trieste Council chamber, Cusin attacked Schiffrer's use of ethno-national criteria for parcelling out Trieste as "unreal." He argued that Schiffrer's demand for a plebiscite at the postwar peace discussions limited political choices to the annexation of Trieste by either Italy or Yugoslavia. These alternatives presupposed that places could only be identified with nations, and that political identity corresponded to ethno-national identity. Cusin also drew the attention of the chamber to the perils of privileging ethno-national identities, reminding them of a topic that had received little discussion in the postwar, the Fascist experience of nationalism in Trieste and the toll it had taken on the community:

> It would be too long and too boring and perhaps too polemical to reconsider the history of the last 30 years now. . . . [T]his city has suffered from seeing all that was beyond and above nationality [*extra-nazionalità e supernazionalità*] and all that was the antithesis of the politics of race—from Mussolini's laws to the Risiera—destroyed. . . . Trieste was born with a cosmopolitan spirit and with the Italian language. If you destroy the first, you will also destroy the city's language.[26]

Cusin's own preference was an alternative form of Italian identification that could equitably reflect and express differences. However, the difficulties Cusin faced are apparent when one considers not only his academic career, but the extent to which, in the second half of the twentieth century, most of Trieste's intellectual and political élite repeated a common tale of the national struggle and survival of Italians against a Slav enemy, and contributed to the elision of the local history of Fascism.

In the decade after the Second World War, when Trieste's political fate was still undecided and uncertain, a particular view of the meaning of the war and its end began to be popularized. In 1946, Silvio Benco, the well-known writer and interwar journalist for the newspaper *Il Piccolo*, published a hostile memoir of the forty days, which he entitled *Contemplazione del disordine* (A Contemplation of Disorder).[27] Benco stated that not even in the twenty years of Fascism, nor in the five hundred years of Austrian dominion, nor in the battle against Austria, had Trieste suffered such a crude deformation of its will and invasion of its sentiments as during May 1945. Tito's "Balkan" soldiers—Bosnians, Montenegrins, and *Morlacchi* (the barbaric figures the Abbé Fortis had written about in the eighteenth century), sporting long beards and Turkish slippers—were more threatening than the Nazi occupying force that they had replaced.[28] As an Italian, Benco claimed, he had no other perspective from which to view the "occupation" than as a tragic carnival, an inversion of the natural order of things.[29] The themes of Benco's memoir were echoed in the recollections of Pier Antonio Quarantotti Gambini's *Primavera a Trieste* (Springtime in Trieste—written in 1948, published in 1951, reprinted 1967 and 1985). *Primavera a Trieste* was an account of the forty days from the perspective of the librarian-director of the Trieste Municipal Library. Gambini's narrative situated the events of May 1945 in a longer-standing history of the threat posed by Slavs to the *civiltà* of Italian Trieste.[30] The publication of *Due anni di storia 1943–45* (Two Years of History 1943–1945, 1948) by the ex-Fascist Triestine historian Attilio Tamaro only reinforced the prevailing intellectual view: the forty days of Slav occupation were "the most shameful, humiliating, saddest scar and insult that the *italianità* of the city ever suffered in the long millennia of its existence."[31] According to the exonerated Fascist ex-Mayor Bruno Coceani, during the Liberation Front government of May 1945 Trieste was subjected to the heights of terror. In *Mussolini, Hitler, Tito alle porte orientali d'Italia* (Mussolini, Hitler, Tito at the Eastern Gates of Italy, 1948), Coceani wrote: "The Slavs abandoned themselves to their predatory and vindictive instincts . . . more than during any other domination undergone by the city, the usurpation, the oppression, the violence were all the worse for the occupiers' lack of *civiltà*."[32] We might dismiss such accounts of the war and liberation as extremist or eccentric but for the postwar rehabilitation of these writers, and the correspondence between their views of Slavs and Trieste and those propounded by locally celebrated democrats, such as Carlo Schiffrer. In a number of postwar works timed to coincide with the 1946 peace talks deciding Trieste's future (most of them reprinted in the 1980s and 1990s), Schiffrer questioned the future of national borders, but he also continued to publish studies in which Slavs were represented as an "amorphous multitude" and the antithesis of "vital" Italian culture. Building on this view, Schiffrer argued that

> [f]or the Italian, sentiments, traditions, education lead to extend the "holy
> soil of the fatherland" as far as the mountain-range of the Alps. . . . [I]f

within these limits there are rustic populations of another tongue, the psychology of the Italian, derived from a thousand years [*sic*] old traditions, finds it quite natural that the country must follow the lot of the towns and not the other way about.[33]

Carlo Sforza, the Italian foreign minister negotiating Trieste's future, commended Schiffrer's work as exposing a lively yet dispassionate understanding of the relationship between "an urban civilisation like the Italian and the Slovene masses."[34] Such comparisons simultaneously reinforced the "reality" of differences between Italians and Slav/Slovenes and the possibility of an utopian line dividing them.

Nationally sanctioned narratives of Trieste's past interwove public and private forms of identification, memory, and history. They enforced not just a particular reading of the past, but the relationship between the territory's fixed national identity and the individual's visceral self. At a time when Cusin argued that Trieste was still waiting to be liberated *from* itself, politically moderate Italian writers such as Giani Stuparich defended national identity and the idea that Trieste was waiting to be free *to be* "its Italian self."[35] Stuparich's *Trieste nei miei ricordi* (My recollections of Trieste, 1948, reprinted in the 1980s) recounted a personal journey from a childhood at the turn of the century when he felt an emotional attachment to things Italian, to an adolescent infatuation with the cosmopolitan socialism of the Habsburg empire, to the liberation of his intuitively Italian inner self and his autochthonous relation to the territory that Italy gained in 1920.[36] Stuparich acknowledged alternative versions of Trieste's history at the same time that he provided the rationale for repudiating them. In a chapter entitled "Dreams and Reality," he described a time when Trieste was part of the Habsburg empire and he had "dreamed" that the city was a crossroads for Europe, a miniature Switzerland. With his brother Carlo and the Triestine writer Scipio Slataper, Stuparich planned to produce a cultural review that would develop Trieste's cosmopolitan tendencies. But when both Scipio and Carlo were killed in the First World War, he converted to Italian patriotism and came to a "consciousness" of the "reality" of the "physiological rapport" between his self and Trieste's topography, manifest in every street through which he wound his way once Trieste was politically united with Italy in 1920: "[A]ll of my city moved inside of me," he explained, Trieste had become "a city, environment no longer separable from its characters, inherent in them."[37] Unlike Cusin, Stuparich wanted the Triestine landscape to speak the historical truths of its *italianità*. It was in this sense that he fought for all "Italians of Trieste, like the Italians of all Italy" to be free, to be themselves.[38] This freedom had gender as well as ethnic limitations. A fundamental feature of Stuparich's narrative of national identity was the masculinity of deep-rooted, authentic national identification. "Few are the women," Stuparich stated, "who abandon themselves without conflict to their instinct, many those who in conflict reach only the half way road, rare the women who are able to reach into their deepest selves or to go as far as it is humanly possible."[39] Stuparich's Triestine women acted out parts in which they were unable to identify or fulfill themselves because they were unable to identify with a nation in any profound way.[40] On this view, characterized both as subverters of reason and order, and as lacking depth of emotion, women shared with Slavs the attributes of superficial non-national selves.[41]

Early in the twentieth century Triestine writers from the Habsburg period had been recognized for their interest in "self-discovery, self-definition, seeking what is their reality—but almost with the presupposition that they will not find it, as one who sees his search as an end in itself, rather than a means."[42] In the second half of the twentieth century, writers such as Stuparich sought the revelation of their innermost national selves in the ethno-national identity of territory and in the reality of the ethno-national past. Schiffrer described the attempt by Triestine intellectuals to anchor a sense of self in national history as "intended first of all to clarify to the authors themselves the basic reasons for their own choices and their own positions, becoming almost the reason for their being."[43] But even Stuparich's narrative was disturbed by the possibility that an alternatively imagined past existed, and that it had ramifications for his own national identification. The other "dream"-like Trieste was populated with a group that Stuparich described as *incroci Triestini* or "mixed" individuals. Stuparich's own "Slavic" name, and his Jewish mother made him an unwilling member of the *incroci*.[44] By reconstructing his personal history around the revelation and unification of an essentially Italian and masculine self, Stuparich was able to suspend the ambiguities of his fragmented "mixed" self, and of Trieste's Habsburg, Slav, and Italian/Fascist past.

It was in the midst of this re-narrativization of overlapping national and individual histories that Fabio Cusin evoked the concept of anti-history as a demand for critical analyses of the nationalist mythologization of the past. By the time of Cusin's death in 1953 (a year before Trieste was returned to Italy), anti-Fascist Triestines who identified with a historical Italian *civiltà* and who sought to defend Trieste's "Italian" history, were firmly reorienting public and private narratives of Trieste's identity and their selves around images of the historic menace of

Slavs, the same images that had been integral to irredentist and Fascist nationalist repertoires in the first half of the twentieth century.[45] In an essay entitled "The Reality of Trieste" (1954), the aim of which was to prove that even Vivante and Slataper thought Trieste should be Italian, Stuparich pressed his view of the relation between Italians, like himself, and Slavs. He described the invasion of Trieste by an alien "Slav race," "strange, with a different language and customs" (and with a predisposition toward those same forms of "discipline" that had characterized Slavic communism for the Allied Military Government):

> We aren't blindly the enemies of the Slavs, to the contrary, we recognize the impulse which animates them, the discipline that unites them, the craftiness that they mix with tenacity in pursuing their intentions, the proud sense that they have of their own nation . . . but we have to be ready to defend ourselves, to not allow ourselves to be obliterated by the Slavs, to reconcile with those who intend to live with us civilly, but to decisively unmask the others who would with the violence and perfidy of barbarians destroy, supplant and eliminate us.[46]

For another decade, Italian intellectuals ignored Cusin's call to reevaluate local chauvinisms and reexamine Trieste's Fascist past. Triestines whose participation in the Italian anti-Fascist resistance had been driven by a democratic idealism were caught between their dismay at the right-wing turn in postwar Italian national politics and the incidents of neo-Fascist violence in Trieste, on the one hand, and their desire to regain Istria for Italy—a desire they shared with right-wing and extremist groups—on the other. Schiffrer was among a number of former left-wing CLNists, including Ercole Miani and Galliano Fogar, who decided to tackle the first problem by creating an Institute for the History of the Liberation Movement in Venezia Giulia the aim of which would be the resuscitation of their resistance ideals.[47] The second problem was dealt with quite differently. Some of the Institute's members (including Schiffrer, Fogar, and Miani) helped create a new English-language political review entitled *Trieste*, which published arguments for the return of Istria to Italy. *Trieste* replicated stereotypes of "foreign" and barbarous Slavs and democratically inclined Italians. Its editors recycled excerpts from *Primavera a Trieste* and the work of Giani Stuparich. They referred to Stuparich as "the typical representative of that Triestine culture which on an ethical and political level goes back to the democratic traditions of the Italian *Risorgimento*."[48] Other articles warned of the "Slav tide" poised at the "last breakwater of our eastern frontier."[49] In 1955, the historian Elio Apih—a protegé of Carlo Schiffrer who would go on to write one of the most important studies of Fascism and anti-Fascism in interwar Venezia Giulia—contributed a critique of Italian-Slav relations that highlighted the "fashions" Italians adopted for discussing Slavs: the nineteenth-century fashion of depicting Slavs according to Romantic ideals of rusticism, or cosmopolitan enthusiasm, and the mid-twentieth-century theme of how Slavs "had grown too big for their boots."[50] But even Apih's final advice was that only a "nationally conscious, strong and stable Italian community . . . can really live side by side and in amity with the Slavs."

In the postwar, efforts by local political bodies to reinforce the "consciousness" and the "stability" of Italian identity were focused on making Trieste's material landscape "speak the historical truths of its *italianità*." Throughout the 1940s and 1950s, municipally and privately funded memorials sprouted in and around Trieste attesting to the national patriotism of the local Italian population. In 1948 the Italian (Christian Democrat) national government awarded the city of Trieste the Gold Medal for Military Valor, an honor marked by a headstone set in the sanctuary of the tree-lined paths of Trieste's *zona capitolina*. The headstone testified to the repeated trials undergone by the city and its population in the defense of Trieste's *italianità*, and the brutality of a "foreign occupation" at the end of the Second World War.[51] In 1956, the Christian Democrat Trieste Council affixed a plaque (1 × 1.5 m approximate size) on the portico wall of the town hall in the Piazza Unità commemorating the Gold Medal and repeating the same historical narrative. By the 1960s, the *Lega Nazionale* and the veterans' *Associazione Grigioverde* had installed an imposing grey marble slab in the fashion of a tombstone at the site of the Basovizza *foibe*. Despite being a communist pro-Yugoslav stronghold during the war, Basovizza village had remained in Italy as the last village before the Italo-Yugoslav border. The Basovizza *foibe* memorial immediately became an object of pilgrimage for nationalists and Istrian exiles who demanded national recognition of the site and its Italian victims. Within a short time, the tombstone erected at Basovizza was complemented by a large vertical marble slab indicating levels of excavation and proposing evidence of human remains.[52] The memorialization of the region's *italianità* was also occurring at other geographical vantage points. In the 1960s, the Triestine archbishop, Monsignor Santin, began building the Santuario S. Maria Regina on Monte Grisa in order to fulfill a promise he had made to the Madonna on the eve of the first of May 1945: if Trieste was saved he would build her a temple.[53] When completed, the imposing modernist triangular church (locals irreverently refer to it as *il formaggino*, or the "little cheese") looked out over the Trieste Gulf and back toward the

eastern hinterland lost to Yugoslavia. At its back entrance an inconspic-
uous bronze plate still attests to the memory of national threat in *"l'ora
tragica* 30.IV.45," "the tragic hour" at the end of Nazi occupation, and
the beginning of the forty days. A foray into the center of Trieste, to the
Questura or police headquarters (originally built in the late 1930s as the
Casa del Fascio and situated opposite the Roman *teatro*), acts as a
poignant reminder of the significance of the memory of national struggle. The *Questura* building, an architectural symbol of Fascism, has a
public foyer which features an imposing sanctum bearing an inscrip-
tion to those police who fell "in the course of their duty" between 1944
and 1945 and listing their names and dates. The sanctum provides no
explicit mention of Slavs or the *foibe*, but it is read by locals as a memorial to the *infoibati*, and eradicates the significance of Fascism in the Second World War.[54]

At different times in the postwar, local evocations of a history of
the Slav threat to *italianità* have been given national validation, and
have been important to the reinvention of what Mabel Berezin has
termed "the memory and meaning of fascism" in Italian national history.[55] In the 1960s, a period of left-wing political renewal in Italy, the Institute for the History of the Liberation Movement began to cooperate
with the Association for the Victims of Nazi and Fascist Deportation
(ANED), and the Slovene Institute for the History of the Workers Movement (now the Slovene Institute for Contemporary History) in order to
focus critical attention in Italy on the history of Fascism.[56] In 1965, the
Institute for the History of the Liberation Movement was successful in
pressing for national recognition of the Risiera di San Sabba in Trieste
(Italy's only wartime concentration camp equipped with cremating
ovens) as a "national monument." As a result, the Risiera was transformed into an impressive memorial and museum.[57] The historians
who identified with the anti-Fascist history of the Second World War
now insisted on a war crimes' trial, hoping that a reinvestigation of the
Risiera's history would establish the identity of the perpetrators and
victims of the deportations and killings that had taken place there.[58] A
trial was eventually granted by the Italian state in 1975, the same year
the Osimo Treaty was signed confirming that Venezia Giulia and Trieste
were Italian territory, and Istria part of Yugoslavia.[59] It was in this political context that during the trial the definition of culpability was given
the narrowest interpretation possible: only German Nazis stood accused, and Italian Fascists remained uncontaminated by any complicity
in the Risiera's history.[60] The court concluded that the Risiera had func-
tioned without the participation of local Italian authorities.[61] The pre-
siding Judge Serbo distinguished between the Risiera's victims as

"innocent" and "non-innocent" by stressing the imperative of national survival, and by questioning the ethical role of local anti-Fascism—which he described as the "so-called 'liberation struggle.'" Non-innocent victims were those engaged in anti-Nazi and anti-Fascist activities, regardless of their age, gender, or civilian status—the same distinction that had operated in the sequestration by Fascist forces of the local Jewish and Slav civilian population.[62] Judge Serbo also identified the anti-Fascist resistance as "Yugoslav," and regarded this assignation as justification for the non-innocent status of anti-Fascists, and for the ferocity of Nazi and Fascist opposition: if some of the "Yugoslav" resistance fighters were killed in the Risiera, the killers could not be blamed.[63] The judicial summing up stated that from the perspective of the Italian state, Germans, a conspiring alien occupying force, were guilty of crimes against Italians, a situation that was repeated when, "[w]ithin a small space of time, the city would once again, in a no less detestable manner, be tragically bloodied," but by a different occupier.[64] Serbo's judgment had substantial precedents, his arguments had been embellished in previous postwar regional trials (some conducted in British-American Military Government courts), which exonerated Nazi collaborators for defending the *italianità* of the border region against "Slavs" and retrospectively criminalized "Slavs" for acts of terrorism against the Fascist Italian state.[65]

Enzo Nizza has recorded that Friuli-Venezia Giulia has, per head, the second-highest number of memorials to the anti-Fascist resistance in Italy, most of them erected by local communities during the early 1970s in the villages surrounding Trieste.[66] These peripheral anti-Fascist memorials seem not to have diminished the influence of chauvinist representations of difference on predominant Italian histories and memories of World War II. In the postwar period, iterations of Italian/Slav hatred and of the foreignness of Slavs in Italy left a seemingly indelible imprint on the political modalities of Italian identity. An article written in the aftermath of the Risiera trial by Simonetta Ortaggi, a schoolteacher from an outlying Triestine settlement, described her experiences teaching in a school near what was then the Italo-Yugoslav (now Slovene) border, and how she and her students began to negotiate their historical understanding of the recent past.[67] Borgo San Mauro, a village north of Trieste, was purpose-built to house Istrian refugees who had been encouraged by the Italian government (and the potency of popular accounts of the *foibe*) to leave Tito's Yugoslavia. Ortaggi called Borgo a ghetto, an island of refugees. It had been part of an area that was under AMG control from 1945 to 1954. She described her students as mixed, although the existence of a separate Slovene-language school in the area meant that all of them were Italian-speaking.[68] When Ortaggi quizzed them about the history of Italian and Slovene relations they responded that the resistance was a peasant affair, and that local Slovenes had all recently emigrated from Yugoslavia to Italy—even though a few of the students actually had Slovene parents or relations who had long been settled in the region. Similar beliefs were expressed by a more advanced class of students from Trieste proper. Ortaggi explained that "accusations launched against the Slovenes exposed most clearly how ignorance and misinformation had fostered antagonism to the local Slovene population."[69] She limited her criticism to the responsibility of the Christian Democrat Party for perpetuating anti-Slav interpretations of the recent past of the area. Ortaggi argued that local conservatives had legitimated their own claims to territorial "ownership" by fostering chauvinism:

> Hatred for the Slavs was a central element in this chauvinist ideology: they were presented as usurpers of Istrian territory . . . Borgo San Mauro was carefully placed as a bastion, an Italian wedge penetrating a predominantly Slav and "red" zone.[70]

Even though the representation of Slovenes as foreign communists was remote from the realities of some of the students' personal experiences or backgrounds, its substance was validated by the authoritative historical narratives they encountered in the everyday material and institutional landscape of Trieste.

In 1980, five years after the Risiera trial, the Italian government decreed the Basovizza *foibe* a "monument of national interest" representing the tragic events of the end of the Second World War, "when a substantial number of civilian and military victims, mostly Italian, were killed and flung into communal graves."[71] In the revisionist climate of the post-Cold War the *foibe* accumulated national status. In 1993, the president of Italy, Oscar Luigi Scalfaro (an ex-anti-Fascist partisan and a conservative Catholic) felt it worthwhile to raise the Basovizza *foibe*'s status from "monument of national interest" to the superior level of "national monument," the Risiera's equal.[72] The following year, a magisterial inquiry into the Istrian *foibe* episode of 1943 was initiated in Rome. Even before the responsible judge, Giuseppe Pittito, had begun to hear evidence, he accepted the estimate of seventeen thousand deaths in the *foibe*, and the "genocide" of Italians as the motivation.[73] Late in 1995, right-wing Italian parliamentary deputies requested that their version of the *foibe* be treated as a special theme in Italian classrooms, as a reminder of Italy's national peril during the Second World

War.[74] In 1996 and 1997, parliamentary representatives from the self-styled "post-Fascist" parties Forza Italia and Alleanza Nazionale (a combination of former neo-Fascist, conservative, and right-wing groups)[75] compared the historical status of the *foibe* to that of the Nazi Ardeatine massacres, and to the practices of ethnic cleansing in 1990s Yugoslavia.[76] They claimed that during the Second World War the objects of "Slavic ethnic cleansing were Italians," and the Slavs were inspired by "motives of cleansing" similar to those they practised against each other half a century later.[77] Their other favorite comparisons were the bloody vengeance exacted by communists against Fascists in Emilia Romagna at the end of the war, and the "Porzus" episode in February 1945, when communists (the "Gappisti" cooperating with the Slovene resistance) killed a score of Catholic anti-Fascists in Friuli.[78] Accompanying interest in both the Istrian and Venezia Giulia *foibe* were the themes of exodus, the Istrian homelands lost to Yugoslavia, and the memories of loss experienced by the Istrian diaspora. In 1997, symposia and commemorations in Venezia Giulia of the fiftieth anniversary of the "exodus" attempted to strike a national chord. The *Società Umanitaria* and *Associazione Nazionale Venezia Giulia e Dalmazia* organized a travelling exhibition entitled, *Immagine di una tragedia: Le foibe e l'esodo*. In these various contexts, some Italian politicians emphasized the nation's need to remember the history of the *foibe*, and to consider its victims as neither Fascists nor anti-Fascists, but as Italians "of every political persuasion."[79] In an article entitled *"Il richiamo dei Balcani"* (The Call of the Balkans), a regular contributor to a major Italian international relations journal enjoined the Italian government to take responsibility for maintaining the "historical memories *(ricordi)*" of the *italianità* of territories lost in the postwar to Yugoslavia, the ethnic cleansing of these territories, and the *infoibati* "who did not fall in the *foibe* by mistake."[80] Although Maria Todorova singles out Italian nationalism as devoid of interest in a Balkan orientalizing discourse, Miles's article is only one example of the ways in which since the Yugoslav wars, the negative connotation of Balkanness has increasingly been exploited in order to reinforce the alterity of a Slav culture across the Italian border, and the essential civilizing traits of Italian national identity.[81]

There is no simple correspondence between national trends and local events in Italy. At the same time that the *foibe* have been used to reinvent the national history of the Italian Fascist past, local writers such as Claudio Magris and Fulvio Tolmizza have been reinventing the "Danubian" or Adriatic qualities of Triestine identity in their fiction, and an independent Triestine mayor has gained local favor for his attempts to reinvent Trieste's economic future as part of a Central European hinterland.[82] Former CLNists such as Galliano Fogar admit however that "the problem of the *foibe* and deportations," "furnished with amplifications and statistics lacking consistency or any critical apparatus which could justify the figures of 10 to 20,000 *infoibati*," has intruded in every "political or administrative event of significance in recent Triestine and Giulian history."[83] Even though in the post–Cold War era some local historians (amateur and professional) continue to amass evidence that challenges the theory that the *foibe* killings were premeditated by communist Slavs to annihilate Italians and Italian culture in the region, a new generation of historians such as Raoul Pupo claim that the *foibe* have become "fixed in the memory of contemporaries."[84] Pupo argues that the *foibe* have remained "an obsession in moments of national and political uncertainty" with "the force to perceptibly determine even the choices made by the masses, such as those carried out by Istrians who decided [in 1954] to abandon the territories that had passed into Yugoslav sovereignty."[85] The force of the *foibe* narrative is evidence of the ways in which individual and local identities are forged from representations of difference with accruing cultural significance and authorized by nationally produced and sanctioned narratives of identity and history. In Italy, as in Trieste, the narratives that have given political and symbolic force to reflections on the *foibe* are deeply anchored in the sociopolitical imaginaries of local and national communities and the relationships between them. As we will see in the following section, these narratives are also insinuated in the international histories that have been written about the problem of Trieste by historians with no personal investment in the identities and differences they have helped reify.

INTERNATIONAL HISTORIES

This history of the problem of Trieste has followed in the path of a small number of important international histories of that problem written since the 1960s—particularly Jean-Baptiste Duroselle's *Le Conflit de Trieste* (1966), Dennison Rusinow's *Italy's Austrian Heritage* (1969), Bogdan Novak's *Trieste: 1941–1954* (1970), and Roberto Rabel's *Between East and West* (1988). While these authors have contributed careful empirical research and critical insights to the political history of Trieste, in each of these histories representations of national differences are intrinsic to the narrativization of the problem of Trieste. In their analyses of political events in the region, Trieste, like the Adriatic as a whole, is, to varying degrees, presented as the confluence of three "racial" groups—Latins, Teutons, and Slavs. It is generally implied that each of these groups requires separate political representation corresponding to their territorial limits—the problem of Trieste is thus the problem of separating out the limits of difference.[86] These histories also tend to validate the motivations of political groups and intellectuals who affirm conventional assumptions of Italian and Slav differences, and the cultural and political antipathy between them.[87] Jean-Baptiste Duroselle's Carnegie-sponsored *Le Conflit de Trieste* includes a study of the foundations of the conflict, a survey of the region's historical and geographical character as the meeting point of the three great groups that divide Europe—Germans, Slavs, and Latins. Although Duroselle dismisses anteriority as a "false problem" because both Italians and Slavs were in the region for centuries, he maintains that two thousand years of history could reveal elements that contributed to conflict between Italians and Yugoslavs after 1914. The important point, he argues, was that Slavs had never assumed sovereign control of Trieste, unlike Italians, whose sovereignty was exercised in the period of Imperial Roman rule. Novak implies that Italian and Slovene are static or pre-given identities, and that national sovereignty is a natural objective of national identification. In *Italy's Austrian Heritage,* Dennison Rusinow argues that the problem of Trieste in the early twentieth century, as in Venezia Giulia, lay in its boundary characteristics. Trieste was "the meeting ground of two of the most important racial groups of Europe," namely German and Italian, to which a third racial group, Slavs, was added in the late nineteenth century.[88] Although Italians and Slavs were "inextricably intermingled" in Istria, Rusinow argues that in the Littoral they were each dominant in particular districts, which in turn meant that the territorial limits of Italian and Slav identities could be defined. Rusinow's criticism of the passions aroused by Italian irredentism among anti-Fascists and Fascists alike is tempered by his sympathy for the "sensitivity" of "history-conscious Italians" "to the vulnerability of their peninsula"—the Littoral is, geographically, an "open door" through which "a dozen of the world's major invasions have come."[89] For Rusinow, among those sensitive Italians who manifest an acceptable nationalism is Gaetano Salvemini, whose writings exemplified the "ethnic and democratic principles" of a Mazzinian tradition. By contrast, I have tried to show that even the historical narrativization of difference and sovereignty in Trieste espoused by "good" Italian nationalists provided a foundation for the destructive (Fascist) forms of Italian nationalism that, as Rusinow states, distorted the democratic tendencies of Italian citizenship. The historical narratives of good nationalists also reinforced the chauvinisms that defined the problem of Trieste in the period after the Second World War, in both Italian and international contexts.

After the ratification of the Italo-Yugoslav border in 1975, when neo-Fascist terrorism against the Slovene minority in Venezia Giulia persisted and Italian authorities continued to exploit conventional representations of the differences between Italians and Slavs, the European West and Balkan East,[90] the postwar history of Trieste began to be presented in English-language literature as exemplary of a successful international resolution to a nationalist territorial dispute that could be used as a model for other similar problems. Christopher Seton-Watson (the son of Robert Seton-Watson) recorded an easy cohabitation between Italy and Yugoslavia: "Traffic across the Italo-Yugoslav frontier is now heavy, and Yugoslavs shop in Trieste while Italians swim on the sandy beaches of Istria."[91] In 1976, John Campbell, who had worked with the Council on Foreign Relations and the American State Department, published *Successful Negotiation*, a collection of interviews with diplomats involved in resolving the problem of Trieste. Campbell sandwiched the interviews between his own account of "the differences between the Italians, heirs of Roman and Venetian tradition," and South Slavs who "had pushed down to the sea."[92] In 1978, Feliks Gross published an "Inquiry into the nature of ethnicity and reduction of ethnic tension in a one-time genocide area." After interviewing hundreds of locals (whom he referred to as either peasants or intellectuals), Gross argued that "for a century, the history books and newspapers wrote of the Slavic-Italian tensions and conflicts in that area," but now locals had successfully forgotten the history of nationalist conflict.[93] This was despite what he described as the extensive influence of a small intellectual elite's "historical memory." That memory seems to have also influenced Gross, who concluded from evidence of the complex and often non-national forms of local identification that Venezia Giulia was "an area of many ethnic or subethnic groups, most of them rooted in the great Italian civilisation," and the Adriatic was "a strategic, limitrophic area of east and west, the historical inroad from the Balkans into the Italian peninsula," a meeting point of three civilizations, Roman-Italian, Slavic, and German.[94] Gross's study was followed a few years later by Colonel Alfred Bowman's memoir of his time in Trieste as the senior civil affairs officer, *Zone of Strain* (1982). Bowman portrayed the problem of Trieste as a historical continuum "involving millennia of conflict between races, nationalities and ideologies."[95] On the eve of the end of the Cold War, Roberto Rabel published *Between East and West* (1988), a more academic history of the role of the United States in Trieste. *Between East and*

West begins with a chapter outlining "[t]he Geohistorical Origins of the Trieste Dispute" describing Trieste and the "Julian Region" as a "zone of strain" where for "two thousand years" "the clash of rival expansionist forces caused frequent changes in sovereignty."[96] For Rabel, like other historians, understanding international relations and the post–Second World War problem of the Italo-Yugoslav border required consideration of the history of Trieste as a meeting place of racial differences, of the region as a site of contest between Italian and Slav nationalisms, of the importance of externally imposed constraints on the local expression of nationalism, and of the role of the United States as a pacifying influence. In *Between East and West,* the roots of Trieste's history as a site of conflict lie in the nineteenth century, when "opposing national and political ideologies" took hold "culminating in the struggle for Trieste and nearby territories after World War II."[97] Rabel states that by the early twentieth century ethnic conflict was not only predictable, it was inevitable because Trieste was "one of the few points of direct contact between all three of Europe's major ethnic groupings: Latins, Slavs, and Germans."[98] He adds that "by the nineteenth century it was difficult to discern clear-cut 'ethnic' distinctions between the so-called Italian and Slavic communities," but that "[t]he Italian ethnic presence originated in Roman times," the Roman legacy persists as an Italian influence through the impact of Venetian culture and the "Italian domination of urban culture," and that the Slavic presence dates from the sixth century. Rabel is as certain of the distinctiveness of Italian and Slavic identities throughout this history as he is of the democratic features of the American identity, which he uses to assess the role of the United States during the Cold War.[99]

Contrary to these international histories, I have argued that depictions of Trieste as the axis of Europe's three major races engaged in a struggle for sovereignty can be traced to late-nineteenth-century views of the Adriatic boundary region. The influence of these views was consolidated during the First World War when European liberals endorsed in principle the democratic value of redrawing borders along lines that separated national and racial identities. The identities they invoked reflected only one strand of the possible discursive representations of the populations under consideration. Difference itself was not the cause of the intractability of the problem of Trieste and an Italo-Yugoslav border in the twentieth century; among relatively dispassionate observers it was, however, a conventional and convenient means of conceptualizing that problem, in part because of the legitimacy afforded to the principle of nationality. During the Cold War the British-American Military Government drew on what had become increasingly authoritative and available representations of difference, of the "British and American way of life" and the foreignness of communist Slavs, to sanction their authority and objectives—objectives influenced in turn by the view of political reality encouraged by those representations.[100] British and American authorities reinforced the political significance of ethno-national differences through their consistent representation of communism as a national-cultural phenomenon—culturally Slavic and nationally Yugoslav. Their representations would have had little force if they did not resonate with widespread Orientalist images of barbarism and Balkanness, and locally reproduced nationalist narratives. The recurring iteration of Trieste's *italianità* and of the foreignness of Slavs in political and historical elaborations of the problem of Trieste over the course of the twentieth century suggests the centrality of an Enlightenment intellectual map of East and West Europe and ethno-nationalist conceptions of sovereignty. As a consequence, in a region conventionally imagined and represented as a cultural and ideological faultline, the possible solutions to that problem were not inevitable, but they were overdetermined.

The history of Trieste offers illustrations of how individuals and governments have assumed cultural and political authority as "Western" by employing narratives of the intrinsic and qualitative differences between nations, between good and bad nationalisms, and between ethno-national and multicultural models of state organization. The "ideological structures of domination constructed out of these distinctions,"[101] have consolidated at different times, for different political purposes, representations of the coherence and democratic nature of national sovereignty in Western states. What became a "Western" attempt to determine sovereignty in Trieste and to locate an Italo-Yugoslav border, was framed in opposition to representations of antinationalism as an unnatural manifestation of communist ambitions. Despite the variety of local support for non-national forms of statehood and citizenship in the aftermath of World War II, and despite the multinational bases of their own states, British and American authorities were able to represent the problem of Trieste as the problem of nationalism and the presence in Trieste of a "Slav minority." In this way those authorities legitimated their presence in the region as "neutral" arbiters, and sanctioned an ideologically driven preference for an Italian solution. Also enmeshed in official British and American perceptions of the problem of sovereignty and the restoration of democracy were gender and class preferences which redefined local forms of citizenship and political agency in a manner requisite to Cold War versions of Western democracy.

Throughout the twentieth century the image of Trieste as a site of national struggle helped reify national identities, legitimate ethno-national forms of sovereignty, and naturalize the idea of ethnic hatred. At the same time, alternative imaginative representations of identities and conceptions of sovereignty that might have provided more inclusive bases for the democratic representation of individuals and groups constituted as "different," assumed a significant, if less successful role in Trieste's history. At various times during this century representations of Trieste as a "hybrid" "theatre of fusions and mixtures," a "no man's land," and a "free territory," and of Triestini as "*incroci*," have been both anxiety inducing and inspiring. The attempts by Angelo Vivante and Fabio Cusin to show how national identities and chauvinist representations of difference were made (and could be remade) within the discourses of history and culture, are exemplary of alternative narrativizations of the connections between difference, identity, and sovereignty.[102] Their lack of success cannot be explained as the simple expression of the overriding identities or national passions of the populations that have made up the Trieste area and boundary region.[103] We can think of patterned representations of sameness and difference and narratives of ethno-national sovereignty as burdens "compelling us to read the past in one way rather than another."[104] This compulsion has been at least partly the responsibility of "Western" historians who have uncritically accommodated those representations and narratives. As I have tried to show, there are other ways of reading and writing Trieste's past. History, as the anthropologist Brackette Williams has argued, "even history made behind men's backs," is "the siren that calls them to particular identities (personal and group) under conditions of territorial nationalism," but "always while, at the same time, pleading the contradictory cases for dissolution *and* maintenance of the specificity of these identities."[105]

Just as changing the way we read the past—in local, national, and international contexts—can have implications for political choices and political representativeness, the cost of not reconsidering the ways in which history provides evidence of both the dissolution and maintenance of the situated specificity of personal and group identities is borne out in recent Italian politics, and influential interpretations of events on the eastern side of the boundary region. In 1993, George Kennan, the same United States statesman who in 1947 advised the United States government of an impending Soviet threat, represented the Balkan nature of Yugoslavia's inhabitants and their "deeper traits of character inherited, presumably from a distant tribal past" as evidence of the inevitability of war in Yugoslavia.[106] From Kennan's perspective, the history of the Balkan Yugoslavs was related to the history of the Adriatic region and both histories provided a lesson for multicultural-ism in America:

> The inhabitants of the onetime Italian cities along the eastern shore of the Adriatic Sea (the scenes of some of Shakespeare's plays) made it a habit, over several centuries to take their menial servants and their ditchdiggers from the Slavs of the poorer villages in the adjacent mountains. Today, fi-nally, the last of the Italians have left; and the beautiful cities in question are inhabited entirely by Slavs, who have little relationship to the sort of city and the cultural monuments they have inherited. They have simply displaced the original inhabitants.[107]

Kennan may no longer be a practicing diplomat, but his reflections of-fer some insight into the ways in which in this century historical as-sumptions about national and racial differences, and about the cultural contest between national and racial groups, became a way of seeing the world and delineating one's self. Kennan's way of seeing the world has had significant implications not only for the so-called culture wars within the United States, and American foreign policy, but for the com-munities of the former Yugoslavia and the Adriatic region.[108]

In the cases of the post–Second World War reinvention of the prob-lem of Trieste and the more dramatic sovereignty disputes in 1990s Yu-goslavia, the privileging by international media, politicians, diplomats, and aggressors of assumptions similar to those informing Kennan's world view have contributed to the marginalization of local support for non-nationalist and more inclusive conceptions of sovereignty and citi-zenship.[109] In both Trieste and Yugoslavia, diplomats and politicians re-duced the democratic implications of the problem of sovereignty to a matter of ethnic representation and the division of territory into ethnic units (a solution also espoused by extremists and aggressor forces). In ef-fect, difference (rather than the chauvinist ways in which differences were imaginatively represented) was presented as the cause of the prob-lem. Conceptions of cultural equality and coexistence became associated with the "ideological" (and therefore artificial) ambitions of communists (just as they were earlier in the century stigmatized as socialist). Because the problem of sovereignty and democracy in Trieste was generally rep-resented by nationalists and the international community as the problem of the natural or inevitable antagonism between ethnic/national groups in a shared territory, the separation of those groups, or the privileging of one of them, became the acceptable resolution of that problem. In the case of post–Cold War Yugoslavia, the international community's assumption that the emergence of nationalism coincided with the decline of communism was accompanied by the premise that the expression of ethno-national identification was more authentic and democratic. The Yugoslav cultural experiment was cast into disrepute not only because it was communist, but because it "repressed" national identities and national narratives.[110] If the problem of Trieste, like Yugoslavia, had been thought of as the problem of how best to represent the diversity of mutable identities and interests (ethnic and otherwise) expressed by the local population, rather than as an exercise in equating ethno-national identity with popular sovereignty, alternative political negotiations and measurements of political success would have been necessary. Viewed from the perspective of the history of the exploitation of discourses of difference, the mid-century appeal in Trieste of the Yugoslav version of national identity and citizenship (despite its contradictions and inconsistencies) seems understandable and even appropriate.

Historical accounts of Trieste written this century have encouraged a nostalgia for what the political theorist William E. Connolly has described as a "coherent politics of place" and identity.[111] The task for historians is to understand how and under what circumstances certain versions of the pasts of nations have been re-collected by specific communities, under the vestiges of what institutionalized authority, and the forms of exclusivity or inclusivity that those recollections of the past may have sustained.[112] The history of the problem of Trieste reminds us that our identities and perceptions of others are both enmeshed in the past and extricable from it. What continues to be central to the identity of Trieste, the most irrepressible part of its history, and what ties all those who find themselves in that place together has always been the ability to pose the questions, what is this place, and who are we who include it in our repertoires of self-identification? It is as if those who refuse to assume too quickly answers to these questions have recognized the fragility of identities, as if Trieste itself embodied all the contradictions of the European political order in the twentieth century. It also suggests that if, in the post–Cold War, we are to take advantage of the possibilities for renegotiating communities and citizenship, historians of twentieth-century Europe need to be attentive to how they represent difference, identity, and sovereignty in the histories that they write.

Notes

INTRODUCTION

1. Yugoslavia was known until 1927 as the Kingdom of Serbia, Croatia, and Slovenia.

2. E. Gellner, *Nationalism* (London: Phoenix, 1998), 56. Gellner added that in the West "[t]he horror of Nazism and Fascism is optional," while to Trieste's east "[t]he horror of nationalism . . . is inherent in the situation."

3. For a discussion of this conception of the boundary, see D. Campbell, *Writing Security: United States Foreign Policy and the Politics of Identity* (Manchester: Manchester University Press, 1992), 8, 78; R. L. Doty, "Immigration and National Identity: Constructing the Nation," *Review of International Studies* 22 (1996): 237–39; M. Canovan, *Nationhood and Political Theory* (Cheltenham, UK: Edward Elgar, 1996), 3.

4. B. Anderson, *Imagined Communities: Reflections on the Origins and Spread of Nationalism* (London: Verso, 1983), and E. Hobsbawm and T. Ranger, *The Invention of Tradition* (Cambridge University Press, 1983).

5. It also tended to obscure historical evidence of the ambivalence ingrained in European discourse about nations and national identity since the early nineteenth century; see N. Stargardt, "Beyond the Liberal Idea of the Nation," in G. Cubitt (ed.), *Imagining Nations* (Manchester: Manchester University Press, 1998), 22 ff.

6. See for example, P. Sahlins, *Boundaries: The Making of France and Spain in the Pyrenees* (Berkeley: University of California Press, 1989), 271; L. Colley, *Britons: Forging the Nation 1707–1837* (New Haven: Yale University Press, 1992); and G. Mosse, *Nationalism and Sexuality: Respectability and Abnormal Sexuality in Modern Europe* (New York: Fertig, 1985); T. Winichakul, *Siam Mapped: A History of the Geo-Body of the Nation* (Honolulu: University of Hawaii Press, 1994).

7. Sahlins, *Boundaries*, 270–71.

8. L. Wolff, *Inventing Eastern Europe: The Map of Civilization on the Mind of the Enlightenment* (Stanford: Stanford University Press, 1994).

9. Ibid., 360.

10. M. Todorova, *Imagining the Balkans* (New York: Oxford University Press, 1997).

11. Wolff, *Inventing Eastern Europe*, 371.

12. Todorova, *Imagining the Balkans*, 38.

13. Campbell, *Writing Security*, 8.

14. T. Todorov, *On Human Diversity: Nationalism, Racism, and Exoticism in French Thought* (Cambridge, Mass.: Harvard University Press, 1993), xiii–xiv; and Campbell, *Writing Security*, 6.

15. R. Kearney, *Postnationalist Ireland: Politics, Culture, Philosophy* (London: Routledge, 1997), 69.

16. The institutional authority of history, vested in the academy has in turn been used to legitimate national borders; See P. A. Bové, *Intellectuals in Power. A Genealogy of Critical Humanism* (New York: Columbia University Press, 1986), 256. For a general commentary on the complacent relationship between the nation and the social sciences, particularly history, see E. R. Wolf, *Europe and the People Without History* (Berkeley: University of California Press, 1982); J. A. Agnew, *Place and Politics: The Geographical Mediation of State and Society* (Boston: Allen & Unwin, 1987); J. Stratton, "Deconstructing the Territory," in *Cultural Studies* 3 (1989): 38–57; and H. K. Bhabha, "Introduction," *Nation and Narration* (London: Routledge, 1990), 1–7.

17. J. G. A. Pocock, "The Politics of History: The Subaltern and the Subversive," *The Journal of Political Philosophy* 6, 3 (1998): 219–34; Jens Bartelson has suggested that "sovereignty and knowledge implicate each other logically and produce each other historically," J. Bartelson, *A genealogy of sovereignty* (Cambridge: Cambridge University Press, 1995), 5.

18. L. Kramer, "Historical Narratives and the Meaning of Nationalism," *Journal of the History of Ideas* 58, 3 (1997): 537. The most influential study of "othering" was Edward Said's *Orientalism* (London: Routledge & Kegan Paul, 1978).

19. T. J. Biesteker and C. Weber, "The Social Construction of State Sovereignty," in T. Biersteker and C. Weber (eds.), *State Sovereignty as Social Construct* (Cambridge: Cambridge University Press, 1996), 2.

20. Campbell, *Writing Security*, 10.

CHAPTER 1. DIFFERENCE, IDENTITY, AND SOVEREIGNTY, BEFORE 1918

1. "Austria-Hungary," *Encyclopedia Britannica*, 11th edition, 1910–1911, Vol. III (Cambridge: Cambridge University Press, 1910), 5; R. Kann, *The Multinational Empire: Nationalism and National Reform in the Habsburg Monarchy 1848–1918, Vols. 1 and 2* (New York: Octagon, 1977).

2. For examples, see chapter 7.

3. R. Oakey, "Austria and the South Slavs," in E. Robertson and E. Timms (eds.), *The Habsburg Legacy: National Identity in Historical Perspective, Austrian Studies V* (Edinburgh: Edinburgh University Press, 1994), 54: "Various factors contributed to the undermining of old supranational perceptions: the dissociation of Habsburg and South Slav goals in the Balkans; the acceptance of linguistic concepts of nationhood; the growing influence of Dualist Hungary; the social malaise of a backward periphery—all this played its part. . . . [T]he old paternalist Austria underwent significant modernisation, admitting important elements of liberal pluralism to its life."

4. Wolff, *Inventing Eastern Europe*, 316, 319.

5. Wolff, *Inventing Eastern Europe*, 319.

6. J. J. Tobin, *Journal of a Tour Made in the Years 1828–9 through Styria, Carniola, and Italy, Whilst Accompanying the Late Sir Humphrey Davy* (1832), 149–150; P. E. Laurent, *Recollections of a Classical Tour through Various Parts of Greece, Turkey, and Italy Made in the Year 1818 and 1819, vol. 2* (1822), 8, cited in C. Carmichael, "Locating Trieste in the Eighteenth and Nineteenth Centuries," in B. Brumer and Z. Smitek (eds.), *Mediterranean Ethnological Summer School* (Ljubljana: Slovene Ethnological Society, 1995), 20.

7. A. A. Paton, *Researches on the Danube and the Adriatic* (1862), 411, cited in Carmichael, "Locating Trieste in the Eighteenth and Nineteenth Centuries," 20.

8. Carmichael, "Locating Trieste in the Eighteenth and Nineteenth Centuries," 21.

9. Wolff, *Inventing Eastern Europe*, 312.

10. Ibid., 314.

11. Ibid., 365–66.

12. See J. B. Allcock, "Constructing the Balkans," in J. B. Allcock and A. Young (eds.), *Black Lambs and Grey Falcon: Women Travellers in the Balkans* (Bradford: Bradford University Press, 1991), 170–91; and Todorova, *Imagining the Balkans*, ch. 5.

13. In the *fin-de-siècle* Italian irredentism was a staple of the foreign policy of the Italian Kingdom. See Richard Bosworth, "Italy's Historians and the Myth of Fascism," in R. Langhorne (ed.), *Diplomacy and Intelligence during the Second World War. Essays in Honour of F. H. Hinsley* (Cambridge: Cambridge University Press, 1985), 85–108; and R. Bosworth, *The Italian Dictatorship: Problems and Perspectives in the Interpretation of Mussolini and Fascism* (London: Edward Arnold, 1998). For a contemporary account of the importance of statistics in this period for nation building, see S. Patriarca, *Numbers and Nationhood: Writing Statistics in Nineteenth-Century Italy* (Cambridge: Cambridge University Press, 1996), 7, 9.

14. G. Marinelli, *Slavi, Tedeschi, Italiani nel Cosidetto <Litorale> Austriaco (Istria, Trieste, Gorizia)* (Venezia: Antonelli, 1885), 6.

15. F. Musoni, *La Vita degli Sloveni* (Palermo-Torino: Carlo Clausen, 1893), 27.

16. B. Auerbach, *Les Races et les nationalités en Autriche-Hongrie* (Paris: Felix Alcan, 1898), 202, 203.

17. Auerbach, *Les Races et les nationalités en Autriche-Hongrie*, 197, 204.

18. Marinelli, *Slavi, Tedeschi, Italiani nel Cosidetto <Litorale> Austriaco*, 3, 4.

19. Auerbach, *Les Races et les nationalités en Autriche-Hongrie*, 204. In the preface to the 1917 edition Auerbach defends the future of Austria-Hungary, *Les Races et les nationalités en Autriche-Hongrie* (Paris: Felix Alcan, 2nd ed. 1914/17).

20. Recently, two Triestine academics, Angelo Ara and Claudio Magris, describe prewar Trieste as "[t]orn between Italy and Austria, divided between spirit and profit, the city seemed subject to a permanent tension"; A. Ara and C. Magris, *Trieste: Un identità di frontiera* (Torino: Einaudi, 1982), 49.

21. G. Stourzh, "Ethnic Attribution in Late Imperial Austria: Good Intentions, Evil Consequences," in Robertson and Timms, *The Habsburg Legacy*, 70–75. Given the power of the emperor to enact laws independent of the parliament or Reichsrat, the efficacy of constitutional rights, like all other rights guaranteed by the constitution, was unclear; B. Jelavich, *Modern Austria: Empire and Republic, 1815–1986* (Cambridge: Cambridge University Press, 1987), 96.

22. Ibid., 67.

23. Ibid., 78.

24. C. A. Macartney, *National States and National Minorities* (London: Oxford University Press, 1934), 142.

25. Kann, *The Multinational Empire*, 265.

26. Ibid., 266.

27. Oakey, "Austria and the South Slavs," 46, 52, 53.

28. See Stourzh "Ethnic Attribution in Late Imperial Austria."

29. For an account of the influence of modernism on conceptions of identity in this period see J. Le Rider, *Modernity and Crises of Identity* (Cambridge: Polity Press, 1993).

30. Kann, *The Multinational Empire, Vol. 2*, 156.

31. Ibid., 159. For an enlightening and more thorough discussion of these ideas, see N. Stargardt, "Beyond the Liberal Idea of the Nation."

32. Kann, *The Multinational Empire, Vol. 2*, 169.

33. See O. Bauer, *Die Nationalitätenfrage und die Sozialdemokratie* (Vienna, 1924); and Macartney, *National States and National Minorities*, 150ff.

34. According to Macartney, "[a]ll members of each nationality, whatever their residence were to form a single public body or association, endowed with legal personality and competent to deal with all its national ('national-cultural') affairs"; Macartney, *National States and National Minorities*, 149.

35. Ibid. See also A. Cobban, *National Self-Determination* (London: Oxford University Press, 1944), 185.

36. Macartney, *National States and National Minorities*, 149.

37. Pietro Pancrazi, cited in J. Cary, *A Ghost in Trieste* (Chicago: University of Chicago Press, 1993), 160.

38. Cary, *A Ghost in Trieste*, 242.

39. S. Slataper, *Il Mio Carso* (Milano, Il Saggiatore, 1965), 11.

40. S. Slataper, *Lettere Triestine* (1909), cited in Cary, *A Ghost in Trieste*, 142. According to his friend Biagio Marin, Slataper thought of himself as "Slavic-German-Italian"; ibid., 243, and Ara and Magris, *Trieste: un identità di frontiera*, 88–89.

41. S. Slataper, *Scritti Politici* (Milano, 1954), 168.

42. D. Zazzi, *Trieste Città Divisa* (Milano: Mazzotta, 1985), 78. According to Angelo Ara, the idea for *Europa* renewed an earlier tradition started by the review *La Favilla*; A. Ara, "The 'Cultural Soul' and the 'Merchant Soul': Trieste between Italian and Austrian Identity," in Robertson and Timms, *The Habsburg Legacy*, 59–62.

43. Slataper, *Scritti Politici*, 168.

44. A. Vivante, *Irredentismo adriatico* (Firenze: Parenti, 1954, 1st ed. 1912), 4.

45. Ibid., 56.

46. Ibid., 136.

47. To varying degrees both experimented with hybrid, *incroci*, or mixed forms of self-identification consonant with the early-twentieth-century modernist view of the dissociated self. Freud added his personal weight to these views of Trieste on a visit when he described it as a place where it was "impossible to confront imaginary passages, and fantasmes with a concrete identification"; cited in J. Nobecourt, "Freud et les Triskelles," in "Les Mysteres de Trieste," *Critique* special issue, Aug.–Sept. 1983, 600. See also B. Gombač, *Trieste/Trst: Ena imena, dva identiteta* (Trst: Tržaška Založba, 1993), 63.

48. See H. Anderson, *Utopian Feminism: Women's Movements in Fin-de-Siècle Vienna* (New Haven: Yale University Press, 1992). To my knowledge no work has been done on the existence of feminist organizations in Trieste and the Littoral at this time.

49. Zazzi, *Trieste Città Divisa*, 89.

50. R. Bosworth, *Italy Least of the Great Powers: Italian Foreign Policy before the First World War* (Cambridge: Cambridge University Press, 1979), 203.

51. Zazzi, *Trieste Città Divisa*, 93.

52. For accounts of the anti-Slovene character of the municipality in the last decades of the nineteenth century see Auerbach who argues that in 1880, "Les Italiens de Trieste affectent à l'égard de la minorité slovene une singuliere arrogance au point de lui interdire l'emploi du mot *ne* au lieu de *non* dans les deliberations de la Diete," *Les Races et les nationalités en Autriche-Hongrie*, 20. See also Ara and Magris, *Trieste: Un identità di frontiera*, 65. For examples of the Slovene nationalist response see Zazzi who states that in 1901 the review *Jug* (South), published in Vienna, argued that Austria had to consign Trieste to the Slovenes, *Trieste Città Divisa*, 46. D. Rusinow provides examples of the most extreme response to these tactics from a 1911 issue of *Edinost*, a Slovene paper: "tomorrow it will be the Slavs of Trieste who will speak. . . . Until now our stuggle has been for equality. Tomorrow we shall say to the Italians that the future struggle will be for dominion"; D. Rusinow, *Italy's Austrian Heritage 1919–1946* (London: Oxford University Press, 1969), 9; see also F. Fölkel and C. K. Cergoly, *Trieste Provincia Imperiale: splendore e tramonto del porto degli Asburgo* (Milano: Bompiani, 1983) and Gombač, *Trieste/Trst*.

53. Until 1914 even outsiders such as R. Seton-Watson believed this was the most realistic scenario for Austria-Hungary, R. W. Seton-Watson, *The Southern Slav Question and the Habsburg Monarchy* (London: Constable, 1911).

54. Bosworth claims that attacks on (Slovene) workers were funded by (Italian) businessmen; Bosworth, *Italy Least of the Great Powers*, 202.

55. E. Apih, *Italia. Fascismo antifascismo nella Venezia Giulia (1918–1943)* (Bari: Laterza, 1966), 15.

56. B. Novak, *Trieste 1941–1954. The Ethnic, Political, and Ideological Struggle* (Chicago: University of Chicago Press, 1970), 20–21.

57. Cited in Zazzi, *Trieste Città Divisa,* 61.

58. Zazzi, *Trieste Città Divisa,* 96.

59. Apih, *Trieste. Storia della città italiana,* 109.

60. S. Sighele, "L'italianità del Garda," *Pagine Nazionaliste* (Milano: Treves, 1910) , 165.

61. S. Sighele, "La lotta per l'autonomia nel Trentino," *Pagine Nazionaliste,* 18.

62. S. Sighele, "L'università italiana a Trieste," *Pagine Nazionaliste,* 81.

63. B. Spackman, *Fascist Virilities: Rhetoric, Ideology, and Social Fantasy in Italy* (Minneapolis: University of Minnesota Press, 1996), 13. In his anticommunist manifesto, *"Al di là di comunismo,"* Marinetti stated that "[t]he negation of *patria* was the equivalent of self-isolation, self-castration, self-diminishment, self-denigration, and suicide" (my translation).

64. S. Sighele, "Irredentismo e Nazionalismo," in *Il Nazionalismo Italiano: Atti del Congresso di Firenze e Relazioni di E. Corradini, M. Marabiglio, S. Sighele* (Firenze: Casa Editrice Italiana di A. Quattrini, 1911), 81.

65. See C. Seton-Watson, "Italy's Imperial Hangover," *Journal of Contemporary History* 15 (1980): 169–70; Patriarca, *Numbers and Nationhood,* 203; R. Bosworth, "Mito e linguaggio nella politica estera italiana," in R. Bosworth and S. Romano (eds.), *Politica Estera Italiana 1860–1988* (Bologna: Il Mulino, 1991), 53; R. Drake, *Byzantium for Rome* (Chapel Hill: University of North Carolina, 1980), 221, 225.

66. Cited in M. Pacor, *Italiani in Balcania dal Risorgimento alla Resistenza* (Milano: Feltrinelli, 1968), 34. See also R. Fauro, *Trieste: Italiani e Slavi; Il Governo Austriaco; l'Irredentismo* (Roma: Garzoni, 1914).

67. "Italian demands to Austria-Hungary by Sonnino," April 1915, in R. Albrecht-Carré, *Italy at the Peace Conference* (Connecticut: Archon Books, 1966, Ist ed. 1938), 332.

68. "Treaty of London," in Albrecht Carré, *Italy at the Peace Conference,* 334.

69. See Fölkel and Cergoly, *Trieste Provincia Imperiale,* 47.

70. Zazzi, *Trieste Città Divisa,* 89.

71. V. Gayda, *Modern Austria: Her Racial and Social Problems with a Study of Italia Irredenta* (London: Fisher Unwin, 1915), 28.

72. Ibid., 7. Even in Dalmatia, where Gayda stated Italians were not a majority, he argued the "country's past has been wholly Italian, as its soul is even now," 38.

73. V. Gayda, *Gli Slavi della Venezia Giulia* (Roma: Rava & Co., 1915), 11.

74. Gayda, *Modern Austria*, 29.

75. Gayda, *Gli Slavi della Venezia Giulia*, 18.

76. Ibid., 28.

77. G. Salvemini, *Delenda Austria* (Milano: Fratelli Treves, 1917).

78. C. Maranelli and G. Salvemini, *La Questione dell'Adriatico* (1918, 1st ed. 1916), 48, 49. For a discussion of the limits of Salvemini's reasonable nationalism, see Bosworth, *The Italian Dictatorship*, 86.

79. Maranelli and Salvemini, *La Questione dell'Adriatico*, 46, 48.

80. Ibid., 50

81. Ibid., 218.

82. K. Calder, *Britain and the Origins of the New Europe 1914–1918* (Cambridge: Cambridge University Press, 1976), 111–13.

83. "Preface," R. W. Seton-Watson, *Europe in the Melting Pot* (London: Macmillan, 1919), ix.

84. "The Future of Bohemia," Lecture at Kings College 1915 in honor of the Quincentenary of John Hus, in Seton-Watson, *Europe in the Melting Pot*, 250; R.W. Seton-Watson, "The Allies' Programme (January 1917), "*The New Europe* ii, 14 (1917); Elsewhere he had claimed that the most important issues were "the reduction of Germany to her national boundaries, the restoration of Polish and Bohemian independence, the completion of Italian, Roumanian, Jugoslav, and Greek national unity, the ejection of the Turks from Europe," Seton-Watson, Editorial "Italy and the Southern Slavs," *The New Europe* i, 2 (1916).

85. Seton-Watson, *Europe in the Melting Pot*, 310.

86. See Stourzh, "Ethnic Attribution in Late Imperial Austria," *passim*.

87. Seton-Watson, *Europe in the Melting Pot*, 311–12.

88. Ibid.

89. *The New Europe*, 2/1/19, in Seton-Watson, *Europe in the Melting Pot*, 311–12.

90. B. Vosnjak, *La Question de Trieste: Essai sur le problème jougoslave dans les pays 'irredente' par Illyricus* (Genève, 1915), 9.

91. Seton-Watson, "The Allies' Programme," 140. Two years later, in 1919, his outlook was more cynical: "the true problem with regard to Trieste and its hinterland" was, in 1915 and still in 1919, "not whether Italians shall destroy the Slavs or Slavs eject Italians, but whether Italians and Slavs will succeed in uniting to keep the Germans away from the Adriatic, or whether the Germans will profit by the quarrels of the two races in order to reduce both to subjection"; Seton-Watson, *Europe in the Melting Pot*, 313.

92. G. Stokes, "The Role of the Yugoslav Committee," in D. Djordevic, *The Creation of Yugoslavia 1914–1918* (Oxford: Clio, 1980), 62.

93. W. Vucinich, "The Formation of Yugoslavia," in Djordevic, *The Creation of Yugoslavia 1914–1918*, 201. See also I. J. Lederer, *Yugoslavia at the Paris Peace Conference: A Study in Frontiermaking* (New Haven: Yale University Press, 1963).

94. Nicolson argued that: "The Congress of Vienna [of 1814] allowed their councils to be dominated by the twin theories of legitimacy and the balance of power. The Conference of Paris [in 1919] was unduly obsessed by the conception of nationality contained in the formula of 'Self-Determination'"; H. Nicolson, *Peacemaking 1919* (London: Methuen, 1964) (1st ed. 1933, rev. ed., 1943), xviii.

95. Nicolson, *Peacemaking 1919*, 134, 135. An avid reader of *The New Europe*, and friend of Seton-Watson's, Nicolson had no difficulty accepting that the city of Trieste was Italian.

96. "Les Revendications de l'Italie sur les Alpes et dans l'Adriatique," Prima stesura del memorandum preparato dalla delegazione italiana alla Conferenza della Pace per esser presentato alla Conferenza stessa, Doc. 574 in *I Documenti Diplomatici Italiani* sesta serie: 1918–1922, vol. 2 (1980), 399.

97. Ibid., 403.

98. "Italian memorandum of Claims, February 7, 1919," Albrecht-Carré, *Italy at the Paris Peace Conference*, 370.

99. Ibid., 374.

100. See Stokes, "The Role of the Yugoslav Committee in the Formation of Yugoslavia," 51.

101. Novak, *Trieste 1941–1954*, 29.

102. Ibid., 31.

103. Ibid., 34.

104. Albrecht-Carré, *Italy at the Paris Peace Conference*, 309. Carré singles out the latecomers to the negotiations, Prime Minister Giolitti and his Foreign Minister Count Sforza.

105. Calder, *Britain and the Origins of the New Europe*, 180–81.

106. Ibid., 42. Alan Sharp argues that British support for Yugoslavia at the conference was a byproduct of dislike of Austria-Hungary, A. Sharp, *The Versailles Settlement: Peacemaking in Paris 1919* (London: Macmillan, 1991), 136. He also claims that "[t]he Yugoslav case for Istria, Dalmatia and Fiume was mainly ethnic and well-founded, but they did spoil their image by their demand for Trieste," 139.

107. M. Dockrill and J. Douglas Goold, *Peace Without Promise: Britain and the Peace Conferences, 1919–1923* (Connecticut: Archon Books, 1980), 105, 106.

108. Sharp, *The Versailles Settlement*, 139.

109. I. Lederer, *Yugoslavia at the Paris Peace Conference*, especially ch. 10.

110. British proponents of national self-determination argued that national self-determination was of limited benefit to less-evolved cultures, such as the Indian and Irish, who were not able to establish sovereign states. Larry Wolff has argued that as a consequence of stock representations of the differences between East and West, Russia was excluded from any influential role in the peace conference itself, despite its role in the war; Wolff, *Inventing Eastern Europe*, 364.

111. R. Seton Watson, "Italy, Jugoslavia and the Secret Treaty," reproduced in Seton-Watson, *Europe in the Melting Pot*, 309; see also Seton-Watson, *Europe in the Melting Pot*, 316.

112. Seton-Watson, *Europe in the Melting Pot*, 315.

113. Maranelli and Salvemini, *La Questione dell'Adriatico*, 58.

114. A. Ghisleri, *Il concetto etnico di nazione e l'autodecisione nelle zone contestate* (Torino: Vega, reprinted 1945), 22. The occasion for this paper was the First National Congress of the Italian branch of the Universal League for the Society of Free Nations. His own suggestion was that determining national borders involved attending to the historic territorial form of the nation as a body, as an entity in itself. Angelo Crespi, on the other hand, believed it was precisely to the people that the peacemakers should turn, marking national boundaries by means of a plebiscite, A. Crespi, "Note politico-sociali, Londra 17 gennaio. I discorsi di Lloyd George e di Wilson," *La Vita Internazionale* 21 (1918): 31.

115. Ghisleri, *Il concetto etnico di nazione*, 34.

116. Ibid., 30. Ghisleri also put the case that the question of "ethnically mixed zones" or "ethnic islands" was irrelevant in Italy because it was one of the most homogenous nations in Europe. Ghisleri's writings on the Adriatic Question were reprinted in the period after the Second World War as important contributions to the newly framed "problem of Trieste"; see A. Ghisleri, *Italia e Jugoslavia* (Roma: Libreria Politica Moderna, 1945).

117. Ghisleri, *Il concetto etnico di nazione*, 24.

118. Sighele, "L'antipatriotismo degli italiani," *Pagine Nazionaliste*, 198.

119. E. Bassi, "Sul futuro assetto territoriale italiano," *La Vita Internazionale* xxii (1919): 10. In the course of the war and in the immediate postwar the contributors to *La Vita Internazionale* included Italy's most prominent pacifists, feminists, reform democrats, and socialists, all of whom, like Moneta, saw no contradiction between pacifism, nationalism, and imperialism and identified as Mazzinian; E. Moneta, "Italia, Europa, Umanità," *La Vita Internazionale* 18 (1915): 261. Angelo

Crespi of the Socialist Democrat Party was among these contributors. In 1916, Moneta confessed that although he was a pacifist he believed in the righteousness of two wars: the Italian war against Libya, and the war against Germany; interview with *Popolo d'Italia*, July 1916, reproduced in *La Vita Internazionale* 21 (1918): 76–77.

120. L. Tancredi, "Le questioni territoriali italiane," *La Vita Internazionale* 22 (1919): 11.

121. C. Errera, *Italiani e Slavi nella Venezia Giulia* (Roma: Istituto Geografico de Agostini, 1919), 13.

122. Errera, *Il concetto etnico di nazione*, 17.

123. This same argument was put in a different form by Walter Lippmann in his study of the peace, *Public Opinion* (New York: Macmillan, 1947; 1st ed. 1922), 81.

124. F. Marston, *The Peace Conference of 1919, Organization and Procedure* (Connecticut: Greenwood Press, 1944), 166.

125. Dockrill and Goold, *Peace Without Promise*, 107.

126. See Nicolson, *Peacemaking 1919*, 138.

127. Ibid., 165.

128. See Macartney, *National States and National Minorities*, 75; Wolff, *Inventing Eastern Europe*, 363; and Todorova, *Imagining the Balkans*. British historians have referred to the Italian Foreign Minister Sonnino as a "slavophobe"; Italian diplomatic correspondence from the period accused their opponents of "italophobia." Dockrill and Goold, *Peace Without Promise*, 106. For the Italian references to italophobia see documents in *I documenti diplomatici Italiani, sesta serie: 1918–1922, vols. 1 & 2* (1980).

129. Nicolson, *Peacemaking 1919*, 258–59.

130. Kann, *The Multinational Empire*, vol. 2, 171.

131. Vivante, *Irredentismo Adriatico*, 154.

132. At a *Convegno del Rinnovamento* in 1920 Pittoni argued the "absolute necessity of an administrative decentralisation, and of the maintenance of the Austrian judicial, social and educational system." Duroselle mentions that some Republicans and Catholics were also autonomists. J. B. Duroselle, *Le Conflit de Trieste 1943–1954* (Bruxelles: l'Institut de Sociologie de l'Université libre de Bruxelles, 1966), 249.

CHAPTER 2. LIBERALISM, FASCISM, AND ITALIAN NATIONAL IDENTITY, 1918–1943

1. Macartney, *National States and National Minorities*, introduction.

2. Rusinow, *Italy's Austrian Heritage 1919–1946*, 192. The other provinces that made up this region were Udine, and Pola, and after 1928, Gorizia, Fiume, and Zara.

3. Maranelli and Salvemini, *La Questione dell'Adriatico,* 290ff.

4. Some authors of nationalism have claimed that the self-identity of nations are "secured partly through the construction of internal Others"; A. M. Alonso, "The Politics of Space, Time and Substance: State Formation, Nationalism, and Ethnicity," *Annual Review of Anthropology* 23 (1994): 379–405, 390; see also E. Balibar, "Paradoxes of Universality," in D. T. Goldberg (ed.), *Anatomy of Racism* (Minneapolis: University of Minnesota Press, 1990), 283–94.

5. Rusinow, *Italy's Austrian Heritage 1919–1946,* 84.

6. Apih, *Italia,* 45.

7. Rusinow, *Italy's Austrian Heritage,* 111.

8. For an example of Nitti's sensitivity to the problem of assimilation, see Rusinow, *Italy's Austrian Heritage,* 93.

9. Ibid., 89.

10. The "Independent Socialist Party of Slovenes and Croats of the Julian Region and Istria" supported a separate Julian Republic, and integration with the Italian Socialist party.

11. Apih, *Italia: Fascismo e antifascismo,* 117.

12. See P. Stranj, *The Submerged Community: An A to Z of the Slovenes in Italy* (Trieste: Stampa Triestina, 1992), 75. Apih argues that Di Roreto was sympathetic to Slavs, and was advised by the government to act with moderation and avoid incidents that could harm the Italian cause at the peace conference, Apih, *Italia,* 45.

13. Rusinow, *Italy's Austrian Heritage,* 97.

14. Ibid.,115.

15. Mosconi, cited in Ibid., 116.

16. A. Mosconi, *I primi anni di governo italiano nella Venezia Giulia Trieste 1919–1922* (Bologna: Cappelli, 1924), 21, 24.

17. Ibid., 7.

18. Ibid., 22. Rusinow states that although Mosconi's accounts of his administration were written retrospectively, his views coincide with the tenor of his administration.

19. For accounts of the "Hotel Balkan" episode see Rusinow, *Italy's Austrian Heritage,* 101–103, and Pacor, *Italiani in Balcania dal Risorgimento all Resistenca,* 64.

20. Apih, *Italia,* 114. The transformation of Slavs into foreigners and aliens was perpetuated by the national press which defended the Fascists' actions and claimed (with no substantiation) that the Balkan was a repository of Slav arms for use in acts of terrorism against the Italian state; Apih, *Italia,* 122.

21. Ibid., 127; Rusinow, *Italy's Austrian Heritage,* 95, 96.

22. Rusinow, *Italy's Austrian Heritage,* 108–109.

23. Apih, *Italia,* chapter 3; A. Vinci, "Il Fascismo nella Venezia Giulia e l'opera di snazionalizzazione delle minoranze," *Il Territorio* 6 (1996): 13; Rusinow, *Italy's Austrian Heritage,* 107, 114, 115.

24. Apih, *Italia,* chapter 3.

25. A. Vinci, "Venezia Giulia e fascismo. Alcune ipotesi storiografiche," *Qualestoria* 16 (1988): 50.

26. In a recent study of Trieste's history, Elio Apih also emphasizes the assimilatory power of Italian culture over *allogeni* (and *alloglotti*) as proof of the robustness of *italianità*. He refers to Slavs as *strati subalterni allogeni,* Apih, *Trieste. Storia della città Italiane,* 15.

27. A. M. Annoni, "Le lingue strainere e gli stranieri in Italia," *La Vita Internazionale* 25 (1922): 310.

28. Annoni conflates Croatians and Serbs.

29. Annoni, "Le lingue strainere e gli stranieri in Italia," 313.

30. E. Bassi, "Il problema delle minoranze allogene," *La Vita Internazionale* 25 (1922): 165.

31. G. I. Abate di Lungarini, "Il proletariato ebraico e il problema del mediterraneo," *La Vita Internazionale* 22 (1919): 217.

32. Rusinow, *Italy's Austrian Heritage,* 163.

33. Decreto: Legge 10, maggio 1923, Numero 1158, Legge 23, giugno 1927, "Toponomastica stradale e monumenti a personnaggi contemporanei," in O. Ravasini, *Compendio di notizie, toponomastica stradale sulla nomenclatura di località e strade di Trieste* (Trieste: La Editoriale Libraria, 1929).

34. For an account of the implementation and impact of these laws in the Alto Adige see Rusinow, *Italy's Austrian Heritage, passim;* and Vinci, "Il Fascismo nella Venezia Giulia e l'opera di snazionalizzazione delle minoranze," 14.

35. "Letter of the President of the Council of Ministers," 22 June 1925, cited in Macgregor Knox, *Mussolini Unleashed, 1939–1941: Politics and Strategy in Fascist Italy's Last War* (Cambridge: Cambridge University Press, 1982), 357; and Rusinow, *Italy's Austrian Heritage,* 164.

36. *Corriere della Sera,* 7 April 1931, cited in G. Salvemini, *Racial Minorities under Fascism in Italy* (The Women's International League for Peace and Freedom, Conference on Minorities, Chicago, 1934), 14. See also Stranj, *The Submerged Community,* 78.

37. A. Lodolino, *Leggi Ordinamenti e Codici del Regime Fascista: Esposizione e commento ad uso delle scuole e delle persone colte: Le vie del Duce, collana di studi Fascista* (Lanciano: Giuseppe Carabba, 1930). These laws were first introduced in the Alto Adige region, and later in Venezia Giulia and Istria.

38. See Lavo Cermelj's *Life and Death Struggle of a National Minority* (Ljubljana: n. p. 1945, 2nd ed.) for a survey of Fascist policies in the area and their claimed effects on the local Slovene and Croat population. Cermelj accuses Fascists of genocide.

39. V. De Grazia, *How Fascism Ruled Women: Italy, 1922–1945* (Berkeley: University of California Press, 1992), 275; D. G. Horn, *Social Bodies: Science, Reproduction, and Italian Modernity* (Princeton: Princeton University Press, 1994).

40. B. Mussolini, "Discorso dell'Ascensione," May 26 1927, in E. Susmel and D. Susmel eds., *Mussolini: Opera Omnia, vol. 22* (Firenze: La Fenice, 1951–1980), 360. See also L. Salvatorelli and G. Mira, *Storia d'Italia nel periodo Fascista, vol. 2* (Milano: Mondadori, 1972), 421–22.

41. Rusinow, *Italy's Austrian Heritage*, 200. As Gaetano Salvemini noted, some of the most prominent of provincial Fascists themselves bore Slavic or German-sounding names, which they in due course Italianized.

42. *Corriere della Sera*, 29 September 1928, cited in Salvemini, *Racial Minorities*, 16. The reference to Slavs as "Slaves" was a common conscious *double entendre*.

43. Salvemini remarks that one case in Tolmino was an absolute failure, the boys fled to Yugoslavia, Salvemini, *Racial Minorities*, 21.

44. Apih, *Italia*, 350.

45. Pagnaccoh "Minoranze nazionale e lotte di popoli," *Italia* 7 (1929): 283–85, 284.

46. "Report of May 7 1931 on the parliamentary bill for the prorogation [*sic*] of the Special Tribunal," cited in Salvemini, *Racial Minorities*, 18.

47. Vinci, "Il Fascismo nella Venezia Giulia e l'opera di snazionalizzazione delle minoranze," 14.

48. See A. Volk, "Una realtà multiforme. Omogeneità e disomogeneità nella memoria degli sloveni di Trieste," in M. Verginella, A. Volk, and K. Colja, *Storia e memoria degli sloveni del Litorale: Fascismo, guerra e resistenza* (Quaderni 7, Istituto regionale per la storia del movimento di liberazione nel Friuli-Venezia Giulia, 1997), 49–121, 63. Salvatorelli argues that local Slovene and Italian workers protested against the tribunal's actions; Salvatorelli and Mira, *Storia d'Italia nel periodo Fascista*, 104.

49. For a discussion using oral history of the impact of communism in the interwar period see M. Verginella, "I vincitori sconfitti. Testimonianze slovene sul movimento di liberazione a Trieste," in Verginella et al., *Storia e memoria degli sloveni del Litorale*, 12–17.

50. See Salvatorelli and Mira, *Storia d'Italia nel periodo Fascista*, 102; Rusinow argues that resistance was nourished from the other side of

the border, but also that the 1930 show trials were held for foreign policy reasons, *Italy's Austrian Heritage,* 207.

51. B. Novak, *Trieste 1941–1954,* 57.

52. *Corriere delle Sera,* 4 April 1931, cited in Salvemini, *Racial Minorities,* 20.

53. Elio Apih describes the Fascist treatment of minorities as an exemplary consequence of traditional nationalist ideologies, and the widespread acceptance in Europe of the idea of assimilation; Apih, *Italia, fascismo e anti-fascismo,* 272–73.

54. Apih, *Italia, fascismo e anti-fascismo,* 124.

55. *Il Fascismo nella Venezia Giulia: Dalle origini alla marcia su Roma* (Edizioni CELVI, 1932), 60.

56. The other two events were 1882, when the Triestine irredentist Guglielmo Oberdan set himself aflame in order to highlight his hatred of Austria; and 1918, when the Italian Navy arrived in Trieste; P. Sartori, G. Veronese, Villa Santa, "La Storia, La Vita, Il Domani," *Trieste,* 1934.

57. Apih, *Trieste. Storia della città italiana,* 134.

58. "Report of May 7 1931 on the parliamentary bill for the prorogation of the Special Tribunal," cited in Salvemini, *Racial Minorities,* 20.

59. B. Coceani, *Il Fascismo nel mondo* (Rocca S. Casciano, 1933), 8. See also Apih, *Italia, fascismo e anti-fascismo,* 274.

60. See for example, G. Gentile, *Che cosa è il fascismo: Discorsi e polemiche* (Firenze: Vallecchi, 1925).

61. D. Horn, *Social Bodies,* 59; V. De Grazia, *How Fascism Ruled Women,* 53.

62. O. Fraddorio, *Il Regime per la razza* (Tumminelle, 1939), 31. David Horn has explained that in the interwar period new forms of state governance contributed to the views of race and nation, *Social Bodies,* 8.

63. E. Corradini, *L'unità e la potenza delle nazioni* (Firenze: Vallechi, 1926, 1st. ed., 1922), 89, 90. Corradini was the founder of the Italian Nationalist Association in 1910.

64. L. Dei Sabelli, *Nazione e minoranze etniche, vol. 1* (Bologna: Zanichelli, 1929), 28.

65. Horn, *Social Bodies,* 59.

66. R. De Felice, *Mussolini il duce, II. Lo Stato Totalitario 1936–1940* (Torino: Einaudi, 1981), 297.

67. R. Ben-Ghiat, "Language and the Construction of National Identity in Fascist Italy," *The European Legacy* 2, 3 (May 1997): 438. Ben-Ghiat argues that Fascism was concerned with independent manifestations of regional cultures as well as *allogene* cultures.

68. A. Cronia, *La Conoscenza del mondo slavo in Italia* (Padova: n. p., 1958), 625.

69. Ibid., 582.

70. T. Amari, "La funzione italiana di Trieste," *Italia* 1 (1929): 27.

71. *Italia* (1929): 9. The review *Italia* was published by the Associazione nazionale fra mutilati ed invalidi di guerra, Delegazione regionale per il Friuli-Le Giulie e la Dalmazia.

72. Ben-Ghiat, "Language and the Construction of National Identity in Fascist Italy," 438.

73. Editore, "Note di politica," *Italia* 2 (1929): 57.

74. Dei Sabelli, *Nazione e minoranze etniche,* 223. Serbia and Montenegro earned some respect as ancient and virile states, see Cronia, *La Conoscenza del mondo slavo in Italia,* 625.

75. Cited in Rusinow, *Italy's Austrian Heritage,* 200.

76. L. Ragusin-Righi, "Politica di confine," *Italia* 3 (1929): 98.

77. Ragusin-Righi's articles in *Italia* were reprinted from a book published that same year. His involvement in the local newspaper, *Il Piccolo,* might explain the articles that appeared in that newspaper in 1925 and 1926 mentioning similar themes: the nonexistence of a nationality problem, and the importance of cleansing, see Apih, *Italia, fascismo e anti-fascismo,* 223, 274.

78. Ragusin-Righi, "Politica di confine," 294.

79. Ibid., 340.

80. *Il Piccolo,* 18 novembre 1930, cited in Apih, *Italia, fascismo e anti-fascismo,* 283.

81. G. Salvemini, "Il fascismo e le minoranze," in N. Valeri and A. Merola (eds.), *Opere, iv: Scritti sul Fascismo, vol. ii* (Milano: Feltrinelli, 1966), 481.

82. Ragusin-Righi, "Politica di confine," 499.

83. Ibid., 499.

84. Ibid., 294.

85. Ibid., 244, 394.

86. A. Pizzagalli, *Per l'italianità dei cognomi nella provincia di Trieste* (Trieste: Treves-Zanichelli, 1929), 100.

87. Ragusin Righi , "Politica di confine," 499.

88. Rusinow, *Italy's Austrian Heritage,* 164. For a comparative discussion of urban planning under Fascism see L. D. Nucci, *Fascismo e spazio urbano: le città storiche dell'Umbria* (Bologna: Il Mulino, 1992).

89. G. Bandelli, "Per una storia del mito di Roma al confine orientale: Archeologia e urbanistica nella Trieste del ventennio," in M. Verzar-Bass (ed.), *Il teatro Romano di Trieste. Monumento, storia, funzione* (Istituto Svizzero di Roma, 1991), 260.

90. The depiction of Trieste's Roman past has become standard in histories of the city and region, see for example, Apih, *Trieste,* and E.

Godoli, *La città nella storia d'Italia: Trieste* (Bari: Laterza, 1984). Godoli begins his history of Trieste as *Tergeste Romana* and ends with a critical commentary on the urban policies of the Fascist period.

91. For a discussion of the importance of the built landscape to the ideals of the Risorgimento in the late nineteenth century, see B. Tobia, *Una patria per gli italiani: spazi, itinerari, monumenti nell' Italia unità, 1870–1900* (Roma: Laterza, 1991).

92. Bandelli, "Per una storia del mito di Roma al confine orientale," 258, 260.

93. *Anonimo*, 1933, 14, cited in Ibid., 253.

94. Ibid., 261.

95. On the construction of the university see also A. Vinci, "Bellicismo e culture diffuse," in A. Vinci (ed.), *Trieste in Guerra: Gli anni 1938–1943* (Trieste: I Quaderni di Qualestoria, 1992), 86.

96. Inauguration speech (1927) by Morpugo, cited in M. E. Viora, "L'università degli studi di Trieste," *Umana: Le istituzioni di cultura della Trieste moderna* VII, 1–8 (1958): 13–27, 20.

97. B. Coceani, "Trieste e la sua università," *Discorso pronunciato alla Camera dei Deputati. Nella 2 tornata del 2 dicembre 1938–XVII* (Roma: Tipografia della Camera dei Deputati, 1938), 10.

98. Salvatorelli and Mira, *Storia d'Italia nel periodo Fascista, vol. 2*, 411.

99. S. Bon Gherardi, *La Persecuzione antiebraica a Trieste (1938–1945)* (Udine: Del Bianco, 1972), 49.

100. E. Ginzburg Migliorino, "L'applicazione delle leggi antiebraiche a Trieste: aspetti e problemi," *Qualestoria* 1 (1989).

101. E. Collotti, "Prefazione," in Bon Gherardi, *La Perzecuzione antiebraica a Trieste*, 12.

102. See for example the first issue of *La Difesa della Razza: Scienza, Documentazione Polemica* 1, 1938.

103 B. Škerlj, "Rapporti di razza fra JugoSlavia e Italia," *La Difesa della Razza* 18 (1940): 48, 49. *La Difesa* occasionally printed correspondence from Yugoslavia; one case concerned the success of Yugoslav attempts to deal with Jews; "Il problema judaica in Jugoslavia," *La Difesa della Razza* 19 (1940): 44. In her study of *La Difesa della Razza*, Sandra Puccini has noted the influence of the racially based ethnographies of Yugoslavia and the Adriatic region published by Francesco Musoni, and Francesco Pullè; S. Puccini, "Tra Razzismo e Scienza: L'Antropologia Fascista e i Popoli Balcanica," *Limes* 1 (1994): 283–94.

104. Vinci, "Trieste in Guerra," 77.

105. Salvemeni, *Racial Minorities*, 30, 31.

106. Cited in Apih, *Italia, fascismo e anti-fascismo*, 338–39.

107. G. Acerbo, *I fondamenti della dottrina Fascista della razza* (Roma: n. p., 1940), 11, 27, 28.

108. Ibid., 28.

109. G. Gaeta, *Trieste ed il colonialismo italiano: Appunti storici giornalistici* (Trieste: Edizioni Delfino, 1943).

110. A. Vinci, "Trieste in Guerra," *Qualestoria* 20 (1992): 75.

111. Ibid.

112. Marco Antonsich has argued that *Geopolitica* reflected the "particular reality of the border," and was only of remote interest to Bottai; M. Antonsich, "La rivista 'Geopolitica' e la sua influenza sulla politica fascista," *Limes* 4 (1994): 269–78. See also A. Vinci, "*Geopolitica* e Balcani: l'esperienza di un gruppo di intellettuali in un Ateneo di confine," *Storia e Società* 47 (1990): 87–127.

113. A. Vinci, "Trieste in Guerra," 75.

114. Macgregor Knox has argued that Mussolini's geopolitical objective to expand East was framed in the early and mid-1920s; M. Knox, "The Fascist Regime, Its Foreign Policy and Its Wars: An 'Anti-Anti-Fascist' Orthodoxy?", *Contemporary European History* 4, 3 (1995): 357, 365.

115. E. Apih, *Italia, fascismo e anti-fascismo*, 219.

116. J. Walston, "History and Memory of the Italian Concentration Camps," *Historical Journal* 40 (1997): 169–83; S. Bon Gherardi, "La politica antisemitica a Trieste negli anni 1940–43," *Qualestoria* 1 (1989): 91–98.

117. Novak, *Trieste 1941–1954*, 57, 58.

118. Vinci, "Il Fascismo nella Venezia Giulia e l'opera di snazionalizzazione delle minoranze," 15.

119. Walston, "History and Memory of the Italian Concentration Camps," 175, emphasis in original. Giacomo Scotti refers to two hundred of these internment camps in Yugoslavia and Italy; G. Scotti, *Bono Taliano: Gli Italiani in Jugoslavia 1941–1943* (Milano: La Pietra, 1977), 89.

120. Walston claims that these figures are comparable with those in the records kept by the Italian army, as is the civilian makeup of the camp populations. Yugoslav sources however claim the figures were twice as high; Walston, "History and Memory of the Italian Concentration Camps," 175.

121. Ibid., 177.

122. Ibid.

123. Ibid., 170. As we will see in the following chapters, during the war and after any criticism of the role of the Italian state and of the military in the war was vulnerable to dismissal as "*filo-slavo*," even by Italian liberal-democrats and socialists.

124. For a useful discussion of the historiography of the impact of German Nazism on Fascism, see N. Zapponi, "Fascism in Italian Historiography, 1986–1993: A Fading National Identity," *Journal of Contemporary History* 29 (1994): 551.

125. See chapter 7.

126. Rusinow, *Italy's Austrian Heritage,* 185; Rusinow argues that in 1936, two years after Salvemini's warning and two years before the racial laws, Slavophobia gained ascendancy in the Italian Foreign Office, and marked "the beginning of Mussolini's sponsorship of revisionism of the 1919 peace settlement."

127. According to Mabel Berezin what distinguished Fascism from liberalism was that Fascism aimed "to recreate the self, to create new identities as citizens of Fascist Italy," particularly by destroying the boundary between the public and private self; M. Berezin, *Making the Fascist Self: The Political Culture of Interwar Italy* (Ithaca: Cornell University Press, 1997), 5, 6.

128. S. Benco, *Trieste* (Firenze: Casa Editrice Nemi, 1932), 8, 11.

129. A. E. Moodie, *The Italo-Yugoslav Boundary. A Study in Political Geography* (London: George Philip & Son, 1945), 162, 163.

130. Ibid.

131. Bandelli, "Per una storia del mito di Roma al confine orientale," 262.

CHAPTER 3. ANTI-FASCISM AND ANTINATIONALISM, 1943–1945

1. "Atlantic Charter," in J. Stone, *The Atlantic Charter: New Worlds for Old* (London: Angus & Robertson, 1943), 240.

2. It only became known as the CLNAI after the liberation of Rome, when it became "the factual leader of resistance in northern Italy," Novak, *Trieste 1941–1954,* 98. In December 1944 the British and American Allies recognized the CLNAI "as the supreme underground authority for northern Italy and the legitimate representative of the Italian government"; Novak, *Trieste 1941–1954,* 99.

3. Rusinow, *Italy's Austrian Heritage,* 277. The Liberation Front's nationalist role in Slovenia made it controversial in Venezia Giulia. Rusinow argues that "[l]ike the Fascists, . . . the [Liberation Front] actively encouraged the polarization of Julian politics into a Slav/Communist or Italian/Fascist antithesis," 278.

4. W. Connor, *The National Question in Marxist-Leninist Theory and Strategy* (Princeton: Princeton University Press, 1984), 147, 155.

5. M. Gombač, "Znanstvene institucije in njihov delez pri mirovnih pogajanjih," *Glasnik: Pariška Mirovna Pogodba, Katalog k razstavi in program mednarodne konference*, 3, 1997, 29, 31.

6. P. Vihar (pseud.), *O Slovenskih Mejah* (Izdala Agitacijsko-propagandistična komisija pri Centralnemu Komitetu Komunistične Partije Slovenije, 1943); See also B. Gombač, "Slovenski intelektualci in Politici v Parizu" (unpublished conference paper).

7. Vihar, *O Slovenskih Mejah*, 12.

8. Novak, *Trieste 1941–1954*, 64. At the same time Slovene intellectuals and members of the middle classes formed a separate clandestine "National Council" later headed by Dr. Jože Ferfolja.

9. See Ibid., 59.

10. Novak argues that "[b]y the summer of 1942 about one hundred Partisans were actually participating in sabotage and approximately one hundred local committees of the Liberation Front existed to spread propaganda and collect food, clothing, medicine, and arms for the Partisan units"; Ibid., 61.

11. Ibid., 64.

12. Duroselle, *Le Conflit de Trieste 1943–1954*, 122.

13. See Novak, *Trieste 1941–1954*, for a discussion of the Istrian region.

14. Tito's newfound legitimacy meant the diminution of the role of the Royalist Chetnik Serbs under Draža Mihajlovic who fought for the reinstitution of the monarchical government that had ruled Yugoslavia in the interwar period and was now acting as a government-in-exile from London.

15. See also "The Yugoslav Frontier," in C. R. S. Harris, *Allied Military Administration of Italy 1943–1945* (London: HMSO, 1957).

16. Cited in Novak, *Trieste 1941–1954*, 123.

17. Ibid., 104. Novak argues that Stalin was sought out as an authority on the respective roles of the Italian and Slovene parties, *Trieste 1941–1954*, 60.

18. Rusinow, *Italy's Austrian Heritage*, 353.

19. Ibid.

20. Cited in N. Troha, "Osvoboditev ali okupacija, narodna osvoboditev ali revolucija—Primorska in Trst v letu 1945," *Slovenija v Letu 1945: Zbornik Referatov* (Zveza Zgodovinskih Društev Slovenije, 1996), 84. See G. Valdevit, *La questione di Trieste 1941–1954. Politica internazionale e contesto locale* (Milano: Franco Angeli, 1987), 63.

21. Troha, "Osvoboditev ali okupacija, narodna osvoboditev ali revolucija," 32.

22. F. Zwitter, "Naš Znanstveni Inštitut," *Slovenski Zbornik 1944* (Ljubljana: Družbena Založba Slovenije, 1945).

23. B. Gombač, "F. Zwitter (1905–1988)," *Glasnik: Pariška Mirovna Pogodba, Katalog k razstavi in program mednarodne konference*, 3, 1997, 39–42.

24. F. Zwitter, "Trst," *Slovenski Zbornik 1944* (Ljubljana: Družbena Založba Slovenije, 1945), 432; Gombač, "Slovenski intelektualci in Politici v Parizu."

25. Zwitter, "Trst," 428. In April 1945 Zwitter took up a position at the Belgrade-based Scientific Institute where border questions for the whole of Yugoslavia were researched, published, and became the basis of the communist Yugoslav leadership's postwar diplomatic negotiations for territory.

26. P. Spriano, *Stalin and the European Communists* (London: Verso, 1985); P. Pallante, *Il PCI e la questione nazionale Friuli Venezia Giulia 1941–1945* (Udine: DelBianco, 1980), 178; P. Sema and C. Bibalo, *Cronaca sindacale triestina 1943–1978* (Roma: Editrice Sindacale Italiana, 1981).

27. See for example, the collection of essays in *Comunista a Trieste: Un 'identità difficile* (Roma: Riuniti, 1983).

28. Spriano, *Stalin and the European Communists*, 189.

29. Istituto regionale per la storia del movimento di liberazione nel Friuli Venezia Giulia (hereafter ISMLVG): "Intervista con la triestina Licia Chersovani 1981," interviewer Franco Giraldi, Busta 101 *Cominform, Storia del PC del TLT*.

30. Interview with Ljubo Strunja, 25 July 1990, Mrše, Slovenia.

31. A. Volk, "Una realtà multiforme. Omogeneità e disomogeneità nella memoria degli sloveni di Trieste," in Verginella et al., *Storia e memoria degli sloveni del Litorale*, 49–121, 116.

32. Ibid., 98. Volk uses pseudonyms for all his interviewees.

33. Ibid.

34. M. Verginella, "I vincitori sconfitti. Testimonianze slovene sul movimento di liberazione a Trieste," in M. Verginella et al., *Storia e memoria degli sloveni del Litorale*, 20.

35. Volk, "Una realtà multiforme," 114.

36. Ibid., 116.

37. Ibid., 115.

38. A. T. Iaccheo, *Donne Armate: Resistenza e terrorismo. Testimoni dalla Storia* (Milano: Mursia, 1994), 59.

39. In her history of the Italian women's movement, Camilla Ravera describes the resistance as a "baptism by fire" for women, and women's "collective and anonymous" contribution to the second Risorgimento and the liberation of *patria*, C. Ravera, *Breve storia del movimento femminile in Italia* (Roma: Riuniti, 1978), 149. See also A. Bravo and A. M. Bruzzone, *In Guerra senza armi: Storie di donne. 1940–1945* (Roma: Laterza, 1995), and P. Gabrielli, "La solidarietà tra

pratica politica e vita quotidiana nell'esperienza delle donne comuniste," *Rivista di storia contemporanea* 22, 1 (1993): 34–56.

40. B. Jančar-Webster, *Women and Revolution in Yugoslavia 1941–1945* (Denver: Arden Press, 1990). The women Jancar-Webster interviewed in the 1980s for her study all had, she argues, a "nationalist" bias in their hopes for the revolution and in their reflections of the relative contributions of their "nations" to the Yugoslav revolution, 16.

41. Volk, "Una realtà multiforme," 112.

42. Z. Vrsčaj-Holly, "Slovenska Žena in Osvobodilni Boj," *Slovenski Zbornik 1944* (Ljubljana: Državna Založba Slovenije, 1945), 249.

43. ISMLVG: PCI document, AIVG: 82.fasc.11.

44. Biographical information can be found in: Slovene National Library, Trieste [hereafter SNL]: AntiFašistične Ženske [AFZ] files, "Mestni Odbor, AFZ, 25 July 1945 to Mestni Odbor UAIS," "Okrožni in Okrajni Odbori ASIZZ za Trž. Okrožje," and "Okrožni Odbor ASIZZ za Goriško"; and Box SIAU/UAIS 2, "Dati personali (UAIS cittadino)."

45. Volk, "Una realtà multiforme," 113.

46. SNL: Box SIAU/UAIS 2, "Attività,' dell'UDAIS dal 1946," 24 March 1948.

47. M. Isenghi, cited in R. Bosworth, *Explaining Auschwitz and Hiroshima* (London: Routledge, 1994), 128.

48. "Il problema nazionale della Venezia Giulia orientamenti repubblicani e del Partito d'Azione," July 1943, Duroselle, *Le Conflit de Trieste*, Annexe 1, 183.

49. ISMLVG: Archivio del Indice Venezia Giulia [AIVG], XLVII/v, Letter to Enzo Collotti dated 14/10/54, "Testimonianza sul Partito d'Azione di Trieste."

50. See chapter 6 for postwar examples of these same ideas.

51. According to Dennison Rusinow, Nazi occupation was "exercised by former Austrians who appeared to be Habsburg officials disguised in Nazi uniforms. The clock was turned back in policy as well as in personnel, pre-1914 answers to still unsolved questions were reapplied as though nothing had changed in twenty-five years"; Rusinow, *Italy's Austrian Heritage*, 4.

52. Novak, *Trieste 1941–1954*, 86–87.

53. ISMLVG: AIVG, 4th/311 XII.869, "Testimonianza del prof. G. Gaeta sull'incontro fra italiani e sloveni a Milano nel 1944," s.d.

54. ISMLVG: AIVG: XXX/2277, "Rapporti C. Schiffrer al PSI: Relazione sul movimento di resistenza italiana a Trieste," 7.

55. F. Verani, "A vent'anni dalla scomparsa di Carlo Schiffrer, presidente dell'Istituto: La sua lezione culturale e politica," *Qualestoria* 2–3 (1989): 223.

56. Ibid., 224.

57. Ibid., 227. The second edition of *Le origini dell'irredentismo* was published in 1978 (DelBianco).

58. E. Apih, "Premessa," *Le origini dell'irredentismo triestino 1813–1860* (DelBianco, 1978), 23. Apih was Schiffrer's student.

59. Apih, *Italia, fascismo e anti-fascismo*, 14.

60. Cf. Todorova, *Imagining the Balkans*, 66.

61. Verani, "A vent'anni dalla scomparsa di Carlo Schiffrer," 227; "Testimonianza del prof. G. Gaeta sull'incontro fra italiani e sloveni a Milano nel 1944." The work that Schiffrer undertook at this time was published in 1946 as an essay and map on the Italo-Yugoslav border (see chapter 5).

62. C. Schiffrer, "La Venezia Giulia. Saggio di una carta dei limiti nazionali italo-jugoslavi," in F. Verani (ed.), *La Questione etnica ai confini orientali d'Italia* (Trieste: Italo Svevo, 1990), 24.

63. Ibid., 77.

64. Ibid., 48.

65. Ibid., 21.

66. Schiffrer reinforced the primacy of language as the determinant of identity in an article entitled "Lingua, cultura e nazionalità italiana nell'Istria e nell'Adriatico orientale," 1956, in Verani (ed.), *La Questione etnica ai confini orientali d'Italia*, 3.

67. Schiffrer, "La Venezia Giulia," 23

68. Ibid., 84.

69. Ibid., 8.

70. ISMLVG: AIVG, IV/311, "Testimonianza di Carlo Schiffrer sulle trattative fra il Comitato di Liberazione Nazionale e l'Osvobodilna Fronta a Trieste dell'Aprile 1945," Stralcio da appunti personali *(s.d.)*.

71. Further attempts at negotiation foundered on Schiffrer's proposal that in areas administered by this mixed committee, flags of both nations would fly in all public places, except on the town halls in Italian cities, where only the Italian flag would be displayed. Novak, *Trieste 1941–1954*, 142.

72. "Testimonianza di Carlo Schiffrer," 4.

73. Ibid., 11.

74. Ibid., 11.

75. E. Collotti, "The Italian Politics of Repression in the Balkans," *In Memory* conference, Arezzo 1994, cited in A. Bravo and A. M. Bruzzone, *In guerra senza armi: Storie di donne* (Roma: Laterza, 1995), 211.

76. G. Secoli, *Il Terzo cinquantennio della 'Minerva' 1910–1960* (Trieste: La società di Minerva, 1965), 37.

77. Novak, *Trieste 1941–1954*, 141. When, in April 1945, Schiffrer was arrested by German forces for his clandestine activities, his old school friend, Pagnini, was able to engineer his release.

78. Ibid.,73.

79. ISMLVG: AIVG: XV/1086, prot.E/1/343, "Lettera di C. Pagnini al governo di Roma," 4/5/45. In the postwar Pagnini and Coceani successfully defended themselves in AMG epuration trials by claiming that they had collaborated in order to protect the *italianità* of Trieste. See C. Vetter, "La Magistratura," *Nazionalismo e neofascismo nella lotta politica al confine orientale 1945–75* (ISMLVG, n.d.), 165; and ISMLVG, AIVG, VIII, Fascicolo Processuale Coceani, "Sentenza Bruno Coceani," Corte Straordinario d'Assize, Trieste 22/10/45.

80. Schiffrer was the branch secretary of the Venezia Giulia Socialist Party.

81. Schiffrer, "Testimonianza di Carlo Schiffrer."

82. See Vetter, "La Magistratura."

83. D. Ward, *Anti-fascisms: Cultural Politics in Italy, 1943–46, Benedetto Croce and the Liberals, Carlo Levi and the Actionists* (New Jersey: Associated University Presses, 1996), 175.

84. Ibid., chapter 3; See also Bosworth, *The Italian Dictatorship*, 86.

85. Salvatorelli and Mira, *Storia d'Italia nel periodo Fascista, vol. 2*, 596.

86. Campbell, *Writing Security*, 55.

CHAPTER 4. IDENTITY AND REVOLUTION, MAY–JUNE 1945

1. Novak, *Trieste 1941–1954*, 123–25.

2. The collaborationist forces included the Slovene National Guard, the Littoral National Guard, Serbian Volunteer Corps and Serbian Chetniks, Italian Republican Army, Trieste's Guardia Civica.

3. E. Maserati, *L'Occupazione jugoslava di Trieste (maggio-giugno 1945)* (Udine: DelBianco, 1963), 58.

4. Novak has a whole section entitled "Who liberated Trieste?" *Trieste 1941–1945*, 156–60.

5. See chapter 7, and G. Sluga, "Italian national identity, memory, and Fascism," in R. Bosworth and P. Dogliani, *Italian Fascism: Memory, History, and Representation* (London: Routledge, 1998).

6. Dennison Rusinow, for example, refers to the intensity of anti-Fascist activity in the region as part of the "Slav Resistance," as irredentist in its aims, and as threatening to Italo-Yugoslav relations; Rusinow, *Italy's Austrian Heritage*, 204.

7. Novak, *Trieste 1941–1945*, 156.

8. UAIS, *Trieste nella lotta per la democrazia* (Trieste: n. p., 1945), 1, 6, 95; and M. Gombač, "Autonomia e decentramento della politica jugoslava alla fine del secondo conflitto mondiale. Un caso specifico: il Comitato regionale di liberazione nazionale per il Litorale sloveno e Trieste," *Annales* 8 (1996): 91.

9. *Svečana predaja civilne oblast: Izvršnemu odboru mesta Trsta. Delovna konferenca vojaškega in civilnega predstavništva mesta Trsta* (Trst: POOF, 1945), 9. The relationship between the Regional and Trieste Council authorities, between Trieste, Slovenia, and the rest of Yugoslavia, was quite confused. Trieste was to be autonomous, but as a city it played a central role in the Primorje area administratively, economically, and culturally; the Primorje being part of Slovenia, another republic, so a republic within a republic. Maserati also has difficulty untangling the threads of authority, see Maserati, *L'Occupazione jugoslava di Trieste*, 62ff. Novak argues that the Liberation Council was executing orders from the Slovene and Yugoslav Communist Parties' Central Committees; Novak, *Trieste 1941–1945*, 179.

10. See N. Troha, "Osvoboditev ali okupacija, narodna osvoboditev ali revolucija," 84; and Novak, *Trieste 1941–1945*, 259.

11. See Maserati, *L'occupazione jugoslava di Trieste*, 97ff.

12. J. Pirjevec, "Gli sloveni a Trieste: 1945–1947," in *Trieste 1941–1947* (Trieste: Dedolibri, 1991), 127.

13. M. Pacor, *Confine orientale. Questione nazionale e resistenza nel Friuli Venezia Giula* (Feltrinelli, 1964), 328. See also Volk, "Una realtà multiforme. Omogeneità e disomogeneità nella memoria degli sloveni di Trieste," 82.

14. Interview with Ljubo Strunja, 25 July 1990, Mrše, Slovenia. Ljubo's account is echoed in the oral histories analyzed by M. Verginella and A. Volk in Verginella et al., *Storia e memoria degli sloveni del Litorale*.

15. ISMLVG: AIVG, Busta XXV/2002, "Primo manifesto ai Triestini del Comitato Esecutivo Antifascista Italo-Sloveno di Trieste."

16. Maserati, *L'occupazione jugoslava di Trieste*, 98.

17. These processes were similar to the epuration that took place under communist CLN committees in Italy: from organized factory committees, to executions authorized by summary judgments. Harris, *Allied Military Administration of Italy 1943–1945*, 301.

18. Maserati, *L'Occupazione jugoslava di Trieste*, 74.

19. Institute for National Questions, Ljubljana, (hereafter INV): "Problemi ki se nanašajo na sodiščečasti," Seja Osvobodilna Svet 26/5/45 (2), 53. There was also a separate category for those referred to

as "arrested lately," and who had to be released because of the threat to the council's credibility.

20. The People's Defense force was under the direct control of the Liberation Council's Department of Interior Affairs.

21. PRO: FO371 [Foreign Office: General Correspondence After 1906 Political], FO371/48953, "Yugoslav Atrocities," Investigating Committee Venezia Giulia, Report Pt. 2, 27/9/45.

22. PRO: FO371/48953, "Yugoslav Atrocities," and "G-5, Fifth Army Rpt for Apr 45, ACC files, 10000/109/436," in H. L. Coles and A. K. Weinberg, *United States Army in World War II, Special Studies, Civil Affairs: Soldiers become Governors* (U. S. Department of the Army, 1964), 564. In Bologna in early June "the number of crimes of violence committed both in the town and in the country continued to be appallingly high, and increased somewhat after the handing over of Emilia to Italian Government administration at the end of July"; Harris, *Allied Military Administration of Italy*, 300.

23. Roberto also stated that confronted with the Fascist who killed his father, or betrayed a member of his family to the Nazis he would have felt legitimated in killing them: "'Quella era ancora guerra, ragazzi miei. No so. Vedi, che uccide tuo fratello e tu, cosa, lo . . . ? Dove lo metti? Dici <No, ti porto in tribunale>, o cosa? Gli spari'"; Volk, "Una realtà multiforme," 111.

24. Volk, "Una realtà multiforme," 111.

25. See PRO: FO371/48953, Broad, "Central Mediterranean to FO," 11/9/45; PRO: FO371/48836, Basovizza Incident 9/8/45; See also PRO: FO371/59359, Sullivan, "Situation Summary 9–15 August," 24/8/46.

26. For further historiographical discussion of the extent of deportations see Troha, "Osvoboditev ali okupacija."

27. G. Cox, *The Road to Trieste* (London: Heinemann, 1947), 231. Novak has argued that a large number of those arrested were Slovenes, and of the deported only two-fifths came from Venezia Giulia; *Trieste 1941–1954*, 180.

28. See N. Troha, "Fra liquidazione del passato e costruzione del futuro. Le foibe e l'occupazione della Venezia Giulia," in G. Valdevit (ed.), *Foibe. Il peso del passato, Venezia Giulia 1943–1945* (Venezia: Marsilio, 1997), 82–86.

29. On 31 July 1945, *The Times* carried a story from Rome entitled "*Foiba* di Basovizza" which stated that the rumors were false, but that Tito's troops had carried off at least 3,000 Italians when they withdrew from Trieste and the western part of Venezia Giulia.

30. For an illuminating survey of historical accounts of these disappearances see G. Fogar, "Venezia Giulia 1943–1945: Problemi e

situazioni," in *Trieste 1941–1947* (Trieste: Edizioni Dedolibri, 1991), 93–124.

31. Novak, *Trieste 1941–1945*, 188.

32. ISMLVG: AIVG, Busta XXVI/2102, Allegato D, "Lettere e memoriali del CLN di Trieste per il commando militare alleato, 11/5–15/6/45."

33. These cultural historical claims also provided Croce with the basis of his argument for Italian sovereignty in the Eliseo speech at Rome in 1944; see Ward, *Anti-fascisms*, 175ff.

34. Allegato D, "Lettere e memoriali del CLN di Trieste," 2–3.

35. Troha, "Osvoboditev ali okupacija," 87.

36. Allegato D, "Lettere e memoriali del CLN di Trieste per il commando militare alleato," 3.

37. PRO: WO204 (War of 1939 to 1945, Military Headquarters Papers, Allied Force Headquarters) WO204/3182, Major F. E. Weidman, "Informal Report based on visit to Trieste 10–13 May," Secret, Air Corps for Brigadier General. Chas. M. Spofford, the Assistant Chief of Staff, Allied Forces HQ G-5 Section APO 512, 14 May 1945.

38. The written use of the slavic "J" for "Y" is quite common in these early documents; see "Informal Report based on visit to Trieste 10–13 May," Secret, 14 May 1945; Similarly: PRO: WO204/913, "TRIESTE is virtually under a military dictatorship a reign of tyranny is operating against the Italian community, and the majority of the civil population is very hungry"; AGWAR for Combined Chiefs of Staff, AMSSO for British Chiefs of Staff, Signed Alexander, Auth. Robert T. Hanley Major, "Report from Chief of Staff," TOP secret For Action, 17/5/45.

39. PRO: WO204/913, For RESMIN from SMITH, From MAIN XIII Corps to AFHQ, Ref 1–12, TOP Secret, 28/5/45.

40. UAIS, *Trieste nella lotta per la democrazia*, 97. At an everyday level the new administration faced the problems of practical survival in a war-ravaged Trieste. There were difficulties with transport, bringing supplies to Trieste, as well as courier services linking Trieste to the Slovene capital, Ljubljana, a source of financial aid; Arhiv Republike Slovenije, Ljubljana (hereafter AS), PNOO 1/i, PNOO Trst, "Zapisnik seje preds. PNOO," 16/5/45. The PNOO established fourteen departments or ministries to deal with the situation regionally. These departments included the following divisions: industry, commerce and supplies, economics, agriculture, forestry, veterinary, finance, transport, navigation, education, construction, health, social welfare, justice, internal affairs, physical education and sport. Three floors in the People's House *(Casa del Popolo/Ljudski Dom)* on the port foreshore housed this

administration; AS:237/ii, PNOO-ZVU, Propaganda Komisija, "Seznam sob in številke telefon 'Ljudskega doma,' Mestni Komitet Trst," 16/5/45. All German and collaborators' goods and unoccupied apartments had been requisitioned, programs for the protection of forests created, and Fascist societies dissolved; AS:77/iii, PNOO-ZVU, ["Report Commission for the Administration of National Property], KUNI [Komisija za Upravo Narodno Imovine]" 559/45, 1945. Tito's new Yugoslavia was to provide raw products, refining, and the loans needed for industrial regeneration; AS:2/iii, PNOO-ZVU, Tajništvo PNOO, "[Letter to the Slovene Finance Minister], Ljubljana, 13/5/45." The finance department had opened up credit institutions and insurance offices. The social welfare department had responsibility for repatriating and rehabilitating soldiers and the politically persecuted, for providing information about the missing, allocating and paying pensions, and providing food. Public soup kitchens were set up distributing a total of 11,000 meals daily of which 1,500 were free, the remainder subsidized; UAIS, *Trieste nella lotta per la democrazia*, 101, and PRO: WO204/6387, HQ 55 (Army) Area Report No. 2, "Report on Conditions in Trieste," 17–23 May 1945, Secret Trieste.

    41. "Memo, Dunlop, RC, Venezia Rgn for Exec Cmsv, AC, 13 May 45, ACC files, 10000/109/312," cited in Coles and Weinberg, *US Army in WW II*, 599.

    42. Amongst the "public manifestoes" that caught Brigadier Eve's eye was one in particular, issued by the Italian Communist Party. He reported that it "laid great stress on the fraternity between the Italian and Jugoslav peoples and acclaimed an autonomous Trieste within the framework of a federated Jugoslavia."

    43. PRO: WO204/6387, Psychological Warfare Branch Reports, Secret D Section Trieste, Trieste 2–16 May 1945, 252.

    44. Novak, *Trieste 1941–1945*, 184.

    45. AS:237/ii, PNOO-ZVU, "Kratko poročilo o Propaganda delu v Trstu," (n.d.).

    46. AS:53: Osvobodilini Svet za Trst Sejni Zapisniki 1945, "Seja Osvobodilnega Svet za Trst," 17/5/45.

    47. Ibid. Regent repeated the same theme at a much later meeting, AS:53, "Seja Osvobodilnega Svet za Trst," 29/5/45: "We wanted to have a Council which was not just made up of workers, but also of experts from all managements. We should not be able to be reproached for not representing the workers on our council. We want to broaden our council with Italians, so that tomorrow no one could say, as they do, that in the Trieste council there only sit communists and Slovenes."

48. UAIS, *Trieste nella lotta per la democrazia,* 93ff; Pacor, *Confine orientale,* 333 cf. Maserati, *L'occupazione jugoslava di Trieste,* 66ff, published under the auspices of the ISMLVG. Maserati either gets the dates wrong, or there is a typographical error; see also, Sema and Bibalo, *Cronaca sindacale triestina 1943–1978,* 52.

49. In the 1960s, the historian Ennio Maserati argued that the presence of British, American, and Soviet military representatives was a blatant betrayal of Triestines; Maserati, *L'occupazione jugoslava di Trieste,* 68–69.

50. *Il Nostro Avvenire,* 18/5/45, as cited in Council of Liberation of Trieste, *The Activity of the Council of Liberation of Trieste (from May 17 to Sep 21 1945) with a short historical introduction* (n. p., 1945, English Edition), appendix, 55.

51. Biographical details from PRO: FO371/48838, "Trial of Giorgio Jaksetich," 13/8/45, Despatch No. 345, British Embassy Rome.

52. Jaksetich later published an anthology of interviews with ex-Garibaldini entitled *La Brigata Fratelli Fontanot: Partigiani Italiani in Slovenia* (Milano: La Pietra, 1982).

53. *Il Nostro Avvenire,* 18 maggio 1945, Allegato I, cited in UAIS, *Trieste nella lotta per la democrazia,* 207–208.

54. UAIS, *Trieste nella lotta per la democrazia,* 208.

55. Council of Liberation of Trieste, *The Activity of the Council of Liberation of Trieste,* 53–55.

56. UAIS, *Trieste nella lotta per la democrazia,* 204.

57. Ibid., 6.

58. PRO: WO204/6387, "Report on conditions in Trieste 17–23 May copy of HQ 55 (Army) Area Report No. 2."

59. Ursic, 17/5/45, cited in UAIS, *Trieste nella lotta per la democrazia,* 202.

60. Troha has argued that even for Slovenes Trieste remained an Italian stronghold, see Troha, "Osvoboditev ali okupacija," 85.

61. ISMLVG: AIVG, XXX/2294, "Velina relativa a una seduta della direzione dell'UAIS e ragguagli politici riguardante gli impiegati del Lloyd redatti dall'UAIS," 17/5/45.

62. There is also evidence of local Jewish groups recognizing the legitimacy of the government and appealing to them for help with the restitution of their rights and property; AS:53, "Seja Osvobodilnega Svet za Trst," 26/5/45, Jewish Council memo.

63. ISMLVG: AIVG, XXX/2286 (2), "Dal giorno dell'occupazione jugoslava," n.n., n.d., 9.

64. These individuals were allowed to carry identification cards that validated their Austrian citizenship; PRO: WO204/3182, B. Smith

Major, Further Memo 7/6/45 and PRO: WO204/913, Main XIII Corps to AFHQ 1-912, 26/5/45.

65. UAIS, *Trieste nella lotta per la democrazia*, 111.

66. SNL: Anti-Fašistične Ženske [AFZ] files, Mestni Odbor, Trst, 18 May 1945.

67. The organization changed its structure and name between 1945 and 1948.

68. *Il Lavoratore*, 6 August 1945.

69. SNL: AFZ files, 1946 report on women's conference, March, n.d..

70. UAIS, *Trieste nella lotta per la democrazia*, 92.

71. Interview with Mira (Karolina Rijavec), Slovene Cultural Centre, Trieste, 10 Sept. 89.

72. UAIS, *Trieste nella lotta per la democrazia*, 94.

73. Harris, *Allied Administration of Italy 1943–1945*, 343.

74. PRO: WO204/6387, "Report on conditions in Trieste 17–23 May Copy of HQ 55 (Army) Area Report No. 2."

75. PRO: WO204/913, Action RESMIN AFHQ INFO GSI, 8th Army, From Main XIII Corps from Smith, 19/5/45, cf. that same day Smith believed that relations "between Partisans and Allied troops" were congenial enough for him to consider arranging a football match, PRO: WO204/913, 8th Army AFHQ, From Rear MacMis, to XIII Corps, "Info 15th Army Group," 20/5/45. Even though he believed the Allied soldiers themselves undoubtedly preferred the Italians for their superior standard of living and charm, relations with the Yugoslavs were NOT, Smith emphasized, bad; PRO: WO204/913, For RESMIN from SMITH, From Main XIII Corps to AFHQ, Ref 1–12, TOP Secret, 28/5/45.

76. PRO: WO204/913, "Report from Chief of Staff," 17/5/45.

77. Coles and Weinberg, *United States Army in World War II*, 600.

78. PRO: WO204/9789, Maj. J. A. Quayle for Brigadier Exec Commission, Copy of HQAMG 8th Army Report on Situation in Venezia Giulia up to 23.59 hours 3 May 45, Top Secret, Ref 152/E, 6/5/45; See also a similar report PRO: WO204/3179, "From HQ Alcom to AFHQ G-5 Section, British Resmin & US Polad, Top Secret," 6 May 1945.

79. PRO: WO204/3182, Major F. E. Weidman, "Informal Report based on visit to Trieste 10–13 May," Secret, Air Corps for Brigadier General Chas. M. Spofford, the Assistant Chief of Staff, Allied Forces HQ G-5 Section APO 512, 14 May 1945; Harris, *Allied Administration of Italy*, 342.

80. AS:53, "Seja Skupščine Osvobodilne Svet," 29/5/45.

81. There was criticism against partisan patrols making random arrests of people and the arbitrary requisitions of cars and cows; AS:29/iii, Upravno Politične Komisije pri PNOO, "Javni Tožilec za mesto Trst M2/45 v Javnemu Tožilcu za Slovensko Primorje," Izredno Poročilo, Trst, 29/5/45.

82. AS:29/iii, "Javni Tožilec za mesto Trst." Peterin was also Professor in International Law and the History of International Relations at the University of Ljubljana; J. B. Duroselle, *Le Conflit de Trieste 1943–1954* (Bruxelles: l'Institut de Sociologie de l'Université libre de Bruxelles, 1966), 14.

83. The AMG were also competing in dealing with the food shortages, the black market, and labor regulations; AS:53, "Seja Osvobodilnega Svet za Trst," 17/5/45.

84. AS:53, "Seja Osvobodilnega Svet za Trst," 21/5/45. The Allied military in Trieste assumed the authority to hear complaints about these arrests made by the local population; AS:53, "Seja Osvobodilnega Svet za Trst," 26/5/45.

85. AS:53, "Seja Osvobodilnega Svet za Trst," 25/5/45.

86. G. Fogar, *Sotto l'occupazione nazista nelle provincie orientali* (Udine: DelBianco, 1968), 61–63.

87. Maserati, *L'occupazione jugoslava di Trieste*, 64–65.

88. AS:53, "Seja Osvobodilnega Svet za Trst," 3/6/45.

89. AS:73/i, Komanda II Sektorja Narodne Milice—Odsek za javni red, Trst, 1/6/45: "Predmet, navodilo za delo," NZ II Sektor.

90. AS:13/i, "Verbale della seduta," 8/6/45, Casa del Popolo, 5–6.

91. D. DeCastro, "Preface," in R. Pupo (ed.), *Trieste diary maggio-giugno 1945* (Gorizia: Editrice Goriziana, 1990), 15.

92. S. Sprigge, "Trieste Diary," October 1945, *The World Today*, Chatham House Review, Royal Institute of International Affairs (Vol. 1, July–December 1945, new series), 159. Sprigge's husband, Cecil, had published *The Development of Modern Italy* (London: Duckworth, 1943).

93. Sprigge, "Trieste Diary," 160.

94. Ibid., 162.

95. Ibid., 160–61.

96. Ibid., 161.

97. Ibid.

98. Ibid.,160. In October of the same year, Sprigge attended the 14th Annual Forum on Current Problems in New York at which she stressed the idea of creating an international region out of Trieste, which would service Central Europe.

99. From 1942 until 1944 Cox had been *Chargé d'Affaires* for the New Zealand Legation to Washington, and then in October 1944 he was

a major with the 2nd New Zealand Division, *Documents relating to New Zealand's Participation in the Second World War 1939–1945 Vol II* (Wellington: N.Z. Dept of Internal Affairs, 1951), 410. *The Road to Trieste* was reissued as *The Race for Trieste* in 1977.

100. Cox, *The Road to Trieste*, 210.

101. Ibid., 231–32

102. Ibid.

103. Ibid., 233.

104. Ibid., 236.

105. Ibid., 231.

106. Ibid., 177.

107. Ibid., 192.

108. Ibid., 236.

109. Ibid., 234–36.

110. Ibid., 234.

111. *28 (Maori) Battalion* (Wellington: War History Branch, Dept of Internal Affairs, 1956), 480.

112. *The Tiger Triumphs: The Story of Three Great Divisions in India* (HMSO for India, 1946), 210–11.

113. PRO: FO371/48953, Investigating Committee Venezia Giulia, Report Pt. 2, "Yugoslav Atrocities," 27/9/45.

114. SNL: AFZ files, Mestni Odbor, Report, 15/7/45.

CHAPTER 5. GENDER, ETHNICITY, AND THE IRON CURTAIN, 1945–1948

1. Churchill coined this image of the iron curtain in his famous 1946 Westminster College speech.

2. D. Campbell, "Violent Performances: Identity, Sovereignty, Responsibility," in Y. Lapid and F. Kratochwil, *The Return of Culture and Identity in IR Theory* (Boulder: Lynne Rienner, 1996), 163.

3. R. Rabel, *Between East and West: Trieste, The United States, and the Cold War, 1941–1954* (Durham, N.C.: Duke University Press, 1988), ix.

4. "They say, that the boundaries (meje) do not only lie between two peoples/nations (narodoma), but between two worlds and that they are defending western culture on this boundary. Thus it is evident that the Italian imperialists are offering themselves to the antisoviet avantguard and on this basis are calculating on the support of the western world over the question of our boundaries. The problem of these boundaries has become a general European political question and it

will have to be resolved in such a manner that it will not be possible to have major discussions regarding this question," cited in Troha, "Osvoboditev ali okupacija, narodna osvoboditev ali revolucija," 77. See also Valdevit, *La questione di Trieste 1941–1954*, 63; and on the PCI and national question Pallante, *Il PCI e la questione nazionale Friuli Venezia Giulia 1941–1945*, 178.

    5. Wolff, *Inventing Eastern Europe*, 371. For a theoretical discussion of the reproduction and transformation of identities in the context of international relations, see A. Wendt, "Identity and Structural Change in International Politics," in Lapid and Kratochwil, *The Return of Culture and Identity in IR Theory*, 62.

    6. Harris, *Allied Military Administration of Italy 1943–1945*, 379.

    7. *AMG Gazette* 1, 15 Sept 1945.

    8. See chapter 4.

    9. Proclamation No. 1, Pt. II, Article iv, 2, *AMG Gazette* 1, 15 Sept 1945.

    10. Article v, 30, *AMG Gazette* 1, 15 Sept 1945.

    11. A. Bowman, *Zones of Strain* (Hoover Press Publication, Stanford, 1982), 66. Bowman argues that Monfort was replaced because he could not get on with the British.

    12. General Order No. 11, Sec. 11, 11/8/45, *AMG Gazette* 1, 15 Sept 1945.

    13. Bowman, *Zones of Strain*, 96.

    14. General Order No. 11, 11/8/45, *AMG Gazette* 1, 15 Sept 1945.

    15. Bowman, *Zones of Strain*, 96.

    16. *Nazionalismo e neofascismo nella lotta politica al confine orientale 1945–1975* (ISMLVG, n.d.), 390. The Allied Official Assistant for Slovene schools in Zone A for example was formerly an information officer for the pro-Nazi Slovene Home Guard who had escaped a death penalty handed down in Tito's courts.

    17. Novak, *Trieste 1941–1954*, 239.

    18. Novak, *Trieste 1941–1954*, 238–39.

    19. PRO: WO204/10989, HQ AMG meeting 12/5/47, "Two general court trials (agenda point 10)." The eighteen-year-old boy received a sentence of twenty-one years imprisonment.

    20. Novak, *Trieste 1941–1954*, 239.

    21. Article 4 stated that "orders will be issued . . . to annul, amend or render inoperative any law in force in the Territory . . . which affects prejudicially any member of the United Nations or the nationals thereof and any law which discriminates against any persons on the basis of race, colour or creed."; cited in PRO: FO371/107425, WE1371/4, Cheetham to Wilson, 13/2/53.

22. Proclamation 6, Article iv, *AMG Gazette* 1, 15 Sept 1945.

23. The AMG also established an alternative union, the Camera del Lavoro.

24. Sullivan explained to the British Foreign Office that the AMG had an obligation to maintain order and security. Its best course was "not to apologise for deviations from normal democratic practice but to affirm our right as a military government to meet subversive activity with effective counter measures"; PRO: FO371/72509, R9230/1013/70, Sullivan, "Legal position of AMG with regard to trial of citizens of Trieste," 6/8/48. Sullivan, later Sir William Sullivan, had served as Acting Consul at Trieste in 1939, and was attached to the U.K. delegation to the Paris Peace Conference and Council of Foreign Ministers in New York, 1946. He remained British Political Adviser to Trieste until 1950, *Who Was Who*, vol. vii, 1971–1980, 769.

25. PRO: FO371/72582, R5607/44/70, Sullivan to Wallinger, "Increased Participation of the Triestini in Local Government," 30/4/48. He defended the AMG's stance against bilingualism in Trieste (despite the 1947 Peace Treaty provisions for both Slovene and Italian as official languages) by citing Italian legislation in force that favored Italian citizens giving them exclusive rights to certain political or legal positions. This was not seen as amounting to discrimination; see PRO: FO371/107426, WE1822/3, Polad to Cheetham, 29/12/53.

26. PRO: WO204/6400, Psychological Warfare Reports, Report No. 14, 17/10/45, "Trieste AIS D Section Secret Report on Conditions in Trieste and the surrounding district."

27. See the "Calendar" or incidents recorded in *Nazionalismo e neofascimo*, 389ff.

28. PRO: FO371/59350, R10465/3/92 "Situation Summary," 28 June to 4 July, Mr. Sullivan 5/7/46.

29. Smith added, "the pro-Yugoslav Press had called upon the Triestini to welcome the Allies"; PRO: WO204/2594, Intelligence and Political Reports, AFHQ Message Center incoming for G-5, 15/6/45, Main XIII Corps Top Secret.

30. PRO: WO204/2329, AMG Directives Venezia Giulia, Director PWB AFHQ, "Central Directive for Venezia Giulia," 2/10/45. The PWB later became the Allied Information Services [AIS].

31. PRO: WO204/2329, "Central Directive for Venezia Giulia," No. 17, 16/8/45.

32. PRO: WO204/2329, "Central Directive for Venezia Giulia," No. 18, 16/8/45.

33. See Coles and Weinberg, *United States Army in World War II*, 157–87.

34. PRO: WO204/2329, "Allied impartiality in Venezia Giulia," Central Directive for Venezia Giulia, No. 3, 2; "Projection of Great Britain and United States," Central Directive for Venezia Giulia, No. 8, 4.

35. E. Wilson, *Europe without Baedeker* (London: Hogarth Press, 1986, 1st ed. 1966), ch.7.

36. B. Alpers, *Love and Politics in Wartime: Letters to my Wife 1943–45* (University of Illinois, 1992), preface, xxi.

37. Cox, *The Road to Trieste*, 149. Allied policy directed their advancing military forces that they were to keep anti-Fascist units well under control and to disband them once the work of liberation had been done.

38. Interview with John Rosselli, 10 June 1989, at Brighton, Sussex.

39. This idea may have been anathema to the formative impulses of the new anti-Fascist Italian republic, but it was emphatically asserted by the University of Trieste's rector. Between 1947 and 1951 the rector challenged AMG sovereignty on the grounds that the university was a site where Italian sovereignty had been uninterrupted. By proposing a thesis on the uninterrupted legal sovereignty of the Italian nation-state in Trieste, Cammarata had endangered the legal armor that protected and defined the AMG presence in Trieste as that of trustee rather than occupier; See M. E. Viora, "L'università degli studi di trieste," *Cenni storici* (Istituto di Storia Medioevale e Moderna, No. 3, 1958), and Valdevit, *La Questione di Trieste*, 238.

40. AS:77/ii, Bevk and Robertson, "Trst 7/9/45."

41. "Central Directive for Venezia Giulia" No. 22, 5/10/45, WO:204/2329, PRO; Valdevit, *La Questione di Trieste*, 135–36. Trieste University was to be approached as a vehicle that could assist the development of closer relationships between the AMG and the pro-Italian groups.

42. See "Min of SCAO's Mtg at Hq AMG, XIII Corps, 28 Jul 45, ACC files, 10000/109/320," in Coles and Weinberg, *United States Army in World War II*, 608.

43. "Central Directive for Venezia Giulia," No. 22.

44. AS:53, "Armstrong discussion with Professor Ferlan, educational representative of the PNOO," 26/6/45.

45. PRO: WO204/6399, "Report No. 4," 5/8/45, Trieste AIS D Section Secret Report, Pt. 1.

46. Ibid., 2.

47. Giuseppe Pogassi was the UAIS president and Franc Štoka its secretary.

48. PRO: WO204/6387, "Situation in Venezia Giulia," 12/8/45, Allied observer present in hall. Appendix 1 to Report No. 6, Trieste AIS D Section Secret Report, 22/8/45.

49. See also New Zealand National Archives: Section 2 NZEF Eyewitness account. Recorder: 280346 Sjt Corrie, RJ; Place: Genigallia; 10 June 45.

50. PRO: FO371/48949, "Report on Venezia Guilia communicated by Local Govt Sub Commission Allied Commission," 20/9/45, R18660/14935/92.

51. In May 1946, Graham Bower of the Foreign Office Research Department passed through Trieste and reported back to the Foreign Office his impression that, at most, only 10 percent of Trieste's industrial workers were of "Slavic" origin, on the basis that few spoke Slav or thought of themselves as Slav; "Report for end May 1946 by Mr. Graham Bower a member of Research Department who was lent to the Austrian Control Commission and is now on leave in Italy," PRO: FO371/59347, R8769/3/92, General Situation in Trieste, 27 May 1946.

52. The Sindicati Unici included shipyard, textile, and transportation workers and longshoremen; PRO: FO371/48949, "Report on Venezia Guilia communicated by Local Govt. Sub-Commission Allied Commission," 20/9/45. An intelligence report from July 1945 estimated that the *Sindacati Unici* had sixty thousand members in the city of Trieste alone (out of a population of 350,000), and that the Communist Party, with the trade union as its base, had more active supporters than all the other existing parties; PRO: WO204/6387, "Report No. 3," 29/7/45, Trieste Secret AIS D Section. See also PRO: WO204/6399, "Report No. 7," 29/8/45, Trieste AIS D Section Secret Report, Pt. 1 summary, 1.

53. Novak, *Trieste 1941–1954*, 258.

54. PRO: FO371/48949, "Report on Venezia Guilia communicated by Local Govt. Sub- Commission Allied Commission," 20/9/45.

55. "Health," HQAMG XIII Corps Monthly Report, month ending 31 August 1945.

56. See Novak, *Trieste 1941–1954*, 228–29; G. Valdevit *La Questione di Trieste*, 125–26.

57. P. Togliatti, *Linea d'una politica* (Milano-Sera, 1948), 63–64.

58. PRO: FO371/59347, R89815/3/92, Sullivan to Rome, Situation in Trieste, 24–31 May 1946.

59. Ibid.

60. ISMLVG: "Intervista con il triestino Galliano Fogar," from "Cominform Storia del PC del TLT": Intervistatore, Franco Giraldi, 1981.

61. Valdevit, *La Questione di Trieste*, 140–41.

62. PRO: WO204/6399, "Report No. 4 Pt. ii," 5/8/45, Trieste AIS D Section Secret Report, 2.

63. Ibid.

64. PRO: FO371/48838, "Trial of Giorgio Jaksetich," 13/8/45.

65. PRO: WO204/6399, "Report No. 4 Pt. ii," 5/8/45.

66. ISMLVG: AIVG, 2306, "Elenco delle manifestazione che hanno avuto luogo dal 1/5 al 4/10/45."

67. PRO: WO204/6405, "News Highlights," Allied Information Services, 22/8/45.

68. PRO: FO371/48838, "Trial of Giorgio Jaksetich," 13/8/45.

69. PRO: FO371/48838, "Trial of Giorgio Jaksetich," 13/8/45, "Background Enclosure," Despatch 345.

70. PRO: WO204/2233, F. T. Hammond Jr., Col. GSC, Arrest and Conviction of G. Jaksetich, 21/8/45.

71. PRO: FO371/48838, "Trial of Giorgio Jaksetich," "2nd note to despatch," 12/9/45, and PRO: FO371/48836, R1365/24/92, Situation in Venezia Giulia, 3–5 August, AMG Intelligence Report, 13/8/45.

72. PRO: WO204/6400, "Report No. 11," 26/9/45, Trieste AIS Secret Reports. After reading an AMG "ethnological survey" a member of the British Foreign Office staff noted that support was being manipulated by the communists "persuading the working class of Trieste and Monfalcone that Yugoslavia will assure the workers' paradise"; PRO: FO371/48949, R18660/14935/92, Note R.G. Staff 2/1/46, "Ethnological survey of North-East Italy," 25/10/45.

73. PRO: FO371/72501, R8825/51/70, Notes GTC Campbell, 23/7/48, Mr. Flynn 29/7/48.

74. PRO: WO204/3178, "AMG Main 8th Army from LUSH to HQ Alcom M1054," 30 May 1945.

75. SNL: Box SIAU 2, "Verbale UAIS riunione," 26/4/47.

76. Ibid.

77. Ibid.

78. Ibid., and SNL: Box SIAU 2, "Comitato Cittadino UAIS riunione," 3/4/47.

79. SNL: Box SIAU 2, "Comitato Cittadino UAIS riunione," 3/4/47.

80. Bowman, *Zones of Strain*, 49.

81. PRO: FO371/48836, R13651/24/92, "Situation in Venezia Giulia, AMI Report," 3–5 August 1945; and PRO: WO204/6387, Report No. 6 22/8/45, "Trieste AIS D Section Secret Report." The Trieste Area General had already defined the FTT as bringing about political regroupings rather than orienting the social and economic situation along national lines. The fear of the influence of the Italian Communist Party is clear in documents in Coles and Weinberg, *United States Army in World War II*, 623ff.

82. PRO: WO204/10989, SCAO Bowman, 12/5/47, "HQ AMG meeting."

83. Bowman, *Zones of Strain*, 48. Although Bowman's account was written retrospectively, it is telling that he expects that his justifications will find sympathy among an anglophone readership. The title "Zones of Strain" was borrowed from Arthur Moodie's description of the Julian Region, see chapter 6.

84. Bowman, *Zones of Strain*, 48.

85. PRO: WO204/623, "From HQ Alcom to AFHQ for G-5 9893," 16 June 1945, XIII Corps.

86. See also Valdevit, *La Questione di Trieste*, 140–41.

87. SNL: AFZ files, "DAT, Comitato Direttivo," 17 August 1945.

88. SNL: AFZ files, "DAT, Comitato Cittadino," 24 July 1945.

89. SNL: AFZ files, "Mestni Odbor, AFZ Trst" sent to "UAIS Mestnemu Odboru," 24 July 1945.

90. Sir Noel Charles described the role of women in the growing resistance: "The black market area near the station in Trieste was overrun and cleared by a working-class demonstration on the 22nd July. On the 24th July a procession of women protested against the inadequacy of wages and 'maladministration'"; PRO: FO371/48836, R13315/24/92, "Sir Noel Charles, 1 August 1945, Situation in Venezia Giulia." Charles's report borrowed from an AMG document.

91. SNL: AFZ files, "DAT, Comitato Cittadino," 17 July 1945.

92. PRO: WO204/6402, Trieste Activities Reports No. 11, 10 November 1945. Unfortunately I have been unable to discover any examples of the display.

93. PRO: WO204/6403, "Radio," Trieste Activities Reports No. 23, 2 February 1946, 3.

94. INV: ZO-39 AISZZ, "Summary of Women's Activities since 1945," 12 June 1948, Comitato Direttivo UDAIS Trieste; SNL: Box SIAU, "Attività dell'UDAIS dal 1946," 24 March 1948.

95. PRO: W0204/11131, Monthly Report HQAMG VG, " Legal report for Venezia Giulia," August 1947. Later in 1949 there was a call for a census controlling "multiple" employment in families, in particular the employment of female as well as male members of the same family—PRO: FO371 78626, R4162/1013/70, Sullivan, Situation Report, 15 April 1949.

96. PRO: WO204/10989, HQAMG VG, Minutes of Economic Meeting, 21 March 1947.

97. PRO: W0204/11131, HQAMG VG Monthly Report, "Legal report for Venezia Giulia," August 1947.

98. For a more detailed discussion of prostitution and the AMG, see G. Sluga, "Cold War Casualties: Gender, Ethnicity and the Writ-

ing of History," *Women's Studies International Forum—From Margins to Centre: Gender, Ethnicity, and Nationalism* [special issue] 19 (1996): 75–86.

99. PRO: WO204/10989, HQ AMG Meeting Reports, A. Bowman, "Top Secret," 12 May 1947. Benedict Alpers complained about this tendency to label all women who associated with Allied men as prostitutes; Alpers, *Love and Politics*, 201.

100. SNL, Box Sindacati, "Comitate UAIS/Odbor SIAU, II rione/II okraj," 18 August 1947, Prot N.re 1563, Oggetto circolare; See also M. E. Reed, "The Antifascist Front of Women and the Communist Party in Croatia: Conflicts within the Resistance," in T. Yedlin (ed.), *Women in Eastern Europe and the Soviet Union* (New York: Praeger, 1980).

101. *Voce del Popolo*, 24 September 1946.

102. Bowman, *Zones of Strain*, 23.

103. ISMLVG: AIVG, XXX/2300, "Servizio informazione dipendento dal CLN. Rapporti informativi," n.d..

104. PRO: WO204/914, "Main XIII Corps to Main 8th Army Info AFHQ For Resmin," 3 July 1945 (period 29 June to 3 July).

105. PRO: FO371/67410, R10105/108/92, W. Sullivan, "Situation Report," 18 July 1947.

106. C. Vetter, "La Magistratura," in *Nazionalismo e neofascismo nella lotta politica al confine orientale 1945–1975*, 214–16.

107. INV: ZO-39 AFSZZ, Comitato direttivo UDAIS, Trieste, 12/6/48.

108. Wolff, *Inventing Eastern Europe*, 2.

109. Valdevit, *La Questione di Trieste*, 131.

110. PRO: FO371/67469, R13416/10882/92, Warner, memo "Proposed cooperation between Allies and Yugoslavs in Trieste," 6/6/47.

CHAPTER 6. "FREE TERRITORY," NATIONALISM, AND THE COLD WAR, 1948–1954

1. Coles and Weinberg, *United States Army in World War II*, 568–70.

2. Ibid., 571–75.

3. Harris, *Allied Military Administration of Italy 1943–1945*, 324.

4. "Memo on recent trip to Northern Italy, Gen Spofford, ACofS, G-5, AFHQ, for Deputy Theatre Comdr, MTOUSA, 9 Jul 45, MTO, HS files, G-5, AFHQ papers," in Coles and Weinberg, *United States Army in World War II*, 574.

5. See for example also, S. W. Boggs, *International Boundaries* (New York: Columbia University Press, 1940); S. B. Jones, *Boundary-*

Making: A Handbook for Statesmen, Treaty Editors, and Boundary Commissioners (Washington, D.C.: Carnegie Endowment for International Peace, 1945); N. L. Hill, *Claims to Territory in International Law and Relations* (London: Oxford University Press, 1945); Harold Nicolson's *Peacemaking 1919* was reissued with a new introduction on his hopes for the postwar territorial settlements.

6. Cited in A. Cobban, *National Self-Determination* (London: Oxford University Press, 1944), 176.

7. For a thorough survey of these investigations see Valdevit, *La Questione di Trieste,* 19–35 *passim.*

8. Cobban, *National Self-Determination,* 176.

9. Ibid., 177.

10. Ibid.

11. Moodie, *The Italo-Yugoslav Boundary,* 158, 187.

12. Ibid., 209.

13. The Foreign Office, warned beforehand, was nervous about Taylor's speech. There was nothing they could do though since the Ministry of Information controlled programming: PRO: FO371/48949, R16674/14935/92, General News Talk, World Affairs by AJP Taylor/GVM (From the Home Service) Pt. II. *The Trieste Issue,* 24/9/45.

14. Ibid.

15. G. Salvemini, "Trieste e Trst," *Il Ponte* 1, 3 (giugno 1945).

16. Ibid.

17. Ibid., 182.

18. James Byrne for the United States, Molotov for the USSR, Ernest Bevin for the British, and Georges Bidault for the French, Novak, *Trieste 1941–1954,* 242.

19. Ibid., 241.

20. J. Campbell, *Successful Negotiation, Trieste 1954: An Appraisal by the Five Participants* (Princeton: Princeton University Press, 1976), 93.

21. Duroselle, *Le Conflit de Trieste 1943–1954,* 201.

22. Ibid., 208, 219; and Novak, *Trieste 1941–1954,* 242.

23. PRO: WO204/6400, "Trieste AIS D Section Reports," Report No. 14, 17/10/45, "Letter to *The Times,* 26/9/45 from Dr. PierPaolo Luzzatto-Fegiz, Professor of Statistics at Trieste University," 9.

24. E. Puecher, "Pro memoria in cui è riepilogata succintamente quella che dovrebbe essere la soluzione ragionevole, perché giusta e conveniente per tutte le parti interessate, del problema politico nazionale della Venezia Giulia," 1946.

25. ISMLVG: AIVG, XXI/2350, G. Paladin, "Scritti vari di G. Paladin sulla questione di Trieste 1945–1946. Schemi di progetti per la costituzione di una 'Unione dei Giuliani,'" circa 1946.

26. Schiffrer, "La Venezia Giulia. Saggio di Una Carta dei Limiti Nazionali Italo-Jugoslavi," 87.

27. PRO: FO371/48949, R18660/14935/92, "Report on Venezia Guilia communicated by Local Govt Sub Commission Allied Commission," 20/9/45.

28. PRO: WO204/6400, "Report No. 16," Trieste AIS D Section Secret Report, 7/11/45; "Report No. 17," Trieste AIS D Section Secret Report, 12/11/45.

29. Novak, *Trieste 1941–1954*, 259.

30. ISMLVG: AIVG, XXVIII/2211/1, Duroselle, *Le conflit de Trieste*, 210; "Comunicato ufficiale di 12/11/45." Gandusio was also president of the Circolo della Cultura e delle Arti to which Trieste intellectuals such as Carlo Schiffrer and Giani Stuparich belonged.

31. See PRO: FO371/59355, R11355/3/9, Sullivan, Situation in Trieste 12–18 July, 19/7/46; ISMLVG: XXVIII/2211, "Scambio di lettere fra Gandusio e Mihelcic 1945–1946 sulle trattative fra italiani."

32. Ibid., "Indirizzo di Gandusio."

33. PRO: FO371/59360, R13008/3/92, "Trieste proposed subcommission of the Italian Political Commission," Brigadier Dove 29/8/46; and PRO: FO371/59341, R440/5/3/9, "Situation in Trieste," 15/3/1946.

34. Duroselle, *Le conflit de Trieste*, 220. Sullivan reported in March 1946 that the commission had adopted the "Report on the Ethnic groups in the Venezia Giulia," printed in Rome January 1946, as a common reference work, and the discredited censuses of 1910 and 1921, PRO: FO371/59341 R440/5/3/9, Situation in Trieste, 8–15 March 1946.

35. Duroselle, *Le conflit de Trieste*, 220.

36. In August 1947, Marshall wrote to the Italian Prime Minister De Gasperi that Italy's ratification of the Marshall Plan had "removed the last barrier created by Fascism between Italy and the other peace-loving sovereign nations"; Marshall to De Gasperi in August 1947, cited in C. Seton-Waton, "Italy's Imperial Hangover," *Journal of Contemporary History* 15 (1980): 177.

37. U.S. National Archives [hereafter NA]: RG286: Agency for International Development Economic Cooperation Administration, "Ivan White to SecState, Washington," 5/5/48 Secret, (Telegram signed Joyce, adding, "Foregoing discussed with and approved by General Gaither, US Army Head AMG"), (ECA) Mission to Trieste, Office of the Director, 1. See NA: RG331: Allied Occupation and Operational HeadQuarters, file 341, H. P. Robertson, Colonel, Dep SCAO, Recommendations, "A Study on Morale and confidence, Free

Territory of Trieste, in connection with the planning and Advisory Staff's memorandum No. AMG/Free Territory/PL/341/1 of 28th October 47," 3.

38. PRO: FO371/57215 U6815/360/g79, "Viability of the Free Territory of Trieste," 17/8/46, Brief No. 10 for the U.K. Delegation to the Peace Conference.

39. Novak, *Trieste 1941–1954*, 256. The new solution was proclaimed during a strike protesting the shooting (one fatal) of three pro-communist demonstrators by AMG police in San Giacomo, after attacks on Slovene and pro-communist institutions.

40. Ibid., 272.

41. PRO: WO204/10988, HQAMG meeting, 12/11/46, Minutes of Misc. Meetings 1 Oct–27 Dec 1946.

42. Article 6 of the peace treaty; Novak, *Trieste 1941–1954*, 272.

43. See PRO: FO371/49757, ZM3232/1/22, Mr Gullman (US Embassy) to Mr Harvey 6/6/45, "Reorganisation of local government in Italy"; and Valdevit, *La Questione di Trieste*, 144–163.

44. The treaty required Italy to safeguard the rights of all persons within its territory, and to prevent the organization of paramilitary groups or antidemocratic groups.

45. PRO: WO264/24, Quarterly Historical Report of AIS, Secret No. 51, AIS Activities 13–27 October 1946, General Summary, Trieste.

46. PRO: FO371/59347, R9220/3/92, W. Sullivan to FO London, 21/6/46, Possible Internationalisation of Trieste; See also NA: RG59: General Records of the Department of State, Diplomatic Branch, letter to Director of Policy Planning Staff, Dept of State, from Robert P. Joyce (app. Consul General Trieste), Subject Trieste, 21 July 1947.

47. PRO: WO204/10988, HQAMG meeting, Col. Bowman, 12/11/46.

48. PRO: FO371/67468, R5637/108/92, W. Sullivan, Situation Report 11–17 April 1947.

49. PRO: FO371/59361R12209/3/9, Sir N. Charles, Situation Summary 23–29 August 1946.

50. PRO: FO371/67468, R5637/108/92, W. Sullivan, Situation Report 11–17 April 1947.

51. According to Seton-Watson, the concept of Italy's civilizing mission in the Mediterranean was still influential, particularly among the Christian Democratic Party, Seton-Watson, "Italy's Imperial Hangover," 171.

52. British Element Trieste Force, Quarterly Historical Reports HQ British Element Trieste Force, 15/9/47 to 31/12/47, quarter ending 30 September 1947.

53. "Top Secret, quarter ending 30/9/47," Quarterly Historical Reports HQ British Element Trieste Force 15/9/47 to 31/12/47. For further discussion of the rise of neofascist groups and the AMG's response, see also Valdevit, *La Questione di Trieste,* 150–51, 251.

54. "Bowman SCAO, VenGiulia, Rpt for Feb 47, Rell 3167 MGD files," in Coles and Weinberg, *United States Army in World War II,* 613.

55. PRO: FO371/67468, R5637/108/92, W. Sullivan, "Situation Summary" 11–17 April 1947. Bowman reported that in Monfalcone "the Italians are for the moment on top and busily repaying in kind past outrages by the pro-Slavs," ("Bowman SCAO, VenGiulia, Rpt for Feb 47, Rell 3167 MGD files," in Coles and Weinberg, *United States Army in World War II,* 613). These migrants would become tragic victims of the Cominform split the following year, living in a Yugoslavia hostile to their internationalist support of Stalin's Soviet Union.

56. NA: RG 331 [Allied Occupation and Operational Headquarters, World War II], AMG BUSZ & Free Territory, Planning and Advisory Staff, Subject - Numerical Files, File 319, "Free Territory Anti-Propaganda Campaign," n.d.

57. Robertson, "A Study on Morale and confidence . . . 28th October 1947," 3; See also PRO: WO204/11208, HQ AMG-BUS Zone Free Territory Monthly Report Jan 1948, AIS Pt. B, 46.

58. Quarterly Historical Reports HQ British Element Trieste Force 1/10/47–31/12/47.

59. Cited in PRO: WO204/10432, HQAMG Trieste Monthly Report, February 1948, 2. Airey took over from Bowman in 1947.

60. See Valdevit, *La Questione di Trieste,* 255ff.

61. "Statement by the Governments of the US, UK, and France," March 20, 1948, reprinted in *Department of State Bulletin* 18, Mar 28, 1948, 425.

62. PRO: FO371/57215 U6815/360/g79, "Viability of the Free Territory of Trieste," 17/8/46.

63. Rabel, *Between East and West,* 87.

64. Novak, *Trieste 1941–1954,* 407.

65. Valdevit, *La Questione di Trieste,* 213.

66. Valdevit argues that Airey's comments were not always well received in London and Washington, even though they shared his general outlook on the problem; Ibid., 184.

67. PRO: FO371/78658, R6352/1821/70, "Airey to Brit & US Polad & DGCA," 21/6/49.

68. The administrative offices opened to election did not affect AMG authority, and were more symbolic than practical and, even then, the AMG attempted to influence the outcome of those elections.

69. NA: RG84, [Records of the Foreign Service Posts of the Department of State], Congressional Files 1949 BX 46, Despatch No. 108 Secret, 29 March 1949, 350 Trieste Baldwin Reports, Rome Embassy and Consulate, C. Baldwin, "Subject Observations on Present and Future Situation in the Trieste Area."

70. NA: RG84, 350 Trieste Baldwin Reports: Records of the Foreign Service Posts of the Department of State, C. Baldwin, "Status of the Trieste Problem in Late 1949," 13/11/49, 2; 350 Trieste Baldwin Reports, "Slav Minority Problems in the Trieste Area," Confidential, Baldwin to Secretary of State, Washington, 11/1/49, 1.

71. C. Baldwin, "Subject Observations on Present and Future Situation in the Trieste Area."

72. "Slav Minority Problems in the Trieste Area," 11/1/49, 14.

73. Dean Rusk to Baldwin, 23/5/49, reproduced in PRO: FO371/78658, R6352/1821/70.

74. PRO: FO371/78658, R10695/1821/70, M. Carlyle, 9/11/49; See also Sullivans's defensive comments PRO: FO371/78658, R12004/1821/70, "Carlyle's outline of the minority problem," 20/12/49.

75. PRO: FO371/107416, WE1371/2, J. A. Grant, Note, 15/1/53, addended to A. D. Wilson (Chargé d'Affaires Belgrade) to Cheetham 7/1/53.

76. Proclamation No. 6, 18/8/45, *AMG Gazette* 1, 15 Sept 1945.

77. PRO: FO371/ 107416, WE1371/41, J. A. Grant, Note 11/2/53 addended to Cheetham to Wilson, 13/2/53.

78. PRO: FO371/107426, WE1822/3, Laurence to Churchill, 24/4/53.

79. PRO: FO371/107426, WE1822/9, "Broad to Foreign Office," 15 February 1954; Wright from the Western and Southern Department in fact was skeptical about Broad's outline, PRO: FO371/107426, WE1822/9, "To Trieste, from Wright," 20/2/54.

80. Bartoli's association with the Committee for the Defense of the Italian Character of Trieste and Istria, as well as his role in the November events organizing demonstrators from outside Trieste was regarded as having encouraged the extreme right wing and neo-Fascism. The history of these negotiations, of the rehearsal by the Yugoslav and Italian governments of ethical and ethnic arguments, have been well documented in Novak's *Trieste 1941–1954*, ch. 14–15.

81. Novak, *Trieste 1941–1954*, 458.

82. PRO: FO371/112737, WE1015/411, "Broad to Foreign Office," 23 September 1954.

83. 1946 poster, see also "L'Italia ritornerà" nella Venezia Giulia," in the Action Party newspaper, *La Voce Libera*, which argued for Tri-

este's return to Italy on the grounds that Italy represented *civiltà* and Yugoslavia stood for *barbarie,* and for the *civiltà delle foibe;* cited in L. Biecker, R. De Rosa, S. Benvenuti, "La stampa," in *Nazionalismo e neofascismo nella lotta politica al confine orientale 1945–1975* (ISMLVG, n.d.), 29, 33.

84. Campbell, *Writing Security,* 69.

85. Coles and Weinberg, *United States Army in World War II,* 589.

86. Rusinow, *Italy's Austrian Heritage,* 2.

87. PRO: FO371/112737, WE1015/335, Sir A. Clarke, 7/8/54.

88. PRO: FO371/11273, WE1015/350, Broad to W&S Dept, 12/8/547.

89. See C. Colummi et al., *Storia di un esodo: Istria 1945–1956* (Trieste: ISMLVG, 1980).

90. V. Vidali, *Ritorno alla città senza pace. Il 1948 a Trieste* (Milano: Vangelista, 1982), 68.

CHAPTER 7. HISTORY AND SOVEREIGNTY, AFTER 1954

1. G. Cervani, "Introduction," in F. Cusin, *Appunti alla storia di Trieste* (Udine: DelBianco, 1983).

2. Cusin, *Appunti alla storia di Trieste.*

3. G. Cervani, *Gli scritti politici di Fabio Cusin nel <Corriere di Trieste>: Gli anni della polemica dura (1946–1948)* (Udine: DelBianco, 1991), 12.

4. F. Cusin, *L'Italiano* (Roma: Atlantica, 1945); F. Cusin, *Introduzione allo storia* (Padova: Cedam, 1946). In his 1943 preface Cusin describes the attack on the first edition of *Introduzione* by the conformist ranks of the Triestine and Italian academy, unwilling to historicize the roots of their own authority. The purpose of history, he replies, exists only in relation to the present, and as such academic history's institutionalized representation of "the truth" is to be regarded with skepticism. The publication of the book's second edition was suspended in October 1945.

5. Ward, *Anti-fascisms,* 78; According to Ward, Croce pronounced the values of Italy as Europe's "first born and most devoted son," of its "ancient civilisation." Italy's location on a political-cultural European map was alongside France and Great Britain, "never with that of Germany or . . . the Slavic countries"; Fascism was thus relegated to the status of "a disease and product of invading barbarian force"; 80, 81.

6. F. Cusin, *Antistoria d'Italia:Una demistificazione della storia ufficiale* (Milano: Mondadori, 1972), xxv.

7. Cusin, *Antistoria d'Italia*, xii.

8. Cusin, *L'Italiano*, 107.

9. F. Cusin, *La liberazione di Trieste* (Trieste: F. Zigiotti, 1946), 12.

10. PRO: WO204/6400, Report No. 17, 2/11/45, "Trieste AIS D Section Secret Report." The report also lists Flora as being expelled with them.

11. PRO: FO371/59357, R12249/3/92, Mr. Sullivan, Situation Report, 19–25 July, 6/8/46; Cervani, *Gli scritti politici di Fabio Cusin nel <Corriere di Trieste>*, 50. Apart from being active in anti-Fascist organizations, including *Giustizia e Libertà*, during the war Pincherle had been one of the few Italians to denounce the Fascist treatment of Venezia Giulian minorities, in his case to the Vatican. When not in enforced exile or in Fascist concentration camps for his antifascism, he was excluded from employment as a doctor because of his Jewishness; M. Coen, *Bruno Pincherle* (Pordenone: Edizioni Studio Tesi, 1995).

12. G. Menasse, *Ponterosso*, 1947, 3; F. Cusin, "La storia d'Italia e la storiografia post-fascista," *Ponterosso*, 1947; and F. Cetineo, "Interpretazione di Slataper," *Ponterosso*, 1947.

13. F. Cusin, *Venti secoli* (Trieste: Gabbiano, 1952), 11.

14. Ibid., 8, 222.

15. Ibid., 11.

16. Ibid., 219.

17. Ibid., 16.

18. Ibid., 70, 73.

19. PRO: FO371/95412, RT1013/24, P. Broad, "Situation Report," 3–16 November 1951.

20. In his anthology of Cusin's contributions to the newspaper *Il Corriere di Trieste*, Cervani describes a whole series of run-ins between Cusin and the university, dating from his time there as a student. When Cusin participated in an anti-Fascist demonstration in 1925, his marks suffered, and later he was denied the position of "assistant"; Cervani, *Gli scritti politici di Fabio Cusin*, 42–46 *passim*. Cervani also argues that despite the fact that that Cusin portrays these episodes as persecutions, they were just a matter of bad luck mostly, part of any academic's career, and were used as excuses by Cusin for his personal failures. For a view of the university in these years that celebrates its nationalist role see M. E. Viora, "L'università degli studi di Trieste," *Cenni storici* 3 (1958).

21. See Cervani, "Introduction," in Cusin, *Appunti alla storia di Trieste*, 23; G. Cervani, "Fabio Cusin storico di Trieste," *Studi Urbinati*, Nuova Serie B XXXII, 1958; E. Sestan, "Giudizio 'Anseatico' sugli Ital-

iani," *Belfagor*, 15 luglio 1946); N. Valeri, "Fabio Cusin," *Rassegna Storica del Risorgimento*, XLII, ii–iii, aprile - settembre 1955; Arduino Agnelli's preface to Cusin, *Antistoria d'Italia*, xvii–xviii, accuses the later Cusin of being asocial, undisciplined, neither conservative nor revolutionary but always factional. Ara and Magris comment on Cusin's "highly personal antinationalist historiography . . . characterised by brilliant intuitions, but not devoid of psychological convolution and rancorous antiitalian-ità"; Ara and Magris, *Trieste: Un identità di frontierà*, 123.

22. ISMLVG: AIVG, 206c, Cusin, Allegato 3, "Verbale delle sedute No. 14," 28 October 1952, Sessione ordinaria autumnale, 29/5/51–14/10/53, Consiglio Comunale di Trieste, 4.

23. E. Apih, *Carlo Schiffrer* (Pordenone: Edizioni Studio Tesi, 1993), 5.

24. PRO: FO371/95425, RT10111/215, P. Broad to Mason, 12/10/51.

25. Ibid. Schiffrer even represented the Socialist Party of Venezia Giulia at a European conference, defending the restitution of the Trieste region to Italy, and the formation of a United States of Europe, at the same time as he accepted his position with the AMG. Verani, "A vent'anni dalla scomparsa di Carlo Schiffrer," 234. See also Valdevit, *La questione di Trieste*.

26. Cusin, Allegato 3, "Verbale delle sedute No. 14," 28 October 1952.

27. S. Benco, *Contemplazione del disordine* (Udine: DelBianco, 1946).

28. Ibid., 7.

29. The prolific local historian Giulio Cervani also described the liberation period as a crisis, "a humiliating disorder." May 1945 had seen "an overturning of history and politics," whereby the economic and ethnic groups that had until then been in the position of subalterns found themselves in control, G. Cervani, Preface to Maserati, *L'Occupazione di Trieste*, 8. In 1953 Diego DeCastro published *Trieste: Cenni riassuntivi sul problema giuliano nell'ultimo decennio* (Bologna: Cappelli, 1953). For him the forty-two days could be encapsulated in the mode of Coceani and Benco as a time of the *foibe*, of massacres, arrests, deportations, and the subversion of all Trieste's *civilissime* institutions.

30. P. Gambini, *Primavera a Trieste* (Trieste: Italo Svevo, 1985), vi.

31. A. Tamaro, *Due anni di storia 1943–45*, 3 Vols. (Roma: Tosi, 1948), 654.

32. B. Coceani, *Mussolini, Hitler, Tito alle porte orientali d'Italia* (Bologna: Cappelli, 1948), 314.

33. C. Schiffrer, *Historic Glance at the Relations between Italians and Slavs in Venezia Giulia* (Instituto di Storia del'Università di Trieste, 1946), 15.

34. ISMLVG: "Letter from Conte Sforza to Schiffrer," Rome, 7/1/46. Another work still lauded for its reasonableness and precision, Ernesto Sestan's *Venezia Giulia: Lineamenti di storia etnica e culturale* (1947), juxtaposed a rejection of the excesses of nationalism, with an explanation of Fascist policy against "Slavs" as natural from the perspective of a psychological rendering of the past, and of the "national struggle" in the region. E. Sestan, *Venezia Giulia: Lineamenti di storia etnica e culturale* (Roma: Edizioni Italiane, 1947).

35. Cusin, *La liberazione di Trieste*, 11; G. Stuparich, *Trieste nei miei ricordi* (Milano: Garzanti, 1948), 111.

36. Stuparich, *Trieste nei miei ricordi*, 8, 9.

37. Stuparich's description of the Triestine Ruggero Fauro relies on this same interdependence of body and *terra*: "aveva nel sangue, nell'anima, nel cervello la sua Istria," 110.

38. Stuparich, *Trieste nei miei ricordi*, 111.

39. Ibid., 184, 216.

40. For a fuller discussion of this theme see G. Sluga, "Cold War Casualties: Gender, Ethnicity, and the Writing of History," *Women's Studies International Forum* 19 (1996): 75–86.

41. Stuparich, *Trieste nei miei ricordi*, 184. The one exception was Anita Pittoni, the daughter of the old Triestine socialist Valentino Pittoni.

42. Pancrazi cited in Cary, *A Ghost in Trieste*, 160.

43. C. Schiffrer, "L'attesa di Trieste," Atti del XLIV Congresso di Storia del Risorgimento Italiano, Trieste, 31/10–4/11/68: "La fine della prima guerra mondiale e i problemi relativi," (Instituto per la storia del Risorgimento Italiano, Roma, 1970), 12.

44. Stuparich, *Trieste nei miei ricordi*, 200. Some *incroci* were "stranger" than others in Stuparich's view, particularly those "crossbred" as he details, "with Levantine and Nordic, with Hungarian, Polish, Swiss, Yugoslav, Sicilian, yet who still succeed occasionally in being very beautiful."

45. E. Collotti, "The Italian Politics of Repression in the Balkans." See also R. Bosworth, "Italy's Historians and the Myth of Fascism," in R. Langhorne (ed.), *Diplomacy and Intelligence during the Second World War* (Cambridge: Cambridge University Press, 1985), 85–108.

46. G. Stuparich, "La Realtà di Trieste," *Il Ponte* x (1954): 553.

47. "Intervista con il triestino Galliano Fogar, Intervistatore Franco Giraldi."

48. "The Trieste Agreement in the Opinion of Personalities from Venezia Giulia," *Trieste* i, 4 (Nov–Dec 1954): 4–5.

49. Ibid.

50. E. Apih, "Italians and Slavs in the Adriatic," *Trieste* 2, 5 (Jan.–Feb. 1955): 1–3.

51. R. Pupo, "Violenza politica tra guerra e dopoguerra," 36. Some of this discussion of the foibe is based on G. Sluga, "The Risiera di San Sabba: Fascism, Anti-fascism, and Italian Nationalism," *Journal of Modern Italian Studies* 1 (1996): 401–12.

52. Claudia Cernigoi has shown that the markings have been altered in the 1990s to indicate the existence of corpses at increasingly greater depths; C. Cernigoi, *Operazione foibe a Trieste: come si crea una mistificazione storica, dalla propaganda nazifascista attraverso la guerra fredda fino al neoirredentismo* (Udine: Kappa Vu, 1997), 180–81.

53. G. Ruaro, *Strolling around Trieste: Practical Guide to the City and Its Surroundings with Many Illustrations* (Trieste: Edizioni B & M Fachin, 1986), 69; M. Walcher, *Il tempio a Maria Madre e Regina di Monte Grisa di Trieste: La storia, e l'architettura* (Trieste: Italo Svevo, 1977).

54. In September 1997 a local police inspector reminded me that regardless of their command, or of the circumstances under which they had disappeared or been killed, they were "Italians" and "infoibati."

55. Berezin, *Making the Fascist Self*, 4.

56. See Nicola Gallerano, "La memoria pubblica del fascismo e dell'antifascismo," in G. Calchi Novati (ed.), *Politiche della memoria* (Manifestolibri, 1993), 7–20.

57. Exhibition Guide: "Risiera di San Sabba, monumento nazionale, Comune di Trieste," (n.d.). An architectural competition was even held to decide its design. For a recent account of the conception of the memorial see: M. Mucci, "La Risiera di San Sabba a Trieste. Un'architettura per la memoria," *Qualestoria* 2 (1996): 69–126.

58. Before the 1960s interest in the wartime history of the Risiera had only been expressed by the pro-Yugoslav anti-Fascist partisans who liberated the camp, the camp's survivors, and individuals on the fringes of the Italian Left, including Cusin, and Pincherle. However, Cusin and Pincherle were marginalized by the local pro-Italian and anticommunist anti-Fascist organisations precisely because of their willingness to question the political implications of a nationalist construction of Italian identity.

59. For a full discussion of the Risiera trial see Sluga, "The Risiera di San Sabba: Fascism, Anti-fascism, and Italian Nationalism."

60. Although historians from Italy and Slovenia testified to widespread local collaboration and the Nazis' administrative and military dependence on local figures and institutions, no collaborators or Fascists were called to give evidence.

61. F. Zidar, "Il processo della Risiera," *Dallo squadrismo Fascista alle stragi della Risiera (con il resoconto del processo) Trieste-Istria 1919–1945* (Trieste: ANED, 1978), 157–80.

62. E. Collotti, "Le stragi di San Sabba trent'anni dopo: il processo dimezzato," in *San Sabba: Istruttoria e processo per il Lager della Risiera* (Milano: Mondadori, 1988), 145; *Idem*, "La sentenza giudicata," in *San Sabba*, 229–34.

63. For the fewer "innocent victims" (those obliquely identified as nonpartisan and usually as Jewish), the Risiera, it was decided, was mostly a transit camp. Consequently there was little need to hunt down their murderers; Zidar, "Il processo della Risiera," 167.

64. Ibid., 177.

65. See C. Vetter, "La Magistratura," in *Nazionalismo e neofascismo*.

66. E. Nizza, *Monumenti alla libertà: Antifascismo, resistenza e pace nei monumenti italiani dal 1945 al 1985* (Milano: La Pietra, 1986). Friuli-Venezia Giulia was the autonomous region created in 1963.

67. S. Ortaggi, "Nationalism and History in an Italian Classroom," *History Workshop Journal* 6 (1978): 186–94.

68. Demonstrations by teachers from Slovene schools in 1973 had led to the introduction of a consultative committee in the regional education authority, but otherwise Slovene-language schools were a minority and undercut by special statutes that limited the kind of schooling they could provide. See Stranj, *The Submerged Community*, 163.

69. Ortaggi, "Nationalism and History in an Italian Classroom," 192.

70. Ibid., and 187.

71. Cited in R. Spazzali, *Foibe: un dibattito ancora aperto* (Trieste: Lega Nazionale, 1990), 280.

72. Cernigoi, *Operazione foibe a Trieste;* and P. Parovel, "Foibe in Neoiredentizem: Zgodovina in politič ni mit," *Delo*, 28/1/1995, 34.

73. Cernigoi, *Operazione foibe a Trieste*, 147–55.

74. This request is referred to in *Atti Parlamentari, Camera dei Deputati, XIII Legislatura, Discussioni*, Seduta del 5 dicembre 1996, M. Gasparri, 8433.

75. Their use of the term *postfascist* nearly half a century after the collapse of the Italian Fascist state referred to the transformation of the neo-Fascist MSI party into the postfascist coalition Alleanza Nazionale that occurred in 1994. For a discussion of the late-twentieth-century use of the term *postfascist*, see Berezin, "Introduction," *Making the Fascist Self*.

76. *Atti Parlamentari, Camera dei deputati, XIII Legislatura, Proposta di legge*, N. 3481, 26 marzo 1997, deputati Malgieri, Fini et al., "Istituzione di una Commissione parlamentare di inchiesta sugli eventi criminosi postbellici verificatisi in Italia tra il 1945 ed il 1948 e sulle cause della mancata individuazione o del mancato perseguimento dei responsabili di eccidi, massacri, stermini e delle stragi ispirate da motivazioni di <pulizia> etnica o politica," 1–8. Their estimates of *foibe* victims is based on the work of an amateur historian, L. Papo. See Cernigoi, *Operazione foibe a Trieste, passim.* When Roberto Menia made a formal request for a national parliamentary commission into the Venezia Giulia *foibe*, he also submitted a demand that the historic national status of the Trieste Civic Guard (a body that had operated under Fascist and Nazi command) be recognized on the basis that there were precedents for acknowledging the Civic Guard's national significance, particularly the state's award of the Gold Medal of Military Valor to Trieste in 1948 for defending the *italianità* of the northeastern frontier against the Slav threat; *Atti Parlamentari, Camera dei deputati, XIII Legislatura, Proposta di legge*, N. 1570, 19 giugno 1996, deputato Menia, "Norme per il riconoscimento della qualifica di ex combattente agli appartenenti alla Guardia Civica di Trieste"; *Atti Parlamentari, Camera dei deputati, XIII Legislatura, Proposta di legge*, N. 1565, 19 giugno 1996, deputato Menia, "Concessione all'Associazione <Comune di Fiume in esilio> della medaglia d'oro al <valor militare> , alla memoria dei suoi cittadini che in guerra e in pace hanno servito la Patria"; and *Senato della Repubblica, XIII Legislatura, Disegno di legge*, N. 1353, Comunicata alla presidenza il 25 sett. 1996.

77. *Atti Parlamentari, Camera dei Deputati, XIII Legislatura, Discussioni*, Seduta del 5 dicembre 1996, C. Giovanardi, 8431.

78. The submitted legislation referred to "la caccia all'italiano," "slavizzazione forzosa," "eccidi, massacri, stermini e delle stragi ispirate da motivazioni di <pulizia> etnica o politica": *Atti Parlamentari, Camera dei deputati, XIII Legislatura, Proposta di legge*, N. 3481, 26 marzo 1997, 1–8.

79. *Senato della Repubblica, XIII Legislatura, Disegno di legge*, N. 1353, Comunicata alla presidenza il 25 sett. 1996, senatori Camber, La Loggia, Schifani, Travaglia, Ventucci, Pera, Baldini, Azzolini, Novi e Tomassini, "Istituzione di una Commissione parlamentare d'inchiesta sulle stragi delle Foibe," 2; Even the center-left coalition, L'Ulivo, accommodated the demands for an investigation into the *foibe* in the name of "pacificazione"; *Atti Parlamentari, Camera dei deputati, XIII Legislatura, Proposta di legge*, N. 3481, 26 marzo 1997; *Senato della Repubblica, XIII Legislatura, Disegno di legge*, N. 1353, Comunicata alla presidenza il

25 sett. 1996, 3. For a discussion of the political context of these investigations see C. Cernigoi, *Operazione foibe a Trieste*, 147–55.

80. "Miles," "Il richiamo dei Balcani: Quali Balcani convegnono all'Italia," *Limes* 3 (1995): 26. When both the themes of exodus and of the *foibe* had been taken up by the media and some academic journals, the Pittito inquiry was still underway, and the educational proposition had been rejected.

81. Todorova, *Imagining the Balkans*, 66: "[M]aybe because of its physical proximity or because it did not become organically afflicted with a *mission civilisatrice*, Italy on the whole did not develop an abstract and hectoring pose toward the Balkans and never lost sight of their concreteness."

82. See for example, C. Magris, *Danube* (London: Collins Harvill, 1990), and F. Tolmizza, *Franziska* (Milano: Mondadori, 1997).

83. G. Fogar, "Venezia Giulia 1943–1945: Problemi e situazioni," 108.

84. Ibid., 118. These studies also tried to reintroduce into the history of the *foibe* the context of Fascism in order to understand civilian complicity and culpability in the *foibe* episodes, by asking what stimulated the acts of summary justice, and whether or not the actions and intentions of the Yugoslav secret police, OZNA, can be distinguished from those of the local partisan pro-Yugoslav authorities.

85. R. Pupo, "Violenza politica tra guerra e dopoguerra, il caso delle foibe giuliane, 1943–45," *Clio* xxx 11 (gennaio–marzo 1996): 35.

86. In the 1980s, Giampoalo Valdevit *(La questione di Trieste 1941–1954)* and Roberto Rabel capitalized on newly accessible American and British state archives to fill out the diplomatic history of the Cold War problem of Trieste. In *Between East and West* (Durham, N.C.: Duke University Press, 1988), Rabel began his analysis of Trieste, the United States, and the Cold War with the depiction of the region as a "zone of strain" where for "two thousand years" "the clash of rival expansionist forces caused frequent changes in sovereignty"; 2.

87. Duroselle referred to the Austrian 1910 census of the Trieste province in order to establish the different language groups, Duroselle, *Le Conflit de Trieste*, 36, 61. See also Rusinow, *Italy's Austrian Heritage*, 69, 407.

88. Rusinow, *Italy's Austrian Heritage*, 12.

89. Ibid.

90. See C. Tonel (ed.), *Dossier sul neofascismo a Trieste 1945–1983* (Trieste: Dedolibri, 1991). Among these incidents was the bombing of a Slovene school in 1974, and, in the aftermath of the Risiera trial, more bombings and molotov cocktail attacks against "Slav" organizations.

91. Seton-Watson, "Italy's Imperial Hangover," 175.

92. Campbell, *Successful Negotiation, Trieste 1954*, 4.

93. F. Gross, *Ethnics in a Borderland: An Inquiry into the Nature of Ethnicity and Reduction of Ethnic Tension in a One-Time Genocide Area* (Connecticut: Greenwood Press, 1978), 11, 45, and 71. He made no reference to the Risiera and *foibe* controversies. His discussions with Slovene scholars and professionals in the Julian Region led him to the conclusion that "[I]n their cultural interest in art or music they were *italianissimi*, but they were also Slovene and sincerely patriotic too," 11. Gross also noted that "they [locals] perceived the situation looking from the windows of a native village or city *toward* the broader universe, instead of defining immediately the entire collective and descending from the collective, national identity to the local level," 9.

94. Ibid., 16.

95. Bowman, *Zones of Strain*, 85.

96. Rabel, *Between East and West*, 2.

97. Ibid., 2.

98. Ibid., 3, 5.

99. Ibid., 4.

100. For a thorough discussion of this argument, see Campbell, *Writing Security*.

101. B. Williams, *Stains On My Name, War In My Veins: Guyana and the Politics of Cultural Struggle* (Durham, N.C.: Duke University Press, 1991), 14.

102. S. Hall, "Cultural identity and cinematic representation," *Framework* 36 (1989): 72.

103. This attitude can be attributed to what David Campbell calls a discursive economy, which allows "some statements and depictions come to have greater value than others," and "investments have been made in certain interpretations"; Campbell, *Writing Security*, 6.

104. Winichakul, *Siam Mapped*, 163.

105. Williams, *Stains on my name.*, 14.

106. Cited in Sluga, "Writing History into Politics: Balkan Boundaries," 199.

107. G. F. Kennan, *Around the Cragged Hill: A Personal and Political Philosophy* (Norton, 1993), 151–56. I am grateful to Lawrence Levine for directing me to this quotation.

108. Todorova, *Imagining the Balkans*, 4–6.

109. For a more detailed discussion of the Yugoslav case, see G. Sluga, "Writing History into Politics: Balkan Boundaries," in L. Holmes and P. Murray (eds.), *Rethinking Boundaries* (London: Ashgate, 1999); and G. Sluga, "Orientalising the Balkan Wars," in G. Ianziti (ed.), *Bosnia-Hercegovina in the Yugoslav Aftermath* (Brisbane: QUT Press, 1997).

110. For a damning commentary on this tendency see. D. Ugrešič, *Culture of Lies* (London: Phoenix, 1998).

111. William E. Connolly, "Democracy and Territoriality," *Millenium: Journal of International Studies* 20, 3 (1991): 463.

112. Many political philosophers and jurisprudists are already experimenting with the idea of postsovereignty as a label that better suits the complexities of late-twentieth-century political modalities, see T. J. Biersteker and C. Weber, *State Sovereignty as Social Construct* (Cambridge: Cambridge University Press, 1996), and the essays in J. Rajchman, *The Identity in Question* (New York: Routledge, 1995).

Bibliography

MANUSCRIPT AND ARCHIVAL SOURCES

Auckland

New Zealand: Official Archives

Section 2 NZEF Eyewitness account. Recorder: 280346 Sjt Corrie, RJ; Place: Genigallia; 10 June 45, given to me by Raoul Pupo.

London

Imperial War Museum

Photographic Archives.

Public Record Office (PRO) Kew Branch

BW97 British Council: Registered Files, Trieste.
FO371 Foreign Office: General Correspondence after 1906 Political.
FO842 Embassy and Consular Archives, Italy, British Political Adviser, Trieste, Correspondence.
WO204 War of 1939 to 1945, Military Headquarters Papers, Allied Force Headquarters.
WO264 Quarterly Historical Reports: British Element Trieste Force.

Ljubljana
Republic of Slovenia Archives (AS)

Inštitut za Narodnosta Vprašanja, (INV)

General Files.
Zahodni Oddelek.

Inštitut za Novejše Zgodovino, (INZ)

Files: Pokrajinskega NOO za Slovenia-Primorje in Trst

Rome

Biblioteca della Camera dei deputati

Atti Parlamentari, Camera dei deputati, 1996–1997.

Trieste

Biblioteca Civica "Hortis"

Manuscript collection.

Istituto regionale per la storia del movimento di liberazione nel Friuli/Venezia Giulia, (ISMLVG)

Archivio dell' Indice Venezia Giulia:
Buste I–LI (no titles available).
Buste 76–206A.
Archivio materiale di Lavoro:
Busta XI, Biografie.
Archivio Photographico, uncatalogued.

Slovenska Narodna in Študijška Knjižnica, Odsek za Zgodovino, (SNL)

(Files uncatalogued)
Boxes:

Isola Box 5	UAIS/SIAU Boxes 1, 2, 3, 4, 5, 6
1948	Simpozij Trst 1941–1947
AFZ-ZSZ-DAT	Sindicati
ASIZZ-UDAIS Razno	Volitve 1949
Notranja in Zunanja Politika	Volitve 1952 Boxes 1, 3
Poročila Zvezne Vojaške Uprave (ZVU)	ZVU SPPZ/OF
Razne	ZVU Stranke

Photo Archive.

USA

National Archives, USA
Diplomatic Branch, Washington, D.C.

RG 59 General Records of the Department of State Central Decimal File Class
    8605.00, confidential file (SDF) Special Files: Harley Notter Papers; Office
    of Western European Affairs relating to Italy; Office of the Assistant Sec-
    retary for Occupied Areas; Office of the Executive Secretariat; Policy Plan-
    ning Staff; Research and Analysis Reports 21.8.47-30.11.48 cc.11.
Washington National Record Center, Suitland (Maryland)
RG 331 Allied Occupation and Operational Headquarters, World War II. Al-
    lied Commission of Control (Italy); Headquarters Allied Commission
    of Control, National; Allied Military Government, British-United States
    Zone, Venezia Giulia, 1945–1947. Allied Military Government, British
    United States Zone, Free Territory of Trieste, 1947–1954: Office of the
    Commander and Military Governor; Allied Secretariat; Planning and
    Advisory Staff.
RG 84 Records of the Foreign Service Posts of the Department of State. Rome
    Embassy. US Political Adviser to the Commander, British-United States
    Zone, Free Territory of Trieste (US Polad Trieste) File 350 Trieste Bald-
    win Reports, File 800 Trieste, US Political Adviser to the Governor and
    Military Commander, BUSZ, FTT.
RG 286 Agency for International Development Economic Cooperation Ad-
    ministration (ECA) Mission to Trieste, Office of the Director.

INTERVIEWS

Sir Robert Andrew (Field Security Officer Intelligence Corps Troops (Betfor) in
    Trieste, 1948): Interview May 1990, London.
Licia Chersovani, 21/9/89, S. Giovanni, Trieste.
"Mira" (Partizanka)- Karolina Rijavec, 10/9/89, Slovene Cultural Center, Trieste.
Neva Lukes, 5/9/89, Slovene Cultural Center, Trieste.
Nadia Pahor, 18/9/89, Slovene Cultural Center, Trieste.
John Rosselli, 10/6/89, Brighton, England.
Anica and Emma, 6/9/89, Slovene Cultural Center, Trieste.

NEWSPAPERS AND PERIODICALS

AMG Gazette
Annali Triestini
Il Corriere di Trieste
La Difesa della Razza: Scienza,
    Documentazione, Polemica
La Fiaccola, settimanale
    dell'Uomo Qualunque
Giornale Alleato
Italia

Libera Parola
The New Europe
Il Nostro Avvenire
Il Piccolo
Ponterosso
Primorski Dnevnik
Razgledi
Razza e Civiltà
Slovenski Zbornik

Tedenska Priloga Primorskega
Dnevnika
Trieste
Trieste Libera

Trieste: The Political Review
Umana
La Vita Internazionale
Žena

SELECTED SECONDARY SOURCES

Acerbo, G. *I fondamenti della dottrina fascista della razza*. Roma: n.p., 1940.

Airey, Maj. Gen. T.S. CB CBE. *Report on the Administration of the British-United States Zone of the Free Territory of Trieste*, Nos. 1–10. 1947–1949.

Aktivist. Mestni Komitet SIAU, Trst st. 1, 2 (1948).

Albrecht-Carré, R. *Italy at the Paris Peace Conference*. Connecticut: Archon Books, 1966, 1st ed. 1938.

Albrecht-Carré, R. "The North-eastern frontier of Italy," *Journal of Central European Affairs* V (April 1945): 230–42.

Alcock, A. E. *The History of the South Tyrol Question*. London: Michael Joseph, 1970.

Alexander, Field Marshal. *The Italian Campaign 12 Dec 1944-2nd May 1945: A Report to the Combined Chiefs of Staff by the Supreme Allied Commander Mediterranean*. London: HMSO, 1951.

AMG. *Report of the Administration of the British United States Zone of the Free Territory of Trieste*, Report Nos.1–11 (1947–1951).

AMG, B/US Zone. *Trieste Handbook* (1st ed. June 1949, revised 1 May 1950).

Angelicus and Ruben. *Sotto due bandiere:tre anni di storia antipatica*. Trieste: F. Zigiotti, 1948.

Apih, E. *Italia. Fascismo e antifascismo nella Venezia Giulia (1918–1943)*. Bari: Laterza, 1966.

———. "Premessa," In C. Schiffrer, *Le origini dell'irredentismo triestino 1813–1860*. Udine: DelBianco, 1978.

———. *Trieste. Storia della città italiana*. Bari: Laterza, 1988.

———. "E` per caso la Risiera nostro passato che non passa?" *Qualestoria* XVII (aprile 1989): 185–92.

Ara, A. and C. Magris. *Trieste. Un'identità di frontiera*. Torino: Einaudi, 1982.

Atkins, E. *Trieste: C'est la guerre?* Paris: Agence continentale d'information, 1954.

Auerbach, B. *Les Races et les nationalités en Autriche-Hongrie*. Paris: Felix Alcan, 1898.

Auty, P., and R. Clogg, eds. *British Policy towards Wartime Resistance in Yugoslavia and Greece*. London: Macmillan, 1975.

Avšič, J. *Our First March into the Venetian Slovenia*. Ljubljana: Ljubljana Research Institute, 1946.

Baroni, R. *Trieste exit: Irredentismo con sentimento*. Trieste: Rino Baroni, 1979.

Bartelson, J. *A genealogy of sovereignty*. Cambridge: Cambridge University Press, 1995.

Bartoli, G. *Italia ritorna. Dieci anni di storia triestina nei documenti, scritti e discorsi del sindaco*. Bologna: Capelli, 1959.

Battisti, G. *Una regione per Trieste: Studio di geografia politica ed economica*. Udine: DelBianco, 1979.

Benco, S. *Trieste*. Firenze: Casa Editrice Nemi, 1932.

———. *Contemplazione del disordine*. Udine: DelBianco, 1946.

Berezin, M. *Making the Fascist Self: The Political Culture of Interwar Italy*. Ithaca: Cornell University Press, 1997.

Bhabha, H. K., ed. *Nation and Narration*. London: Routledge, 1990.

Biber, D., ed. *Konec druge svetovne vojne v Jugoslaviji, Bovec* 12, xxxviii, (1986).

Biesteker, T. J., and C. Weber, eds. *State Sovereignty as Social Construct*. Cambridge: Cambridge University Press, 1996.

Bon Gherardi, S. *La Persecuzione antiebraica a Trieste (1938–1945)*. Udine: Del Bianco, 1972.

Bosworth, R. *Italy Least of the Great Powers: Italian Foreign Policy Before the First World War*. Cambridge: Cambridge University Press, 1979.

———. *Explaining Auschwitz and Hiroshima*. London: Routledge, 1994.

———. *The Italian Dictatorship*. London: Edward Arnold, 1998.

———. "Italy's Historians and the Myth of Fascism." In R. Langhorne, ed., *Diplomacy and Intelligence during the Second World War. Essays in honour of F. H. Hinsley*. Cambridge: Cambridge University Press, 1985.

———. "Mito e linguaggio nella politica estera italiana." In R. Bosworth and S. Romano, eds., *Politica Estera Italiana 1860–1988*. Bologna: Il Mulino, 1991.

Botteri, G., ed. *Il comunismo a Trieste*. Udine: DelBianco, 1961.

Botteri, C., and S. Marchetti, eds. *Trieste e la sua storia: Il rapporto difficile fra cattolici e comunisti—La rivista "Trieste"—Il centro-sinistra e il caso Hreščak*. Udine: Dedolibri, 1986.

Bowman, A. C. *Zones of Strain*. Stanford: Hoover Press Publication, 1982.

Bravo, A., and A. M. Bruzzone. *In Guerra senza armi: Storie di donne. 1940–1945*. Roma: Laterza, 1995.

Brecelj, A. *I gruppi politici autonomi sloveni a Trieste 1949–1952*. Trieste: Krožek za družbene vprašanje, Virgil Scek, 1983.

Cadorna, R. *La riscossa. Dal 25 luglio alla liberazione*. Milano: Rizzoli, 1948.

Calder, K. *Britain and the Origins of the New Europe 1914–1918*. Cambridge: Cambridge University Press, 1976.

Campbell, D. *Writing Security: United States Foreign Policy and the Politics of Identity*. Manchester: Manchester University Press, 1992.

Campbell, J. C. *Successful Negotiation: Trieste 1954: An Appraisal by the Five Participants*. Princeton: Princeton University Press, 1976.

Carpi, D. "The Origins and Development of Fascism—Anti-semitism in Italy (1922–1945)." In Y. Gutman and L. Rothkirche, *The Catastrophe of European Jewry—Selected Papers*. New York: Ltvav Publishing House Inc., 1976.

Cary, J. *A Ghost in Trieste*. Chicago: University of Chicago Press, 1993.

Catalano, F. *Storia del CLNAI*. Bari: Laterza, 1956.

Cermelj, L. *Life and Death Struggle of a National Minority (The Jugoslavs in Italy)*. 2nd. ed. Ljubljana, 1945.

————. *Il vescovo Antonio Santin e gli sloveni e croati*. Ljubljana, 1953.
Cernigoi, C. *Operazione foibe a Trieste: come si crea una mistificazione storica, dalla propaganda nazifascista attraverso la guerra fredda fino al neoirredentismo*. Udine: Kappa Vu, 1997.
Cervani, G. *Gli scritti politici di Fabio Cusin nel "Corriere di Trieste": Gli anni di polemica dura (1946–1948)* Civiltà di Risorgimento series, no.44. Udine: DelBianco, 1991.
CLNVG et l'Association des Partisans Italiens de Trieste. *Le mouvement italien de la resistance dans la Venetie Julienne*. Trieste: Stabilimento Tipografico Nazionale, 1946.
Coceani, B. *Il Fascismo nel Mondo*. Rocca S. Casciano, 1933.
————. *"Trieste e la sua università." Discorso Pronunciato alla Camera dei Deputati. Nella 2 tornata del 2 dicembre 1938-XVII*. Roma: Tipografia della Camera dei deputati, 1938.
————. *Mussolini, Hitler, Tito alle porte orientali d'Italia*. Bologna: Cappelli, 1948.
Cody, J. F. *Official History of New Zealand in The Second World War 1939–45: 28 (Maori) Battalion*. Wellington: War History Branch, Department of Internal Affairs, 1956.
Coen, M. *Bruno Pincherle*. Pordenone: Edizioni Studio Tesi, 1995.
Cokelj, B. *Zgodovinski razvoj narodnostnega stanja v Trstu*. Trst: Slovenska Prosvetna Matica, 1949.
Coles, H. L., and A. K. Weinberg. *US Army in WWII, Special Studies Civil Affairs: Soldiers become Governors*. Washington, D.C.: Office of the Chief of Military History, Dept of the Army, 1964.
Colummi, C. et al. *Storia di un esodo: Istria 1945–1956*. Trieste: ISMLVG, 1980.
Comitato Cittadino dell'UAIS. *Trieste nella lotta per la democrazia*. Trieste: UAIS, 1945.
Committee for the Defense of the Italian Character of Trieste and Istria. *Trieste November 1953: Facts and Documents*. Trieste, 1953.
Committee of National Liberation of Istria. *Trieste: Political and Ethnical Aspects of the Trieste Problem*. Trieste, 1954.
————. *Trieste: Zone "B." Land Without Liberty*. Trieste, 1954.
————. *Italy's Eastern Border*. Trieste, 1954.
Confederate Chamber of Labour in Trieste. "Report on the Situation of the Working Classes of Zone 'B' of the Free Territory from May 1945 up to date" (April 1950).
Connor, W. *The National Question in Marxist-Leninist Theory and Strategy*. Princeton: Princeton University Press, 1984.
Coppola, F. *Fascismo e Bolscevismo*. Roma: Istituto Nazionale di Cultura Fascista, 1938.
Corradini, E. *L'Unità e la potenza delle nazioni*. Firenze: Vallechi, 1926, 1st. ed. 1922.
Council of Liberation of Trieste. The *Activity of the Council of Liberation of Trieste (from May 17 to September 21 1945) (with a short historical introduction)*. Trieste, 1945, English edition.
Cox, G. *Defence of Madrid*. London: Victor Gollancz, 1937.
————. *The Road to Trieste*. London: Heinemann, 1947.

———. *The Race for Trieste*. London: William Kimber, 1977.

Critique. "Les Mystères de Trieste," Special Issue (août–sept. 1983).

Cronia, A. *La conoscenza del mondo slavo in Italia*. Padova: n.p., 1958.

Cusin, F. *Il confine orientale d'Italia nella politica europea del XIV e XV secolo* 2 Vols. Trieste: Lint, 1977, 1st ed. 1937.

———. *L'Italiano. Realtà e illusioni*. Roma: Atlantica, 1945.

———. *Introduzione allo studio della storia*. Padova: Cedam, 1946.

———. *La liberazione di Trieste, contributo alla storiografia non nazionalistica di Trieste*. Trieste: F. Zigiotti, 1946.

———. *L'Italia unità 1860–1876. Saggio di una nuova sintesi storica*. Udine: DelBianco, 1952.

———. *Venti secoli di bora sul Carso e sul Golfo*. Trieste: Gabbiano, 1952.

———. "Autocritica," *Studi Urbinati* 1–2 (anno XXIX nuova serie B, 1956).

———. *Antistoria d'Italia. Una demistificazione della storia ufficiale*. Milano: Arnoldo Mondadori, 1972.

———. *Appunti alla storia di Trieste*. Udine: DelBianco, 1983, Ist ed.1938.

Dalla liberazione agli anni '80: Trieste come problema nazionale. PCI, 1982.

Dallo squadrismo Fascista alle stragi della Risiera (con il resoconto del processo) Trieste-Istria 1919–1945. Trieste: ANED, 1978.

De Castro, D. *Trieste. Cenni riassuntivi sul problema giuliano nell'ultimo decennio*. Bologna: Cappelli, 1953.

———. *La questione di Trieste: L'azione politica e diplomatica italiana dal 1943 al 1954*. Trieste: Lint, 1981.

———. "Ricordo di quei giorni." In *Trieste diary maggio–giugno 1945*. Gorizia: Goriziana, 1990.

De Felice, R. *Mussolini il duce, II. Lo Stato Totalitario 1936–1940*. Torino: Einaudi, 1981.

De Grazia, V. *How Fascism Ruled Women: Italy, 1922–1945*. Berkeley: University of California Press, 1992.

Dei Sabelli, L. *Nazione e minoranze etniche, Vol. 1*. Bologna: Zanichelli, 1929.

Desico, E. *La passione di Trieste: Ottobre 1914–maggio 1915*. Roma: Edizioni di Storia e Letteratura, 1981.

Djordevic, D. *The Creation of Yugoslavia 1914–1918*. Oxford: Clio, 1980.

I Documenti Diplomatici Italiani sesta serie: 1918–1922, Vol. 2. Roma, 1980.

Documents Relating to New Zealand's Participation in the Second World War 1939–45, Vol. II, Official History of New Zealand in the Second World War. Wellington: War History Branch, Department of Internal Affairs, 1951.

Dollot, R. *Trieste et la France*. Paris: A. Pedone, 1961.

Duroselle, J.-B. *Le conflit de Trieste 1943–1954*. Bruxelles: L'Institut de Sociologie de l'Université libre de Bruxelles, 1966.

Ellwood, D. W. *Italy 1943–1945*. Leicester: Leicester University Press, 1985.

Esposito, G. *Trieste e la sua odissea*. Roma: Comitato Italiano Pro Bacino Adriatico, 1952.

European Recovery Program: Trieste Country Study. U.S. Economic Cooperation Administration, Feb. 1949.

Il Fascismo nella Venezia Giulia: Dalle origini alla marcia su Roma. Trieste: CELVI, 1932.

Fauro, R. *Trieste: Italiani e Slavi; Il Governo Austriaco; l'irredentismo.* Roma: Garzoni, 1914.

Fogar, G. *Sotto l'occupazione nazista nelle provincie orientali.* Udine: DelBianco, 1968.

———. "Foibe e deportazione," *Qualestoria,* XVII (agosto–dicembre, 1989): 11–20.

———. "Venezia Giulia 1943–1945: Problemi e situazioni." In *Trieste 1941–1947.* Udine: Dedolibri, 1991.

Fölkel, F., and C. K. Cergoly. *Trieste Provincia Imperiale: splendore e tramonto del porto degli Asburgo.* Milano: Bompiani, 1983.

Fraddorio, O. *Il Regime per la Razza.* Tumminelle, 1939.

Furlani, V. *Trieste 1947,* script. Milano: Gastaldi Editore, 1955.

Gabrielli, P. "La solidarietà tra pratica politica e vita quotidiana nell'esperienza delle donne comuniste," *Rivista di storia contemporanea* 22, 1 (1993): 34–56.

Gaeta, G. *Trieste ed il colonialismo italiano: Appunti storici giornalistici.* Trieste: Delfino, 1943.

Gambino, A. *Storia del dopoguerra dalla liberazione al potere DC.* Bari: Laterza, 1978.

Ganapini, L., ed. *"anche l'uomo doveva essere di ferro": Classe e movimento operaio a Trieste nel secondo dopoguerra.* Milano: Franco Angeli, 1986.

Gayda, V. *Modern Austria: Her Racial and Social Problems with a Study of Italia Irredenta.* London: Fisher Unwin, 1915.

———. *Gli Slavi della Venezia Giulia.* Roma: Rava & Co. 1915.

Ghisleri, A. *Il concetto etnico di nazione e l'autodecisione nelle zone contestate.* Vega-Torino, reprinted 1945.

———. *Italia e Jugoslavia.* Roma: Libreria Politica Moderna, 1945.

Godoli, E. *La città nella storia d'Italia: Trieste.* Bari: Laterza, 1984.

Gombač, B. *Trieste/Trst: Ena imena, dva identiteta.* Trst: Tržaška Založba, 1993.

———. "F. Zwitter (1905–1988)," *Glasnik: Pariška Mirovna Pogodba, Katalog k razstavi in program mednarodne konference* 3 (1997): 39–42.

Gombač, M. "Znanstvene institucije in njihov delez pri mirovnih pogajanjih," *Glasnik: Pariška Mirovna Pogodba, Katalog k razstavi in program mednarodne konference* 3 (1997): 29–38.

———. "Autonomia e decentramento della politica jugoslava alla fine del secondo conflitto mondiale. Un caso specifico: il Comitato regionale di liberazione nazionale per il Litorale sloveno e Trieste," *Annales* 8 (1996): 87–110.

Gratton, G. *Trieste. The Password to Peace.* Paris: Guy LePrat, 1947.

Grindrod, M. *The New Italy: Transition from War to Peace.* London: Royal Institute of International Affairs, 1947.

Gross, F. *Ethnics in a Borderland: An Inquiry into the Nature of Ethnicity and Reduction of Ethnic Tension in a One-Time Genocide Area.* Connecticut: Greenwood Press, 1978.

Gustinčič, D. *Trieste o il problema della delimitazione dei confini fra la Jugoslavia e l'Italia.* Ljubljana: Ljudske Pravice, 1946.

Hall, D. O. W. *Women at War.* Wellington: War History Branch, Department of Internal Affairs, 1948.

Harris, C. R. S. *Allied Military Administration of Italy 1943–1945.* London: HMSO, 1957.

Hill, N. L. *Claims to Territory in International Law and Relations.* London: Oxford University Press, 1945.

HQAMG XIII Corps. *Monthly Report* (agosto 1945–agosto 1946).

Hobsbawm, E. *Nations and Nationalism Since 1870: Programme, Myth, Reality.* Cambridge: Cambridge University Press, 1990.

Horn, D. G. *Social Bodies: Science, Reproduction, and Italian Modernity.* Princeton: Princeton University Press, 1994.

Illyricus. *La questione de Trieste: Essai sur le Problème jougoslave dans les pays "irredente."* Geneva, 1915.

Inaugurazione dell'anno accademico 1983/84, Università degli studi di Trieste. Trieste: Lint, 1984.

Interviews and Articles. The Clergy of the Slovene Littoral for the Federative People's Republic of Yugoslavia. Ljubljana: Gregorčičeva Založba, 1946.

Isnenghi, M. *Intelletuali militanti e intelletuali funzionari.* Torino: Einaudi, 1979.

Jaksetich, G., ed. *La brigata "Fratelli Fontanot": Partigiani italiani in Slovenia.* Milano: La Pietra, 1982.

Jančar-Webster, B. *Women and Revolution in Yugoslavia 1941–1945.* Denver: Arden Press, 1990.

Jeri, J. *Tržaško vprašanje po drugi svetovni vojni, Tri faze diplomatskega boja.* Ljubljana: Cankarjeva Založba, 1961.

Jeri, J., ed. *Slovenci v Italiji po drugi svetovni vojni.* Ljubljana: Cankarjeva Založba, 1975.

Jones, S. B. *Boundary-Making: A Handbook for Statesmen, Treaty Editors, and Boundary Commissioners.* Washington, D.C.: Carnegie Endowment for International Peace, 1945.

The Julian March. The Memorandum of the Regional National Liberation Committee for the Slovene Littoral and Trieste (in Croatian, Slovene, English, Serbian, French, and Italian, n.d.).

Kann, R. *The Multinational Empire: Nationalism and National Reform in the Habsburg Monarchy 1848–1918, Vols. 1 and 2.* New York: Octagon, 1977.

Kearney, R. *Postnationalist Ireland: Politics, Culture, Philosophy.* London: Routledge, 1997.

Keating, M. *State and Regional Nationalism: Territorial Politics and the European State.* Brighton: Harvester Wheatsheaf, 1988.

Knox, M. "The Fascist Regime, its Foreign Policy, and its Wars: An 'Anti-Anti-Fascist' Orthodoxy?" *Contemporary European History* 4, 3 (1995).

———. *Mussolini Unleashed, 1939–1941: Politics and Strategy in Fascist Italy's Last War.* Cambridge: Cambridge University Press, 1982.

Kos, M. *Historical Development of the Slovene Western Frontier.* Ljubljana: Slovene Research Institute, Section for Frontier Questions, 1946.

Kocovic, B. *Territoire Libre de Trieste*. Paris: University of Paris, 1949, published 1984.

Kogan, N. *A Political History of Italy. The Postwar Years*. New York: Praeger, 1983.

Krleža, M. *La Thème Adriatique*. La societé pour la cooperation culturelle Yougoslavie-France, 1946).

Lapid, Y., and F. Kratochwil. *The Return of Culture and Identity in IR Theory*. Boulder: Lynne Rienner, 1996.

Lederer, I. J. *Yugoslavia at the Paris Peace Conference: A Study in Frontiermaking*. New Haven: Yale University Press, 1963.

Leprette, J. *Le Statut Internationale de Trieste*. Paris: A. Pedone, 1949.

Linklater, E. *The Campaign in Italy*. London: HMSO, 1951.

Lodolino, A. *Leggi Ordinamenti e Codici del Regime Fascista: Esposizione e commento ad uso delle scuole e delle persone colte: Le vie del Duce, Collana di Studi Fascista*. Lanciano: Giuseppe Carabba, 1930.

Luzzato, G. "Fabio Cusin e la storia di Trieste," *Studi Urbinati* 1–2 (anno XXIX, nuova serie B, 1956): 16–21.

Macartney, C. A. *National States and National Minorities*. London: Oxford University Press, 1934.

Macciocchi, M. A. *La Donna Nera: "Consenso" femminile e fascismo*. Milano: Feltrinelli, 1976.

Mack-Smith, D. *Italy: A Modern History*. Ann Arbor: University of Michigan Press, 1959.

MacLean, F. *Eastern Approaches*. London: Penguin 1991, 1st ed. 1949.

Maganja, N. *Trieste 1945–1954: Nascita del movimento politico autonomo sloveno*. Trieste: Krožek Scek, 1980.

Maier, B. *Gli scrittori triestini e il fascismo*. Trieste: Italo Svevo, 1975.

Maranelli, C., and G. Salvemini. *La Questione dell'Adriatico*. Roma: Libreria della Voce, 1918, 1st published in 1916.

Marinelli, G. *Slavi, Tedeschi, Italiani nel Cosidetto <Litorale> Austriaco (Istria, Trieste, Gorizia)*. Venezia: Antonelli, 1885.

Maserati, E. *L'occupazione jugoslava di Trieste (maggio–giugno 1945)*. Udine: Del-Bianco, 1963.

Melik, A. *Trieste and North Yugoslavia*. Ljubljana: Slovene Academy of Arts and Sciences, 1946.

Millo, A. *L'élite del potere a Trieste: Una biografia collettiva 1891–1938*. Milano: Franco Angeli, 1989.

Memorandum of the Government of the Federative People's Republic of Yugoslavia concerning the ethnical structure of the Julian March (n.d.).

Memorandum of the Government of the Federative People's Republic of Yugoslavia on the economic problem of Trieste. Belgrade, 1946.

M.K.G. "The Venezia Giulia Question," *The World Today*, Chatham House Review, Royal Institute of International Affairs 1 (new series, 1945): 147–59.

Moodie, A. E. *The Italo-Yugoslav Boundary. A Study in Political Geography*. London: George Philip and Son, 1945.

Mosconi, A. *I primi anni di governo italiano nella Venezia Giulia Trieste 1919–1922*. Bologna: Cappelli, 1924.

Mucci, M. "La Risiera di San Sabba a Trieste. Un'architettura per la memoria," *Qualestoria*, 2 (1996): 69–126.

Musoni, F. *La Vita degli Sloveni.* Palermo-Torino: Carlo Clausen, 1893.

"Les Mystères de Trieste," *Critique* special issue (Aug–Sept 1983.

Nazionalismo e neofascismo nella lotta politica al confine orientale 1945–75 (ISML Ts, n.d.).

Negrelli, G. *Al di qua del mito: Diritto storico e difesa nazionale nell'autonomismo della Trieste asburgica.* Udine: DelBianco, 1978.

Nicolson, H. *Peacemaking 1919.* London: Methuen, 1964 rev. edition.

Nizza, E. *Monumenti alla Libertà: Antifascismo, resistenza e pace nei monumenti italiani dal 1945 al 1985.* Milano: La Pietra, 1986.

Novak, B. C. *Trieste 1941–1954. The Ethnic, Political, and Ideological Struggle.* Chicago: University of Chicago Press, 1970.

Nucci, L. D. *Fascismo e spazio urbano.* Bologna: Il Mulino, 1992.

Ortaggi, S. "Nationalism and History in an Italian Classroom," *History Workshop* 6 (1978): 186–94.

Pacor, M. *Confine orientale. Questione nazionale e resistenza nel Friuli Venezia Giulia.* Milano: Feltrinelli,1964.

———. *Italia e balcani dal risorgimento alla resistenza.* Milano: Feltrinelli, 1968.

Pallante, P. *Il PCI e la questione nazionale Friuli Venezia Giulia 1941–1945.* Udine: DelBianco, 1980.

Patriarca, S. *Numbers and Nationhood: Writing Statistics in Nineteenth-Century Italy.* Cambridge: Cambridge University Press, 1996.

Patterson, E. M., ed. *The World Trend towards Nationalism.* The Annals of the American Academy of Political and Social Science (Vol. 174, July 1934).

Pearson, R. *National Minorities in Eastern Europe 1848–1945.* London: MacMillan Press, 1983.

Pellegrini, E. *Trieste dentro Trieste.* Firenze: Vallecchi Editore, 1985.

Peterin, Dr. S. *Zahodne velesile in tržaško vprašanje.* Ljubljana, 1953.

Pirjevec, J. *Tržaški vozel: O zgodovinskih dogodkih in političnem razvoju v letih 1945–1980.* Trieste: Založništvo Tržaškega Tiska, 1985.

Pittoni, A. *L'anima di Trieste.* Firenze: Vallechi Editore, 1968.

Pizzagalli, A. *Per l'italianità dei cognomi nella provincia di Trieste.* Trieste: Treves-Zanichelli, 1929.

Polson, C. E. *Yugoslavia: West or East?* (London Group of European Studies - reprinted from "The Month," January–February 1946).

Powell, N. *Travellers to Trieste.* London: Faber and Faber, 1977.

Prescott, J. R. V. *Political Frontiers and Boundaries.* London: Allen and Unwin, 1987.

Pupo, R. *La rifondazione della politica estera italiana: la questione giuliana (1944–46).* Udine: DelBianco, 1979.

Pupo, R, ed. *Trieste diary maggio–giugno 1945.* Gorizia: Goriziana, 1990.

Quarantotti Gambini, P. A. "Un antifascista epurato," (1946, pamphlet).

Quarantotti Gambini, P. A. *Primavera a Trieste.* Trieste: Italo Svevo, 1985.

Quazza, G. "The Politics of the Italian Resistance." In S. J. Woolf, *The Rebirth of Italy 1943–50.* London: Longman, 1972.

Questione dell'UAIS (Edito a cura del Comitato Regionale dell'UAIS, Nov.1945).

Rabel, R. *Between East and West: Trieste, The United States, and the Cold War, 1941–1954*. Durham, N.C.: Duke University Press, 1988.

Ravasini, O. *Compendio di notizie, toponomastica stradale sulla nomenclatura di località e strade di Trieste*. Trieste: La Editoriale Libraria, 1929.

Ravera, C. *Breve storia del movimento femminile in Italia*. Roma: Editori Riuniti, 1978.

Reed, M. E. "The Antifascist Front of Women and the Communist Party in Croatia: Conflicts within the Resistance." In T. Yedlin, ed., *Women in Eastern Europe and the Soviet Union*. New York: Praeger, 1980.

Renton, B. "The Three Days of Trieste," *World Review* (40 June 1952): 23–28.

Robertson E., and E. Timms. *The Habsburg Legacy: National Identity in Historical Perspective, Austrian Studies V*. Edinburgh: Edinburgh University Press, 1994.

Roletto, G. *Trieste ed i suoi problemi: Situazione—tendenze—prospettive*. Trieste: Borsati, 1952.

Rusinow, D. I. *Italy's Austrian Heritage 1919–1946*. Oxford University Press, 1969.

Rutteri, S. *Trieste. Spunti dal suo passato*. Trieste: Lint, 1968.

Salvatorelli, L., and G. Mira. *Storia d'Italia nel periodo Fascista, vol. 2*. Milano: Mondadori, 1972.

Salvemini, G. "Il fascismo e le minoranze." In N. Valeri and A. Merola, eds., *Opere, iv: Scritti sul Fascismo, vol. ii*. Milano: Feltrinelli, 1966.

———. *Racial Minorities under Fascism in Italy*. Chicago: The Women's International League for Peace and Freedom, Conference on Minorities, 1934.

San Sabba: Istruttoria e processo per il Lager della Risiera. Milano: Mondadori, 1988.

Sapelli, G. *Trieste italiana. Mito e destino economico*. Milano: Franco Angeli, 1990.

Schiffrer, C. *Historic Glance at the relations between Italians and Slavs in Venezia Giulia*. Istituto di Storia dell'Università di Trieste, 1946.

Schiffrer, C., and E. Apih. "Il socialismo triestino nella lotta antifascista e nella difesa dell'italianità (1942–1948)." Trieste: PSVG publication, 1948.

Schiffrer, C. "L'attesa di Trieste." *Atti del XLIV Congresso di Storia del Risorgimento Italiano, Trieste, 31/10–4/11/68*. Roma: Istituto per la storia del risorgimento italiano, 1970.

———. *Le origini dell'irredentismo triestino (1813–1860)*. Udine: DelBianco, 1978, 1st ed. 1937.

Scotti, G. *Bono Taliano: Gli Italiani in Jugoslavia 1941–1943*. Milano: La Pietra, 1977.

Secoli, G. *Il terzo cinquantennio della "Minerva" 1910–1960*. Trieste: La Società di Minerva, 1965.

Sema, P., and C. Bibalo. *Cronaca sindacale triestina 1943–1978*. Roma: Editrice Sindacale Italiana, 1981.

Sestan, E. "Guidizio 'Anseatico' sugli Italiani," *Belfagor* 4 (15/7/46): 487–94.

———. *Venezia Giulia. Lineamenti di storia etnica e culturale*. Roma: Edizione Italiane, 1947.

Seton-Watson, C. "Italy's Imperial Hangover," *Journal of Contemporary History* 15 (1980): 169–70.

Seton-Watson, H., and C. Seton-Watson. *The Making of a New Europe: R. W. Seton-Watson and the last years of Austria-Hungary*. London: Methuen, 1981.

Seton-Watson, R. W. *The Southern Slav Question and the Habsburg Monarchy*. London: Constable, 1911.

———. *Europe in the Melting Pot*. London: Macmillan, 1919.

Sighele, S. *Pagine Nazionaliste*. Milano: Treves, 1910.

Silvestri, C. *Dalla redenzione al fascismo. Trieste 1918–1922*. Udine: DelBianco, 1966, 2nd. ed.

Skerl, Dr. F. *The Struggle of the Slovenes in the Littoral for the People's Authority* (n.p. 1945).

The Struggle of the people of the Julian March for freedom and self-determination (1947).

Slataper, S. *Il mio Carso*. Milano: Il Saggiatore, 1965.

———. *Scritti Politici*, ed. G. Stuparich. Milano: Mondadori, 1954.

Slovenci v Italiju včeraj in danes. Trieste: Založništvo Tržaškega Tiska, 1974.

Sluga, G. "Inventing Ethnic Spaces: 'Free Territory,' Sovereignty and the 1947 Peace Treaty," *Acta Histriae* 4 (1998): 173–86.

———. "Identity and Revolution: The History of the Forty Days of May 1945," *Annales: Annals for Istrian and Mediterranean Studies* 8 (1998): 125–40.

———. "The Risiera di San Sabba: Fascism, Anti-Fascism, and Italian Nationalism," *Journal of Modern Italian Studies* 3 (1996): 401–12.

———. "Inventing Trieste: History, Anti-History, and Nation," *The European Legacy: Towards New Paradigms* 1 (1996): 25–30.

———. "Cold War Casualties: Gender, Ethnicity, and the Writing of History," *Women's Studies International Forum—From Margins to Centre: Gender, Ethnicity, and Nationalism* [special issue] 19 (1996): 75–86.

———. "No Man's Land: the Gendered Boundaries of Postwar Trieste," *Gender and History* 6 (1994): 184–201.

———. "Trieste: Ethnicity and the Cold War," *Journal of Contemporary History* 29 (1994): 285–303.

———. "<Terra di Nessuno>: i confini di <genere> nella Trieste del dopoguerra," *Qualestoria* 2–3 (1993): 165–86.

———. "Fascism, Anti-fascism, and italianità: Contesting Memories and Identities." In R. Bosworth and P. Dogliani, eds., *Italian Fascism: Memory, History, and Representation*. London: Macmillan, 1998.

———. "Orientalising the Balkan Wars." In G. Ianziti, ed., *Bosnia-Hercegovina in the Yugoslav Aftermath*. Brisbane: Queensland University of Technology Press, 1997.

Spackman, B. *Fascist Virilities: Rhetoric, Ideology, and Social Fantasy in Italy*. Minneapolis: University of Minnesota Press, 1996.

Spazzali, R. *Foibe: un dibattito ancora aperto*. Trieste: Lega Nazionale, 1990.

Spinelli, M. A *Trieste italiana*. Pistoia: Stabilimento Grafico Niccolai, 1954.

Spriano, P. *Stalin and the European Communists*. London: Verso, 1985.

Sprigge, S. "Trieste Diary," October 1945, *The World Today*, Chatham House Review, Royal Institute of International Affairs, 1 (July–December 1945, new series): 159–86.

————. "The Lure of Trieste and Istria," *Twentieth Century* 154 (December 1953): 406–13.

St. John, R. *The Silent People Speak*. New York: Doubleday and Co. Inc., 1948.

Stella, A. "Il comune di Trieste." In G. Galasso, *Storia di Italia*, Vol. 17 (UTET, 1979).

La Storia della Slavia Italiana. Secondo ciclo di conferenze degli incontri culturali 1974–75 a Pulfero, San Pietro al Natisone. Trieste: Stampa Triestina, 1978.

Stranj, P. *The Submerged Community: An A to Ž of the Slovenes in Italy*. Trieste: Stampa Triestina, 1992.

Stuparich, G. *Trieste nei miei ricordi*. Milano: Garzanti, 1948.

Svečana predaja civilne oblasti, Izvršnemu odboru mesta Trsta. Delovna konferenca vojaškega in civilnega predstavništva mesta Trsta. Maribor: POOF, 1945.

Tamaro, A. *Due anni di storia 1943–45*, 3 Vols. Roma: Tosi, 1948.

Tamborra, A. "L'Europa orientale." In *Bibliografia dell'età del Risorgimento, vol. III*. Firenze: Leo S. Olschki Editore, n.d.

Tarchiani, A. *Dieci anni tra Roma e Washington*. Milano: Mondadori, 1956.

Taylor, A. J. P. *Trieste*. New York: United Committee of South Slavic Americans, 1945.

The Tiger Triumphs: The Story of Three Great Divisions in Italy (HMSO, for India, 1946).

Tobia, B. *Una Patria per gli italiani: spazi, itinerari, monumenti nell' Italia unità, 1870–1900*. Roma: Laterza, 1991.

Todorova, M. *Imagining the Balkans*. London: Oxford University Press, 1997.

Togliatti, P. *Linea d'una politica*. Milano-Sera, 1948.

Tonel, C., ed. *Dossier sul neofascismo a Trieste 1945–1983*. Trieste: Dedolibri, 1991.

Trieste 1941–1947. Trieste: Dedolibri, 1991.

Trieste and the Julian March: The Original Yugoslav Government Memorandum on these subjects and subsequent official statements with Maps. London Yugoslav Embassy Information Office, 1946.

Trieste e la Venezia Giulia. Roma: Istituto Editoriale Julia Romano, 2nd ed. 1951.

Troha, N. "Osvoboditev ali okupacija, narodna osvoboditev ali revolucija—Primorska in Trst v letu 1945," *Slovenija v Letu 1945: Zbornik Referatov* (Zveza Zgodovinskih Društev Slovenije, 1996): 77–137.

Tuta, A. R. *La questione nazionale a Trieste in un'inchiesta tra gli operai sloveni*. Trieste: Slovenski Raziskovalni Institut, Stampa Triestina, 1980.

Udina, M. *Scritti sulla questione di Trieste: sorta in seguito al secondo conflitto mondiale ed i principali atti internazionali ed interni ad essa relativi*. Milano: Dott. A. Guiffre, 1969.

L'università di Trieste nella luce della libertà democratica. Trieste: n.p., 1945.

Valdevit, G. *La questione di Trieste 1941–1954. Politica internazionale e contesto locale*. Milano: Franco Angeli, 1987, 2nd edition.

Valdevit, G., ed. *Foibe. Il peso del passato. Venezia Giulia 1943–1945*. Venezia: Marsilio, 1997.

Valussi, G. *Gli sloveni in Italia*. Trieste: Lint, 1974.

Vare, D. *East Wind on the Adriatic* (Italian Centre of Studies and Publications for International Reconciliation, Rome, 1st ed. August 1945, newly revised February 1946).

Venaille, F. *Trieste,* Series "des Villes." Paris: Aux Editions du Champ Vallon, 1985.

Verani, F., ed. *La questione etnica ai confini orientali d'Italia. Antologia.* Trieste: Italo Svevo, 1990.

Verginella, M. A. Volk, and K. Colja. *Storia e memoria degli sloveni del Litorale: Fascismo, guerra e resistenza.* Quaderni 7, Istituto Regionale per la Storia del movimento di liberazione nel Friuli-Venezia Giulia, 1997.

Verzar-Bass, M., ed. *Il teatro Romano di Trieste.* Monumento, storia, funzione. Istituto Svizzero di Roma, 1991.

Vidali, V. *Ritorno alla città senza pace. Il 1948 a Trieste.* Milano: Vangelista, 1982.

Vinci, A. "Il Fascismo nella Venezia Giulia e l'opera di snazionalizzazione delle minoranze," *Il Territorio* 6 (1996).

———. "Venezia Giulia e fascismo. Alcune ipotesi storiografiche," *Qualestoria* 16 (1988): 39–60.

———, ed. *Trieste in Guerra: Gli anni 1938–1943.* Trieste: i Quaderni di Qualestoria, 1992.

———. "*Geopolitica* e Balcani: l'esperienza di un gruppo di intellettuali in un Ateneo di confine," *Storia e Società* 47 (1990): 87–127.

Viora, M. "L'Università degli studi di Trieste. Cenni Storici," *Cenni Storici.* Trieste: No. 3, Istituto di Storia Medioevale e Moderna, 1958.

Vivante, A. *Irredentismo adriatico.* Firenze: Parenti, 1954, 1st ed. 1912.

Vrščaj-Holly, S. "Slovenska Žena in Osvobodilni Boj," *Slovenski Zbornik 1944.* Ljubljana: Državna Založba Slovenije, 1945.

Walston, J. "History and Memory of the Italian Concentration Camps," *Historical Journal* 40 (1997).

Ward, D. *Anti-fascisms: Cultural Politics in Italy, 1943–46, Benedetto Croce and the Liberals, Carlo Levi and the "Actionists."* New Jersey: Associated University Presses, 1996.

Whittam, J. R. "Drawing the Line: Britain and the Emergence of the Trieste Question, January 1941–May 1945," *English Historical Review* 419 (April 1991): 346–70.

Williams, B. F. *Stains on My Name, War in My Veins: Guyana and the Politics of Cultural Struggle.* Durham, N.C.: Duke University Press, 1991.

Wolff, L. *Inventing Eastern Europe: The Map of Civilization on the Mind of the Enlightenment.* Stanford: Stanford University Press, 1994.

Zapponi, N. "Fascism in Italian Historiography, 1986–1993: A Fading National Identity," *Journal of Contemporary History* 29 (1994).

Zazzi, D. *Trieste Città Divisa.* Milano: Mazzotta, 1985.

Ženam. Svobodnega Tržaškega Ozemlja. Antifašistična Slovenska-Italijanska Ženska Zveza, Trieste, 1948.

Zwitter, F. *To Destroy Nazism or to Reward It? An Aspect of the Question of Slovene Carinthia.* Belgrade: Yugoslav Institute for International Affairs, 1947.

Index

Acerbo, Giacomo, 57, 196n 107
Action Party (*Partito d'Azione*), 76, 122, 124, 137, 139, 159
Adriatic, 1, 2, 3, 11, 14–38 *passim*, 52, 111, 136, 141, 160, 171, 173, 177
Adriatic boundary, 2, 4, 13, 39, 66, 83, 135, 174
Adriatic question, 1914–1920, 1, 25–38, 136, 137
Airey (Governor), 113, 145, 147, 150
Albanian, 44, 45, 46, 56, 95
Albrecht-Carré, René, 34, 187n 104
Alexander (Field-Marshall), 68, 99, 113
Alleanza Nazionale, 170
Alliance of Slovene-Italian Anti-Fascist Women, 67, 74
Allied Information Service, 128
allogene/allogeno, 32, 42, 45, 48, 49, 50, 52, 54, 58
Alpers, Benedict, 117, 118, 130, 213n 36
Alto Adige, 35, 36, 45, 48, 133, 138
anarchists, 139
Anderson, Benedict, 4

Annoni, Antonio Marcello, 45, 191n 27
anthropologists/anthropology, 16, 17, 21, 52, 53, 120, 176
Anti-Fascist Italian Youth, 67
Antifascist Union, 119, 125
Anti-Fascist Women, 67, 73, 74, 86, 97, 109, 127, 128
anti-history, 158–171
anti-Semitism, 47, 56
Apih, Elio, 42, 165
Ardeatine, 170
Armenians, 27
Armstrong (Lieutenant Colonel), 119
assimilation, 6, 7, 27, 32, 42–52 *passim*, 57, 59, 78, 79
Association for the Victims of Nazi and Fascist Deportation, 167
Associazione Nazionale Venezia Giulia e Dalmazia, 170
Atlantic Charter, 63, 66
Attlee, Clement, 119, 120, 124
Auerbach, Bertrand, 17, 182n 16, n 17
Australia, 155

Austria/Austrian, 38, 50, 65, 66, 70, 82, 83, 90, 96, 104, 133, 144
Austrian Committee of Liberation, 96
Austrian Social Democratic Party, 19, 24
Austro-Hungarian empire: *See* Habsburg empire
Austro-Marxists, 19, 20–24 *passim*, 75, 158, 163

Baldwin, Charles, 147–149
Balkans, 2–6 *passim*, 9, 13, 15, 36, 44, 47, 51, 52, 53, 54, 58, 59, 60, 64, 78, 82, 91, 99, 102, 104, 108, 135, 139, 162, 170, 173, 175, 177
Bandelli, Gino, 55, 194n 89
Banne, 72
Barcola, 152
Bartoli, Gianni, 151
Basovizza, 77, 90–91, 109, 150, 166, 167, 168, 169
Bassi, Ercole, 36, 45, 188n 119, 191n 30
Bauer, Otto, 19–20, 23
Belgrade Agreement, 99, 101, 114
Benco, Silvio, 60, 161–162, 197n 128, 225n 27
Berezin, Mabel, 167, 197n 127
Bevk, France, 118
bilingualism, 27, 74, 79, 80, 97, 145, 147, 151
Bimillenario Augusteo (1937–1938), 54
Blocco Trestino, Il (The Trestine Bloc), 139
Bolshevik(s), 2, 44, 58, 72, 103
borders (boundary regions), 13, 14, 63, 66, 82, 95, 99, 102, 108, 132, 133, 135, 136, 138, 162, 174; *mentioned*, 1–8, 24–42, 50–59, 69–78
Borgo San Marco, 168–169
Bosnia, 65, 162
Bosworth, Richard, 23, 184n 50
Bottai, Guiseppe, 57
Bowman, Alfred, 113, 126, 129, 130, 143, 173, 211n 11

British-American Allied Military Government of Trieste, 1, 3, Chapters 4–6, 158, 168, 174
British 8th Army, 83
British Foreign Office, 29, 114, 115, 123, 124, 132, 135, 141, 143, 146, 149, 151, 154
British Intelligence, 91, 98
British Labour Party, 119
British Royal Navy, 86, 99
British War Office, 143
Broad, Phillip, 151, 152, 154
Bruch, Giordano, 139

Calder, Kenneth, 34, 186n 82
Campbell, David, 5, 111, 179n 3, 210n 2
Campbell, John, 173
Caporetto, Battle of, 31
Carinthia, 65, 68
Carlyle, Margaret, 149
Carmichael, Cathie, 15, 181n 6
Carniola, 13
Carr, E. H., 135, 218n 6
Carso/Karst/Kras, 11, 20, 36, 86, 90, 109
Casa del Popolo, 112
Catholicism, 12, 76, 98, 169, 170
censi, 13, 18, 30, 59, 120, 141
Centre for Political Culture, 159
Četniks, 63, 73, 82
Charles, Sir Noel, 124
chauvinism, 71, 97, 148, 158, 165, 168, 169, 173, 176, 177
Chersovani, Licia, 71, 74
Christian Democrats, 150, 169
Christian Socialists, 66
Christianity, 92
Churchill, Winston, 63, 86, 151
Civil Affairs Officer, 113, 117, 126
Civil Commissioner-Generals, 41
Civil Police, 131
Civiltà, 24, 25, 42, 47, 53, 55, 57, 59, 78, 81, 92, 162, 164
class, 3, 8, 15, 19, 25, 38, 41, 44, 64, 65, 71, 74, 75, 86, 97, 104, 108, 115,

121, 123, 125, 126, 130, 131, 132, 153, 175
Classification of cultural differences, nineteenth-century, 16
cleansing, 6, 170
Cobban, Alfred, 135, 218n 6
Coceani, Bruno, 48, 49, 51, 55, 77, 81, 162
Cognale, 90
cohabitation, 77
Cold War, 3, 7, 108, 109, 111, 112, 117, 131, 132, 133–155, 173, 174, 175
collaboration/collaborators, 83, 91, 101, 102, 122, 168
Collotti, Enzo, 80
Comeno, 72
cominformist, 149, 150
Comitato Fronte Nazionale d'Azione, 67
Communal Council, 114, 139
communism, 5, 65–75, 115, 121, 132, 133, 146, 148, 175, 178
Communist Party, 98, 121, 122
communists, 1, 3, 5, 7, 43, 44, 50, 57, 58, 64, 71, 73, 76, 77, 89, 92, 94, 97, 98, 102, 103, 104, 109, 111, 115, 119, 122, 123, 124, 125, 126, 138, 144, 145, 147, 166, 170, 171, 177
concentration camps, 58, 59, 81, 90, 117, 167
Concordat, Italy and the Vatican (1929), 53
Congress of Vienna, 29
Connolly, William E., 178, 232n 11
Connor, Walker, 65, 197n 4
Consulta, 94, 95, 97
Corradini, Enrico, 51, 193n 63
Corte d'Appello, 123
Council of Foreign Ministers, 137, 138, 143
    Boundary Commission, 138, 140, 152
counternarratives, 8, 109
Cox, Geoffrey, 91, 104–109, 111, 117
Cres, 34

Cripps, R. R., 120
Croatia/Croats, 20, 30, 36, 42, 48, 58, 59, 65, 73, 95
Croce, Benedetto, 82, 144
Cronia, Arturo, 52, 193n 68
Cusio, Fabio, 8, 158–160, 163, 164, 165, 176, 223n 1
Cvijič, Jovan, 52
Cyril and Methodius Society, 23

Dachau, 140
Dalmatia, 26, 32–59 *passim*, 83, 95
D'Annunzio, Gabriele, 23, 43, 76
De Grazia, Victoria, 51, 192n 39
Dante, 13
Dante Alighieri Society, 23
Danubian hinterland, 2, 11, 20, 31
Danzig, 34, 37
Darwinian, 16
Dei Sabelli, Luca, 51, 53, 193n 64
De Gasperi, Alcide, 138, 140
democracy, 6, 14, 20, 37, 63, 96, 97, 98, 109, 112, 116, 120, 126, 130, 147, 150, 165, 175, 177
democrats, 47, 82
De Winton, Robin, 144
dialect, 12, 27
difference, 2, 3, 4–8, 14, 16, 17, 19, 20, 24, 42, 47, 85, 92, 102, 104, 108, 109, 112, 136, 153, 157–178; *mentioned*, 27–37, 50–56
    ambiguity, 4
    anthropological (Italian) classifications, 16
    British/American/Yugoslav, 104
    categories, 17
    classification, 18
    East/Balkan and the West, 5, 13, 37, 70, 133, 173
    ethno-national, 3
    history, 7
    imaginative representation, 7
    Italy, political and cultural, 3
    Italian/Jewish, 59
    Italians/Slavs, 2, 5, 8, 9, 13, 30–38 *passim*, 54, 59–60, 64, 70, 75,

difference, (*continued*)
  Italians/Slavs, (*continued*) 78–79,
     80, 82, 92, 98, 101, 158–178,
     158, 163, 172, 173
  narratives of, 6, 8
  national, 29–3 0
  "scientific" classification, late
     nineteenth-century, 13
  Slav, 56
  sovereignty, 3
  stereotypes, 9, 27, 30, 31, 32–33, 35
Dinaric, 52
Di Roreto, Carlo Petiti, 41
discourse, 5, 14, 43, 149, 159, 170, 176,
   178
dissent, working-class, 43, 44
diversity, 2, 3, 4, 13–25 *passim*, 38, 44,
   51, 97, 98, 136, 178
Dockrill, M., 34, 37, 187n 107, 189n
   125
Dodecanese, 26
Dubrovnik, 11
Duino, 151
Duroselle, Jean-Baptiste, 140, 141,
   171, 172, 189n 132

Eden, Anthony, 83
elections, 24, 43, 44, 94, 95, 96, 116,
   123, 124, 129, 147, 150
emancipation, 74, 75
Emilia Romagna, 170
Enlightenment, 2, 5, 25, 112, 175
epuration, 83–109, 115
Errera, Carlo, 36, 189n 121
ethnicity, 4, 7, 18, 83, 111–132, 138
ethnography/ethnographers, 16, 17,
   30, 36, 52, 56, 78–80, 120, 152
eugenics, 51
Europe/European, 1, 4, 11, 14, 15, 20,
   21, 28–38 *passim*, 47, 56, 69, 71,
   73, 124, 131, 132, 136, 137, 139,
   141, 163, 178
  admixture of races, 51
  Central, 6, 11, 21, 29, 135, 170–171
  East West, 1, 13, 14, 25, 69, 92, 107,
     108, 175

Eastern (or Balkan), 2, 4, 5, 6, 15,
     29, 39, 44, 112, 116
  federated, 76, 137, 138, 139
  historicizing of broad cultural op-
     positions within, 4
  Western, 5, 15, 16, 21, 38, 112
evolutionary theory, 16

Fascism/Fascists, 5, 7, 8, 27, 43, 44,
     47, 53, 55, 71–78 *passim*, 80, 81,
     82, 89, 90, 91, 94, 95, 98, 101,
     102, 109, 115, 138, 159, 161, 163,
     166, 167, 170, 172
  Italian/Italy, 3, 7, 39–61, 88, 89,
     109, 133, 148, 158, 162, 167
  racial laws, 59
  republican, 63
  Slovene, 89
Fascist anti-Semitism, 56
Fascist death squads, 58
Fascist experiment, 161
Fascist Federal Secretaries, 48, 49
Fascist Prefects, 47
federalism, 19, 23, 24
feminism/feminists, 22, 44, 74
Ferlan (Comrade), 101
Festa del Lavoro, 78
Fiume, 13, 26, 32–38 *passim*, 43, 68, 76,
     86, 138, 143
flags, 94, 98, 104 fig. 4.5, 112, 119, 120,
     125, 141
Flora, Emmanuel, 76, 137
Florence, 28, 78
Fogar, Galliano, 122, 123, 165
foibe, 77, 90–91, 109, 150, 166, 167, 168,
     169, 170, 171
Forti, Bruno, 139
Forti, Fulvio, 95
Fortis, Abbé Alberto, 14, 162
forty days, the, 83–109, 148, 161, 162,
     167
Forza Italia, 170
France/French, 27, 32, 34, 36, 44, 57,
     65, 104, 133, 137, 138, 140, 141,
     145, 146
franchise, 18

fraternity, 8, 41, 68, 70, 72, 74, 86, 94,
   97, 99, 103
Free Territory of Trieste, 141–146, 149,
   150, 151, 154, 160
French Popular Fronts, 65
Friuli/Friulian, 17, 45, 68, 144, 168,
   170
Friuli CLN, 78

Gaeta, Gaetano, 77
Gambini, Pier Antonio Quarantotti,
   81, 162
Gandusio, Ferdinando, 139, 140, 144
Gappisti, 170
Garibaldi, 120
Garibaldi Brigades, 67, 94, 96, 123
Gayda, Virginio, 27, 36, 186n 73
gender, 3, 7, 8, 23, 64, 75, 86, 97–98,
   104, 108, 111–132, 164, 175
geography/geographers, 15, 30, 32,
   35, 36, 60, 70, 80, 120, 135
Geopolitica, 57
Germany/Germans, 2, 5, 11–32 *pas-
   sim*, 35, 36, 38, 44, 48, 55, 56, 74,
   78, 82, 172, 173, 174
   Nazi Germany, 1, 8, 56–71 *passim*,
      75, 81, 82, 83, 90, 91, 94, 96,
      112, 123, 133, 138, 162, 167,
      168, 170
Gestapo, 91
Ghisleri, Arcangelo, 35–36, 188n 114,
   n 116
Giampiccoli, Mario, 139
Gibbon, Francis, 15
Giolitti government, 43
Giunta, Franceso, 43
Giustizia e Libertà, 78, 117
Goold, Douglas J., 34, 37, 187n 107,
   189n 125
Gorizia, 11, 26, 28, 31, 33, 41, 42, 66,
   68, 76, 83, 91, 112, 113, 138, 143,
   144
Gotha line, 83
Gradisca, 11, 26
Gramsci, Antonio, 94
Grant, J. A., 151

Great Britain
   Britain/British, 5, 29, 32, 33, 34, 37,
      38, 63, 68, 83–109, 111–132,
      133–155, 175
   English, 15, 34, 37, 57, 60, 70
   Scots, 119
Greek/Greeks, 8, 15, 22, 27, 38, 44, 45,
   56, 90, 121
Greek Liberation Front, 96
Gross, Feliks, 173
Guardia Civica, 89
Guardia di Finanza, 89
Gurkhas, 108

Habsburg Empire (Austria), 76, 96,
   120, 137, 162, 163, 164; *mentioned*, 1–42, 49–55
Hammond (Colonel), 124
Harding (General), 113
Harris, C. R. 5., 98, 112, 198n 15
Herder, 16
heterogeneity, 2, 3, 6, 51
Higher People's Court for the
   Slovene Littoral, 101
history/historians, 13, 14, 18, 34, 37,
   42, 44, 64, 65, 66, 84–85, 86, 91,
   95, 98, 102, 115, 135, 141, 146,
   149, 151, 157–178; *mentioned*,
   1–8, 50–59, 69–81
Hitler, Adolf, 162
Hobsbawm, Eric, 4
homogeneity, 2, 4, 19, 20, 29, 39, 47,
   51, 52, 59, 60, 66, 114
Hotel Balkan, 43, 50, 152
Horn, David, 51, 192n 39
hybridity, 7, Chapter 1, 53, 61, 68,
   176

Iaccheo, Anna Teresa, 73, 199n 38
identification, 2–8 *passim*, 12, 20, 23,
   25, 64, 70, 72, 75, 79, 80, 82, 103,
   111, 136, 161, 163, 164, 173, 178
identity, 3, 4–8, 14, 17, 33, 38, 42, 47,
   48, 50, 54, 55, 58, 60, 61, 64, 65,
   68, 80, 82, 83–109, 111, 118, 123,
   136, 140, 143, 157–158, 160, 161,

identity, (*continued*)
  170, 171, 172, 174; *mentioned*,
    19–29, 70–75
  American, 115, 174
  Balkans, 5
  British, 115
  community, 6
  ethnic, 7
  ethno-national, 14, 161
  European, 21
  gender, 7
  history, 7
  hybrid, 14
  Italian, 41, 44, 45, 47–60 *passim*, 64,
    71, 72, 80, 81, 82, 92, 95, 111,
    115, 123, 166, 168, 170, 172
  linguistic, 47
  multiple, 21
  narratives, Trieste, 7
  national, 5, 7, 39–61, 64, 72, 80, 97,
    119, 135, 163, 164, 176, 178
  political, 7
  Slav/Slovene, 50, 72, 86, 111, 115,
    123, 172
  struggle, 24
  territory, 6
ideological conflict, 24
incroci, 164
Independentist Front, 114, 121, 139,
    145, 151, 160
Indian 43rd Gurkha Regiment, 83,
    108, 131
Indians, 108
Institute for the History of the Libera-
    tion Movement in Venezia Giu-
    lia, 165, 167
intellectuals, 5, 14, 25, 31, 35, 44, 52,
    77–82 *passim*, 135, 157, 159, 161,
    162, 164, 172, 173
  anti-Fascist, 8, 64
  Austrian Socialist, 38
  British, 29, 30, 141
  centre-left, 76
  communist, 70, 124
  Enlightenment, 175
  European, 29, 35

  Democrats, 136
  Fascist, 7, 25, 51
  futurist, 25
  Italian, 16, 26, 29, 44, 52, 61, 80, 82,
    124, 136, 144, 160, 165
    anti-nationalists, 44
    early twentieth-century moder-
      ates, 27
    extreme right, 82
    Fascist, 7
    Liberals, 64, 73
    Marxist, 19
    Mazzinian, 28, 44, 54, 64, 70
    moderates, 27
    nationalist, 132
    Socialist, 7, 158
  liberal democrats, 7, 28, 44
  liberals, 29, 44
  Liberation Front, 65
  Marxist, 19, 136
  pro-Italian, 44, 109
  radicals, 158
  social democrats, 28
  Socialist, 7, 14, 19, 44, 158
  Triestine, 14, 19–21, 23, 42, 44, 57
  Viennese, 19, 23
  Western, 2, 5, 57, 135
International Court of Justice, 137
internationalism, 76
Irish, 119
Iron Curtain, 1, 111–132, 135
Isnenghi, Mario, 75–76, 200n 47
Isonzo River, 83, 107, 108, 144
Istria, 11, 36, 41, 66, 77, 101, 136, 141,
    143, 144, 151, 152, 171, 173;
    mentioned, 26–34, 165–169
  Croat, 114
  foibe, 169, 170
Italia, 49, 52, 53
Italian
  culture, 45
  intellectuals, 7
  nation building, 47, 48, 50
  national aspirations in the Adri-
    atic, 21
  national consciousness, 25, 42, 78

spazio vitale, 58
terra irrendenta, 16, 21–28 *passim*,
        31, 36, 78, 158, 165, 172
Italian Anti-Fascist Women, 67, 74
Italian Communist Party, 43, 66–76
        passim, 96, 122
Italian Liberal National Party (of Tri-
        este), 23, 76
Italian Nationalist Association, 23
Italian Socialist Party, 41, 76, 78, 82,
        161
italianità, 8, 21–28 *passim*, 36, 41, 45,
        47, 51, 52, 55, 57, 60, 61, 75, 79,
        81, 86, 102, 122, 123, 140, 158,
        159, 162, 163, 165, 167, 168, 170,
        175
Italianness, 17, 102
Italianization, 47, 48, 50, 54, 133, 148
Italo/Slav (Italo/Slovene), 4, 8, 43,
        67–75 *passim*, 89, 102
    brotherhood, 3, 64, 67, 68, 73, 75,
        81, 82, 95, 98, 116, 118, 124,
        126
    historical enmity, 4, 8, 29, 77, 82,
        102, 148, 149, 151, 153
Italo-Croat, 68
Italo-Slav Soviet Republic, 41
Italo-Slovene Antifascist brother-
        hood, 102
Italo-Slovene Anti-Fascist Coordina-
        tion Committees, 67
Italo-Slav Antifascist Union, 119, 125,
        140
Italo-Slovene women, 97
Italy/Italians, 17, 18, 26, 27, 32, 37,
        39–61, 88, 90, 95, 111, 112, 114,
        115, 120, 122–123, 124, 132, 144,
        145, 146, 148, 151, 152, 158,
        159, 161, 163, 164, 168, 169,
        170, 171; *mentioned*, 98–108,
        136–141
    communists, 58, 84
    cultural identity, 7
    democrats, 44, 47
    heterogeneity, 51, 57
    imperialism, 3, 57

kingdom of, 1, 3, 8, 16, 41, 44
liberal period (1918–1922), 1, 7,
        39–61, 64
national corpus, 3
national identity, 8
nationalist discourse,
        (1918–1943), 7
Risorgimento (unification), 13, 22,
        25, 55, 76, 165
World War One, 25–26

Jaksetich, Giorgio, 85, 94–95, 123
Jančar-Webster, Barbara, 73, 200n 38
Jews/Jewish, 8, 12, 18, 20, 22, 38,
        55–57, 58, 59, 81, 96, 115, 151,
        158, 164, 168
Julian region, 2, 13, 22, 33, 136, 174

Kann, Robert, 18, 181n 1
Kardelj, Edvard, 68, 69, 70, 111, 137
Kearney, Richard, 6, 180n 15
Kennan, George, 176–177
Klagenfurt, 66
Küstenland, 11, 76
Kveder, Dušan, 85

language, 11, 12, 36, 68, 73, 86, 92, 94,
        96, 97, 108, 114, 119, 122, 124,
        126, 133, 141, 147, 161, 168–169;
        mentioned, 16–30, 42–48, 76–80
Latin peoples, 2, 16, 35, 36, 136, 172,
        174
Lastovo, 34
League of Nations, 37, 41
Lederer, Ivo, 34, 35, 188n 109
Legionari, 76
Liberals, 5
    American, 28, 29
    British, 28, 29
    discourses of democracy, 14
    Italians, 39, 43, 45, 47, 76
    Western, 6
liberation, 83, 84, 86, 97
Liberation Councils, 67, 83–109, 112,
        114, 116, 123
    Propaganda Commission, 89

Littoral, 12–28 *passim*, 32, 35, 36, 38,
    68, 86, 172
    Adriatic, 11, 14, 16, 24, 26, 29
    Austrian, 16, 18
    Habsburg, 12, 13, 16
    Illyrian, 31
    Slovene, 101, 114
Littoral National Guard, 63
Ljubljana, 31, 58, 66, 68, 69, 71, 90
London, Treaty of, 34
Lošinj, 34
Luzzatto-Fegiz, Pierpaolo, 138, 218n
    23

Macartney, C. A., 18, 20, 183n 24
Maganj, Mario 127–128
Magris, Claudio, 170
Malalan, (Don), 90–91
Maoris. *See* New Zealand
mapping/maps, 29, 30, 36, 66, 70, 111
Maranelli, Carlo, 28, 39
Marinelli, Giovanni, 16, 17, 182n 14
Marinetti, F. T., 25
Marshall Plan, 141
marxism, 19, 65
Masons, 12, 56
May Day (1946), 132
May Day (1947), 125, 126–127
Mazzini, 28, 76
Mazzinians, 44, 172
Memorandum of Understanding, 152
mezzadria system, 115
Miani, Ercole, 165
Miani, Michele, 139
Mihelčič, Giuseppe, 140
Milan, 44, 57, 64
Milan CLNAI, 78
Minerva, 81
Ministry for the Interior, 48
minorities, 8, 30, 32, 36, 44, 58, 96,
    133, 141, 147–149, 152, 173, 175;
    mentioned, 39–42, 47–56
mixed marriages, 79
Mohammedans, 104
Monfalcone, 33, 66, 72, 86, 96, 103,
    104, 112, 143, 144, 145, 152

Montenegro/ Montenegrins, 95, 162
Montfort, Nelson, 113
Moodie, Arthur, 60, 135, 197n 129
Morgan, William D., 99
Morgan line, 99, 112, 144
Morlacchi, 15, 162
Muggia, 152
multicultural, 8, 18, 21, 98, 177
Musconi, Antonio, 41, 42, 43
Musoni, Francesco, 16–17, 53, 182n 15
Mussolini, Benito, 48, 51–59 *passim*,
    63, 80, 81, 90, 161, 162

Narodni Dom (National Home), 43
narratives, 14, 26, 50, 64, 82, 85, 102,
    108, 109, 118, 157, 158, 171, 172,
    175, 176, 178; *mentioned*, 4–8,
    160–169
nation, 4, 19, 25, 36, 47, 52, 55–61, 79,
    96, 104, 157, 161, 175, 178
    American, 15
    English, 15
    German (Teutonic), 15, 16, 18, 21
    Greek, 15
    ideal, 47
        Ghisleri, 36
        Salvemini, 36
        Seton-Watson, 36
    Italian (Italian), 15, 16, 18, 21, 39,
        52
    Jewish, 18
    Polish, 18
    presumptions, 16
    Slav, 15, 16, 18, 21
    Turks, 15
National Council (Trieste), 67
National Fascist Institute of Culture,
    Legal and Historical Section, 51
National Fascist Party, 58
national identity, 2, 4, 5, 7, 14, 15, 19,
    79, 82
    American, 5
    Austro-Marxist view, 19
    British, 5
    conceptions, 2
    core, bases of representation, 5

creation
   by elites, 4
   specific circumstances, 4
formation, 4
German, 5
Habsburg, 5
historical analysis, 4
imaginative representation, 7
   construction of, 4, 7, 13
Italian
   before the Italian nation-state, 5
   between the wars, 8
language, 17
oppositional discourses, 5
political, 2
Slovene/Slav, 5, 30, 66, 71, 72
Yugoslav, 5
National Liberation Committee, 64,
   76–81 *passim*, 89, 91, 92, 95, 96,
   98, 102, 114, 122, 123, 133, 139,
   140, 153, 165, 171
National Liberation Committee for
   Upper Italy, 64, 77
nationalism, 1, 2, 9, 19, 24, 28, 65,
   71–72, 73, 77, 78, 101, 109,
   133–155, 157, 174, 175, 178
nationalists, 14, 17, 19, 31, 59, 86, 132,
   166, 177; *mentioned*, 24–26, 71–73
   Italian, 4, 7, 13, 21, 24, 25, 39–61,
      64, 70, 75, 114, 117, 118, 131,
      172
   Slovene, 13, 24, 41, 95, 147, 149
nationalities struggle, 13, 14–25
nationality, 13, 18, 20, 30, 96, 133
Natisone valley, 27, 36, 45
Nazifascists, 76
Nazism, 75, 81
neo-Fascism, 116, 123, 131, 140, 148,
   150, 165, 170, 173
New Zealand Expeditionary Force
   2nd Division, 83–109
   28th Maori Battalion, 83–109
Nicolson, Harold, 32, 35, 37, 187n 94
Nitti, Francesco, 41, 42, 43
Nizza, Enzo, 168
Novak, Bogdan, 34, 115, 171, 185n56

Novo Mesto, 70
Nucleo d'Azione Patriottica, Il, 102

Oakey, Robin, 18, 181n 3
occupation, 31, 41, 43, 60, 63, 64, 65,
   69, 83, 97, 99, 102, 133, 160, 162,
   166, 167, 168
   AMG, 112–118
   Yugoslav, 109
Office of Minority Affairs, 146
Orlando, 34, 37
ORJUNA, 50
Ortaggi, Simonetta, 168–169
Osimo Treaty, 167
Ottoman empire, 11, 15, 29

Padua, 137
Pagnini, Cesare, 77, 81
Paladin, Giovanni, 139
Palagruža, 34
Pagnacco, Federico, 49
Paris Peace Conference/Treaty, 32,
   140, 143
   World War One, 3, 7, 29, 32–37 *pas-
      sim*, 42, 47
   World War Two, 83, 101, 141, 144,
      145, 147
Parri, Ferrucio, 139
Pasquinelli, Maria, 144
partisans, 8, 63–82, 83–109
   anti-Fascist, 117, 169
   Italian Communist, 94
   pro-Yugoslav, 83, 85, 103, 107
   Slovene Liberation Front, 83–109
   Tito, 84
   Yugoslav, 104
patriotism, 20, 26, 71, 73, 75, 76, 82,
   123, 150, 163
peasants, 6, 15, 27, 48, 74, 77, 86, 103,
   111, 114–115, 121, 127, 132, 167,
   173
People's Court, 112
People's Defense, 89, 90
People's Guard, 102
Peterin, Stanko, 101
Piazza Unità, 125, 166

Piccolo, Il, 53, 161
Pincherle, Bruno, 158, 159
Pirjevec, Jože, 86
Pisa-Rimini, 113
Pittito, Giuseppe, 169
Pittoni, Valentino, 24, 38, 41
Pocock, J. G. A., 6, 180n 17
Poland/Poles, 18, 30, 34, 52
Ponterosso, 159
Ponzo, 96
population, 5, 6, 12, 13, 16, 25, 28, 70,
        118, 140, 174
Porzus, 170
post-Cold War Yugoslavia, 177
post-Structuralism, 4
post-Communism, 114
post-Fascism, 170
Potsdam, 137
principle of nationality, 3, 8, 26, 29–35
        passim, 38, 39, 47, 60, 69, 174
principle of sovereignty, 152
prostitution, 130, 131
proletariat, 72, 75
provisional government, 79
Psychological Warfare Branch, 116
Pubblica Sicurezza, 89, 90
Puecher, Edmondo, 41, 139
Pula, 101, 112, 113, 144
Pullé, Francisco, 52
Pupo, Raoul, 171

Quarnero Gulf, 13
Questura, 89, 90, 167

Rabel, Robert, 111, 171, 173–174
race, 3, 16, 17, 21, 22, 24–25, 27, 30, 36,
        47, 51, 52, 55–61, 99, 102, 104,
        108, 111, 158, 161, 172, 174
    biological theory, 51, 55
    evolutionary theory, 2, 16, 24
    classification, 56
races, 2
    European, 56
    German (Teuton), 2, 15, 172
    Italian (Latin), 2, 57, 172
        Aryan origins, 55

purity, 55
    soul, 36
    spirit, 51
    Slovene (Slav), 2, 172
racism, Italian, 55
radicals, 22, 23, 29, 33–34, 52, 158
Ragusin-Righi, Livio, 53, 54, 194n 76
Rapallo, Treaty of (November 1920),
        33–34, 41, 42, 43, 70, 137
Regent, Ivan, 41, 94
Regional National Liberation Com-
        mittee, 85, 86, 102, 118, 119–120,
        121, 124, 140
Renan, Ernest, 15, 33, 181n 11, 187n
        98
Rendall (Captain), 117
Renner, Karl, 19–20, 23
Republic of Venezia Giulia, 41
Republican Party, 76
resistance, 8, 50, 57, 58, 61, 63–82, 139,
        165, 168, 169, 170
Risiera di San Sabba, 81, 161, 167–168,
        169
Robertson (Colonel), 118–119, 145
romanità, 57
Rome/Roman, 50, 54, 78, 150, 169
    ancient, 13, 22, 27, 35, 44, 45, 54,
        55, 92, 160, 172, 173, 174
Rome-Berlin Axis, 56
Rome Exhibition of the Fascist Revo-
        lution (1932), 50
Roosevelt, Franklin Delano, 63
Rosselli, John, 117, 213n 38
Rosetti, Domenico, 94, 96
Rusinow, Dennison, 42, 47, 59, 65,
        171, 184n 52

Sahlins, Peter, 4
Said, Edward, 4
Salvemini, Gaetano, 27–31 *passim*, 35,
        36, 39, 49, 54, 56, 59, 78, 186n
        77–78, 136–137, 172, 191n 36,
        194n 81
San Giacomo, 128
San Giusto, 54
San Sabba, 81

Santin, (Monsignor), 166
Scalfaro, Oscar Luigi, 169
Schiffrer, Carlo, 77, 78–79, 81–82, 138, 139, 158, 160, 161, 162–163, 165
Schmitz, Ettore: *See* Svevo, Italo
Secret Treaty of London, 31, 32, 33, 34, 41
Serbia/Serbian, 30, 38, 44, 45, 52, 56
Serbian-Orthodox, 8, 12, 38
Serbo (Judge), 167–168
Serbo-Croat, 17, 124
Seton-Watson, Christopher, 173
Seton-Watson, Robert, 29–30, 31, 34, 35, 36, 37, 173, 186n 84, n 85, 188n 111
Sforza, Carlo, 144, 163
Sharp, Alan, 34, 187n 106
Sindacati Unici, 121
shortages, 89, 103, 127
Sighele, Scipio, 24, 25, 26, 36, 188n 118
Škerlj, Božo, 56
Slataper, Scipio, 20, 21, 23, 26, 44, 163, 165
Slav-Bolshevik threat, 43–44, 57
Slav-Communist, 147, 165
Slavic, 15, 21, 27, 44, 48, 70, 91
Slavness, 140
Slavs, 2, 5, 6, 7, 23, 24, 26, 27, 80, 81, 82, 86, 89, 91, 94, 95, 98, 111–155, 136, 137, 140, 141, 144, 145, 146, 148, 151, 153, 159, 172, 174, 177; *mentioned*, 13–18, 30–57, 64–77, 101–104, 161–170
Slavification, 27
Slavs/threat, 162, 167
Slovene, 2, 7, 13, 16, 17, 27, 33, 36, 64–66; *mentioned*, 42–50, 56–59, 70–81
Slovene 9th Corps, 68, 69, 83
Slovene Catholics, 150
Slovene Communist government, 86
Slovene Communist Party, 65, 66, 74
Slovene Home Guard, 63, 76, 82
Slovene Institute for the History of the Workers Movement, 167

Slovene Liberation Front, 64, 65, 66, 69, 70, 71, 74, 77, 79, 82, 83–104, 113, 116, 118, 127, 139, 149, 162
Border Committee, 65–66
City Command, 83
Scientific Institute, 69, 70, 78
Slovene liberals, 150
Slovene/Yugoslav Communist Party, 65, 66, 67, 69, 71, 73, 74
Slovenia, 4, 65, 67, 70, 73, 144
Smith (Major), 92–93, 99, 116
Socialist Party, 124
Smuts (Lieutenant Colonel), 132
socialists, 3, 14, 19, 20, 23, 24, 25, 37, 41, 43, 44, 51
Austrian, 19, 24
Croatian, 43
Italian, 43, 44, 45, 76, 136, 139, 151
Slovene, 24, 42, 43
Triestine, 41, 42, 43
Società Umanitaria, 170
Sonnino, Sidney, 26, 37
sovereignty, 9, 14, 24, 25, 26, 35, 38, 59, 73, 75, 77, 81, 82, 98, 102, 109, 130, 132, 135, 136, 153, 157–178; *mentioned*, 1–6, 17–21, 28–32, 60–71
alternative conceptions of, 3, 4
AMG, 112, 118
Austro-Marxist view, 19
concepts of, 2, 6, 14
ethno-national, 6, 7, 139, 146
national, 125, 146
non-national, 121
popular, 118–132
Spackman, Barbara, 25, 185n 63
Spanish Civil War, 94, 96
Spanish Popular Front, 65
Special Italian Inspectorate of Public Security, 58
Sporer, Teodoro, 139
Sprigge, Cecil, 123
Sprigge, Sylvia, 102–104, 108, 109, 112, 123
Sproiano, Paolo, 71, 199n 26
Stalin, Josef, 86, 120

Starace, Achille, 57
stirpe, 17, 22, 51, 53, 55, 57
Stocca, Mario, 139
Štoka, Franc, 72, 85, 96
Stourzh, Gerard, 18, 182n 22
Strunja, Ljubo, 71
Stuparich, Carlo, 21
Stuparich, Giani, 21, 81, 163, 165
Sullivan, William, 115, 143, 145
Sušak, 34
Suvich, Fulvio, 49, 59
Svevo, Italo, 20
Switzerland, 136, 137, 163

Tamaro, Attilio, 55, 162
Tancredi, Libero, 36, 189n 120
Taylor, A. J. P., 136, 218n 13
Temple (Major), 120
Terza Forza, 139
TIGR, 50
Tito, Josip Broz, 1, 65, 68, 80, 83, 86,
     89, 94, 98, 99, 101, 104, 108, 120,
     149, 162, 168
Todorova, Maria, 5, 78, 170, 180n 12
Togliatti, Palmiro, 68, 122
Tolmizza, Fulvio, 170
toponomy laws (1923), 47, 55
Toynbee, Arnold, 135
Treaty of Friendship and Co-
     operation between Italy and
     Yugoslavia, 53
Trentino, 16, 26, 34, 35
Trento, 133
Tribunale Popolare, 89
*Tribunale Speciale per la Difesa della
     Stato*, 49, 51
Trieste, 165
Trieste City Military Command, 85
Tripartite Declaration, 145, 146, 148
Truman, Harry S., 120
Turin, 94
Tuntar, Guiseppe, 41
Turks, 15, 96
Tyrol, 16

Union of Italian Women, 73

Union of the Soviet Socialist Re-
     publics, 52, 70, 71, 103, 128, 131,
     131, 137, 138, 140, 141, 146, 149,
     176
     Bolshevism/Bolsheviks, 37, 42, 44,
          72
*Unione delle Donne Antifasciste Italo-
     Slavo*, 127–128, 129, 131, 132
United Nations, 76, 121
     Security Council, 141, 143, 145
United States of America, 5, 15, 29,
     32, 33, 34, 37, 38, 63, 68, 83–109,
     111–132, 137, 140, 141, 151, 173,
     174, 175, 177
     State Department, 114, 123
United States 5th Army, 89–90
United States Main 13 Corps, 83, 92,
     113, 116, 117, 131
United States 2nd Corps, 86
Urals, 64
Ursič, Rudi, 67, 95, 102
Ustaše, 63

Val d'Aosta, 36, 76, 133
Valdevit, Giampaolo, 123, 146
Valussi, Pacifico, 22
Velebit, Ivan, 137
Venezia Giulia, 13, 22, 28, 29, 34, 36,
     81 82, 85, 89, 92, 98, 99, 101, 103,
     111, 112, 119, 120, 124, 133, 135,
     136, 137, 140, 141, 144, 158, 160,
     161, 165, 166, 167, 168, 170, 171,
     172, 173; *mentioned*, 39–59,
     60–76
Venezia Giulia CLN, 84, 85, 91, 94,
     101, 121, 131
Venezia Giulia Communist Party, 122,
     131
Venezia Giulia police force, 115, 116,
     126, 140
Venezia Giulia Socialist Party, 114
Venezia Mestre, 104
Venice, 11, 14, 22, 70, 173, 174
Ventimiglia, 133
Verginella, Marta, 72, 199n 34
Vidali, Vittorio, 155, 223n 90

Vidussoni, Aldo, 58
Vienna, 23, 104
Vinci, Anna Maria, 50, 56, 57, 191n 23
Vivante, Angelo, 21–22, 23, 26, 38, 44,
    158, 160, 165, 176, 183n 44
Volk, Allessandro, 71, 74, 199n 31
Voranc, Prežihov, 66, 70
Vosnjak, Bogumil, 31, 186n 90

Walston, James, 58, 59, 196n 119
war crimes/criminals, 89, 167
Weidman, Floyd E., 92
White, Ivan, 141
Williams, Brackette, 176
Wilson, Edmund, 117n 213, n 35
Wilson, Woodrow, 34, 35–36
  "Wilson line" on Fiume, 33, 137,
    138
Wolff, Larry, 4, 15, 180n 11, 181n 9
women, 49, 58, 67, 73–75, 79, 80, 86,
    87 fig. 4.2, 88 fig. 4.3, 90, 95, 96,
    97–98, 104, 106, 107, 109, 111,
    120, 125, 127–132, 149–150, 159,
    164
Women's Hour, 129
Workers Unity, 66, 67, 96
World War One, 1, 3, 6, 11, 14, 18, 20,
    23, 25, 27, 64, 70, 137, 139, 140,
    141, 143, 152, 153, 161, 162, 174
  Allies, 68, 71, 63–82
  Big Four, 37
  Central Powers, 25, 26
  Entente, 25, 26, 31
  post war peace process, 3, 7, 29,
    32–3 7 *passim*, 42, 47
    Memorandum of Italian territo-
      rial claims, 32
    Memorandum of Yugoslav ter-
      ritorial claims, 32, 33
    Slovene participation, 26
    Supreme Allied War Council, 31

World War Two, 1, 3, 8, 41, 55–61, 66,
    85, 96, 109, 112, 133, 135, 161,
    167–170 *passim*
  Allies, 133–155, 133, 137, 139, 143
  "Big Four", 137
  Paris Peace Conference, 83, 101,
    141, 144, 145, 147

Yalta Conference, 83
youth/youth groups, 49, 71, 72, 74,
    125
  Communist, 72, 90, 96
Yugoslav (Yugoslavia), 1, 3, 4, 5, 8, 42,
    56, 58, 60, 63, 65, 66, 67, 70, 80,
    82, 90, 92, 95, 97, 98, 99, 101,
    102, 103, 104, 108, 117, 120, 121,
    122, 123, 131, 132, 133, 135, 137,
    138, 141, 143, 144, 149, 150, 151,
    152, 154, 161, 167, 168, 169, 170,
    171, 176, 177, 178; *mentioned*,
    30–39, 50–54
  Kingdom of Serbs, Croatians and
    Slovenes, 28, 36, 39
Yugoslav Executive-Supreme Sloven-
    ian-Command City of Trieste
    Command, 84
Yugoslav military, 89, 92, 98, 99, 101,
    102, 104, 108, 109, 123, 143, 146
  4th Army, 83, 85, 86, 89, 90, 95
Yugoslav Military Administration,
    114
Yugoslav Secret Police, 89, 90, 91, 117
Yugoslav wars, 170

Zadar, 138
Zionism, 47
Zoratti (Dr), 102
Zone A, 101, 111–132, 143, 144
Zone B, 101, 111–132, 138, 143, 144
Zone Council, 139, 144
Zwitter, Fran, 69–70